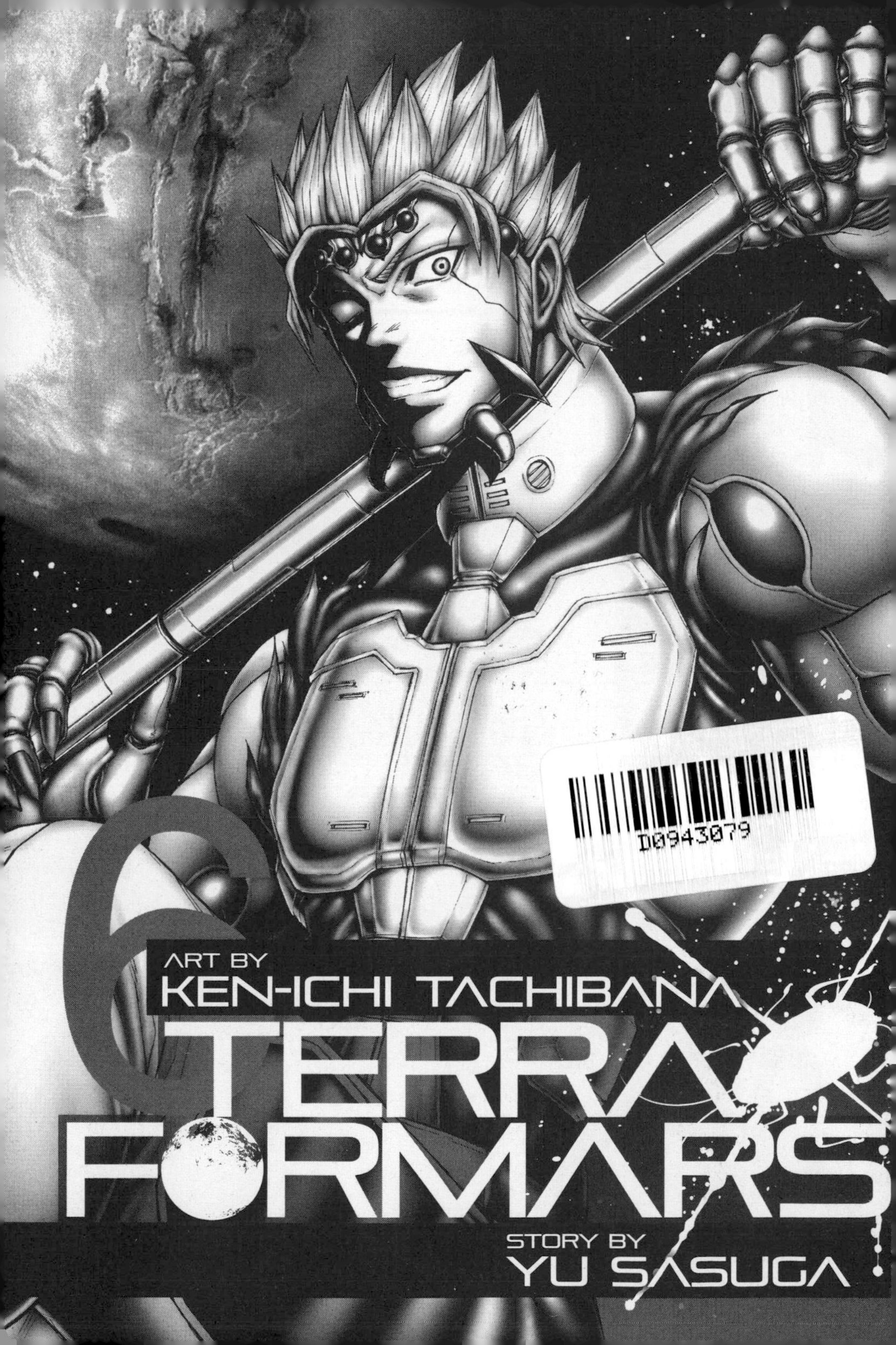
ART BY
KEN-ICHI TACHIBANA
6
TERRA FORMARS
STORY BY
YU SASUGA

TERRA FORMARS 6

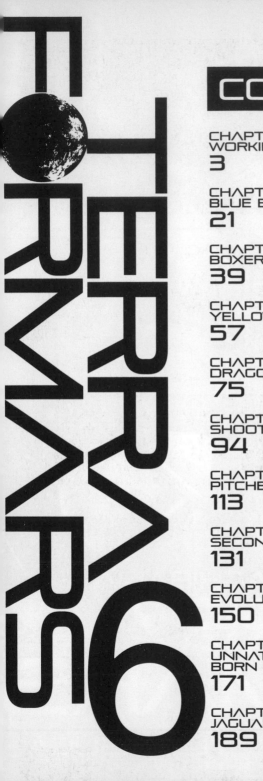

CONTENTS

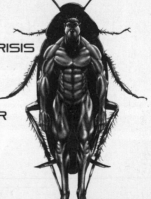

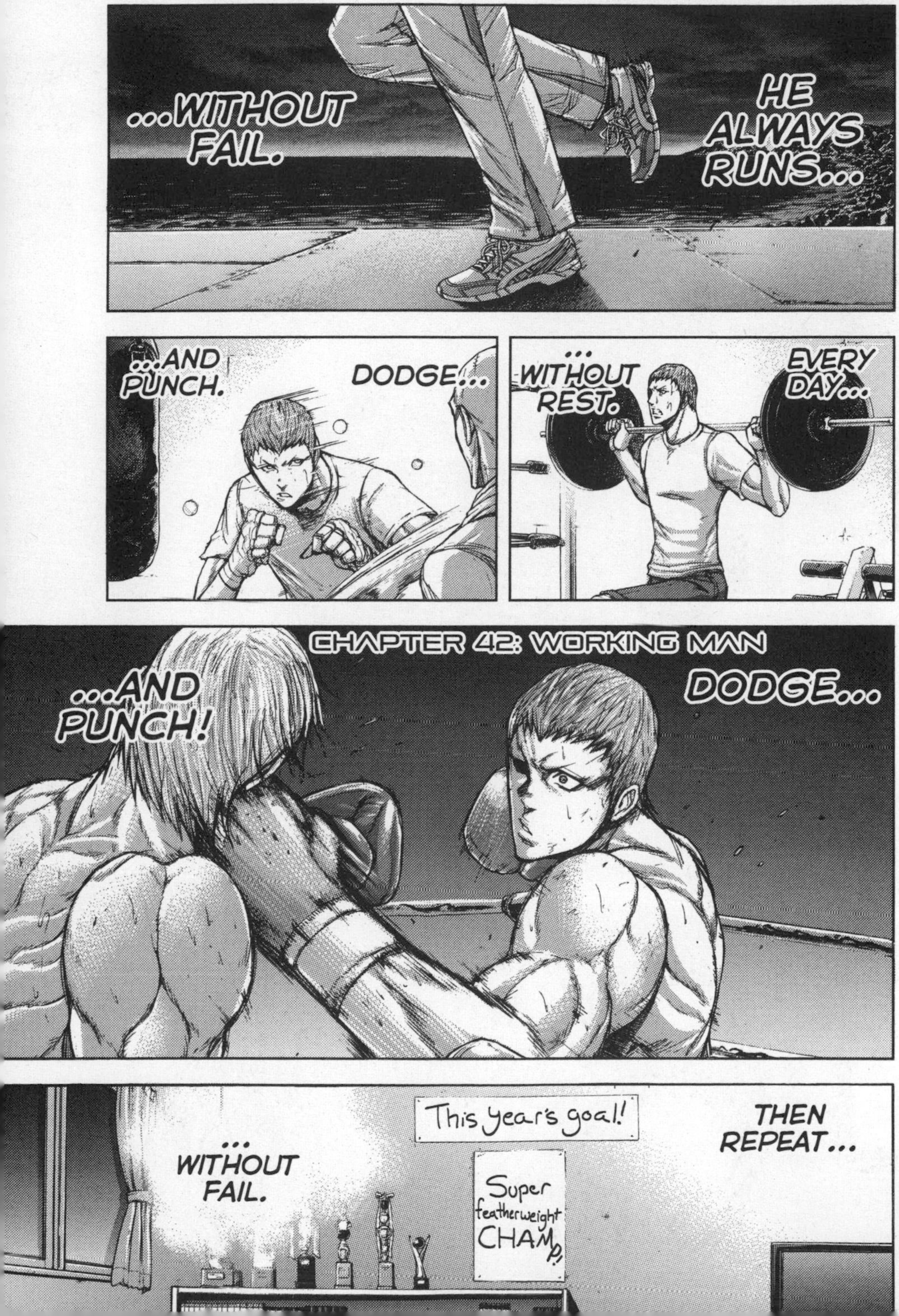
HE ALWAYS RUNS...
...WITHOUT FAIL.
EVERY DAY...
...WITHOUT REST.
DODGE...
...AND PUNCH.
CHAPTER 42: WORKING MAN
DODGE...
...AND PUNCH!
THEN REPEAT...
This year's goal!
Super featherweight CHAMP!
...WITHOUT FAIL.

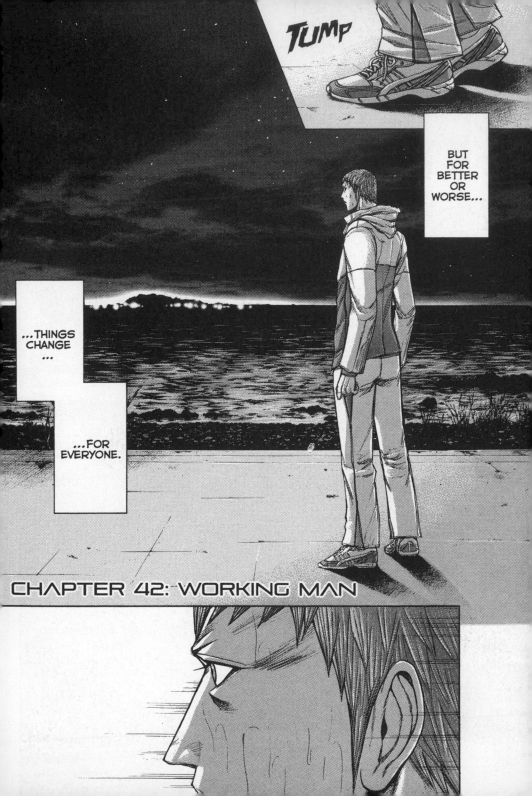

TUMP

BUT FOR BETTER OR WORSE...

...THINGS CHANGE...

...FOR EVERYONE.

CHAPTER 42: WORKING MAN

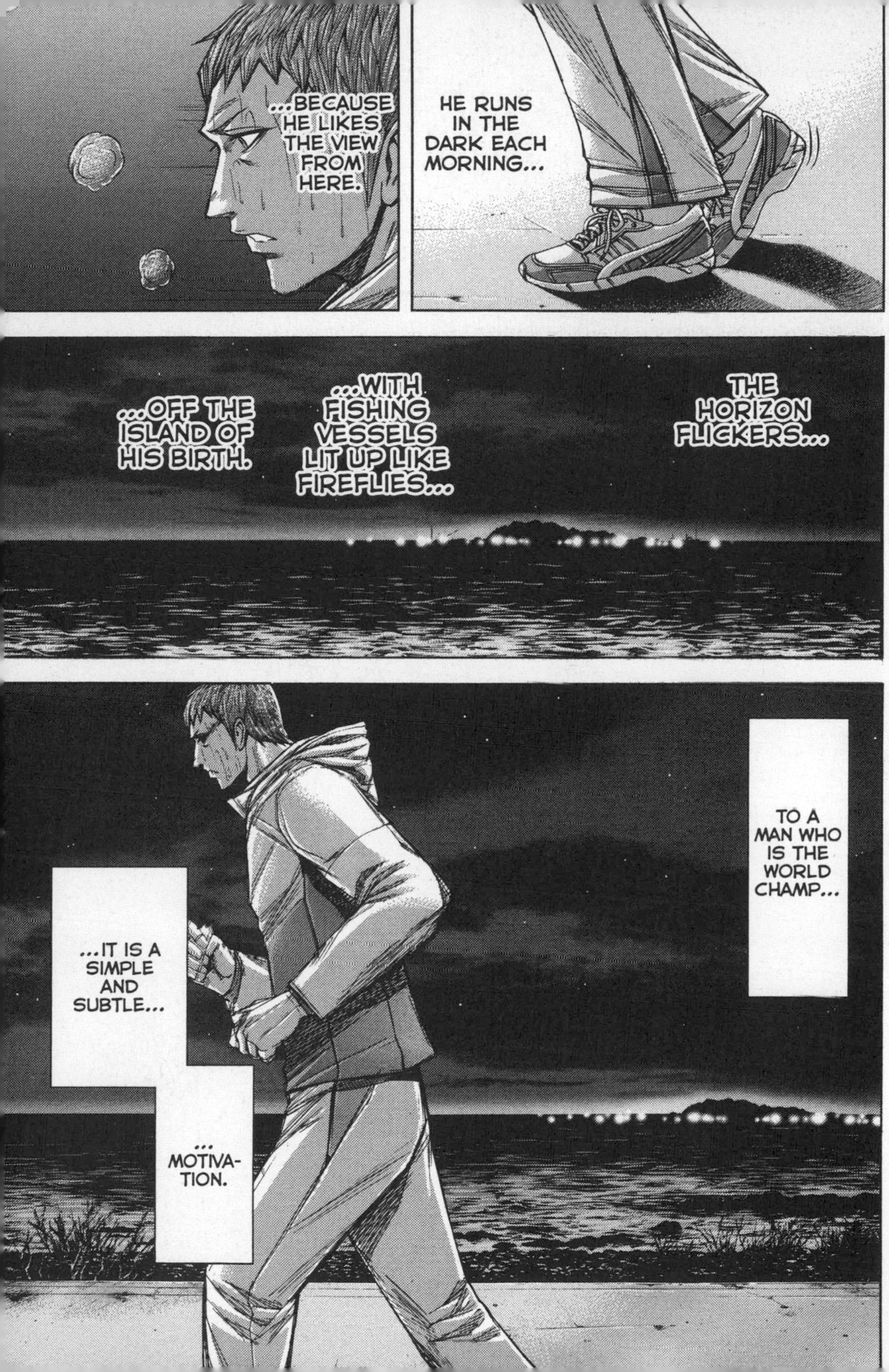
HE RUNS IN THE DARK EACH MORNING...
...BECAUSE HE LIKES THE VIEW FROM HERE.
THE HORIZON FLICKERS...
...WITH FISHING VESSELS LIT UP LIKE FIREFLIES...
...OFF THE ISLAND OF HIS BIRTH.
TO A MAN WHO IS THE WORLD CHAMP...
...IT IS A SIMPLE AND SUBTLE...
... MOTIVATION.

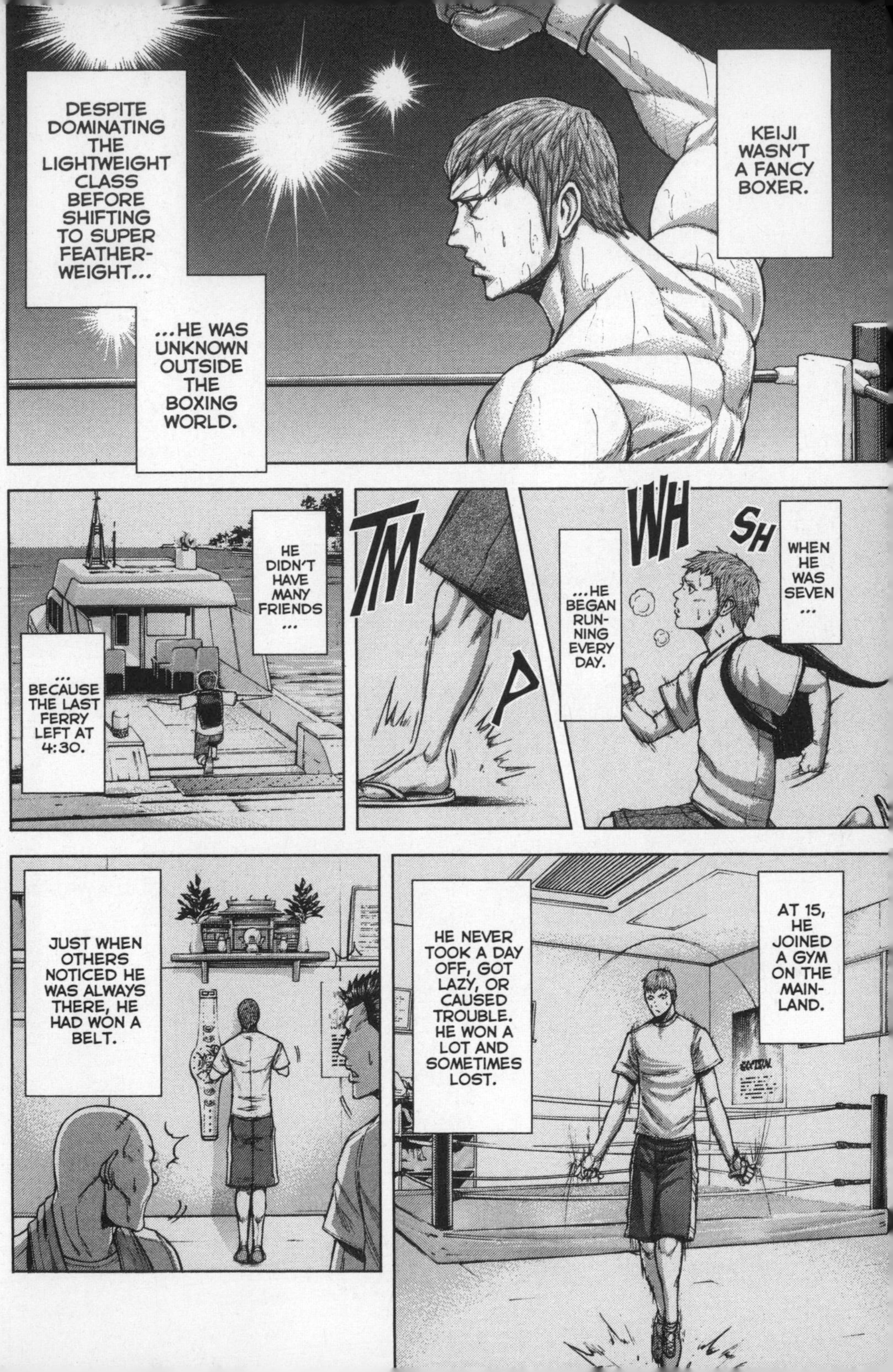
KEIJI WASN'T A FANCY BOXER.
DESPITE DOMINATING THE LIGHTWEIGHT CLASS BEFORE SHIFTING TO SUPER FEATHER-WEIGHT...
...HE WAS UNKNOWN OUTSIDE THE BOXING WORLD.
WHEN HE WAS SEVEN...
SH
WH
...HE BEGAN RUN-NING EVERY DAY.
TM
P
HE DIDN'T HAVE MANY FRIENDS...
...BECAUSE THE LAST FERRY LEFT AT 4:30.
AT 15, HE JOINED A GYM ON THE MAIN-LAND.
HE NEVER TOOK A DAY OFF, GOT LAZY, OR CAUSED TROUBLE. HE WON A LOT AND SOMETIMES LOST.
JUST WHEN OTHERS NOTICED HE WAS ALWAYS THERE, HE HAD WON A BELT.

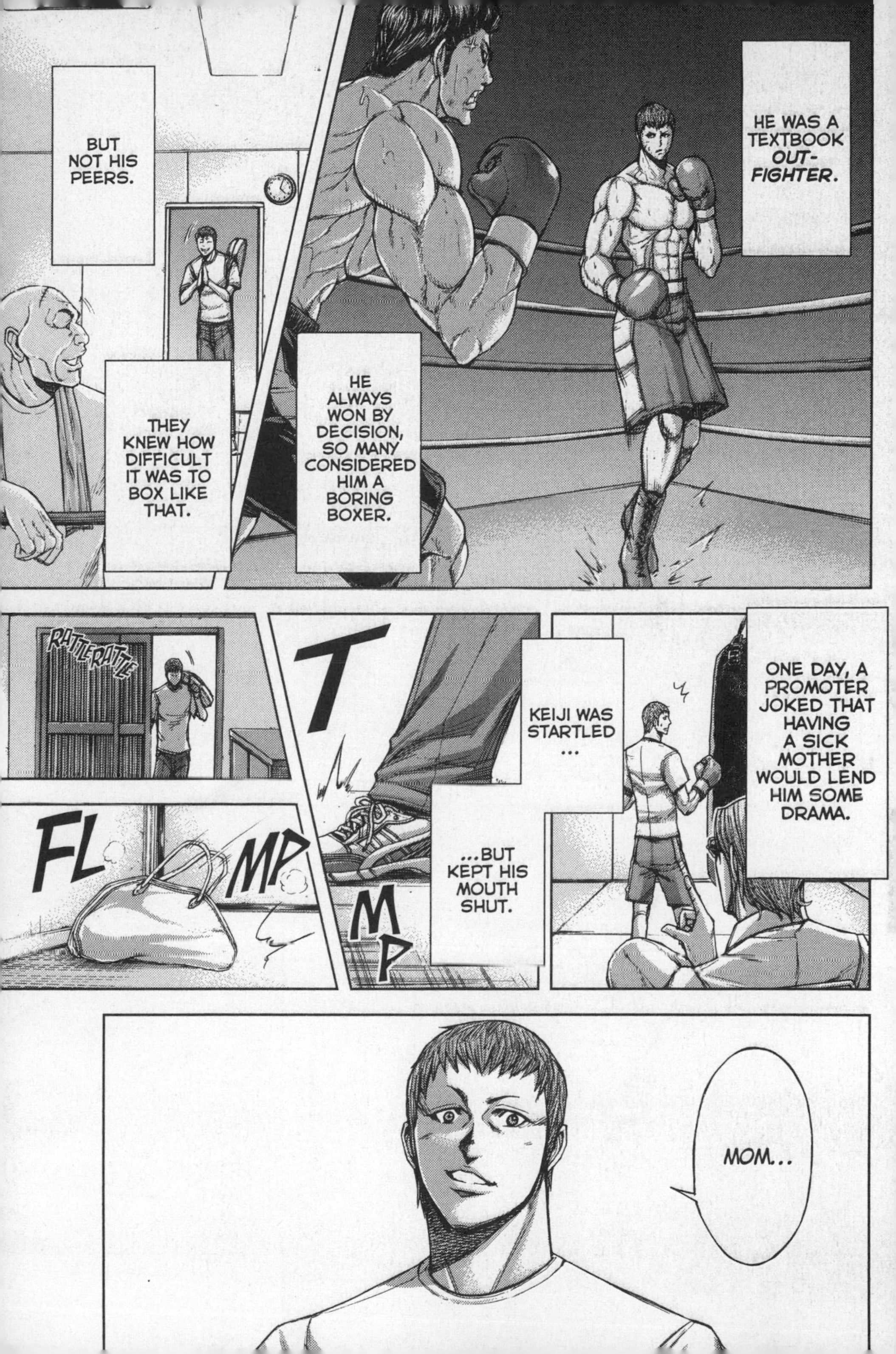
HE WAS A TEXTBOOK OUT-FIGHTER.
HE ALWAYS WON BY DECISION, SO MANY CONSIDERED HIM A BORING BOXER.
BUT NOT HIS PEERS.
THEY KNEW HOW DIFFICULT IT WAS TO BOX LIKE THAT.
ONE DAY, A PROMOTER JOKED THAT HAVING A SICK MOTHER WOULD LEND HIM SOME DRAMA.
KEIJI WAS STARTLED ...
...BUT KEPT HIS MOUTH SHUT.
TMMP
RATTLE RATTLE
FLMP
MOM...

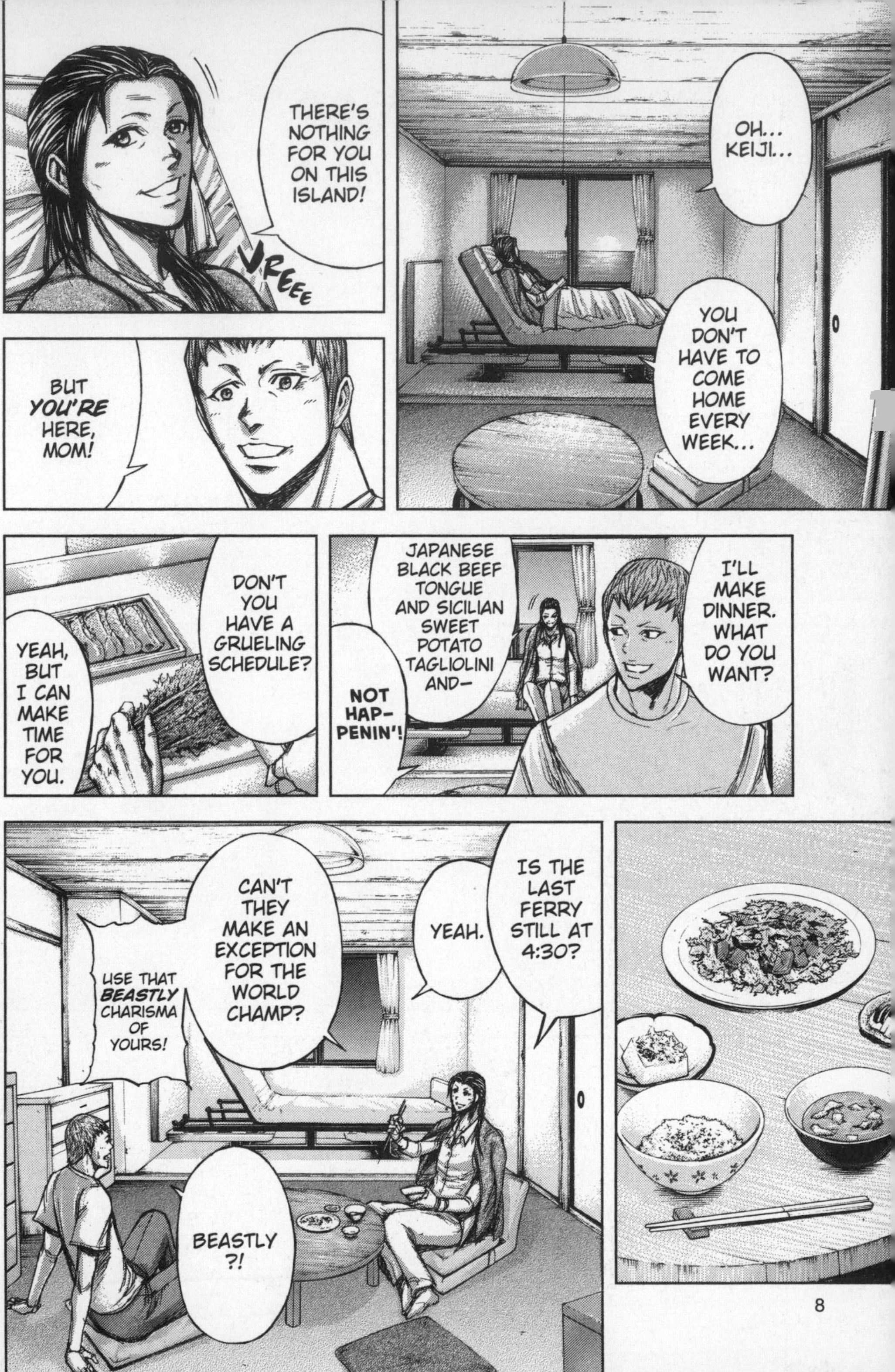
OH... KEIJI...
YOU DON'T HAVE TO COME HOME EVERY WEEK...
THERE'S NOTHING FOR YOU ON THIS ISLAND!
VREEEE
BUT YOU'RE HERE, MOM!
I'LL MAKE DINNER. WHAT DO YOU WANT?
JAPANESE BLACK BEEF TONGUE AND SICILIAN SWEET POTATO TAGLIOLINI AND–
NOT HAP-PENIN'!
DON'T YOU HAVE A GRUELING SCHEDULE?
YEAH, BUT I CAN MAKE TIME FOR YOU.
IS THE LAST FERRY STILL AT 4:30?
YEAH.
CAN'T THEY MAKE AN EXCEPTION FOR THE WORLD CHAMP?
USE THAT BEASTLY CHARISMA OF YOURS!
BEASTLY?!

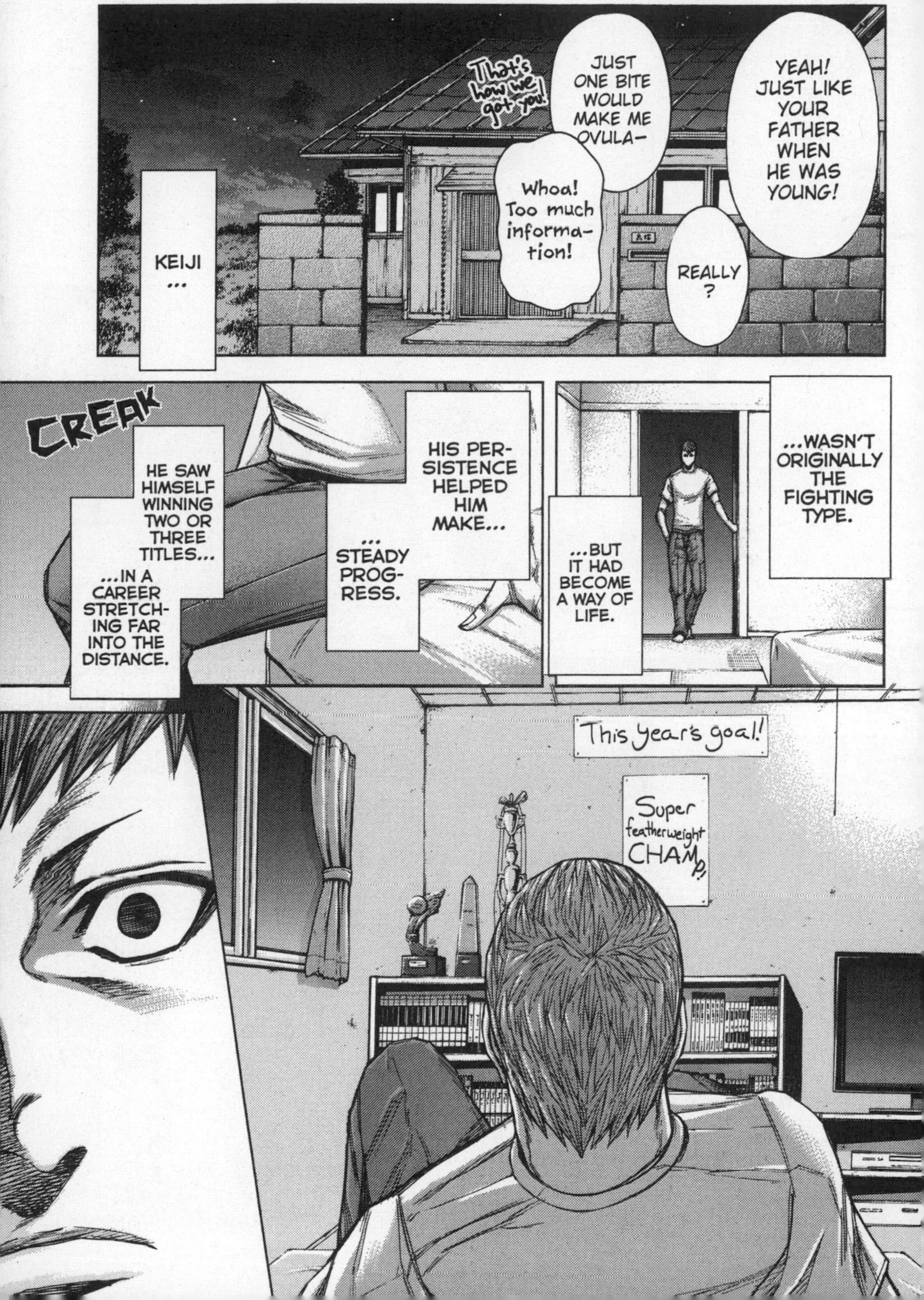
YEAH! JUST LIKE YOUR FATHER WHEN HE WAS YOUNG!
REALLY?
JUST ONE BITE WOULD MAKE ME OVULA-
Whoa! Too much information!
That's how we got you!
KEIJI ...
...WASN'T ORIGINALLY THE FIGHTING TYPE.
...BUT IT HAD BECOME A WAY OF LIFE.
HIS PERSISTENCE HELPED HIM MAKE...
... STEADY PROGRESS.
CREAK
HE SAW HIMSELF WINNING TWO OR THREE TITLES...
...IN A CAREER STRETCHING FAR INTO THE DISTANCE.
This year's goal!
Super featherweight CHAMP!

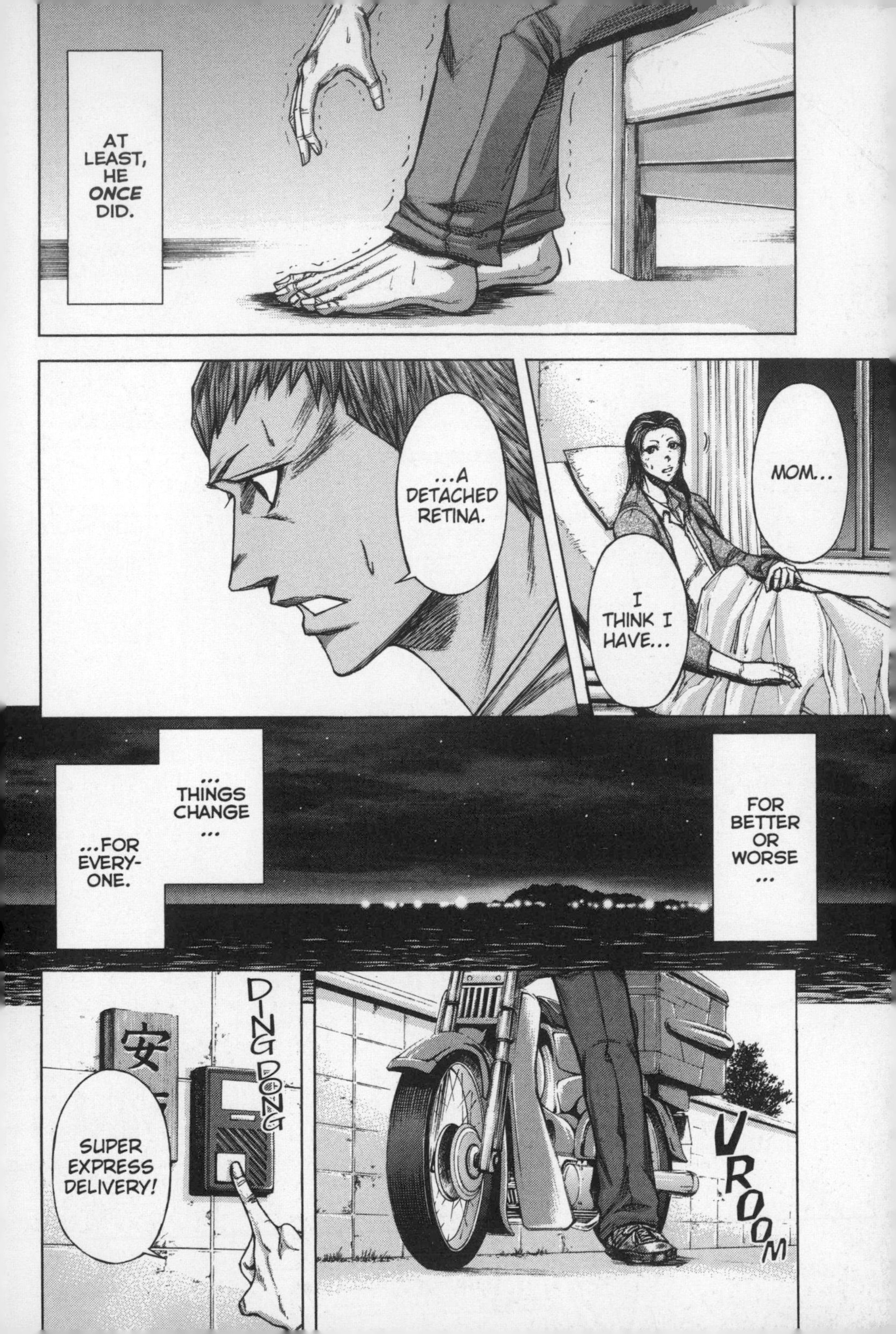
AT LEAST, HE ONCE DID.
MOM...
I THINK I HAVE...
...A DETACHED RETINA.
FOR BETTER OR WORSE ...
... THINGS CHANGE ...
...FOR EVERY- ONE.
VROOM
安
DING DONG
SUPER EXPRESS DELIVERY!

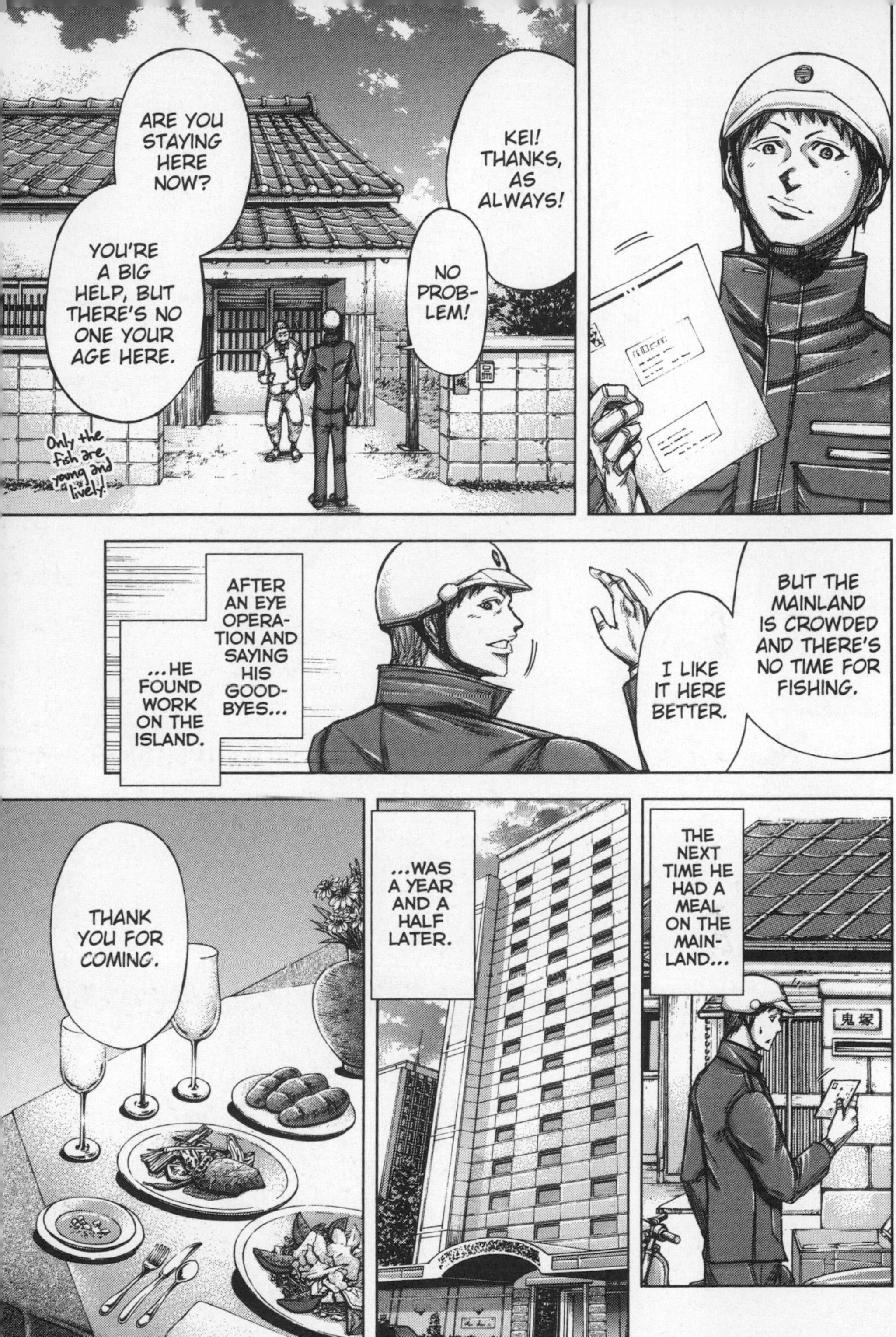
KEI! THANKS, AS ALWAYS!
NO PROB-LEM!
ARE YOU STAYING HERE NOW?
YOU'RE A BIG HELP, BUT THERE'S NO ONE YOUR AGE HERE.
Only the fish are young and lively!
BUT THE MAINLAND IS CROWDED AND THERE'S NO TIME FOR FISHING.
I LIKE IT HERE BETTER.
AFTER AN EYE OPERA-TION AND SAYING HIS GOOD-BYES...
...HE FOUND WORK ON THE ISLAND.
THE NEXT TIME HE HAD A MEAL ON THE MAIN-LAND...
鬼塚
...WAS A YEAR AND A HALF LATER.
THANK YOU FOR COMING.

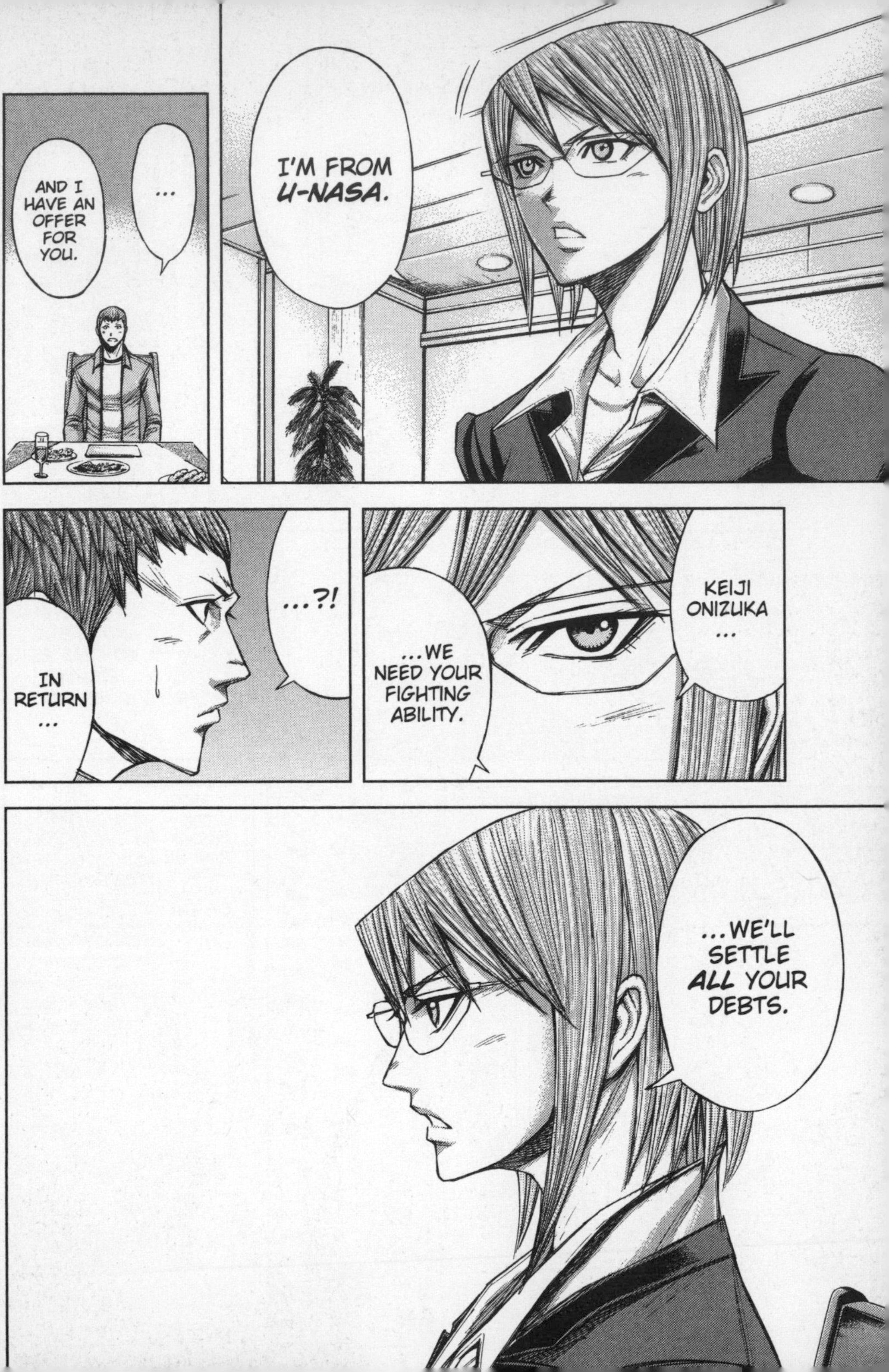
I'M FROM U-NASA.
...
AND I HAVE AN OFFER FOR YOU.
KEIJI ONIZUKA ...
...WE NEED YOUR FIGHTING ABILITY.
...?!
IN RETURN ...
...WE'LL SETTLE ALL YOUR DEBTS.

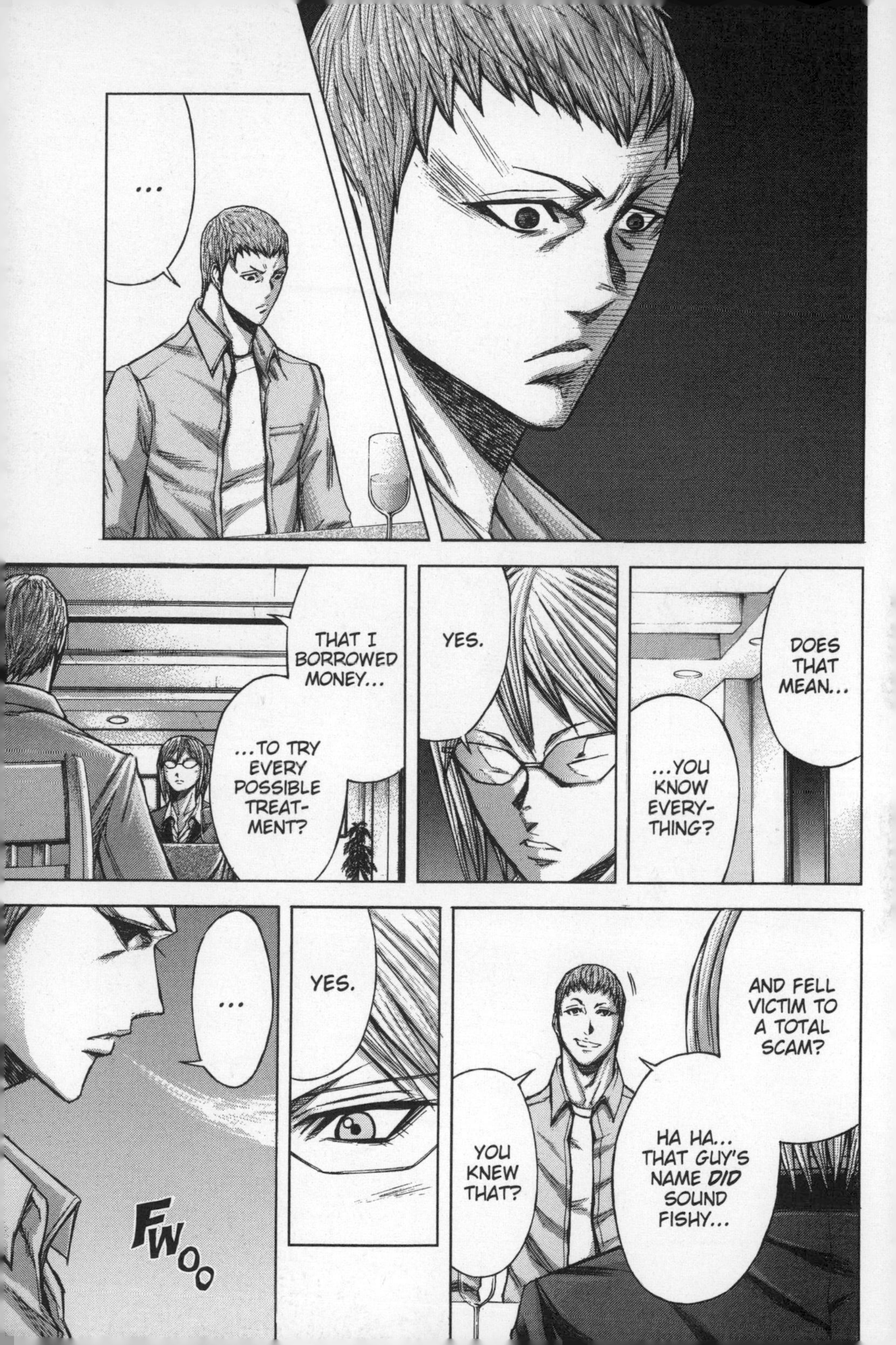
...
DOES THAT MEAN...
...YOU KNOW EVERYTHING?
YES.
THAT I BORROWED MONEY...
...TO TRY EVERY POSSIBLE TREAT-MENT?
AND FELL VICTIM TO A TOTAL SCAM?
HA HA... THAT GUY'S NAME *DID* SOUND FISHY...
YOU KNEW THAT?
YES.
...
FWOO

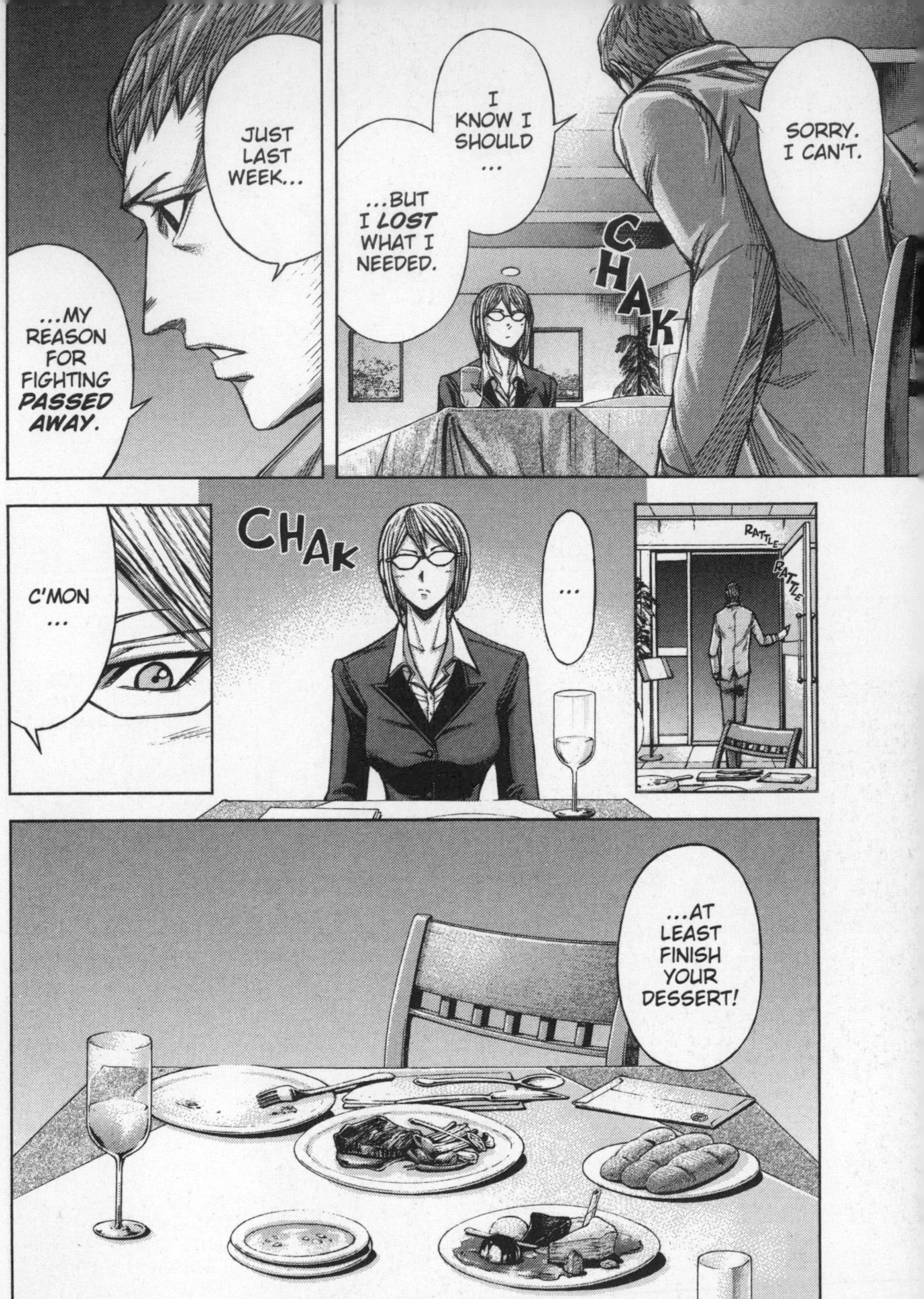
SORRY. I CAN'T.
CHAK
I KNOW I SHOULD ...
...BUT I LOST WHAT I NEEDED.
JUST LAST WEEK...
...MY REASON FOR FIGHTING PASSED AWAY.
RATTLE RATTLE
CHAK
...
C'MON ...
...AT LEAST FINISH YOUR DESSERT!

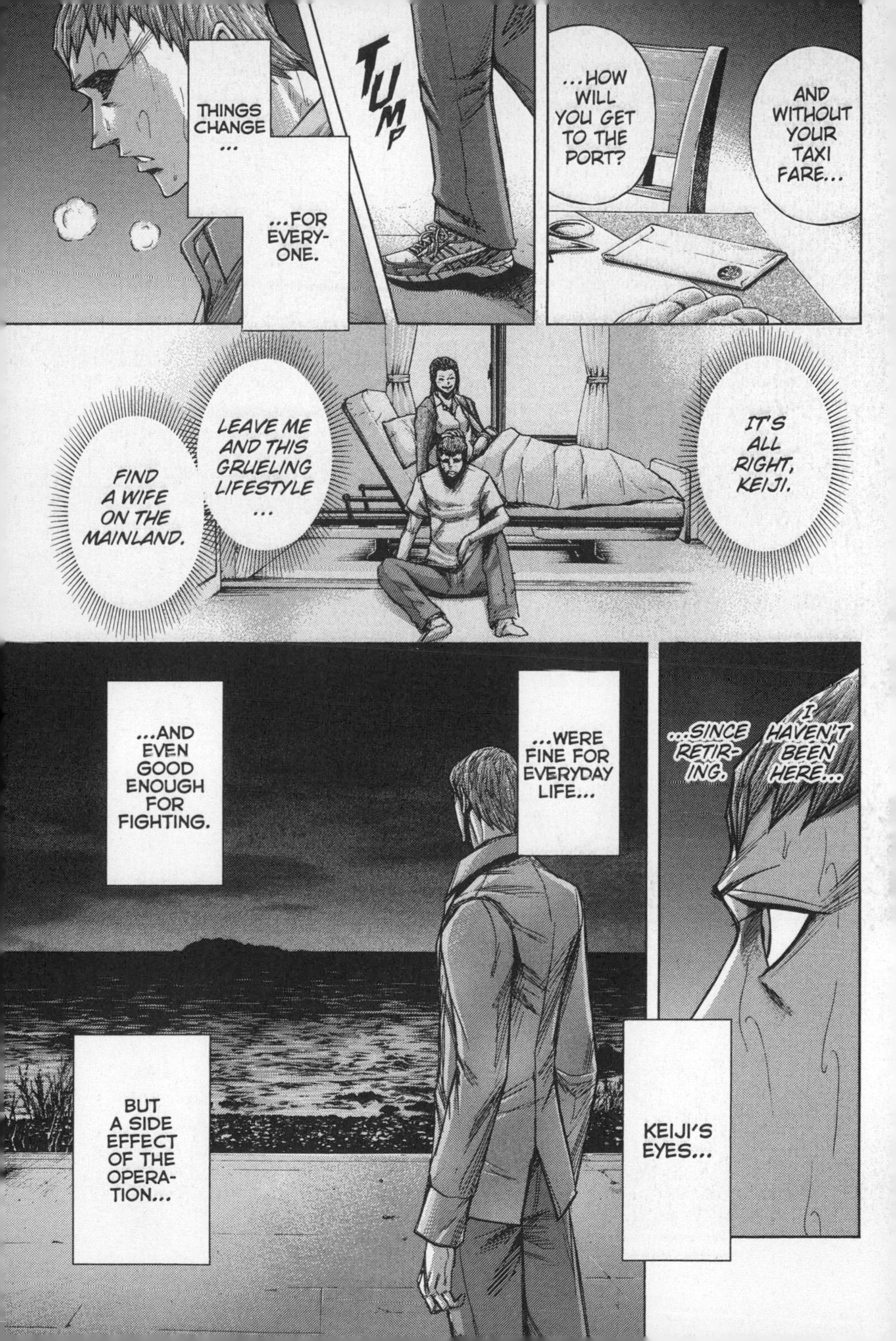
AND WITHOUT YOUR TAXI FARE...
...HOW WILL YOU GET TO THE PORT?
TUMP
THINGS CHANGE ...
...FOR EVERYONE.
IT'S ALL RIGHT, KEIJI.
LEAVE ME AND THIS GRUELING LIFESTYLE ...
FIND A WIFE ON THE MAINLAND.
I HAVEN'T BEEN HERE...
...SINCE RETIRING.
KEIJI'S EYES...
...WERE FINE FOR EVERYDAY LIFE...
...AND EVEN GOOD ENOUGH FOR FIGHTING.
BUT A SIDE EFFECT OF THE OPERATION...

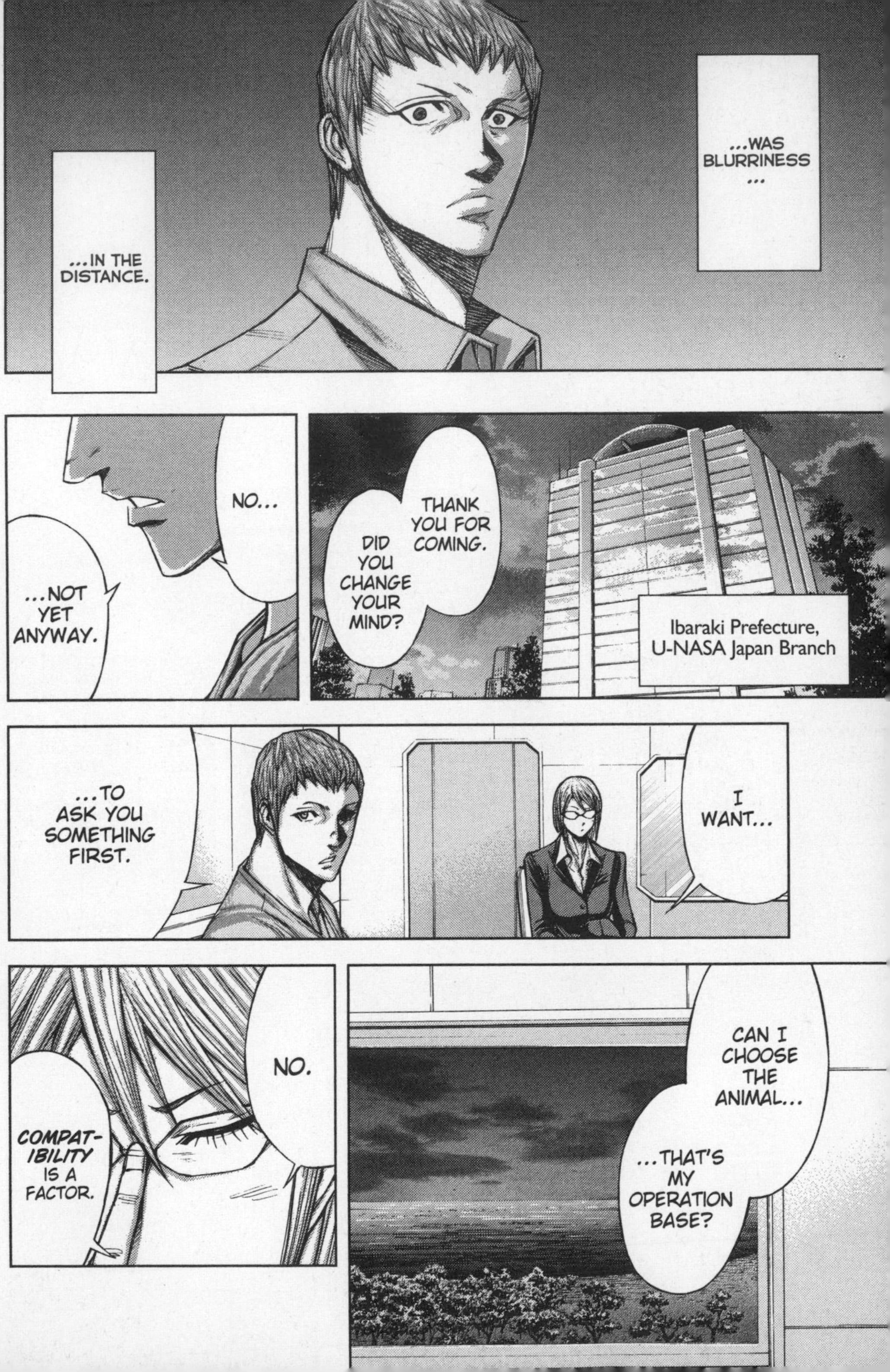
...WAS BLURRINESS ...
...IN THE DISTANCE.
Ibaraki Prefecture, U-NASA Japan Branch
THANK YOU FOR COMING.
DID YOU CHANGE YOUR MIND?
NO...
...NOT YET ANYWAY.
I WANT...
...TO ASK YOU SOMETHING FIRST.
CAN I CHOOSE THE ANIMAL...
...THAT'S MY OPERATION BASE?
NO.
COMPAT-IBILITY IS A FACTOR.

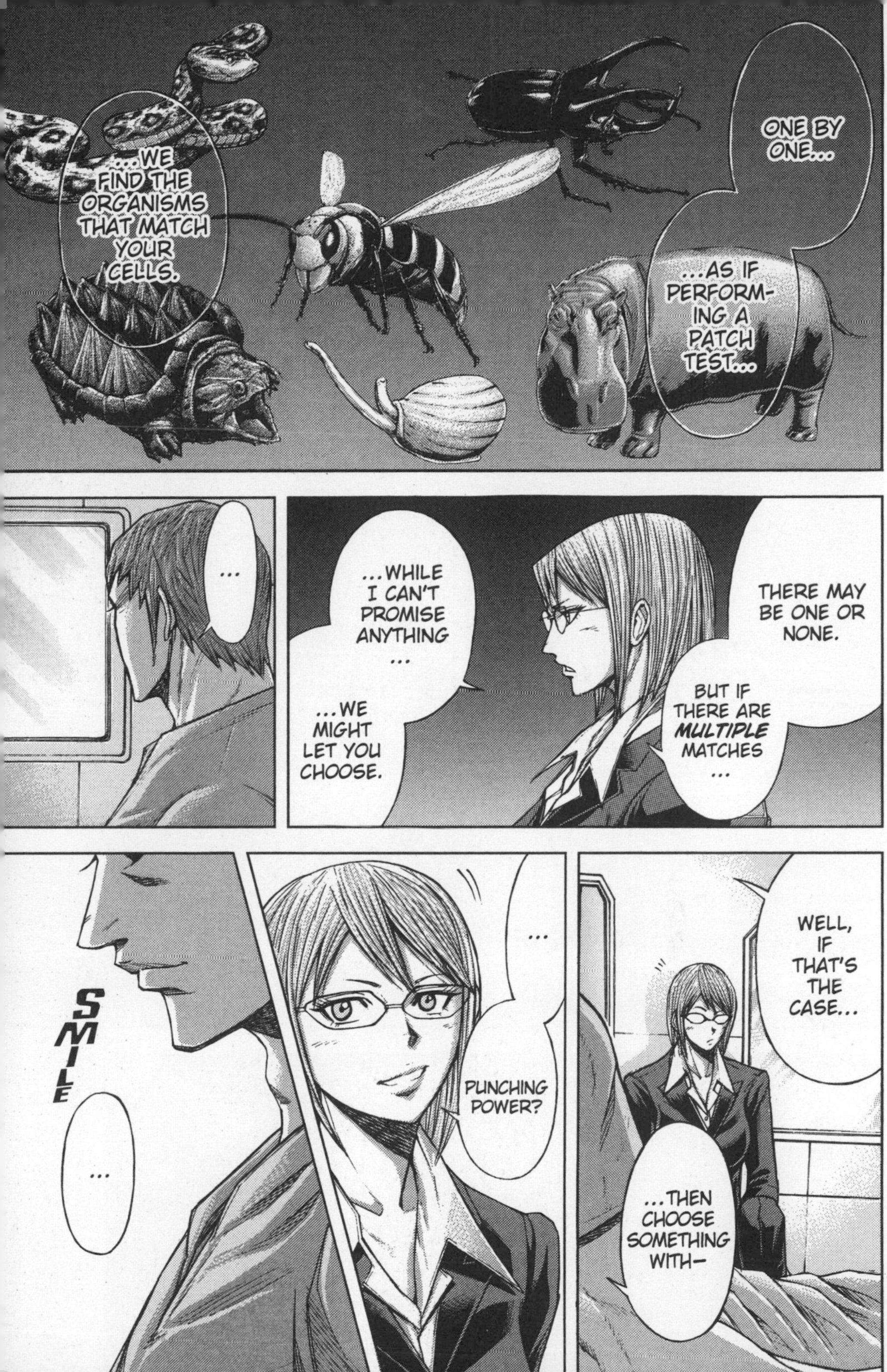
ONE BY ONE...
...AS IF PERFORMING A PATCH TEST...
...WE FIND THE ORGANISMS THAT MATCH YOUR CELLS.
THERE MAY BE ONE OR NONE.
BUT IF THERE ARE *MULTIPLE* MATCHES ...
...WHILE I CAN'T PROMISE ANYTHING ...
...WE MIGHT LET YOU CHOOSE.
...
WELL, IF THAT'S THE CASE...
...THEN CHOOSE SOMETHING WITH—
...
PUNCHING POWER?
SMILE
...

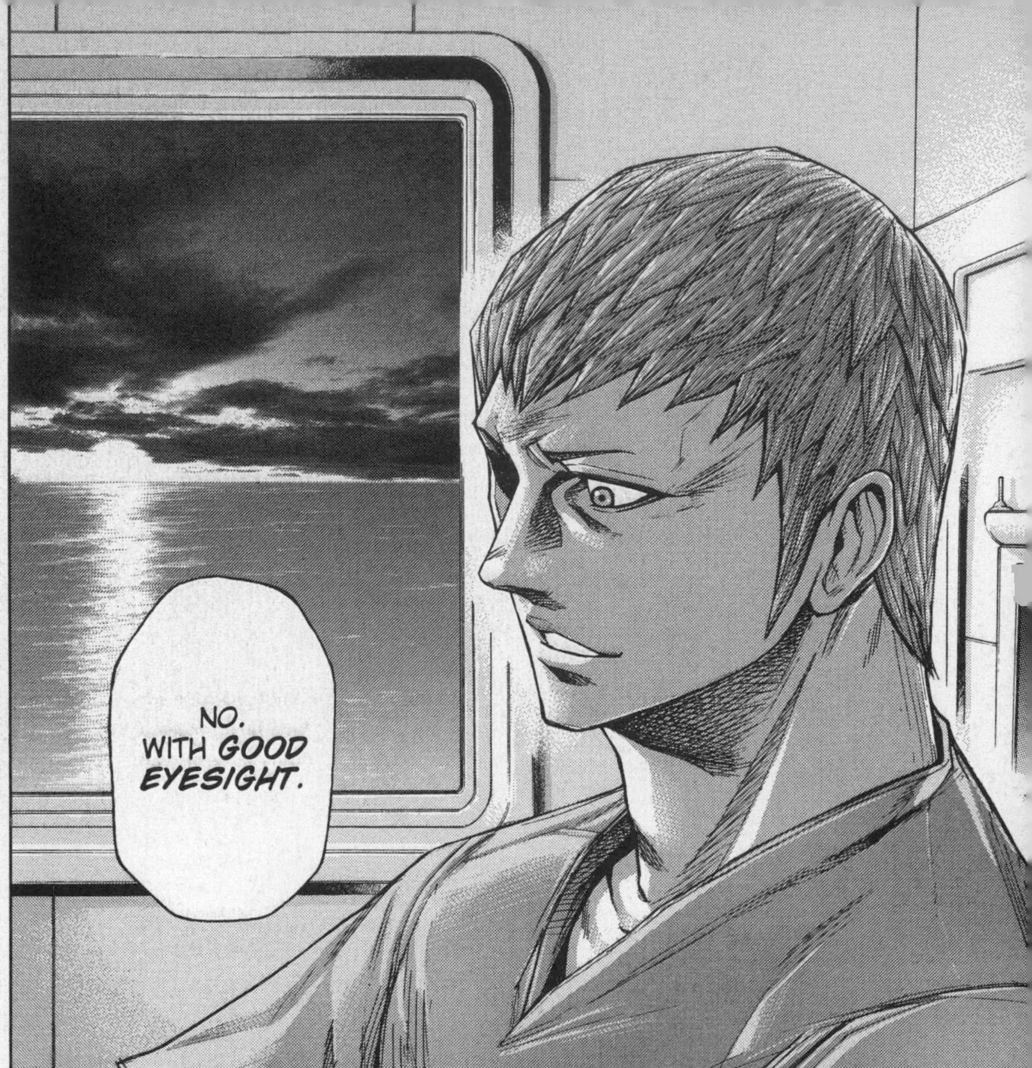
NO. WITH GOOD EYESIGHT.
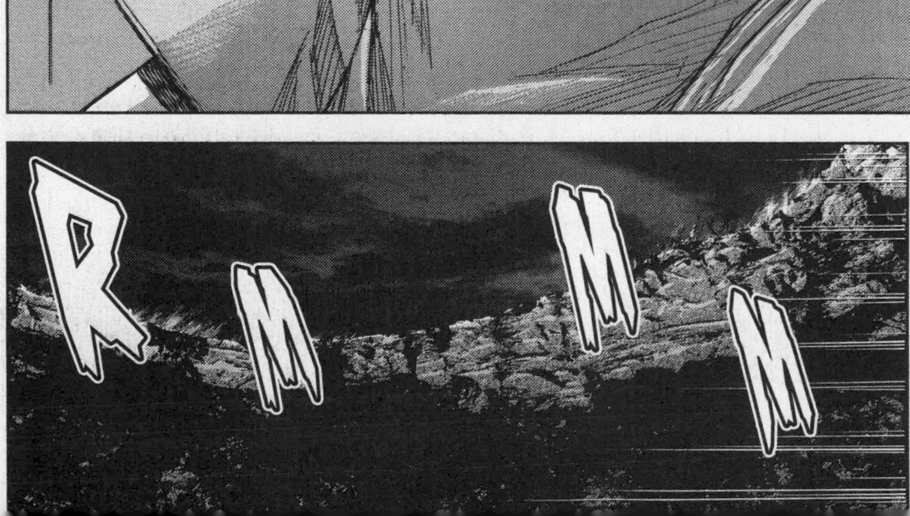
RMMM

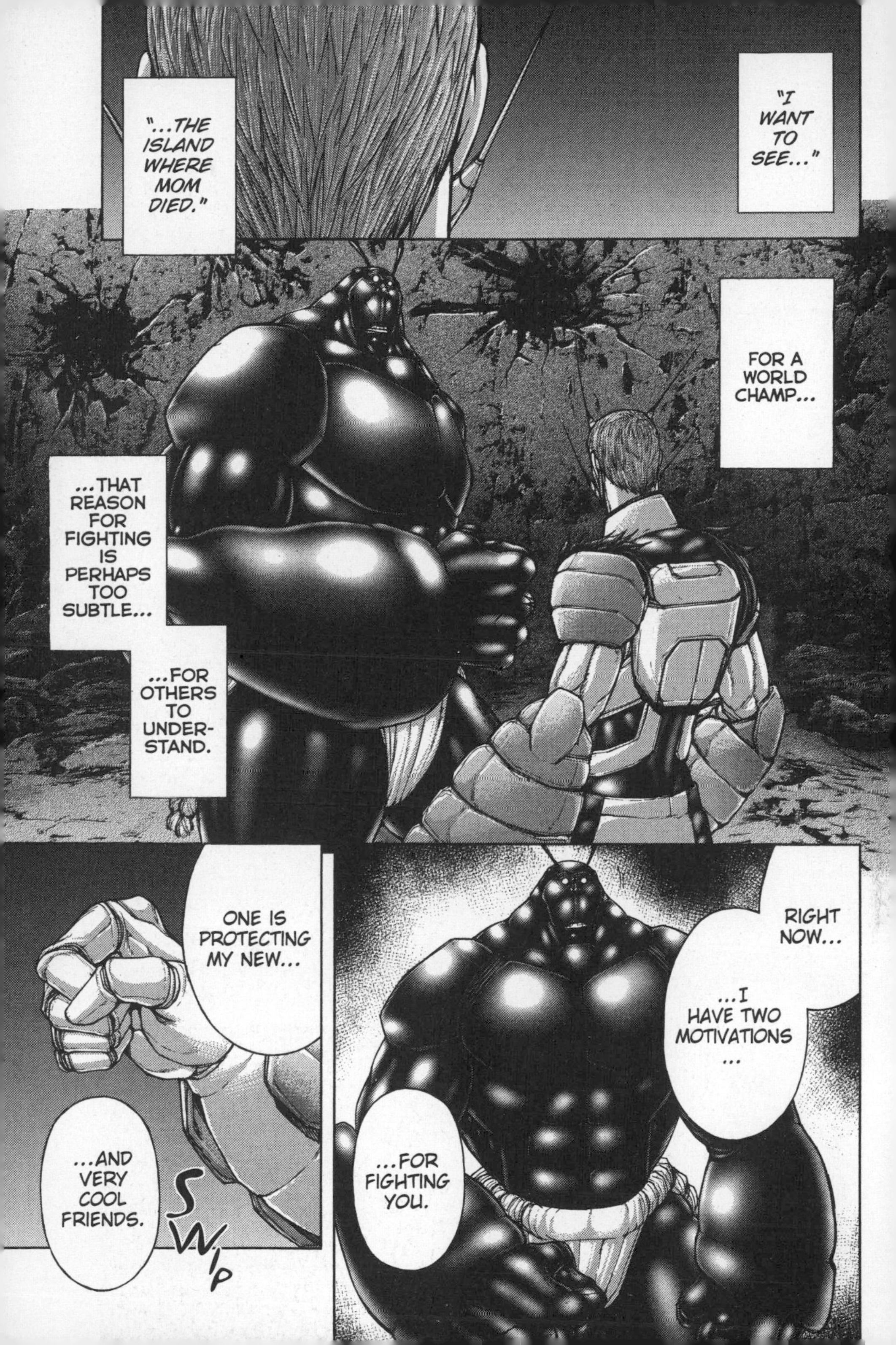
"I WANT TO SEE..."
"...THE ISLAND WHERE MOM DIED."
FOR A WORLD CHAMP...
...THAT REASON FOR FIGHTING IS PERHAPS TOO SUBTLE...
...FOR OTHERS TO UNDERSTAND.
RIGHT NOW...
...I HAVE TWO MOTIVATIONS ...
...FOR FIGHTING YOU.
ONE IS PROTECTING MY NEW...
...AND VERY COOL FRIENDS.
SWIP

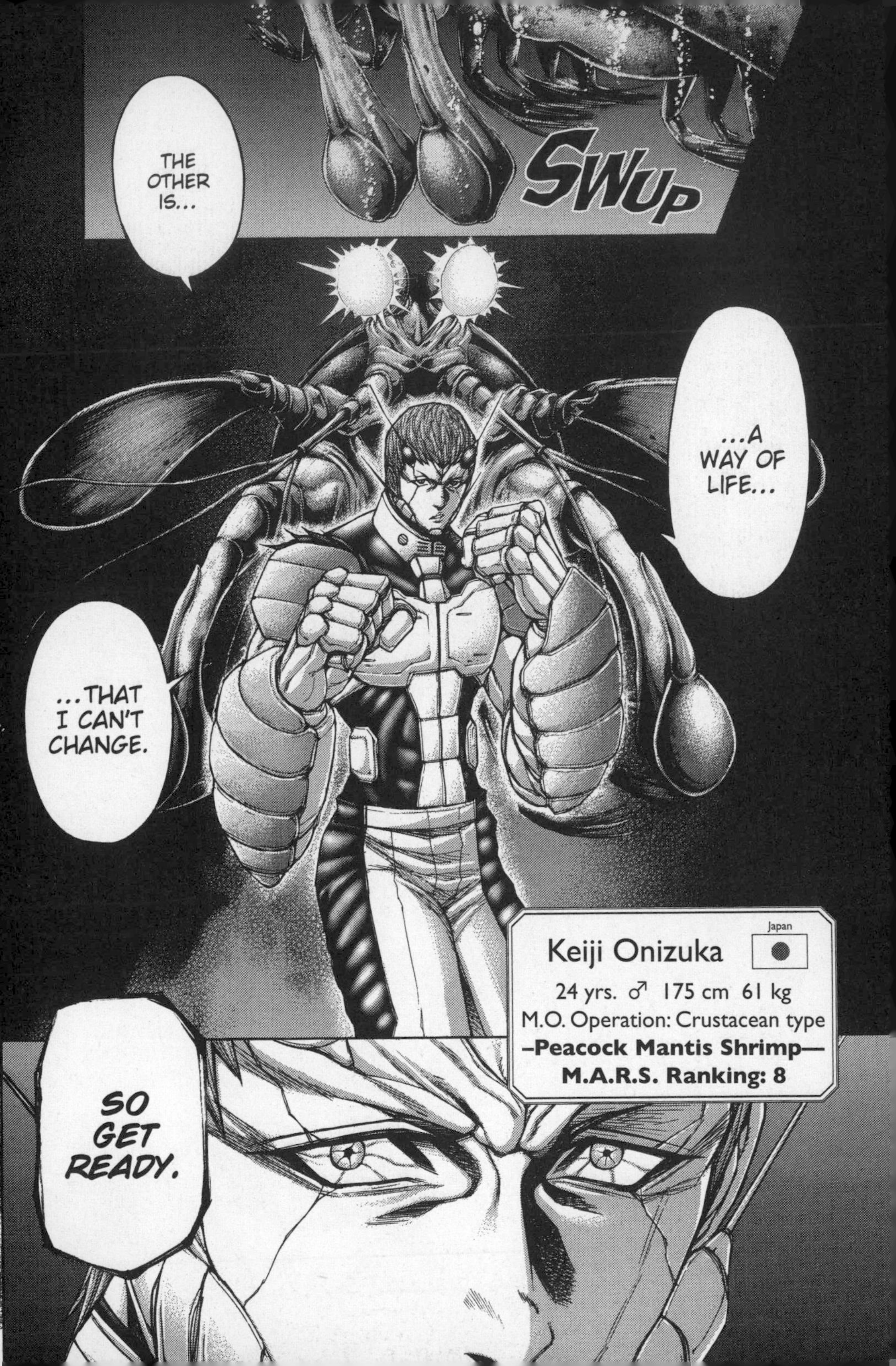
SWUP
THE OTHER IS...
...A WAY OF LIFE...
...THAT I CAN'T CHANGE.
Keiji Onizuka
Japan
24 yrs. ♂ 175 cm 61 kg
M.O. Operation: Crustacean type
–Peacock Mantis Shrimp—
M.A.R.S. Ranking: 8
SO GET READY.

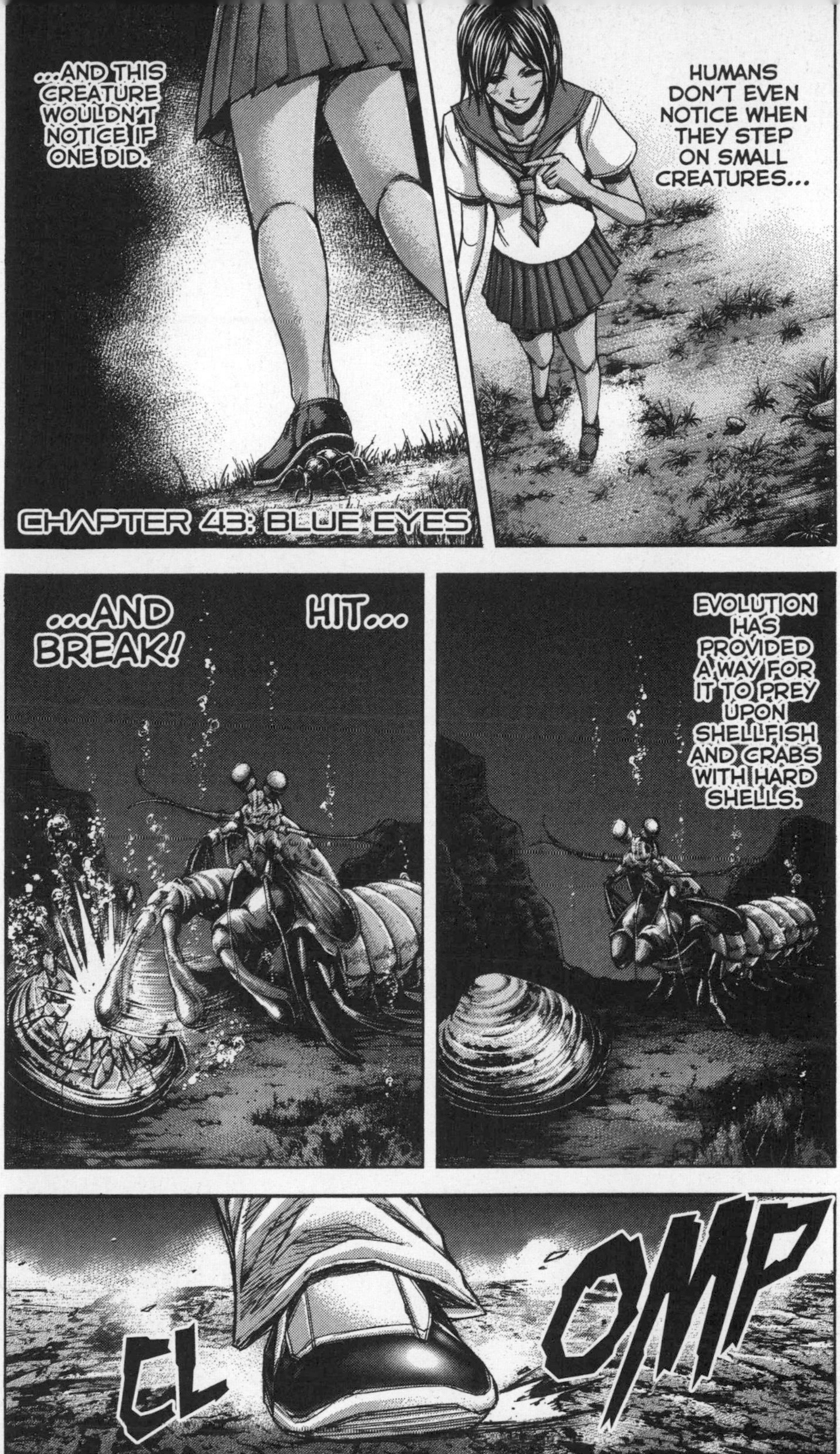
HUMANS DON'T EVEN NOTICE WHEN THEY STEP ON SMALL CREATURES...
...AND THIS CREATURE WOULDN'T NOTICE IF ONE DID.
CHAPTER 43: BLUE EYES
EVOLUTION HAS PROVIDED A WAY FOR IT TO PREY UPON SHELLFISH AND CRABS WITH HARD SHELLS.
HIT...
...AND BREAK!
CL
OMP

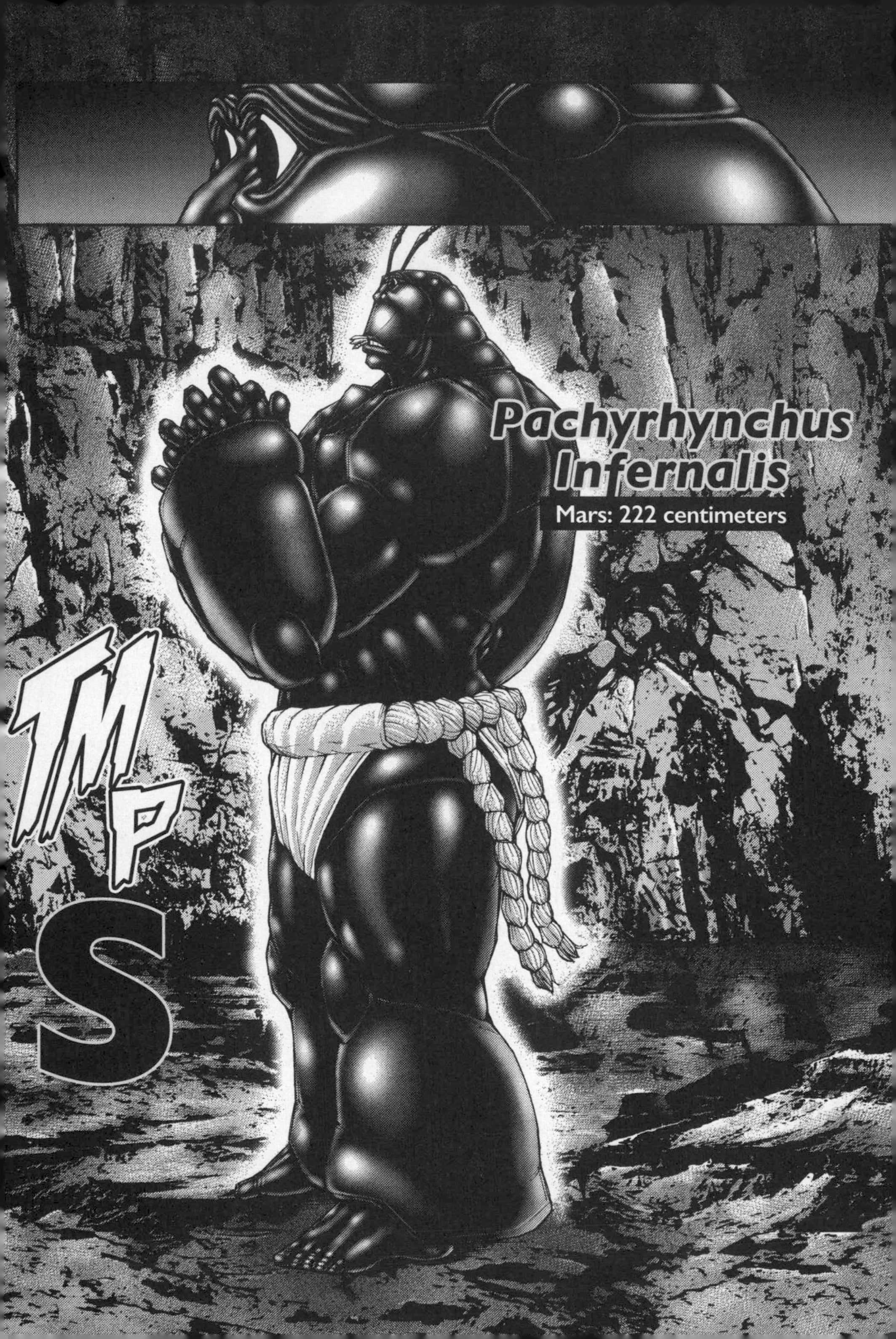
Pachyrhynchus Infernalis
Mars: 222 centimeters
TMPS

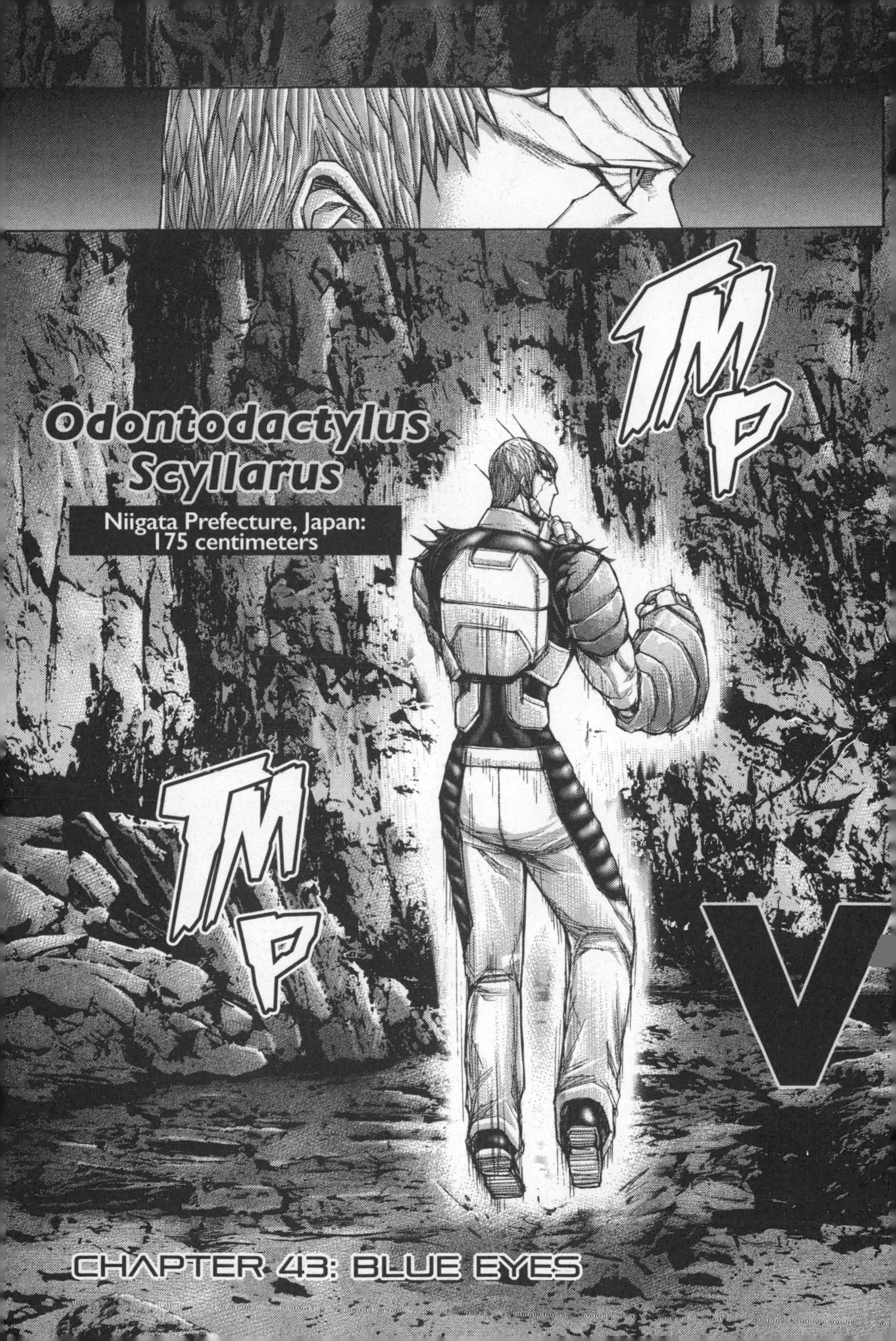
TMP
Odontodactylus Scyllarus
Niigata Prefecture, Japan: 175 centimeters
TMP
V
CHAPTER 43: BLUE EYES

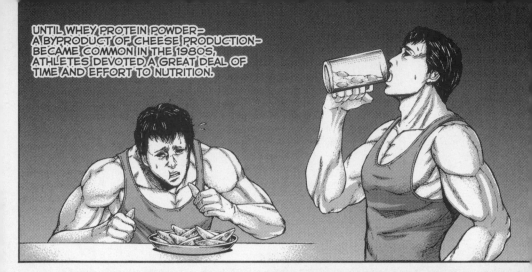

UNTIL WHEY PROTEIN POWDER— A BYPRODUCT OF CHEESE PRODUCTION— BECAME COMMON IN THE 1980S, ATHLETES DEVOTED A GREAT DEAL OF TIME AND EFFORT TO NUTRITION.
PROTEIN IS INDISPENSABLE FOR GAINING AND MAINTAINING MUSCLE, AS WELL AS FOR HEIGHT GROWTH IN CHILDREN.
THE GREEK WORD *PROTEIOS* DESIGNATES SOMETHING OF UTMOST IMPORTANCE.
ACCORD- INGLY, THIS SUBSTANCE ...
GWUMP
... GENERATES *PHYSICAL ABILITY*.

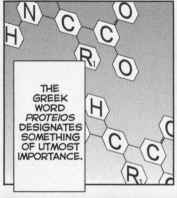

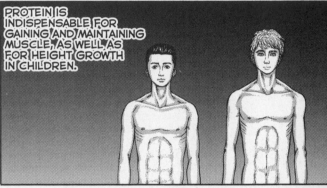

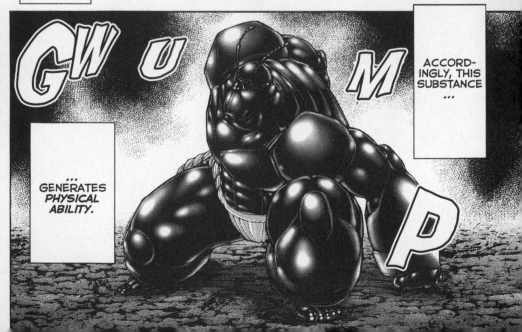

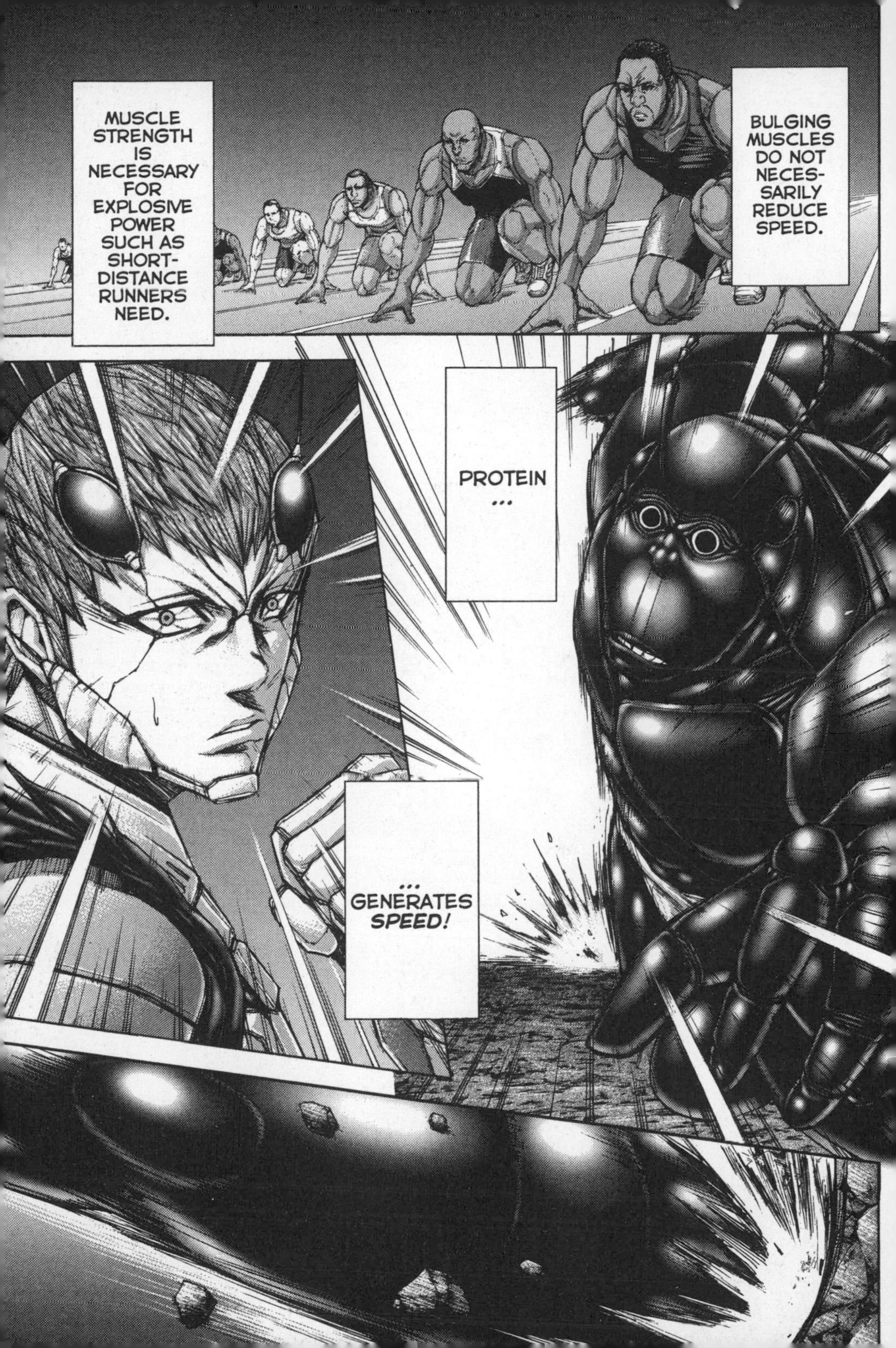
BULGING MUSCLES DO NOT NECES-SARILY REDUCE SPEED.
MUSCLE STRENGTH IS NECESSARY FOR EXPLOSIVE POWER SUCH AS SHORT-DISTANCE RUNNERS NEED.
PROTEIN...
...GENERATES SPEED!

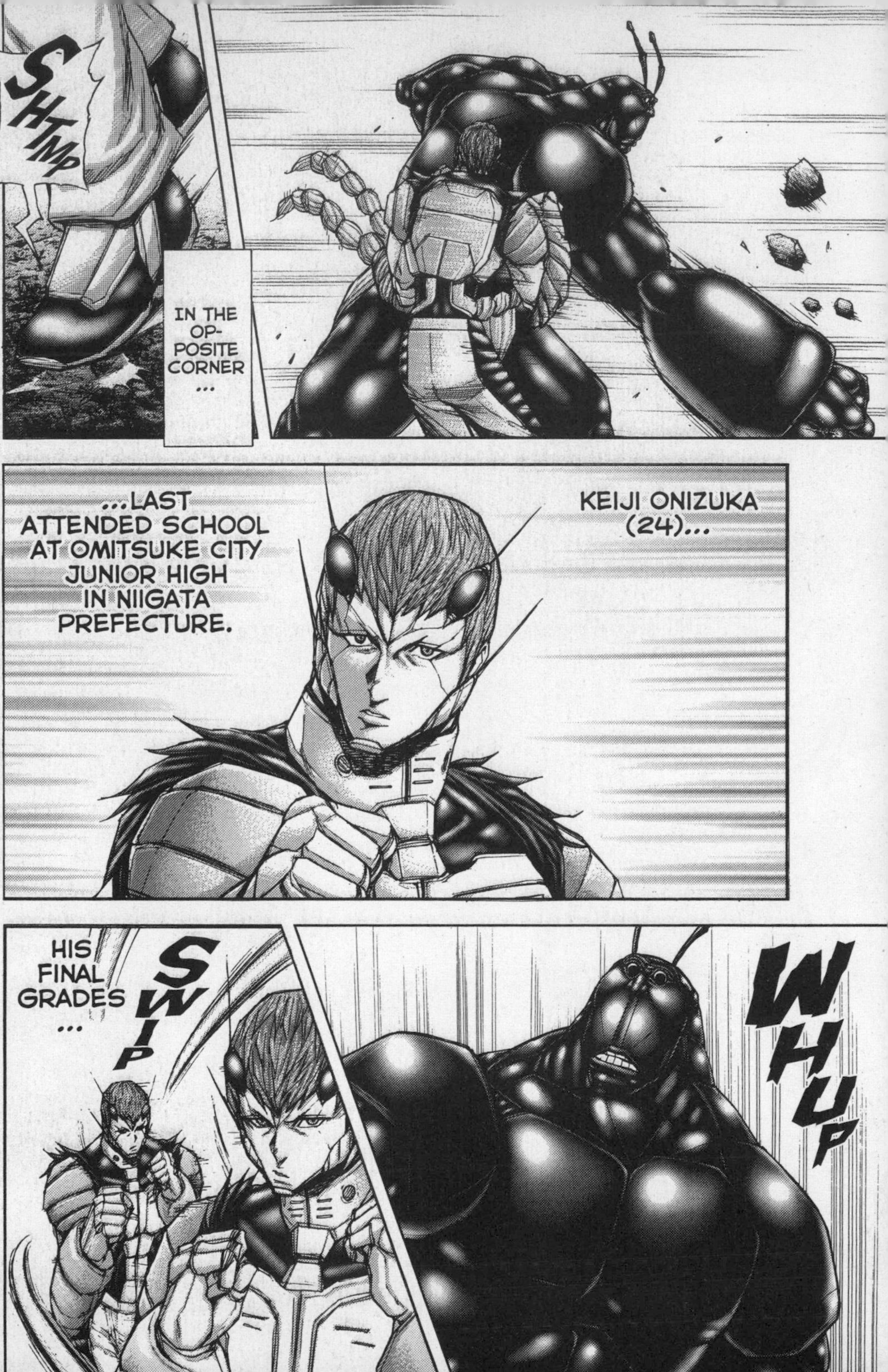
IN THE OP-POSITE CORNER ...
SHTMP
KEIJI ONIZUKA (24)...
...LAST ATTENDED SCHOOL AT OMITSUKE CITY JUNIOR HIGH IN NIIGATA PREFECTURE.
WHUP
HIS FINAL GRADES ...
SWIP

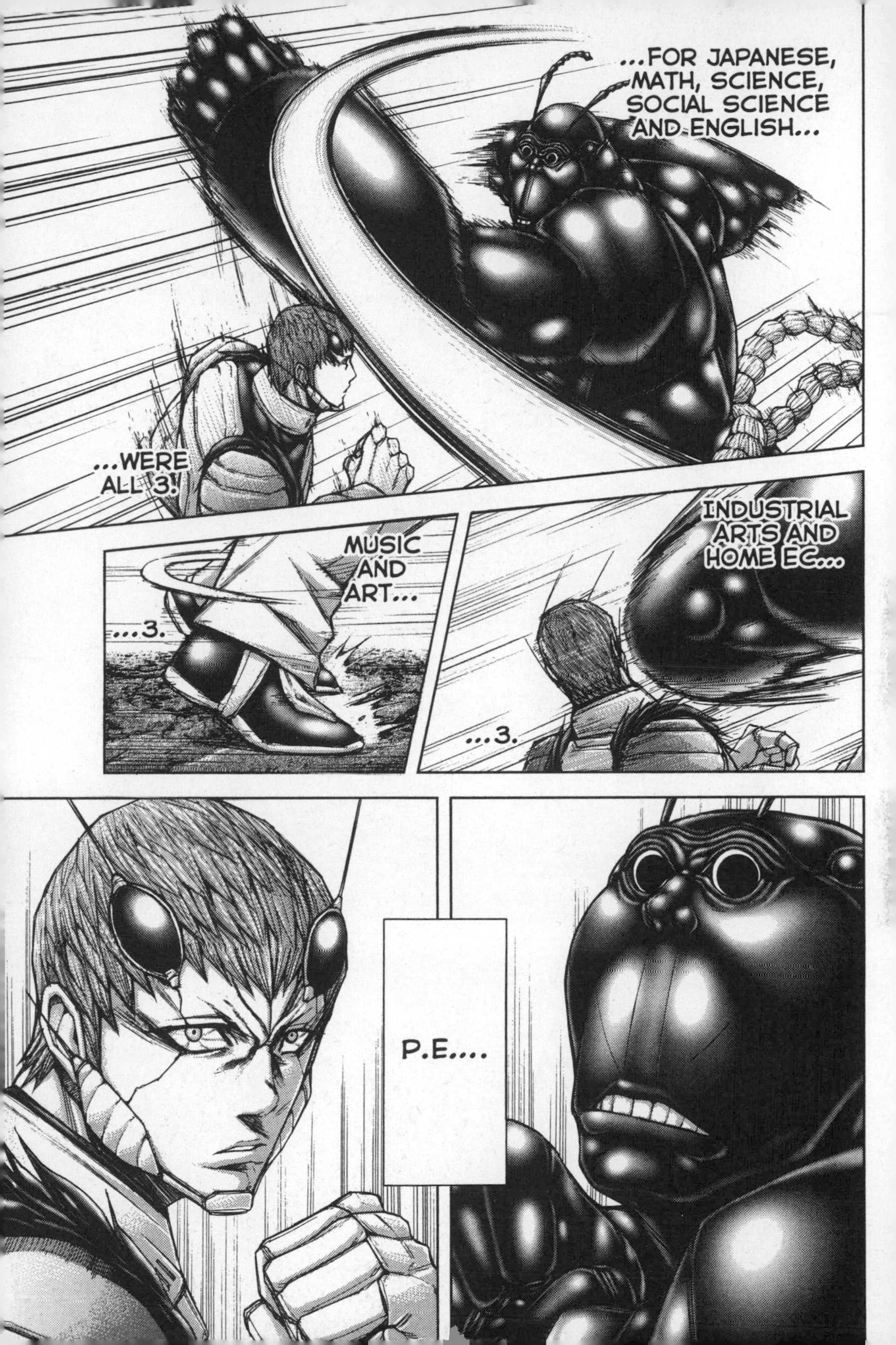
...FOR JAPANESE, MATH, SCIENCE, SOCIAL SCIENCE AND ENGLISH...
...WERE ALL 3!
INDUSTRIAL ARTS AND HOME EC...
...3.
MUSIC AND ART...
...3.
P.E....

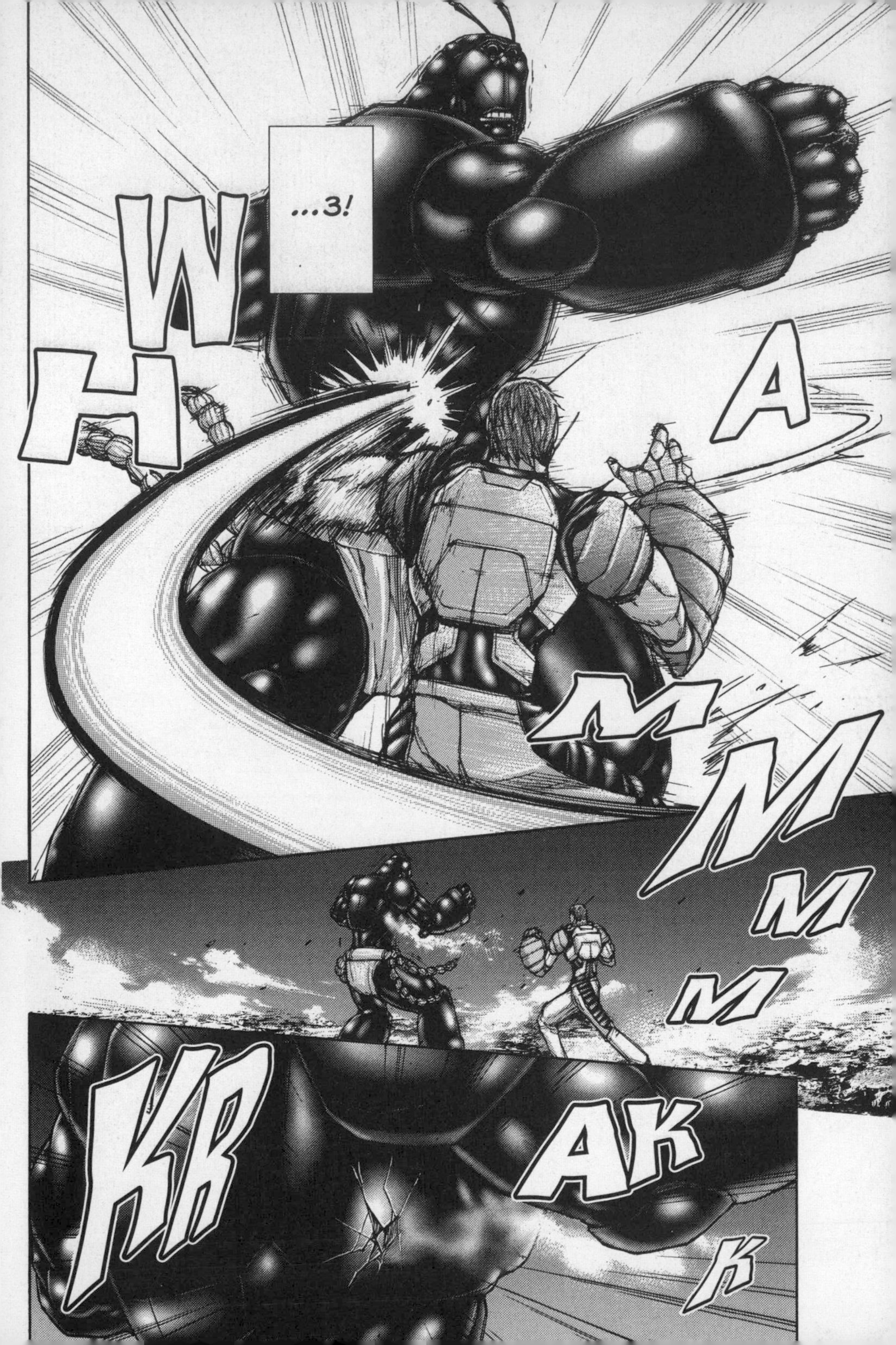
...3!
WHAMMMMM
KRAKK

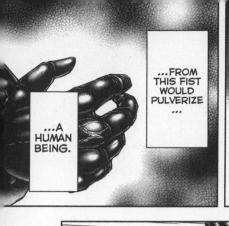

...A HUMAN BEING.

...FROM THIS FIST WOULD PULVERIZE...

A SINGLE BLOW...

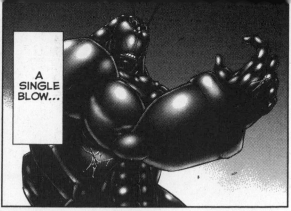

...BUT ITS FIST...

...DOESN'T HIT!!

KEIJI'S OPPONENT HAS A WEEVIL'S HARDNESS, INCREASED MUSCLE BULK...

...AND A COCK-ROACH'S SPEED...

...IS NO SURPRISE.

AND THAT...

WHAM

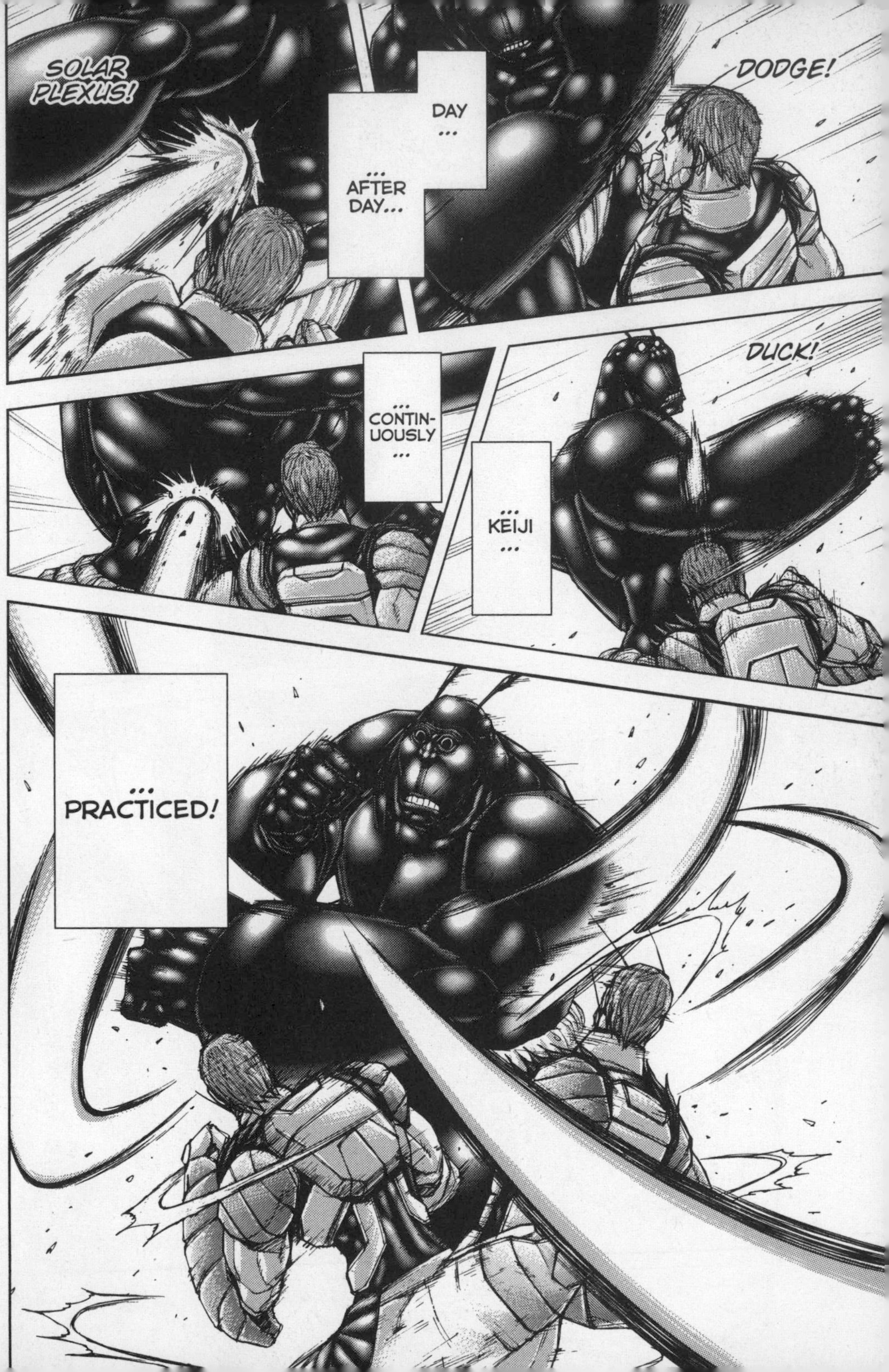
DODGE!
DAY ...
... AFTER DAY...
SOLAR PLEXUS!
DUCK!
... KEIJI ...
... CONTIN-UOUSLY ...
... PRACTICED!

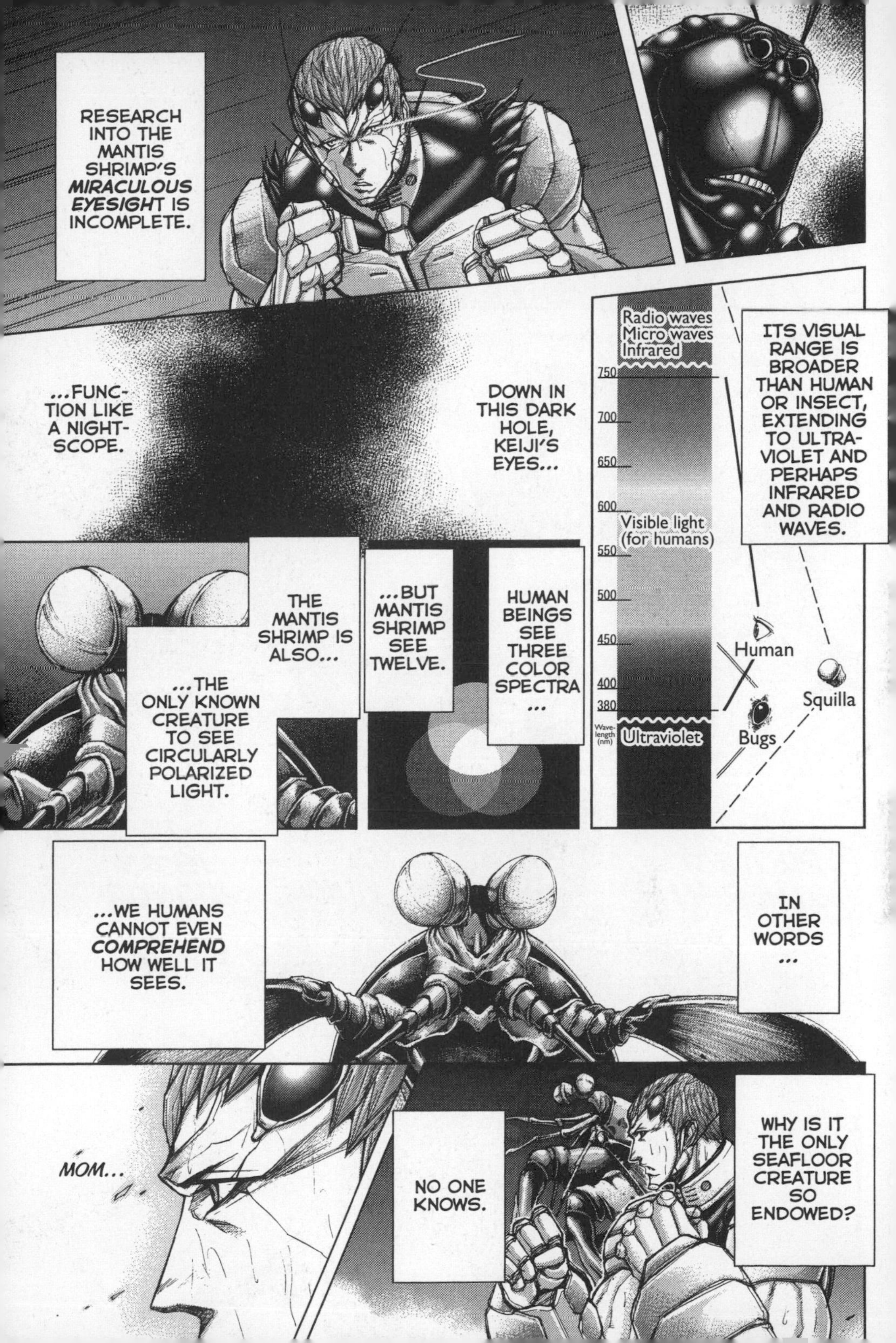
RESEARCH INTO THE MANTIS SHRIMP'S *MIRACULOUS EYESIGHT* IS INCOMPLETE.
ITS VISUAL RANGE IS BROADER THAN HUMAN OR INSECT, EXTENDING TO ULTRAVIOLET AND PERHAPS INFRARED AND RADIO WAVES.
Radio waves
Micro waves
Infrared
750
700
650
600
Visible light (for humans)
550
500
450
400
380
Wave-length (nm)
Ultraviolet
Human
Squilla
Bugs
DOWN IN THIS DARK HOLE, KEIJI'S EYES...
...FUNCTION LIKE A NIGHT-SCOPE.
HUMAN BEINGS SEE THREE COLOR SPECTRA...
...BUT MANTIS SHRIMP SEE TWELVE.
THE MANTIS SHRIMP IS ALSO...
...THE ONLY KNOWN CREATURE TO SEE CIRCULARLY POLARIZED LIGHT.
IN OTHER WORDS...
...WE HUMANS CANNOT EVEN *COMPREHEND* HOW WELL IT SEES.
WHY IS IT THE ONLY SEAFLOOR CREATURE SO ENDOWED?
NO ONE KNOWS.
MOM...

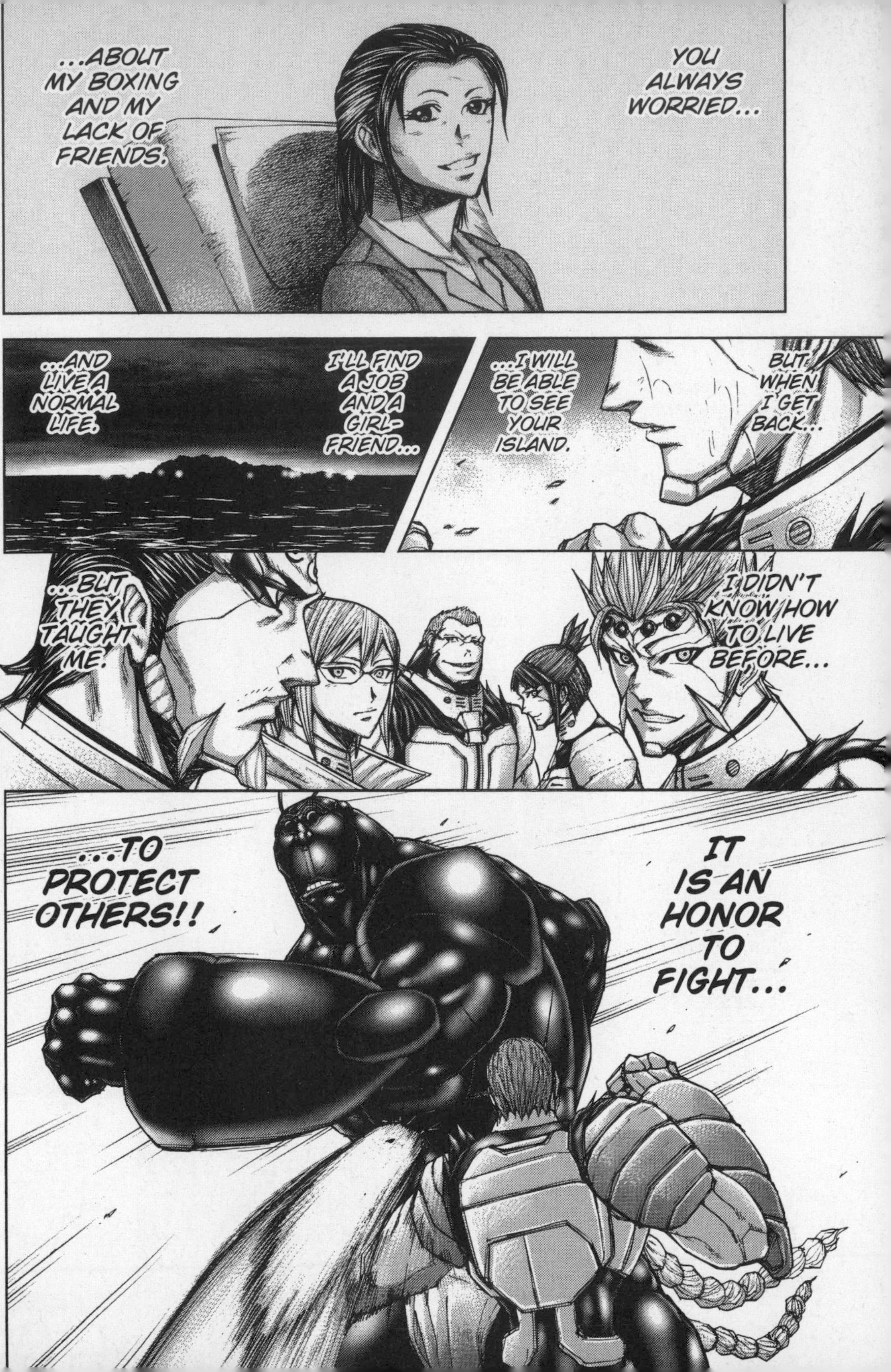
YOU ALWAYS WORRIED...
...ABOUT MY BOXING AND MY LACK OF FRIENDS.
BUT WHEN I GET BACK...
...I WILL BE ABLE TO SEE YOUR ISLAND.
I'LL FIND A JOB AND A GIRL-FRIEND...
...AND LIVE A NORMAL LIFE.
I DIDN'T KNOW HOW TO LIVE BEFORE...
...BUT THEY TAUGHT ME.
IT IS AN HONOR TO FIGHT...
...TO PROTECT OTHERS!!

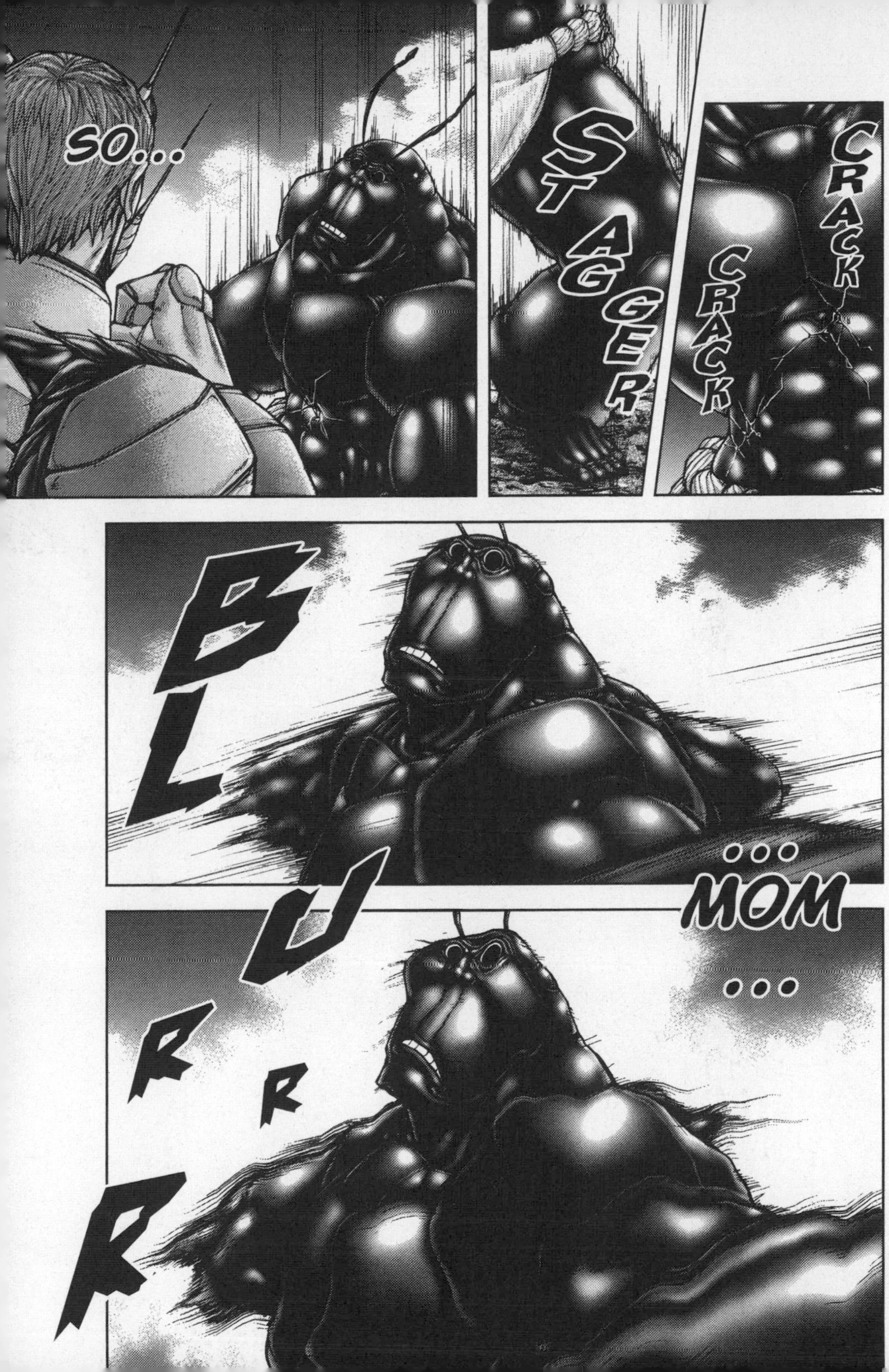
CRACK
CRACK
STAGGER
SO...
BLURRR
...MOM...

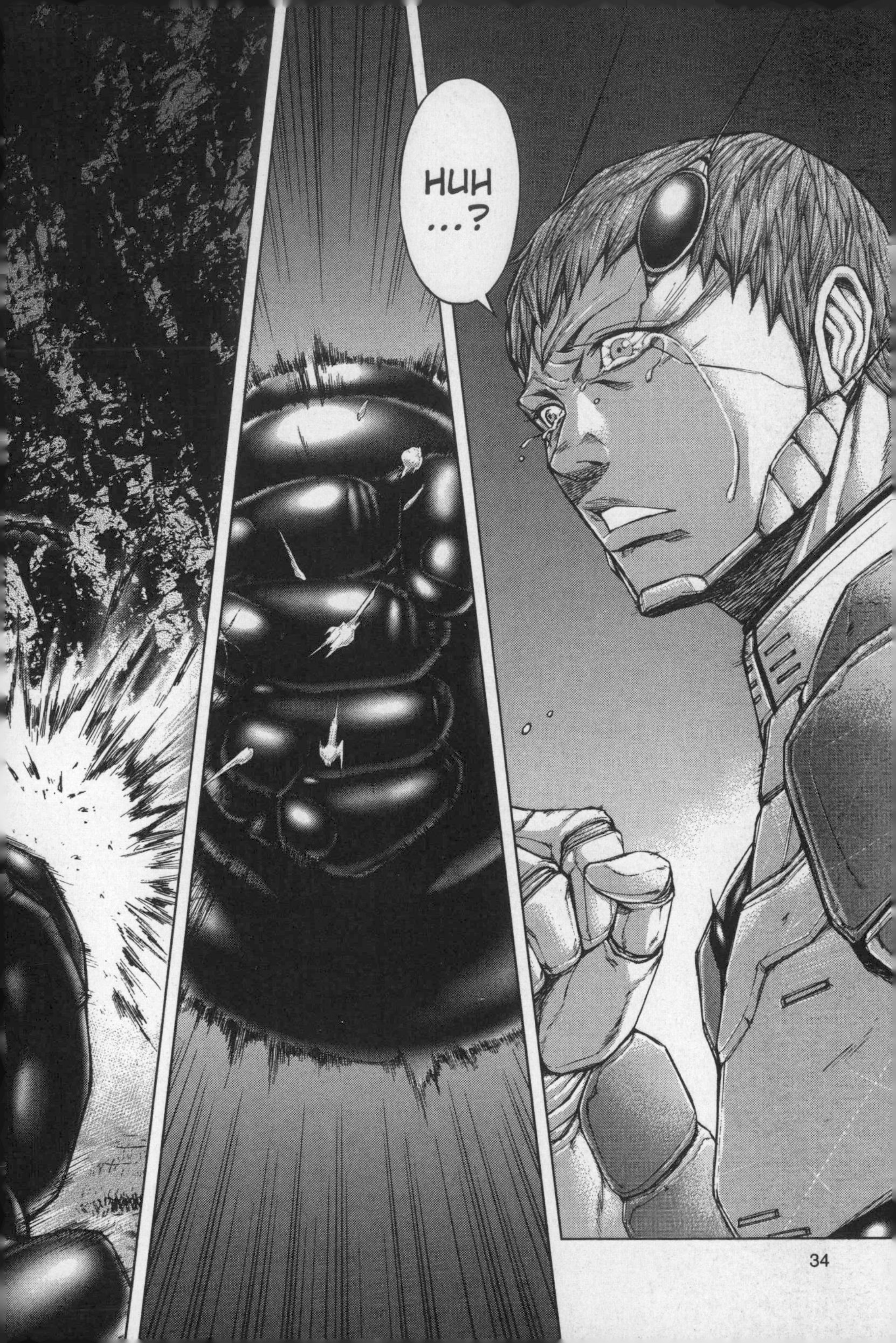
HUH ...?

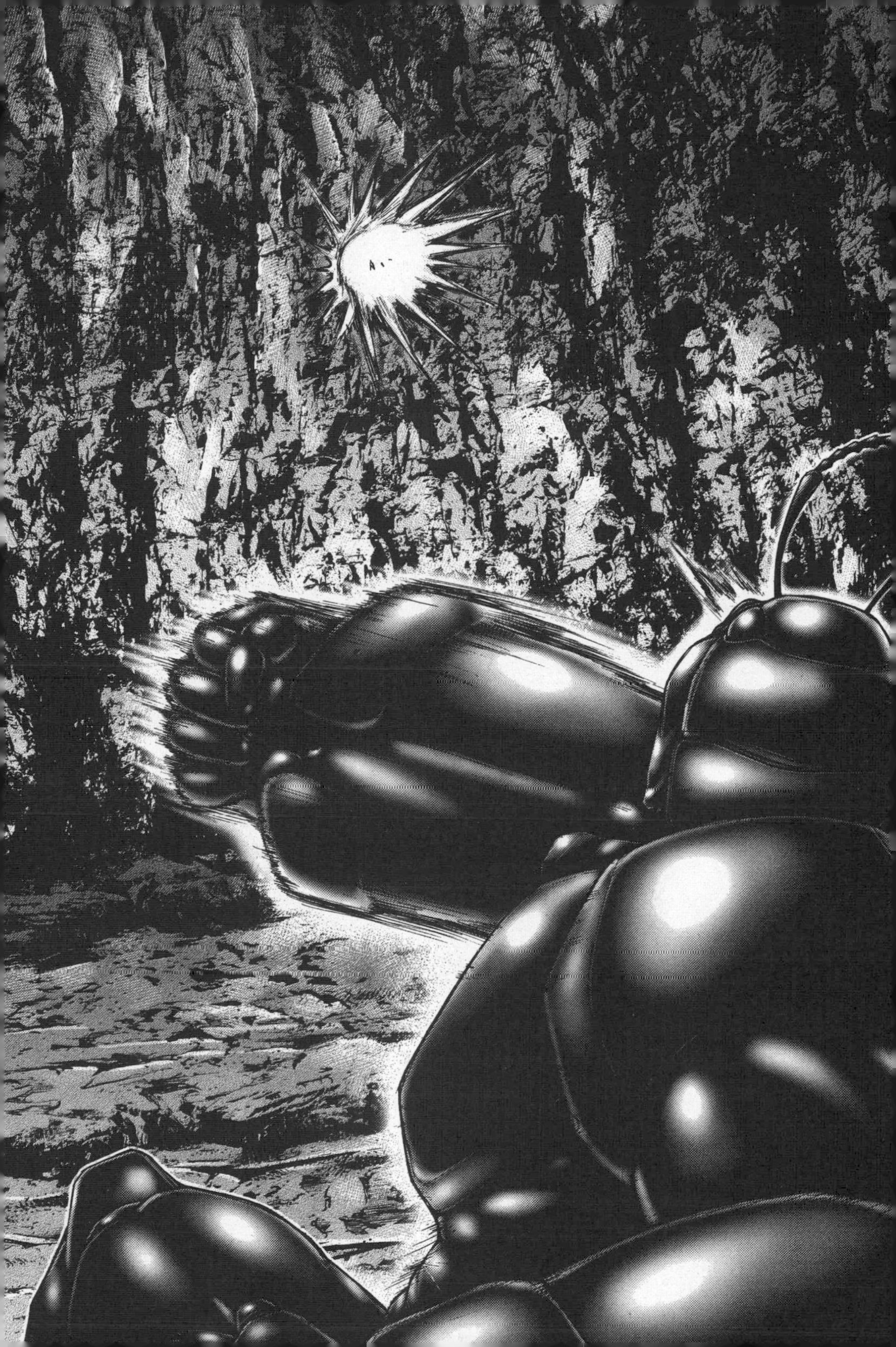

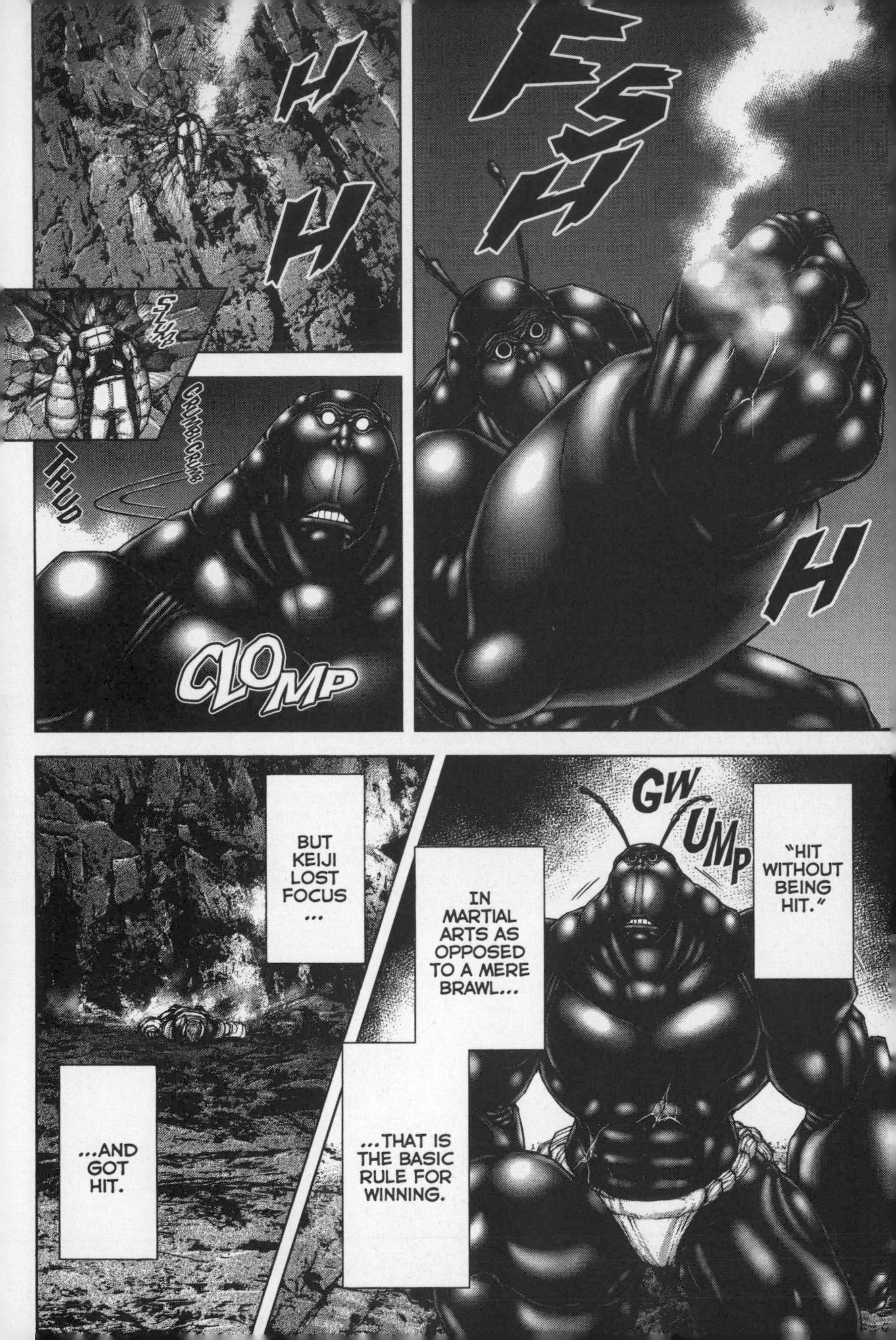
FSHH
H
HH
THUD
CLOMP
GWUMP
"HIT WITHOUT BEING HIT."
IN MARTIAL ARTS AS OPPOSED TO A MERE BRAWL...
...THAT IS THE BASIC RULE FOR WINNING.
BUT KEIJI LOST FOCUS ...
...AND GOT HIT.

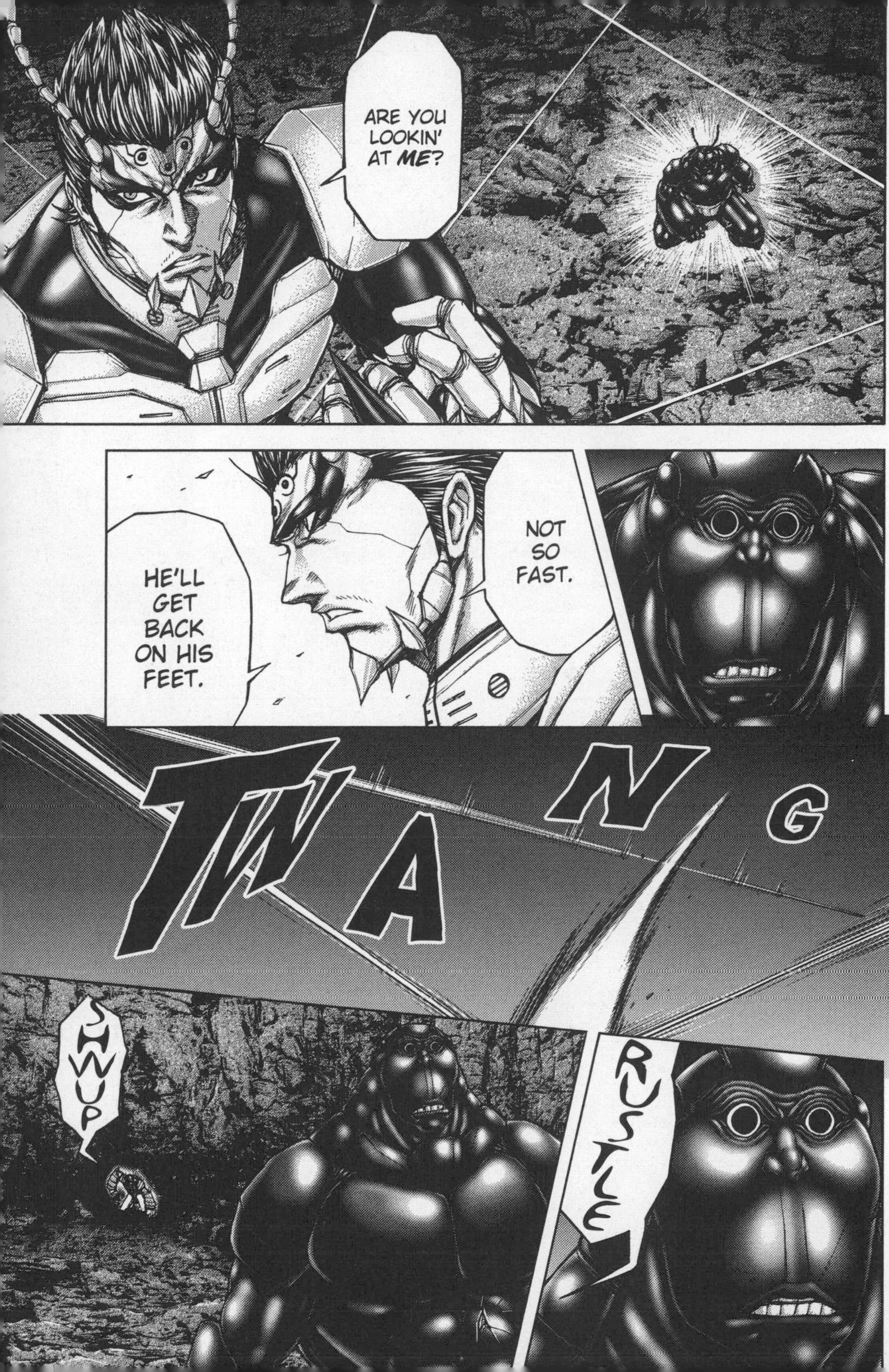
ARE YOU LOOKIN' AT *ME*?
NOT SO FAST.
HE'LL GET BACK ON HIS FEET.
TWANG
RUSTLE
SHWUP

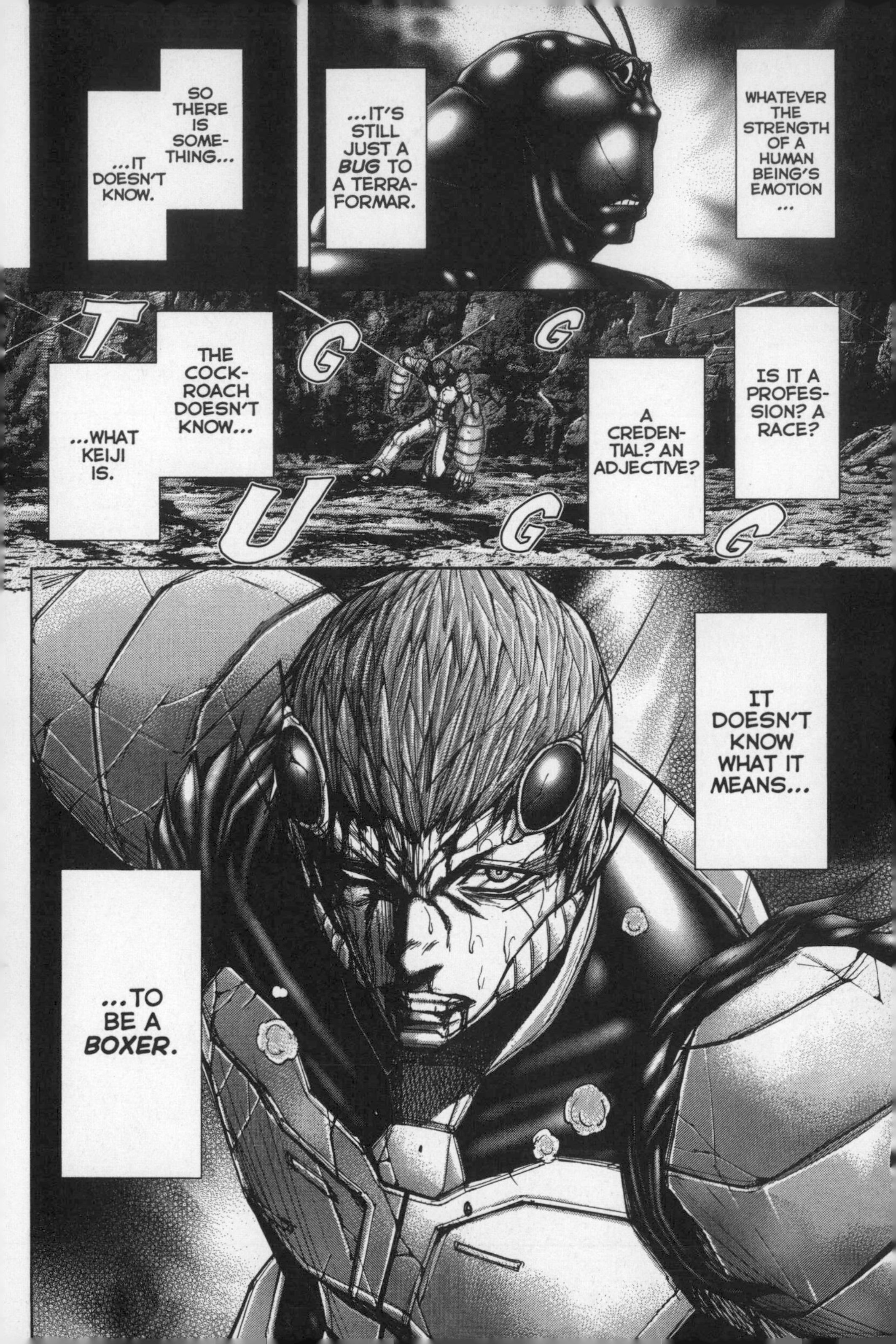

WHATEVER THE STRENGTH OF A HUMAN BEING'S EMOTION...
...IT'S STILL JUST A BUG TO A TERRAFORMAR.
SO THERE IS SOMETHING...
...IT DOESN'T KNOW.
IS IT A PROFESSION? A RACE?
A CREDENTIAL? AN ADJECTIVE?
TUGGGG
THE COCKROACH DOESN'T KNOW...
...WHAT KEIJI IS.
IT DOESN'T KNOW WHAT IT MEANS...
...TO BE A BOXER.

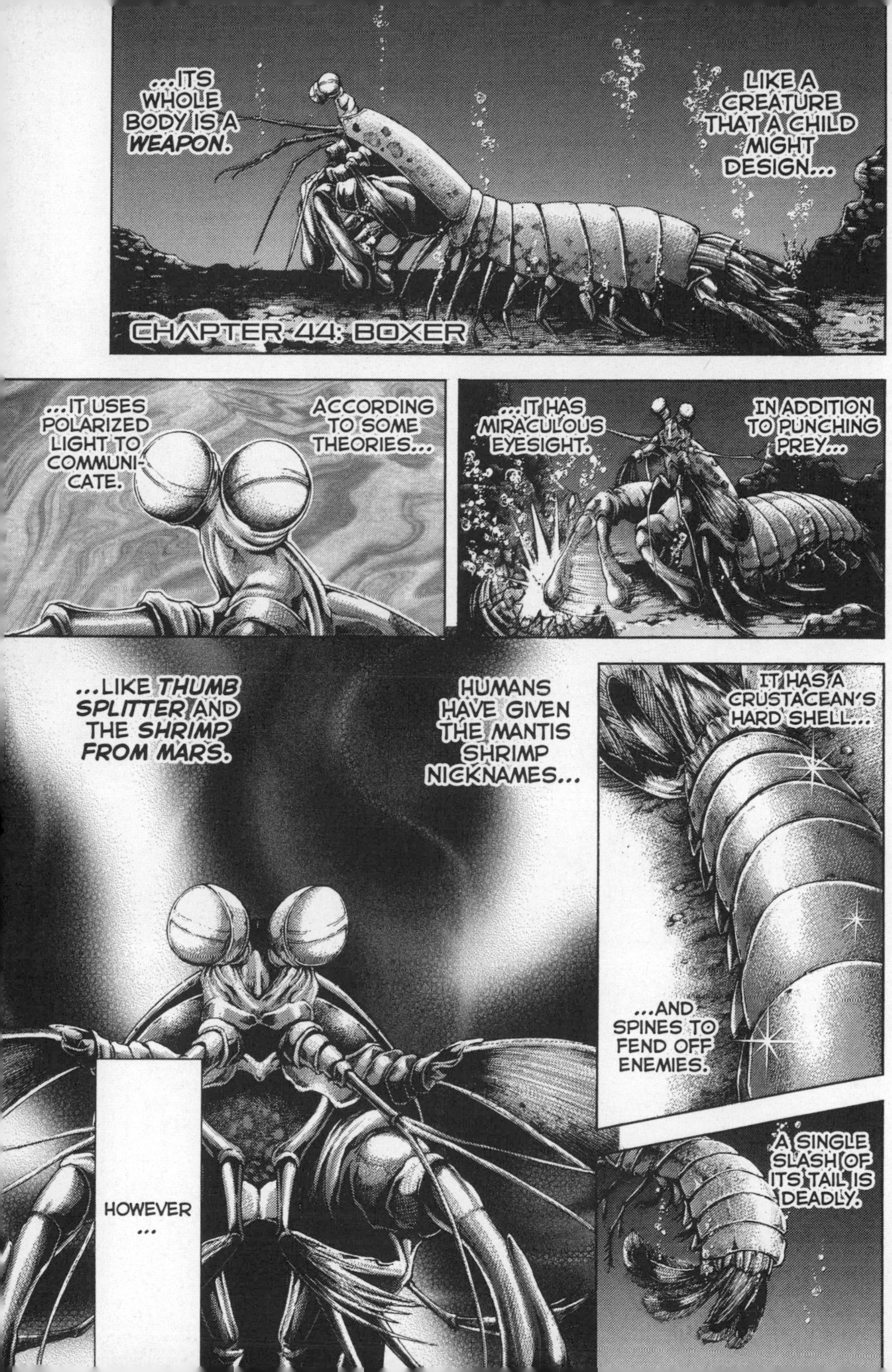
LIKE A CREATURE THAT A CHILD MIGHT DESIGN...
...ITS WHOLE BODY IS A WEAPON.
CHAPTER 44: BOXER
IN ADDITION TO PUNCHING PREY...
...IT HAS MIRACULOUS EYESIGHT.
ACCORDING TO SOME THEORIES...
...IT USES POLARIZED LIGHT TO COMMUNI-CATE.
IT HAS A CRUSTACEAN'S HARD SHELL...
...AND SPINES TO FEND OFF ENEMIES.
A SINGLE SLASH OF ITS TAIL IS DEADLY.
HUMANS HAVE GIVEN THE MANTIS SHRIMP NICKNAMES...
...LIKE THUMB SPLITTER AND THE SHRIMP FROM MARS.
HOWEVER...

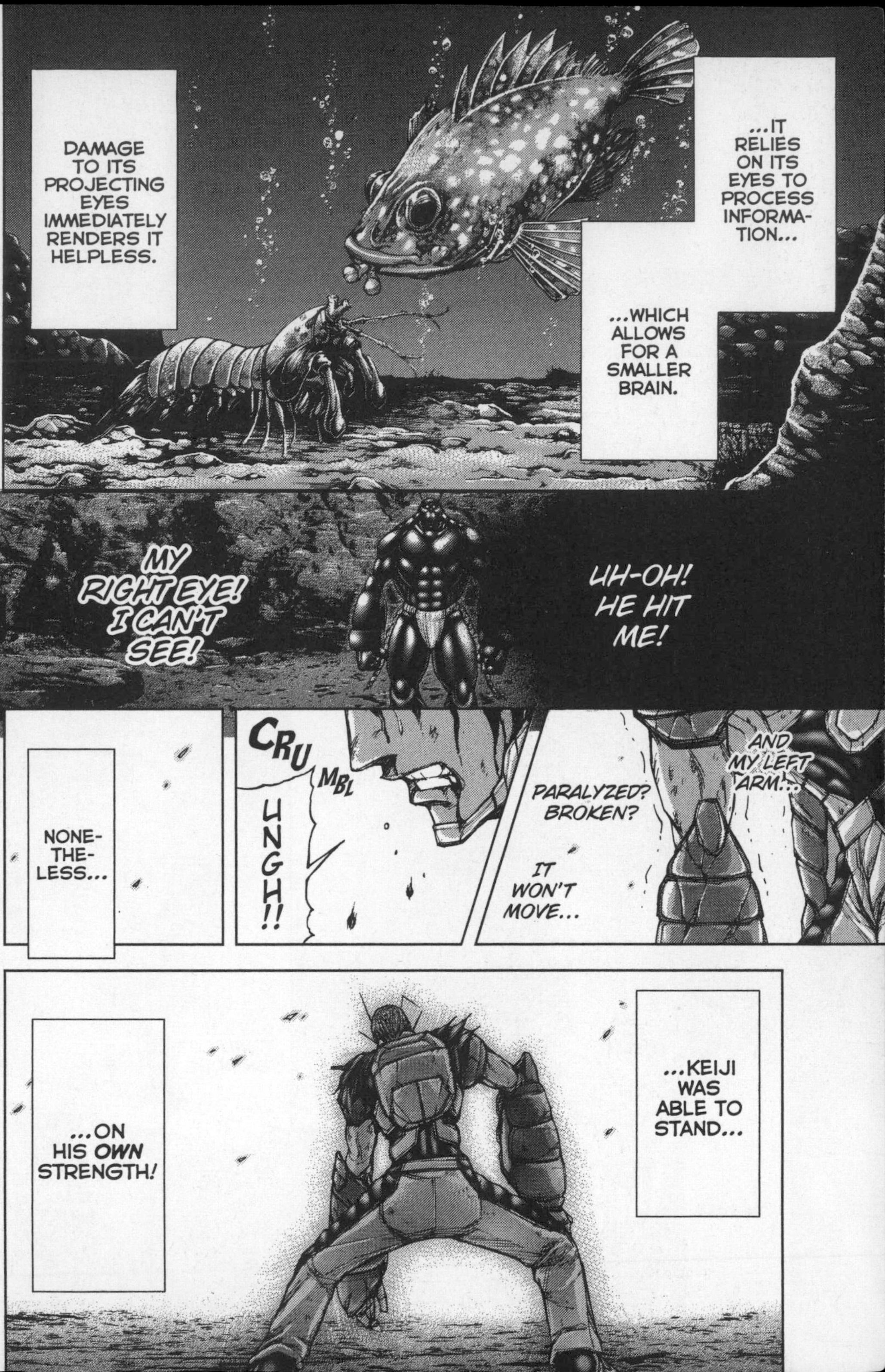
...IT RELIES ON ITS EYES TO PROCESS INFORMATION...
...WHICH ALLOWS FOR A SMALLER BRAIN.
DAMAGE TO ITS PROJECTING EYES IMMEDIATELY RENDERS IT HELPLESS.
UH-OH! HE HIT ME!
MY RIGHT EYE! I CAN'T SEE!
AND MY LEFT ARM...
PARALYZED? BROKEN?
IT WON'T MOVE...
CRUMBL
UNGH!!
NONE-THE-LESS...
...KEIJI WAS ABLE TO STAND...
...ON HIS *OWN* STRENGTH!

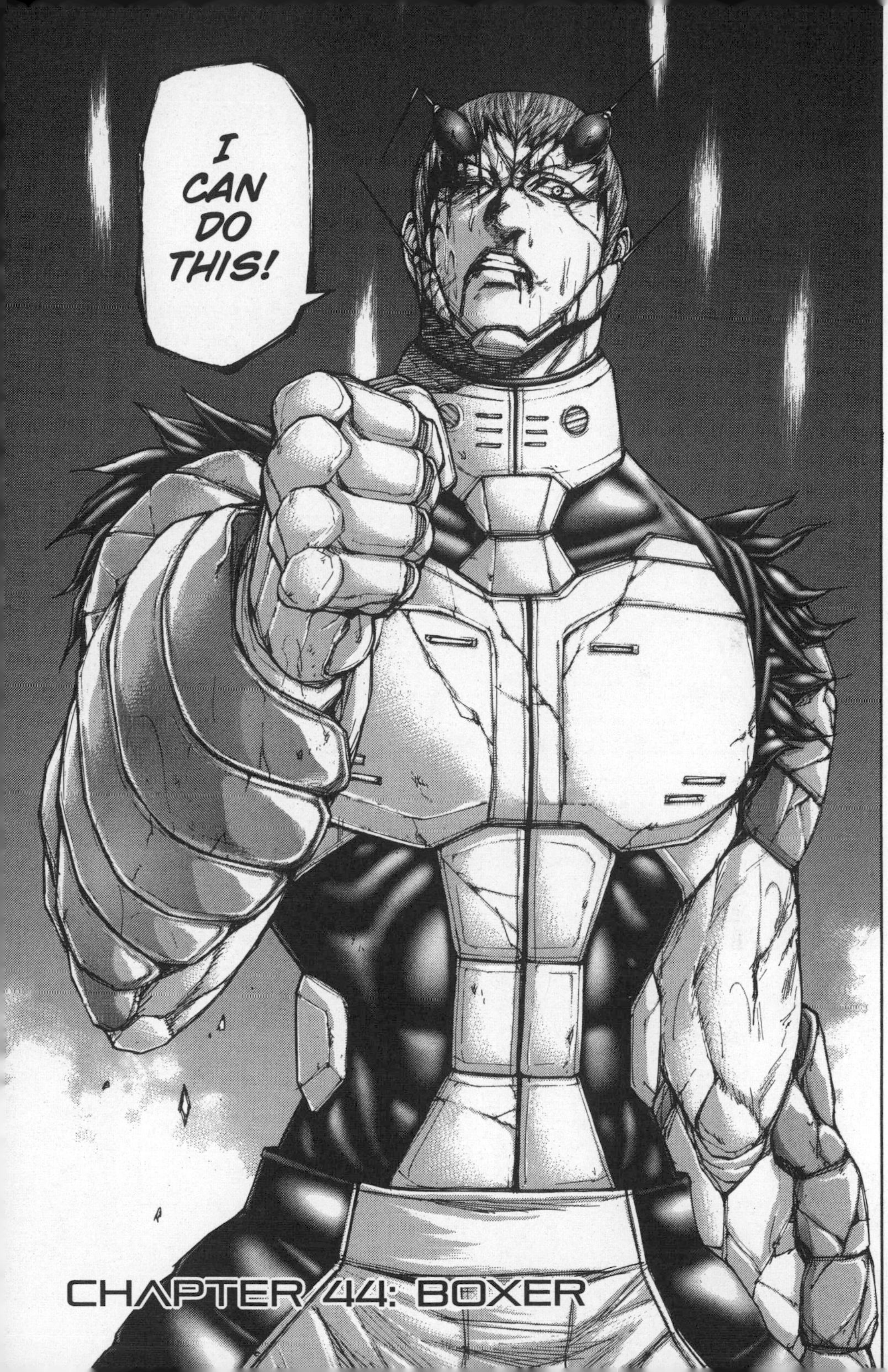
I CAN DO THIS!
CHAPTER 44: BOXER

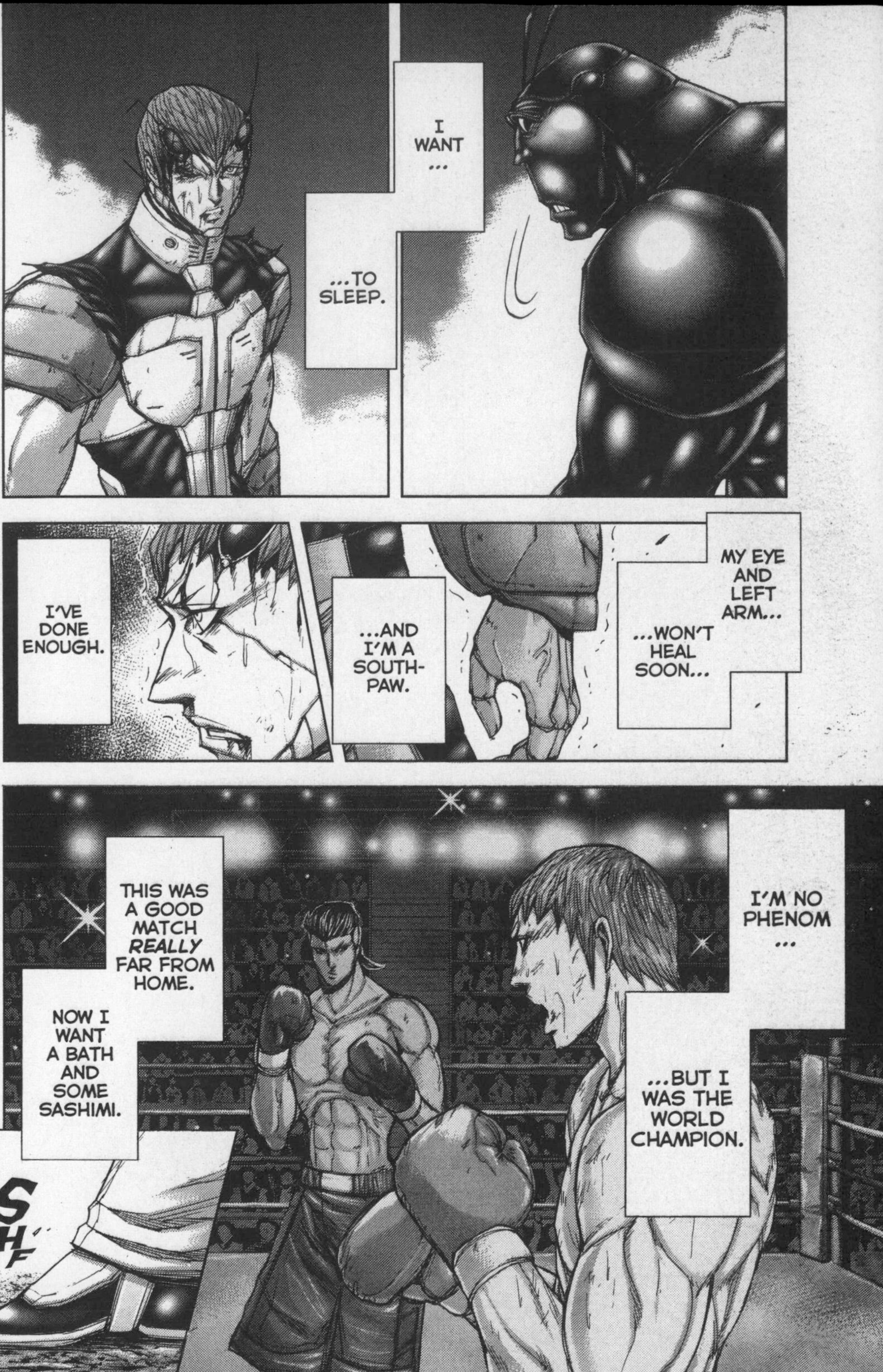
I WANT ...
...TO SLEEP.
MY EYE AND LEFT ARM...
...WON'T HEAL SOON...
...AND I'M A SOUTH-PAW.
I'VE DONE ENOUGH.
I'M NO PHENOM ...
...BUT I WAS THE WORLD CHAMPION.
THIS WAS A GOOD MATCH *REALLY* FAR FROM HOME.
NOW I WANT A BATH AND SOME SASHIMI.
SHF

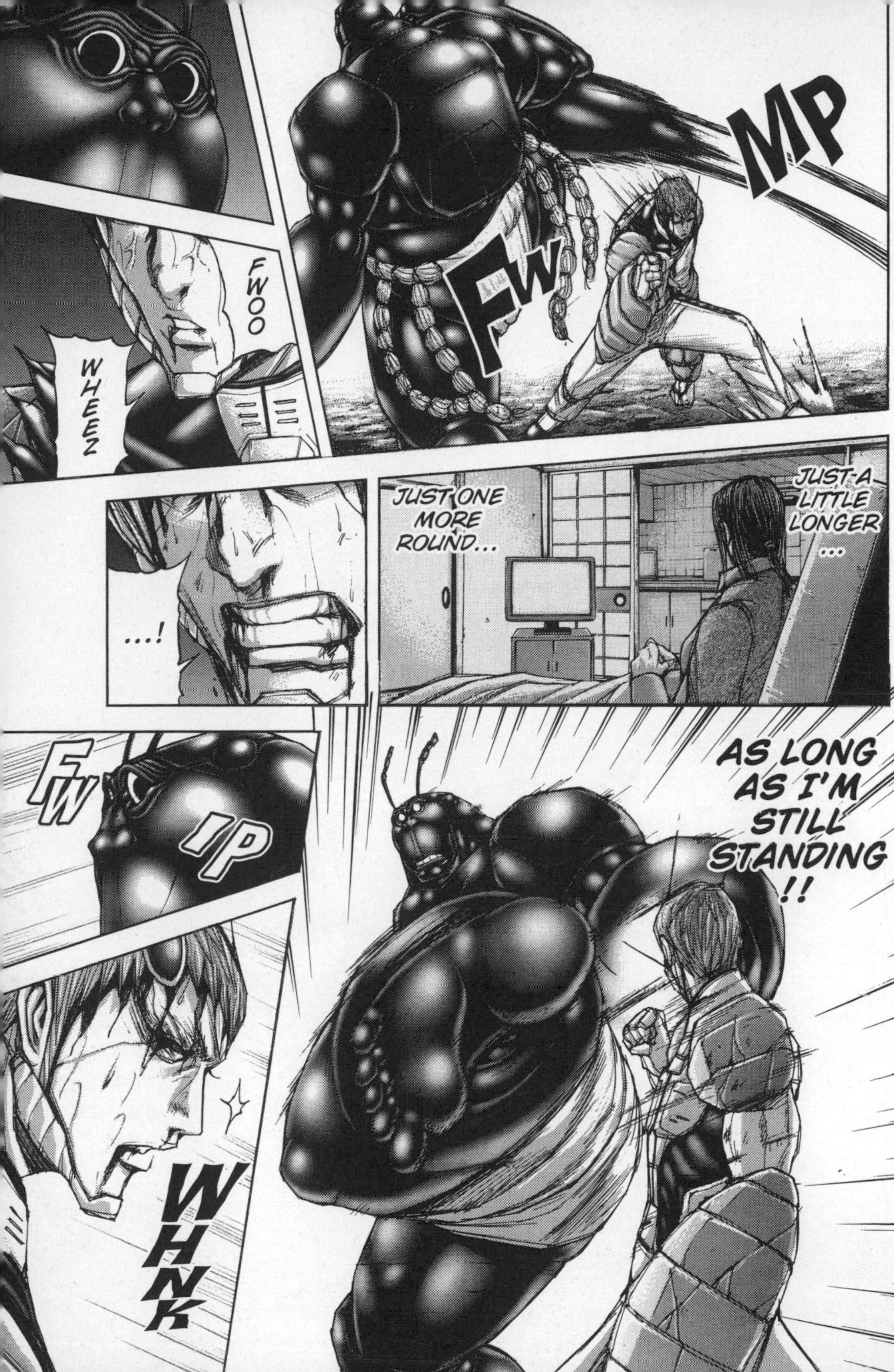

FW
MP
FWOO
WHEEZ
JUST A LITTLE LONGER...
JUST ONE MORE ROUND...
...!
AS LONG AS I'M STILL STANDING!!
FW
IP
WHNK

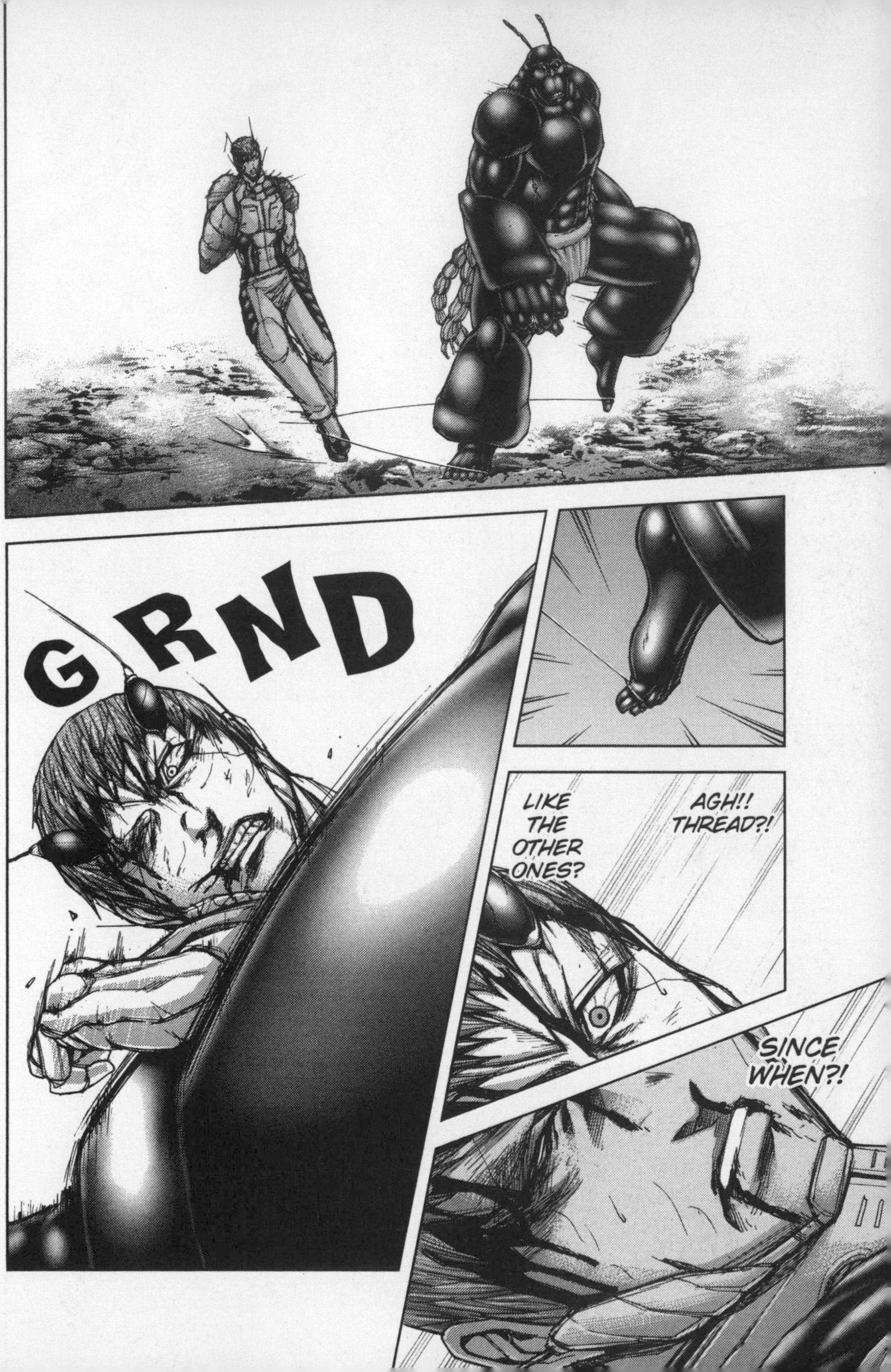
AGH!! THREAD?!
LIKE THE OTHER ONES?
SINCE WHEN?!
GRND

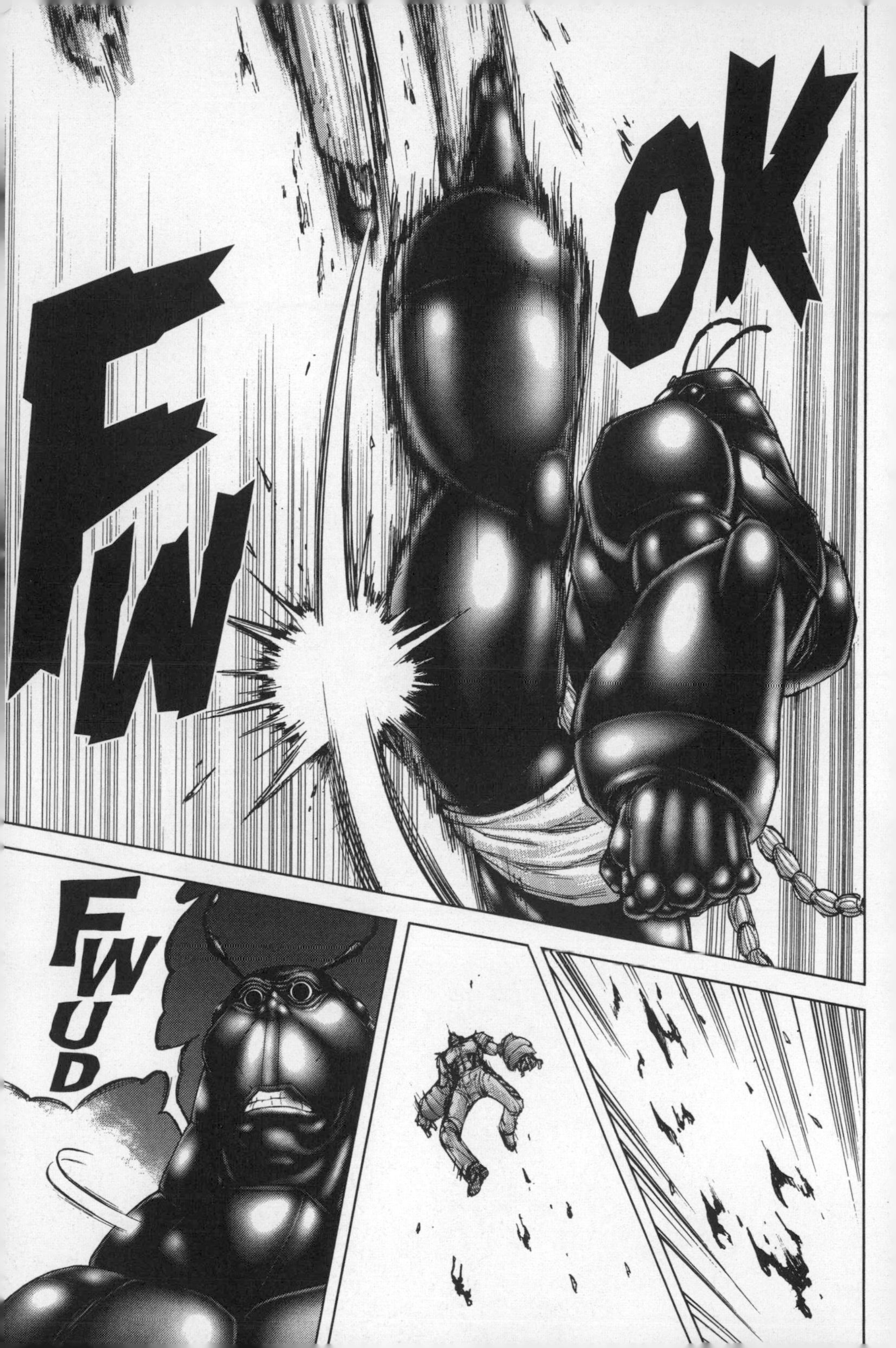
FWOK
FWUD

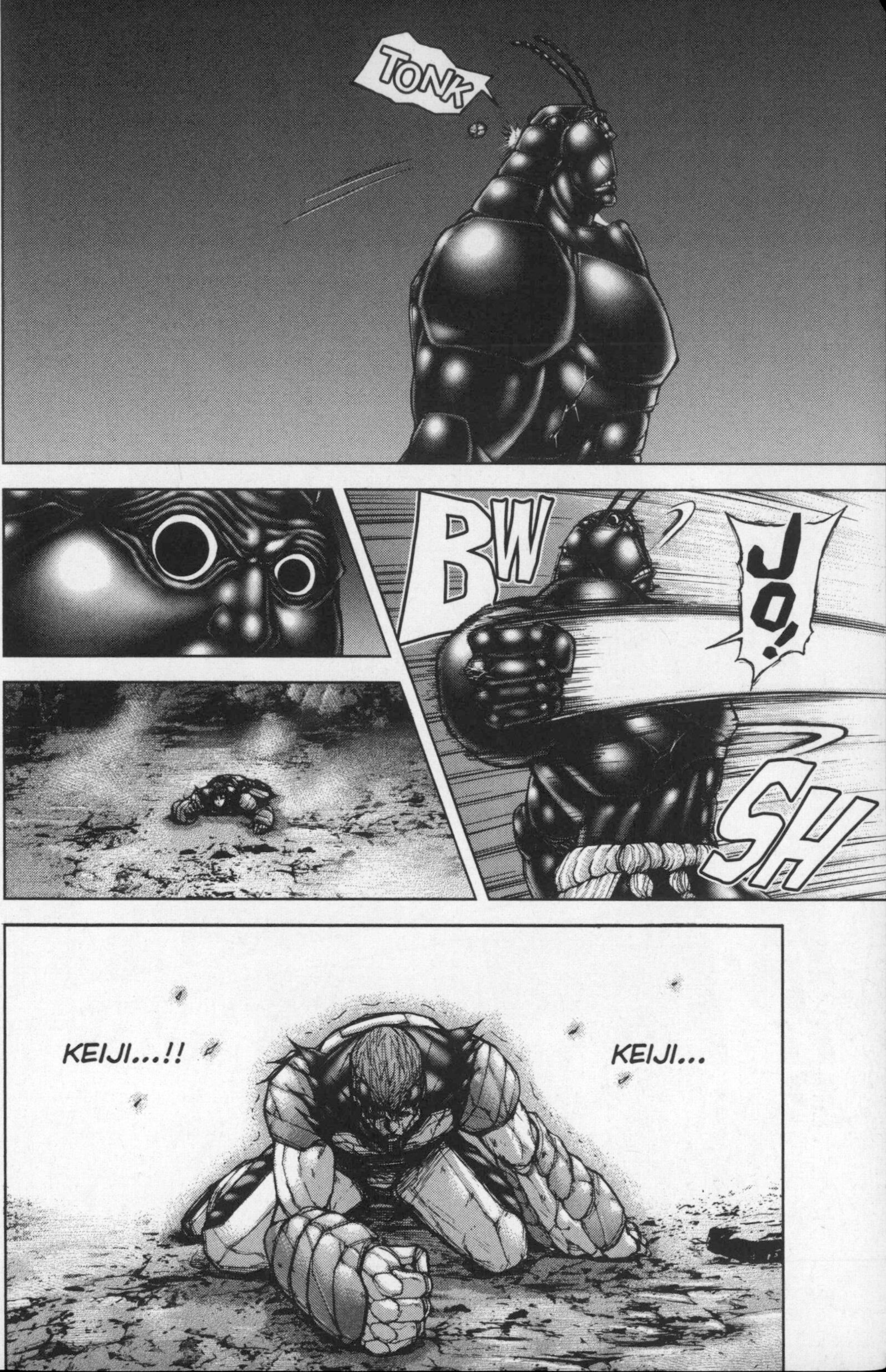
TONK
BW
JO!!
SH
KEIJI...
KEIJI...!!

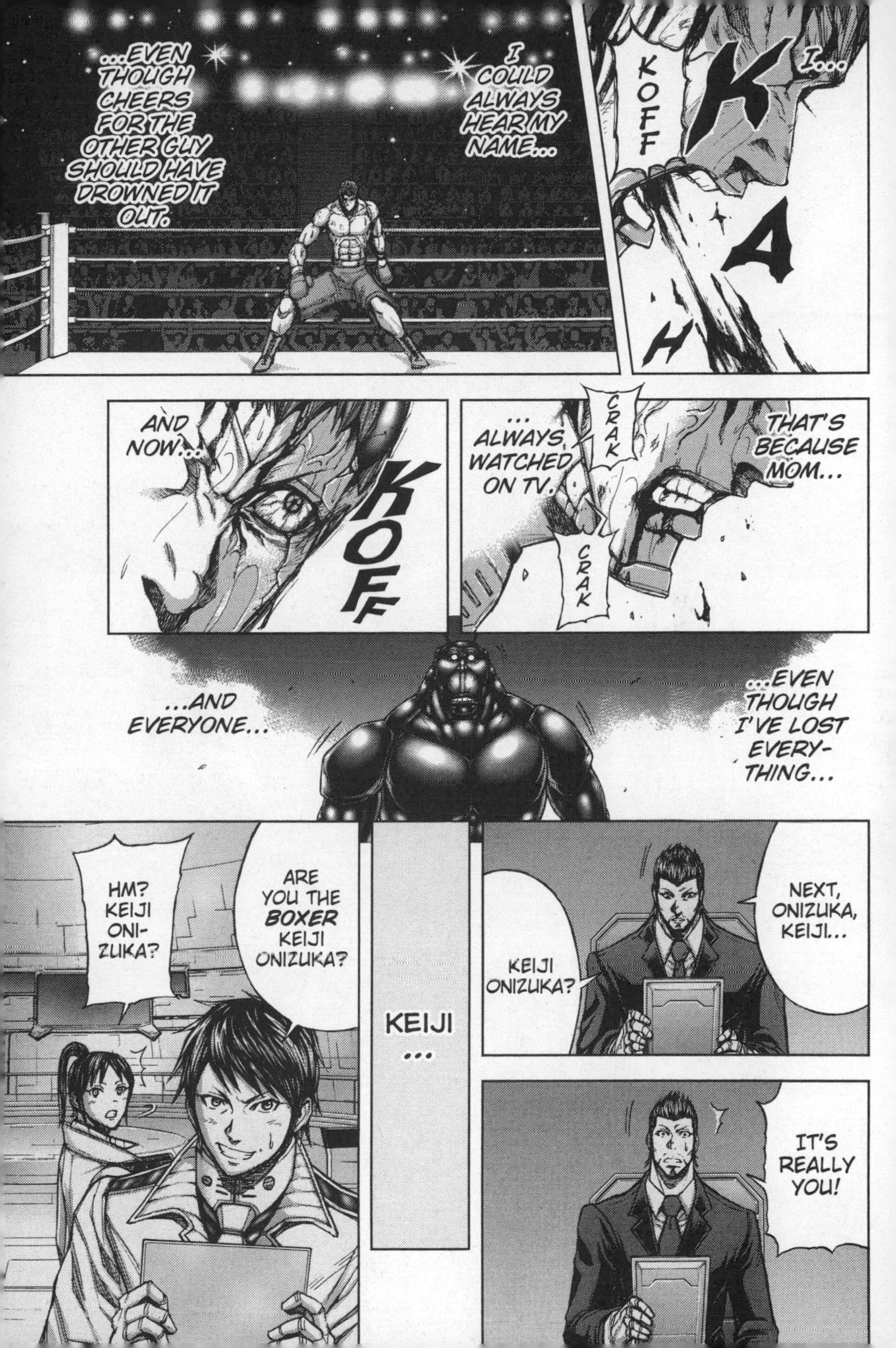
I...
KOFF
KAH
I COULD ALWAYS HEAR MY NAME...
...EVEN THOUGH CHEERS FOR THE OTHER GUY SHOULD HAVE DROWNED IT OUT.
THAT'S BECAUSE MOM...
CRAK
...ALWAYS WATCHED ON TV.
CRAK
AND NOW...
KOFF
...EVEN THOUGH I'VE LOST EVERY-THING...
...AND EVERYONE...
NEXT, ONIZUKA, KEIJI...
KEIJI ONIZUKA?
IT'S REALLY YOU!
KEIJI...
ARE YOU THE BOXER KEIJI ONIZUKA?
HM? KEIJI ONI-ZUKA?

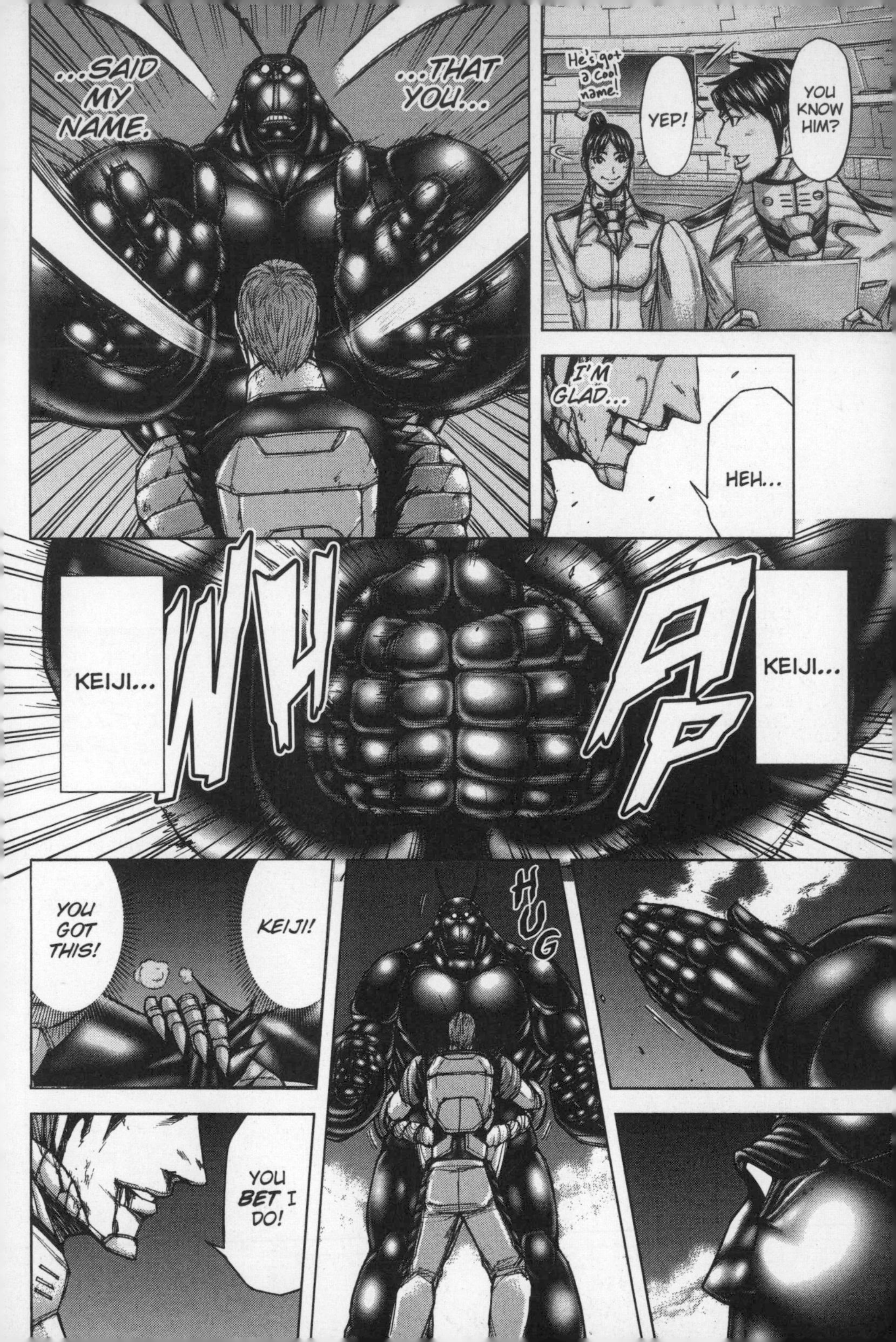
YOU KNOW HIM?
YEP!
He's got a cool name!
HEH...
I'M GLAD...
...THAT YOU...
...SAID MY NAME.
KEIJI...
WHAP
KEIJI...
HUG
KEIJI!
YOU GOT THIS!
YOU BET I DO!

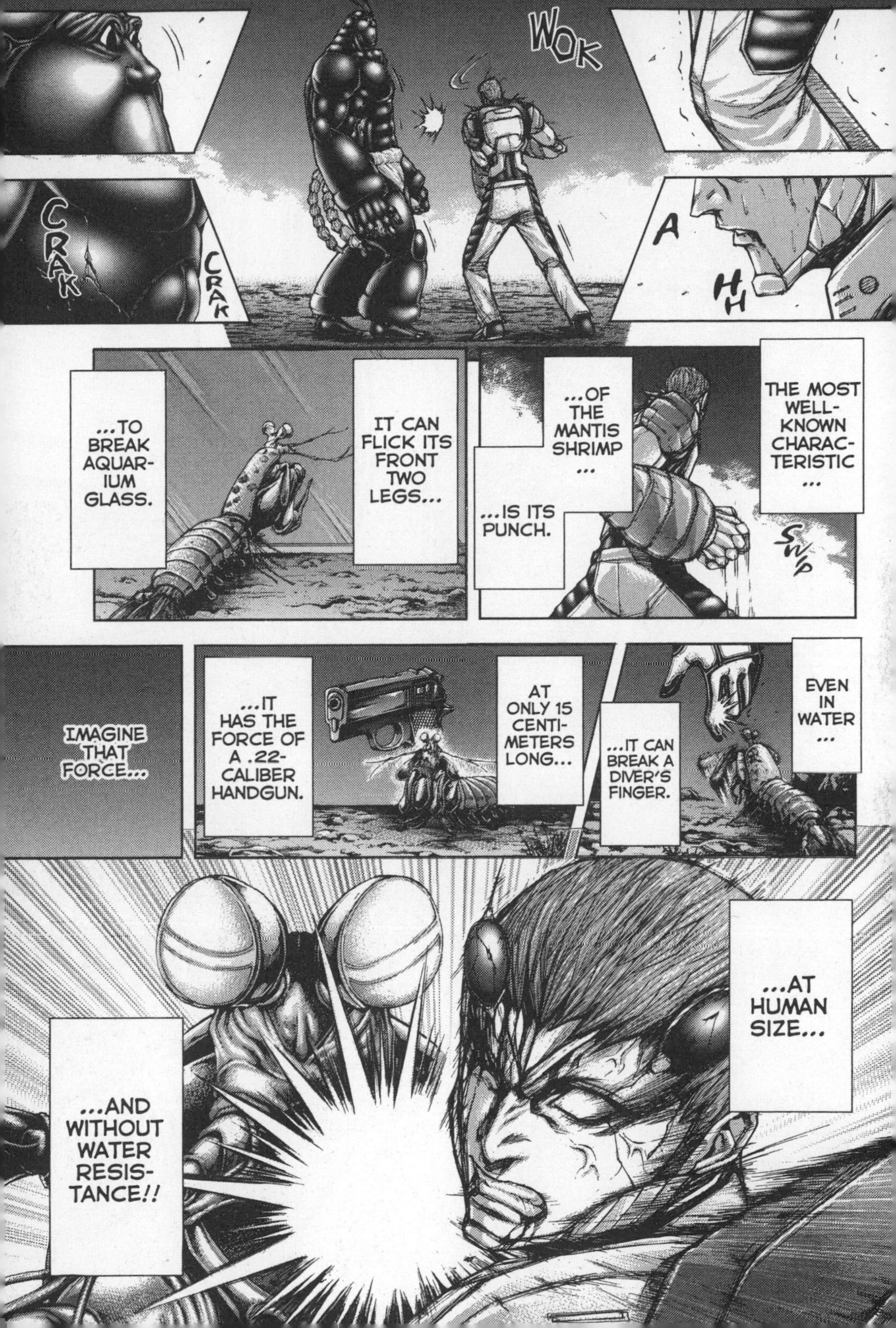
A HH
WOK
CRAK CRAK
THE MOST WELL-KNOWN CHARACTERISTIC...
...OF THE MANTIS SHRIMP...
...IS ITS PUNCH.
SWIP
IT CAN FLICK ITS FRONT TWO LEGS...
...TO BREAK AQUARIUM GLASS.
EVEN IN WATER...
...IT CAN BREAK A DIVER'S FINGER.
AT ONLY 15 CENTIMETERS LONG...
...IT HAS THE FORCE OF A .22-CALIBER HANDGUN.
IMAGINE THAT FORCE...
...AT HUMAN SIZE...
...AND WITHOUT WATER RESISTANCE!!

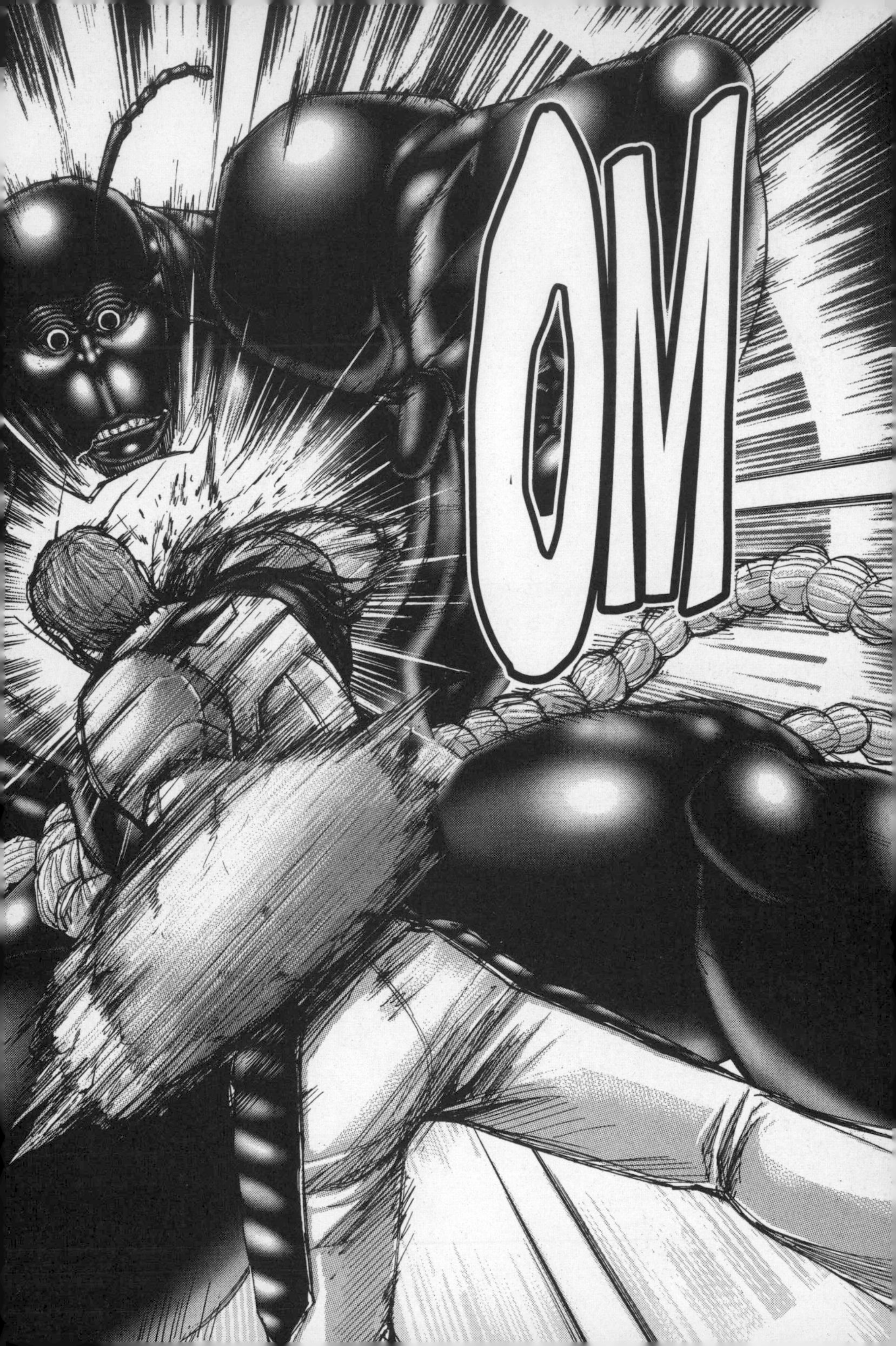
OM

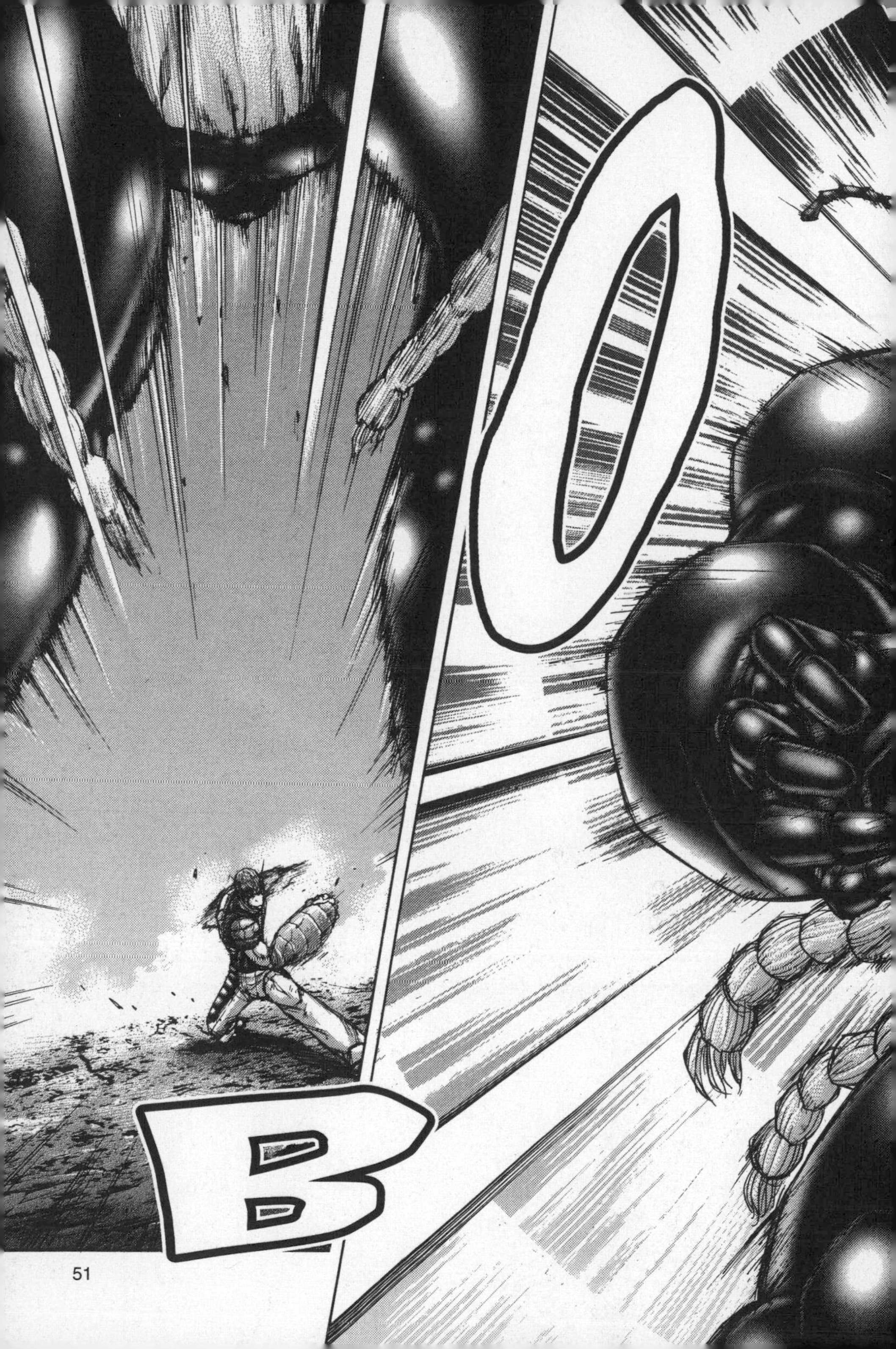
BO

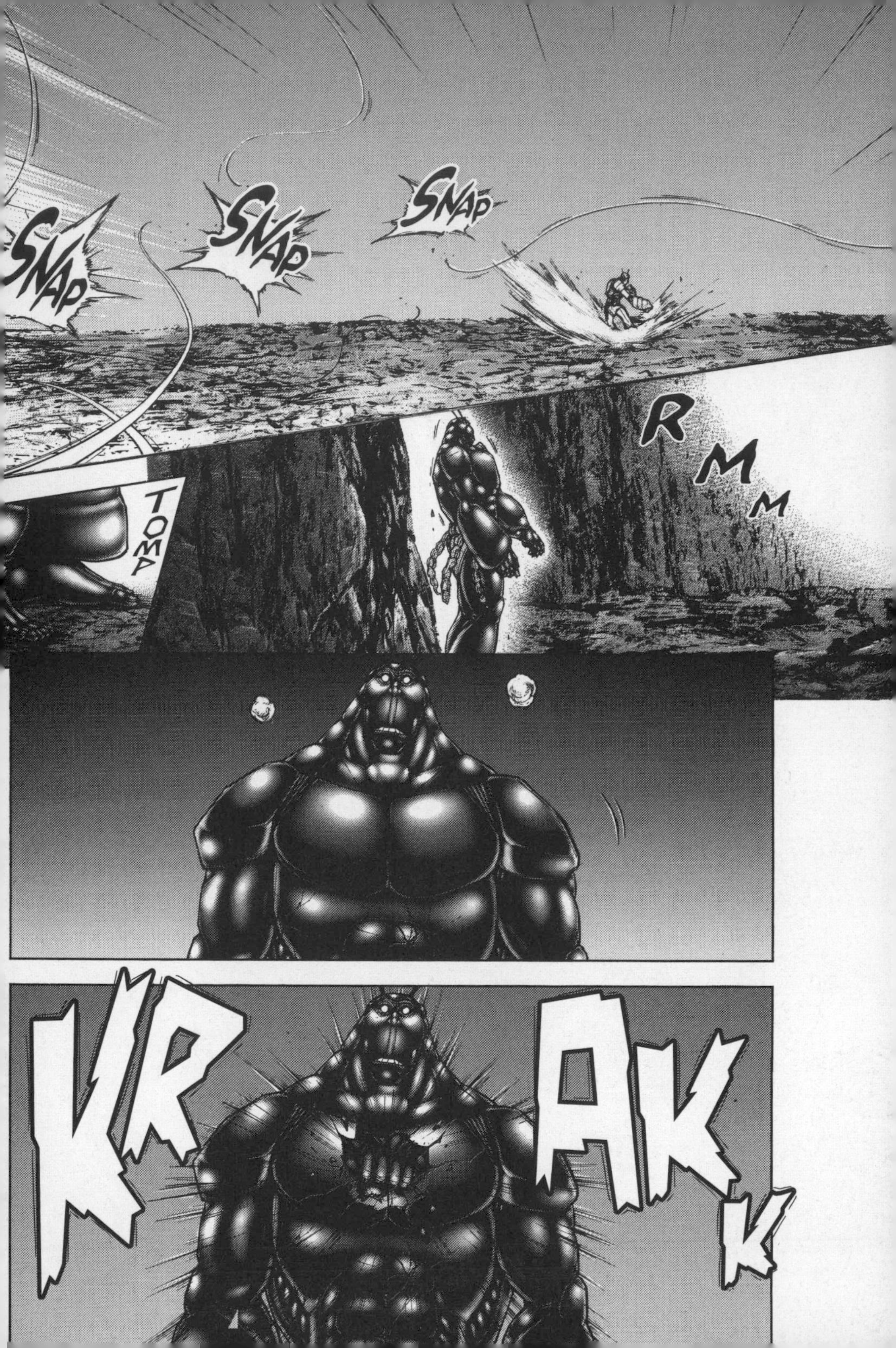
SNAP
SNAP
SNAP
RMMM
TOMP
KRAKK

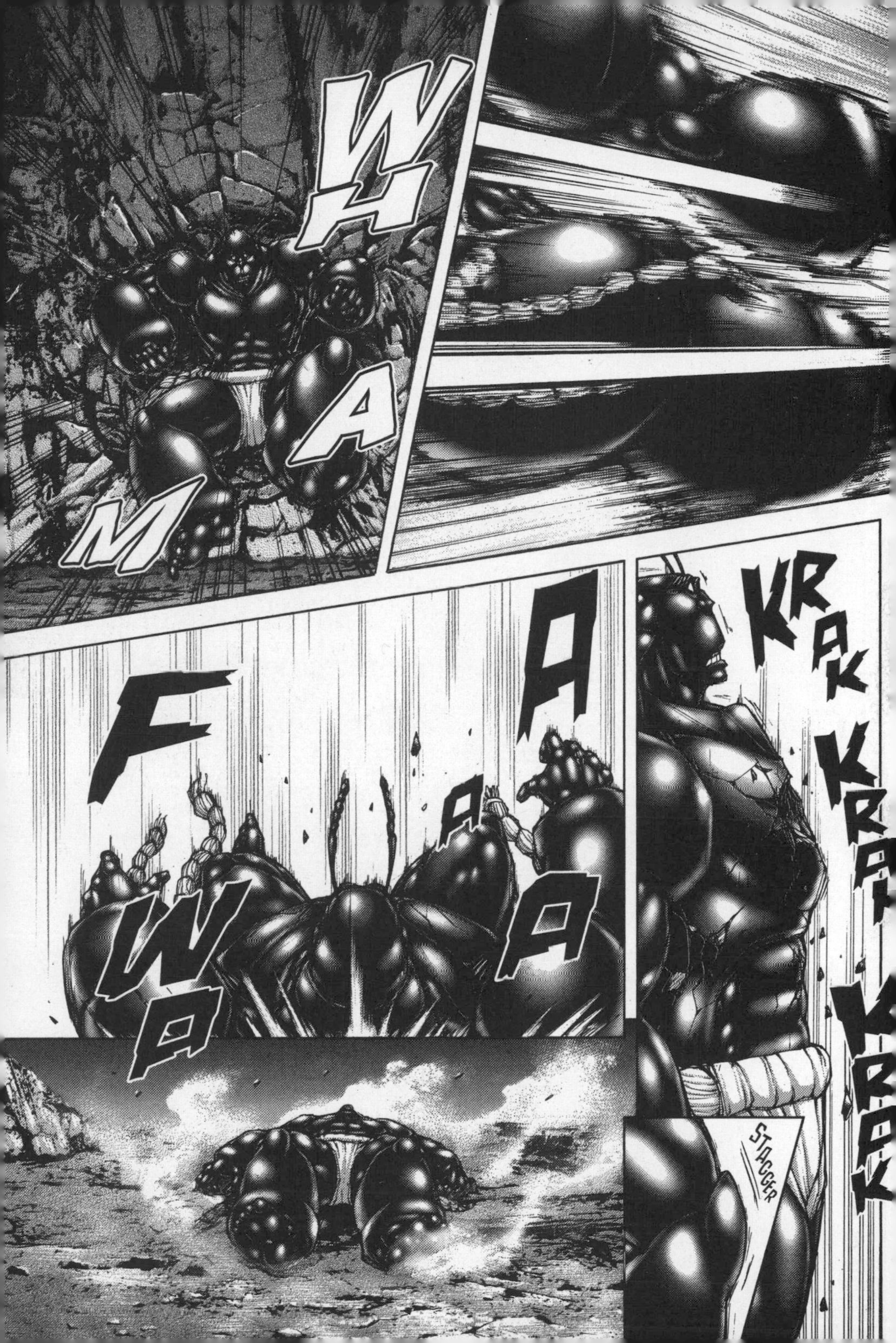
WHAM
KRAK
KRAK
KRAK
STAGGER
FWAAAA

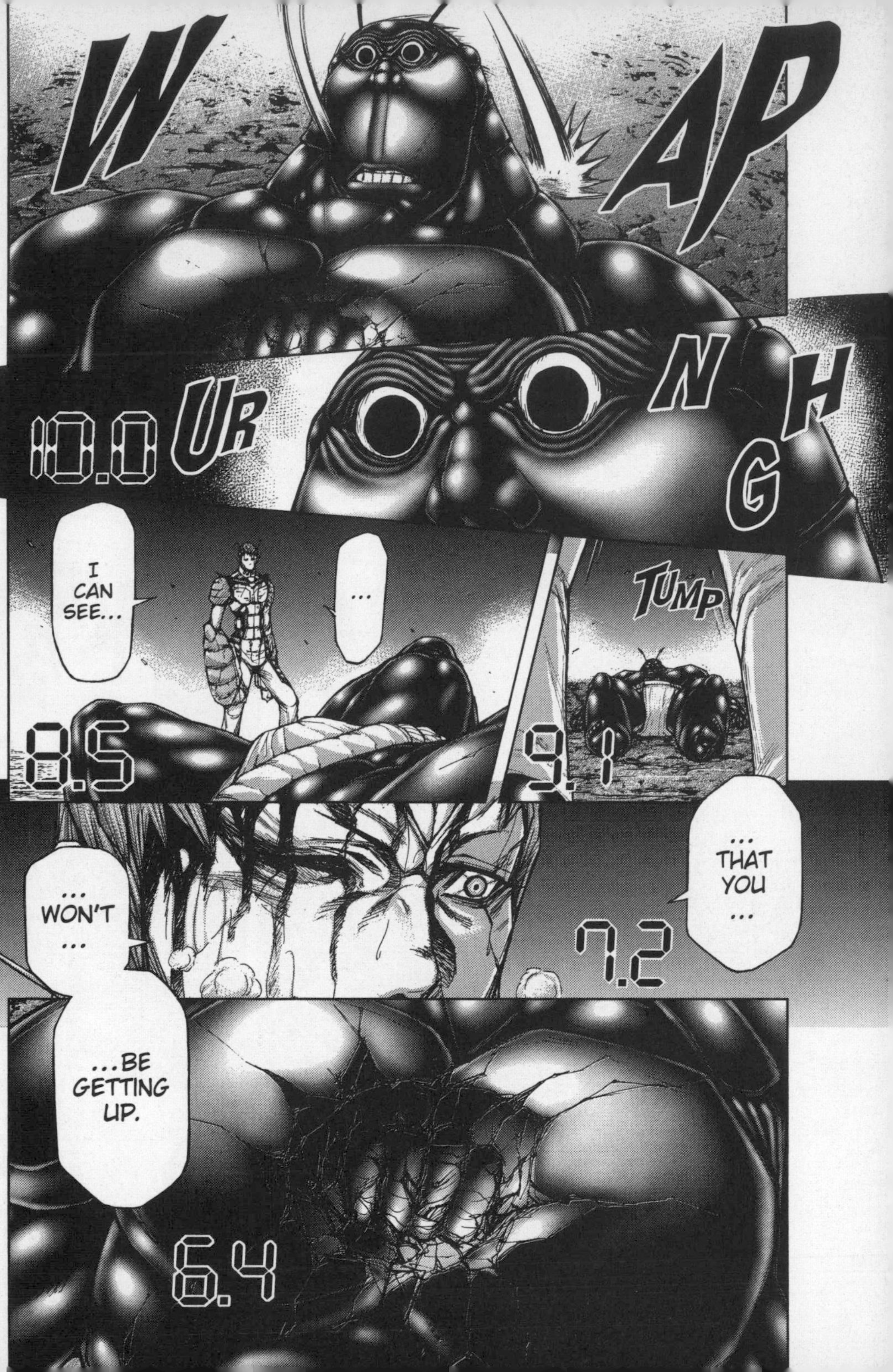
WAP
10.0
URNGH
TUMP
9.1
...
I CAN SEE...
8.5
...THAT YOU...
7.2
...WON'T...
...BE GETTING UP.
6.4

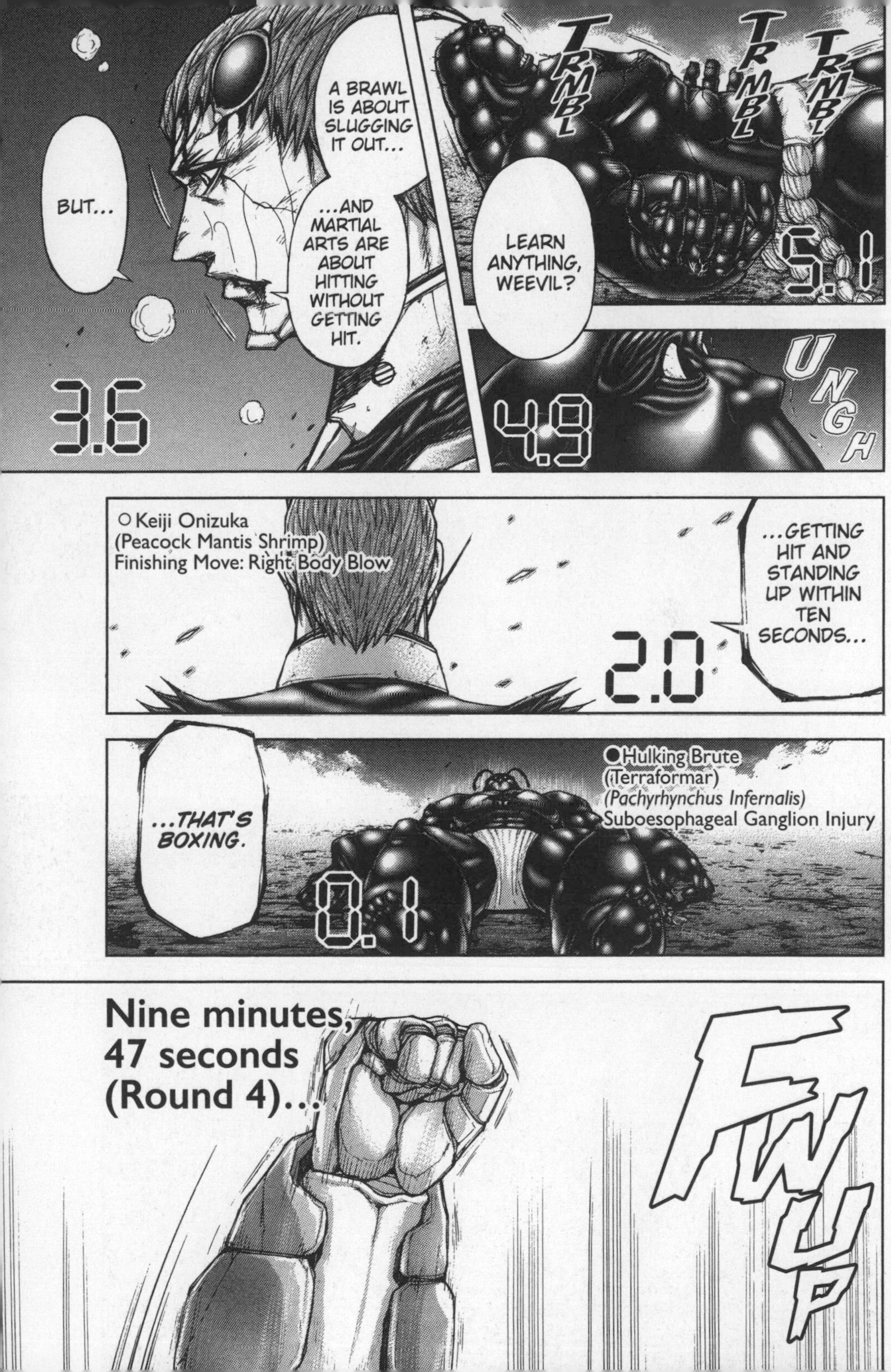

TRMBL
TRMBL
TRMBL
LEARN ANYTHING, WEEVIL?
5.1
UNGH
4.9
A BRAWL IS ABOUT SLUGGING IT OUT...
...AND MARTIAL ARTS ARE ABOUT HITTING WITHOUT GETTING HIT.
BUT...
3.6
○Keiji Onizuka
(Peacock Mantis Shrimp)
Finishing Move: Right Body Blow
...GETTING HIT AND STANDING UP WITHIN TEN SECONDS...
2.0
●Hulking Brute
(Terraformar)
(Pachyrhynchus Infernalis)
Suboesophageal Ganglion Injury
...THAT'S BOXING.
0.1
Nine minutes, 47 seconds (Round 4)...
FWUP

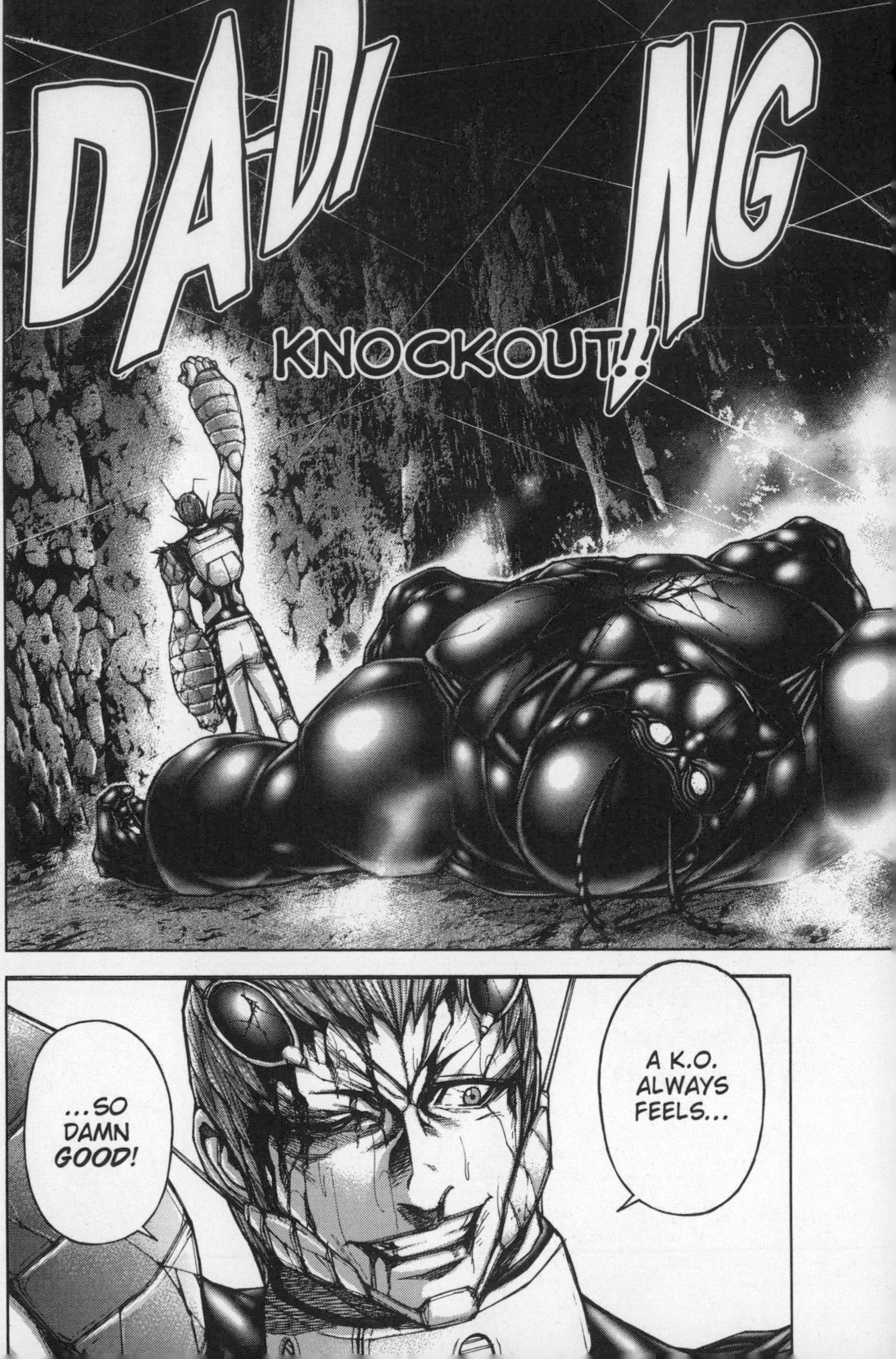
DADING
KNOCKOUT!!
A K.O. ALWAYS FEELS...
...SO DAMN GOOD!

HUFF

SHUMP

OW...

TWITCH

TWITCH

CHAPTER 45: YELLOW JACKET ARMS BUG

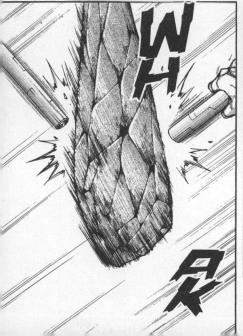

WH

AK

NOW I'VE GOT MASSIVE RESPECT...

...FOR HEAVY-WEIGHT FIGHTERS...

OUCH...

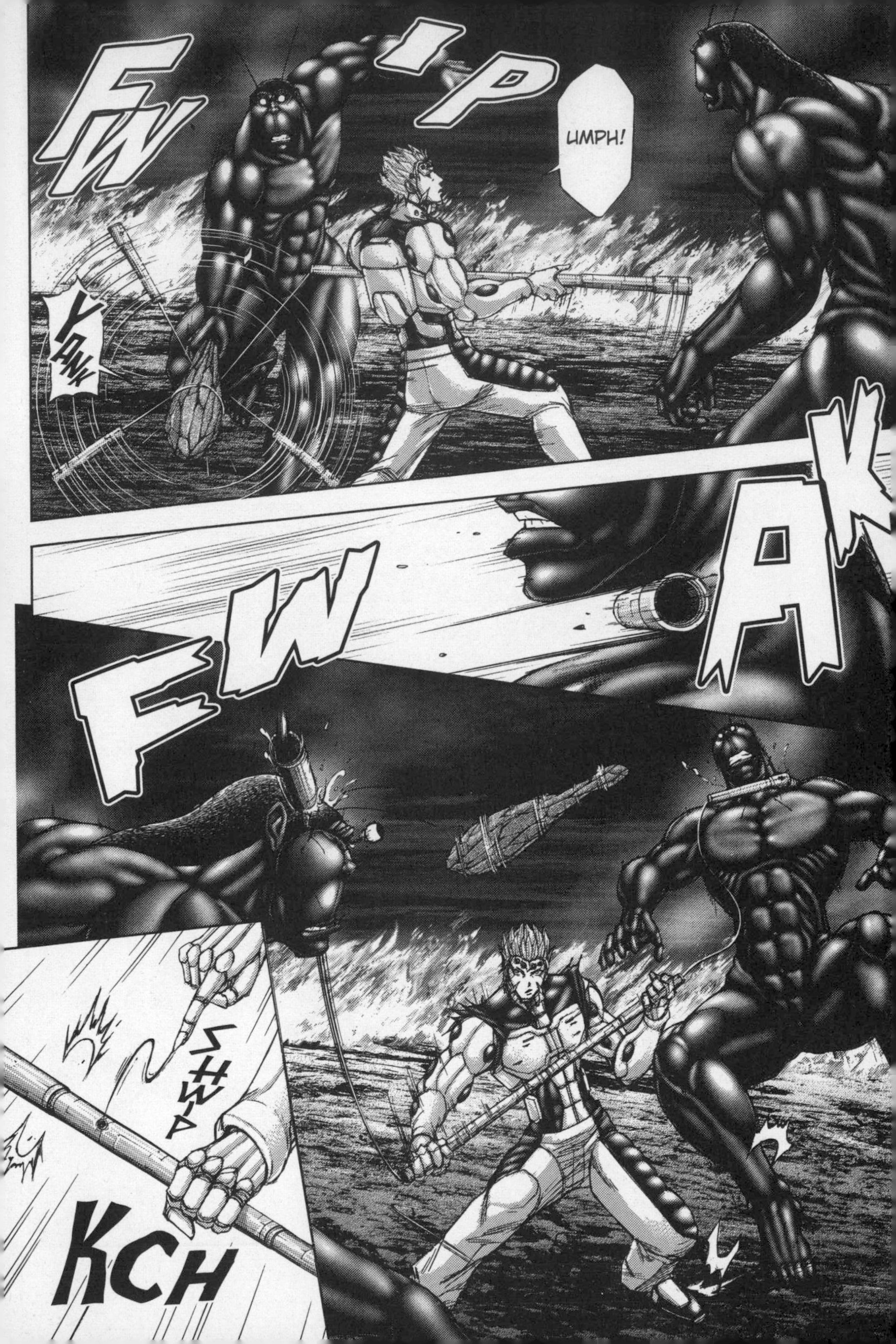
UMPH!
FWIP
YANK
FWAK
SHWIP
KCH

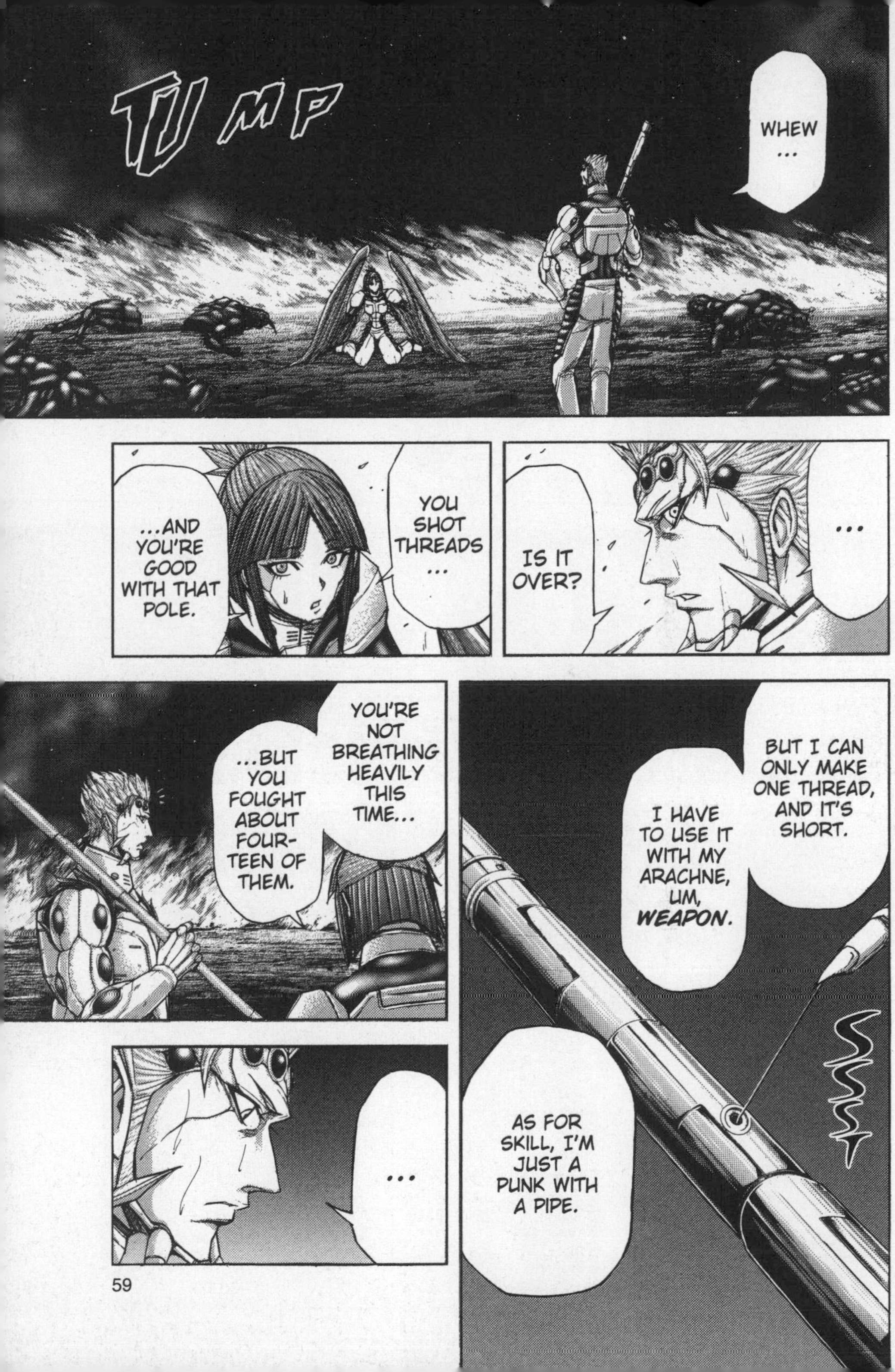
WHEW ...
TUMP
...
IS IT OVER?
YOU SHOT THREADS ...
...AND YOU'RE GOOD WITH THAT POLE.
BUT I CAN ONLY MAKE ONE THREAD, AND IT'S SHORT.
I HAVE TO USE IT WITH MY ARACHNE, UM, **WEAPON**.
AS FOR SKILL, I'M JUST A PUNK WITH A PIPE.
YOU'RE NOT BREATHING HEAVILY THIS TIME...
...BUT YOU FOUGHT ABOUT FOUR-TEEN OF THEM.
...

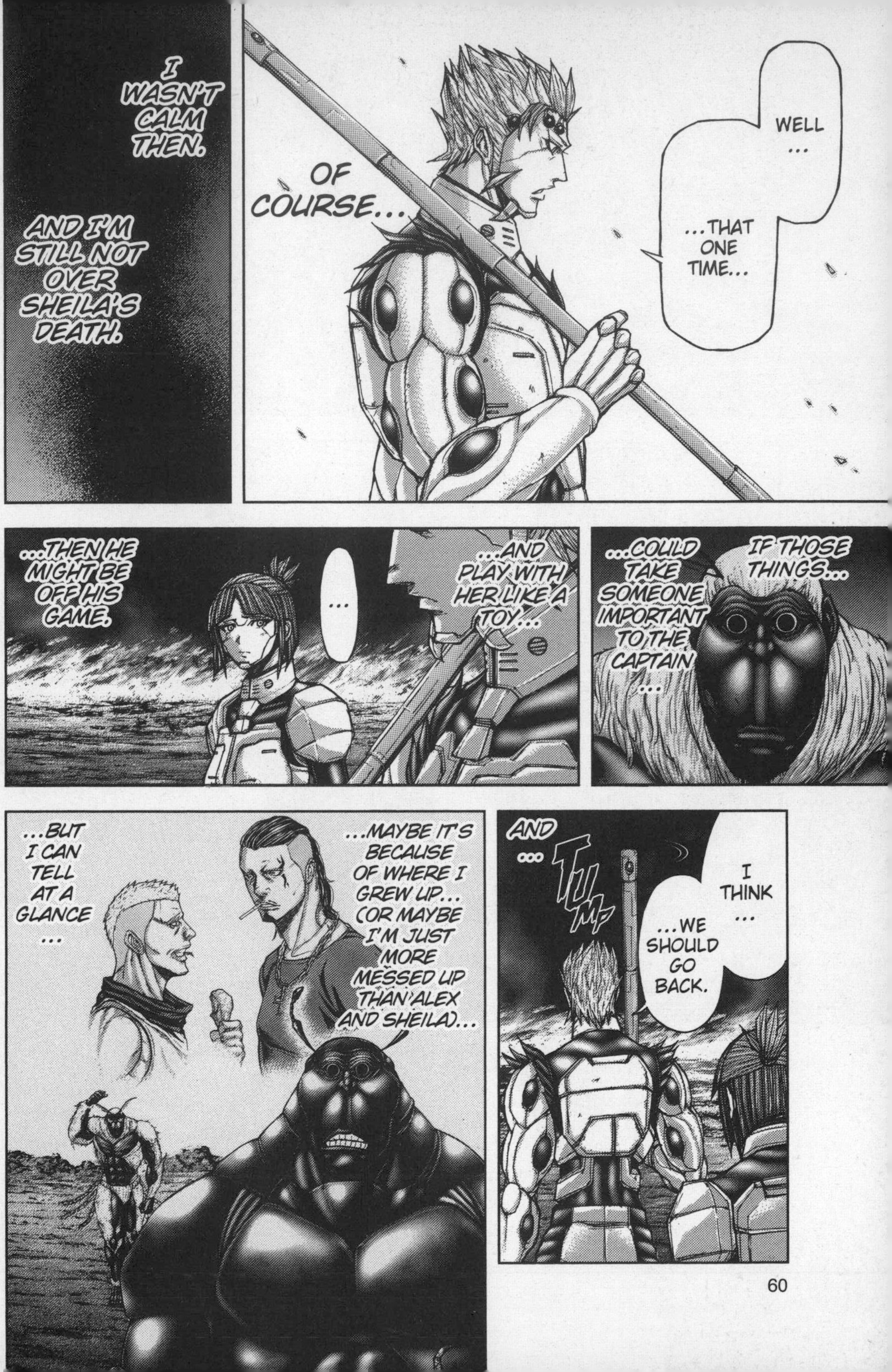

WELL...
...THAT ONE TIME...
OF COURSE...
I WASN'T CALM THEN.
AND I'M STILL NOT OVER SHEILA'S DEATH.
IF THOSE THINGS...
...COULD TAKE SOMEONE IMPORTANT TO THE CAPTAIN...
...AND PLAY WITH HER LIKE A TOY...
...
...THEN HE MIGHT BE OFF HIS GAME.
AND...
TUMP
I THINK...
...WE SHOULD GO BACK.
...MAYBE IT'S BECAUSE OF WHERE I GREW UP... (OR MAYBE I'M JUST MORE MESSED UP THAN ALEX AND SHEILA)...
...BUT I CAN TELL AT A GLANCE...

...THAT THE SPIDERWEB SILKWORM...

...IS HIGHER THAN THE OTHER IN STATUS OR COMBAT ABILITY.

CAP-TAIN!!

I'VE GOT A BAD FEELING ABOUT THIS.

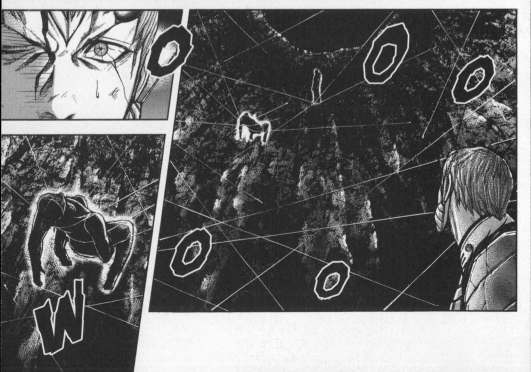

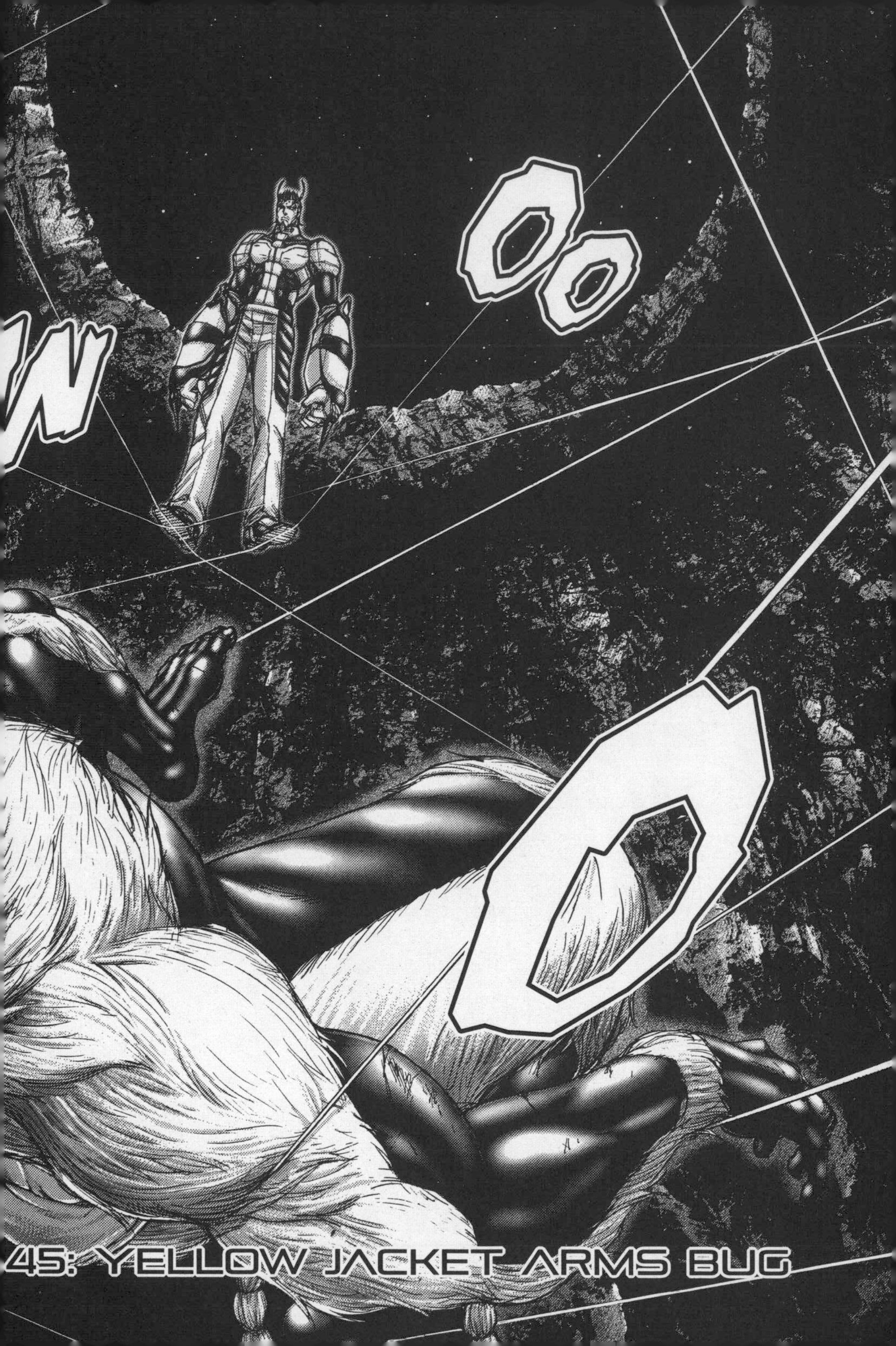
OO
O
45: YELLOW JACKET ARMS BUG

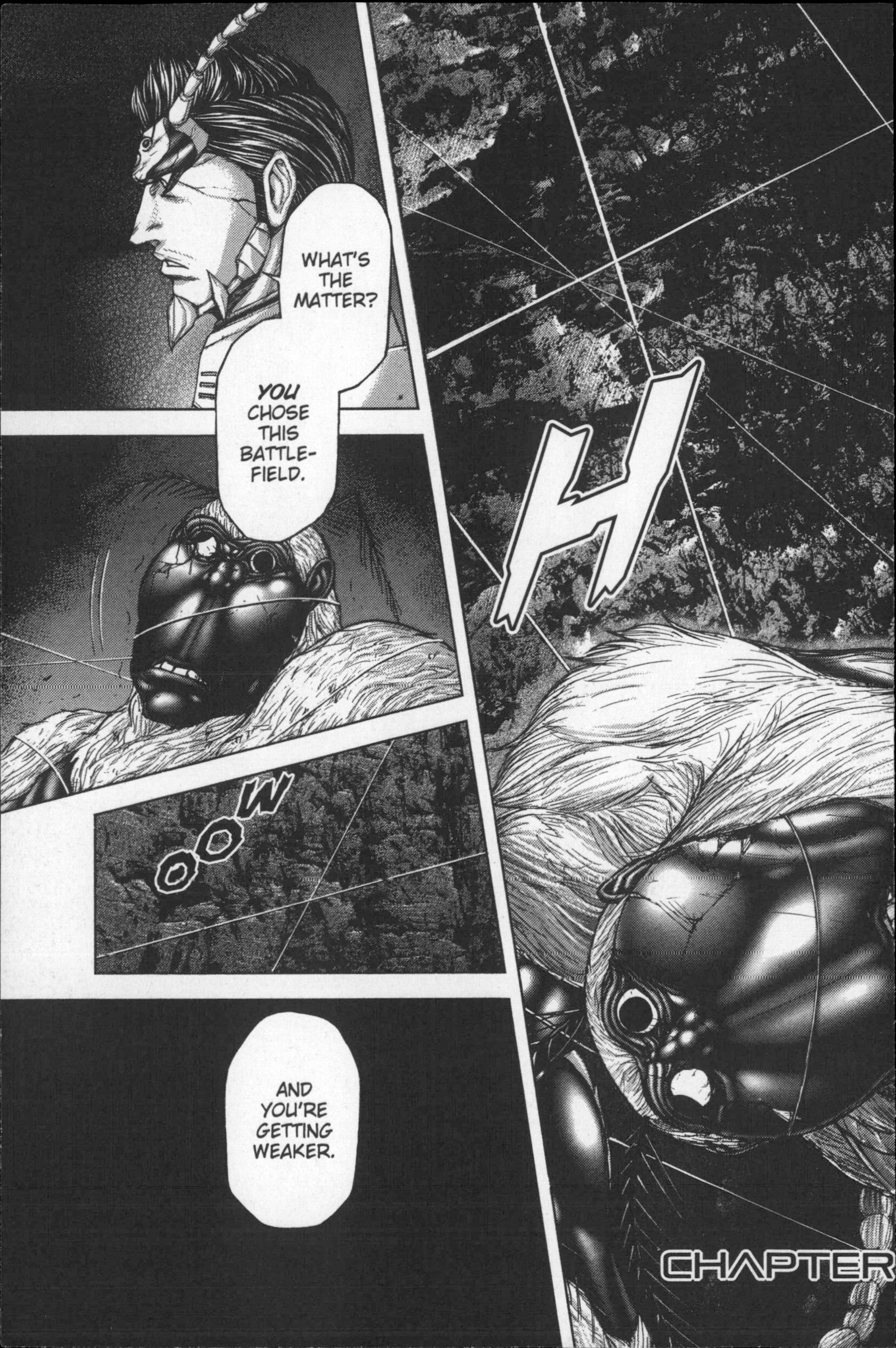
H
CHAPTER
WHAT'S THE MATTER?
YOU CHOSE THIS BATTLE-FIELD.
OOOW
AND YOU'RE GETTING WEAKER.

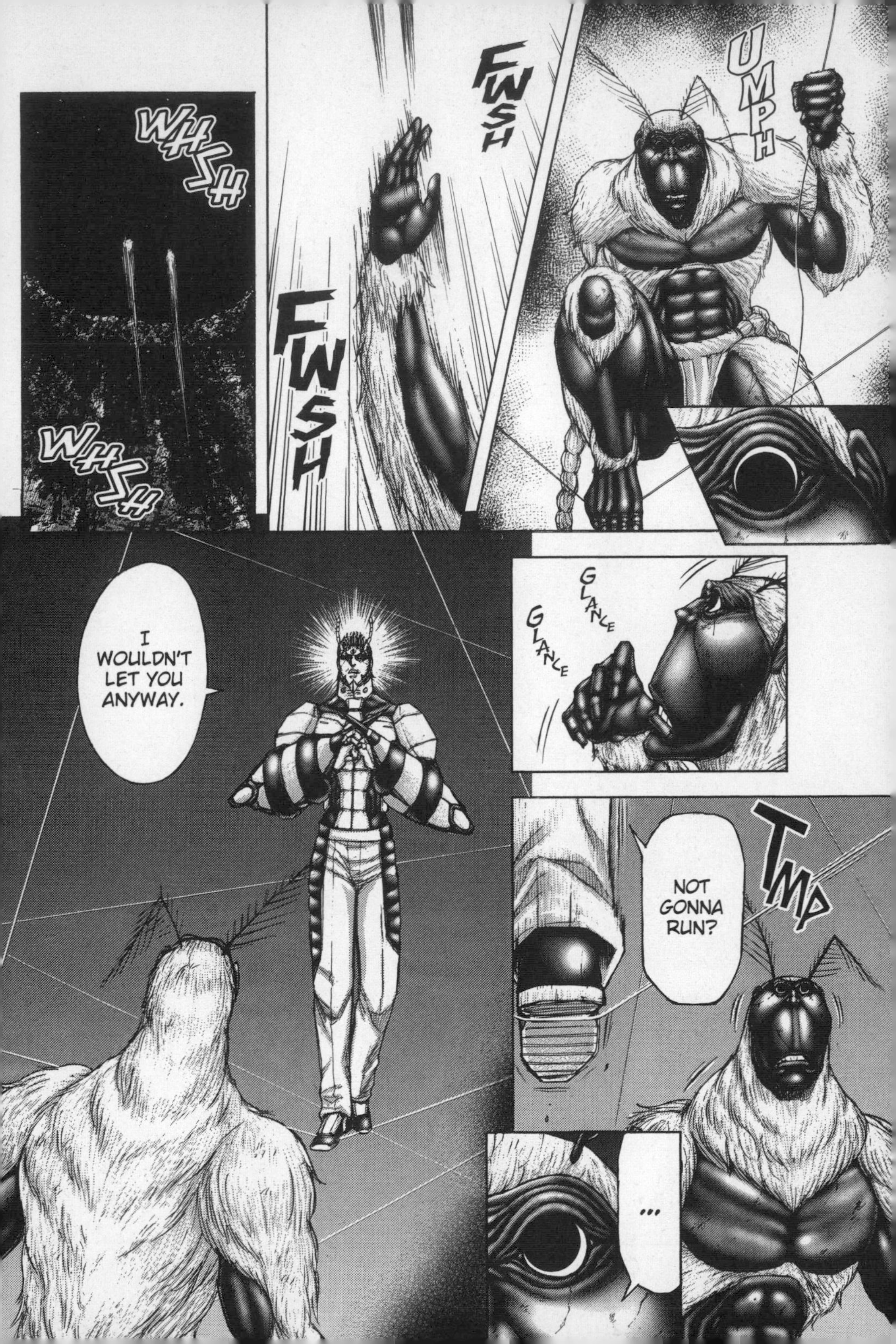
UMPH
FWSH
FWSH
WHSH
WHSH
GLANCE GLANCE
TMP
NOT GONNA RUN?
...
I WOULDN'T LET YOU ANYWAY.

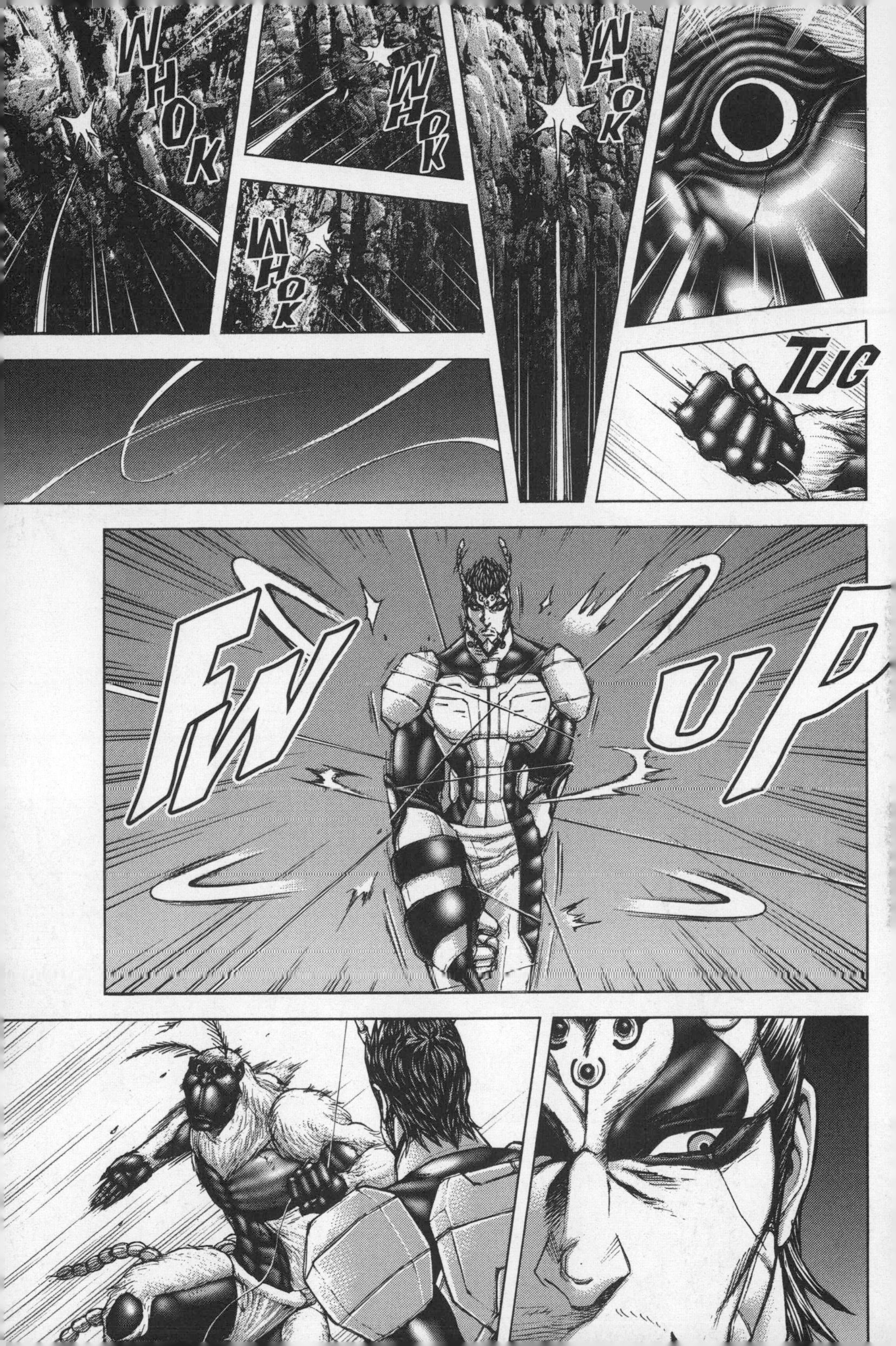
WHOK
WHOK
WHOK
WHOK
TUG
FWUP

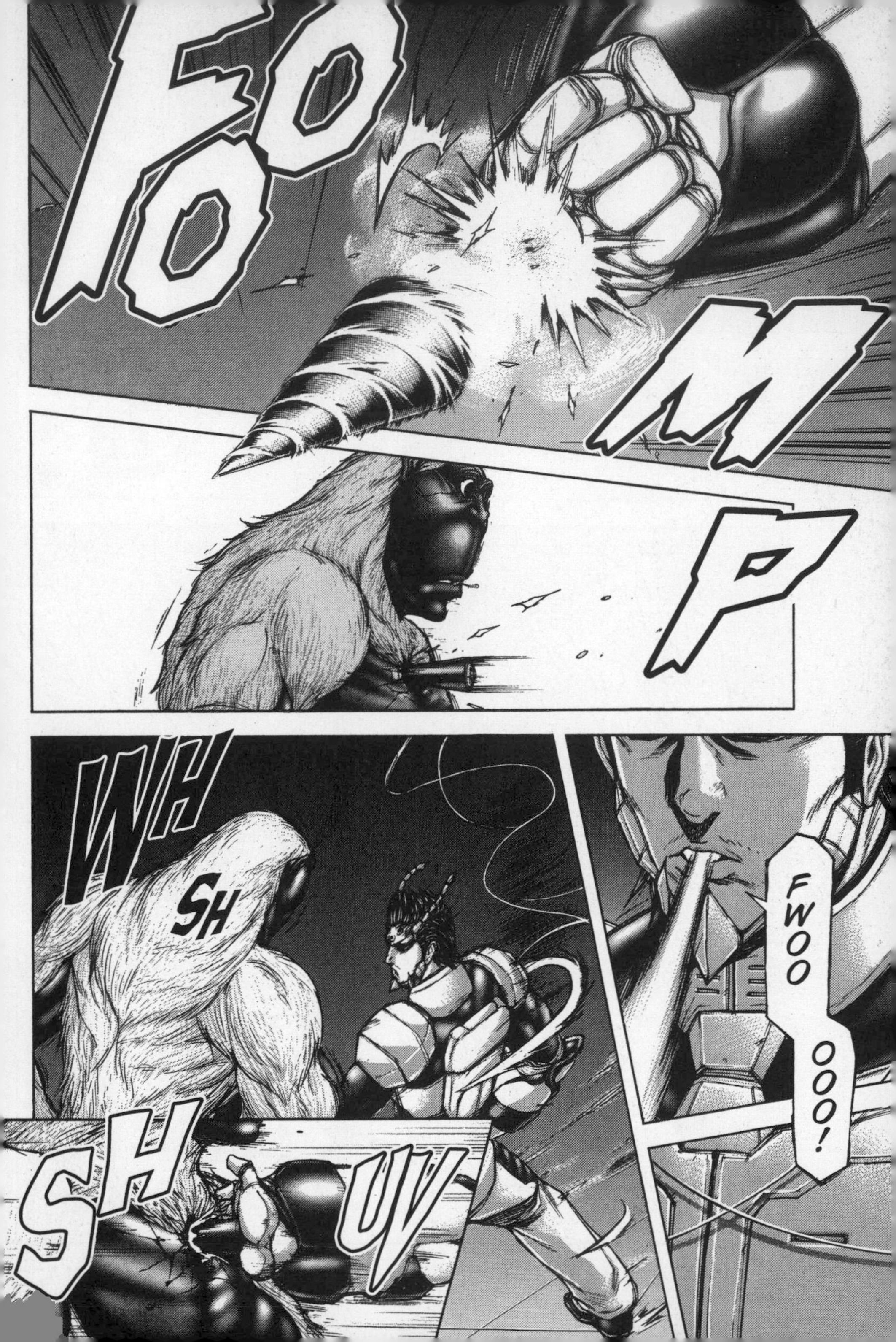
FOOMP
FWOO OOO!
WHSH
SHUV

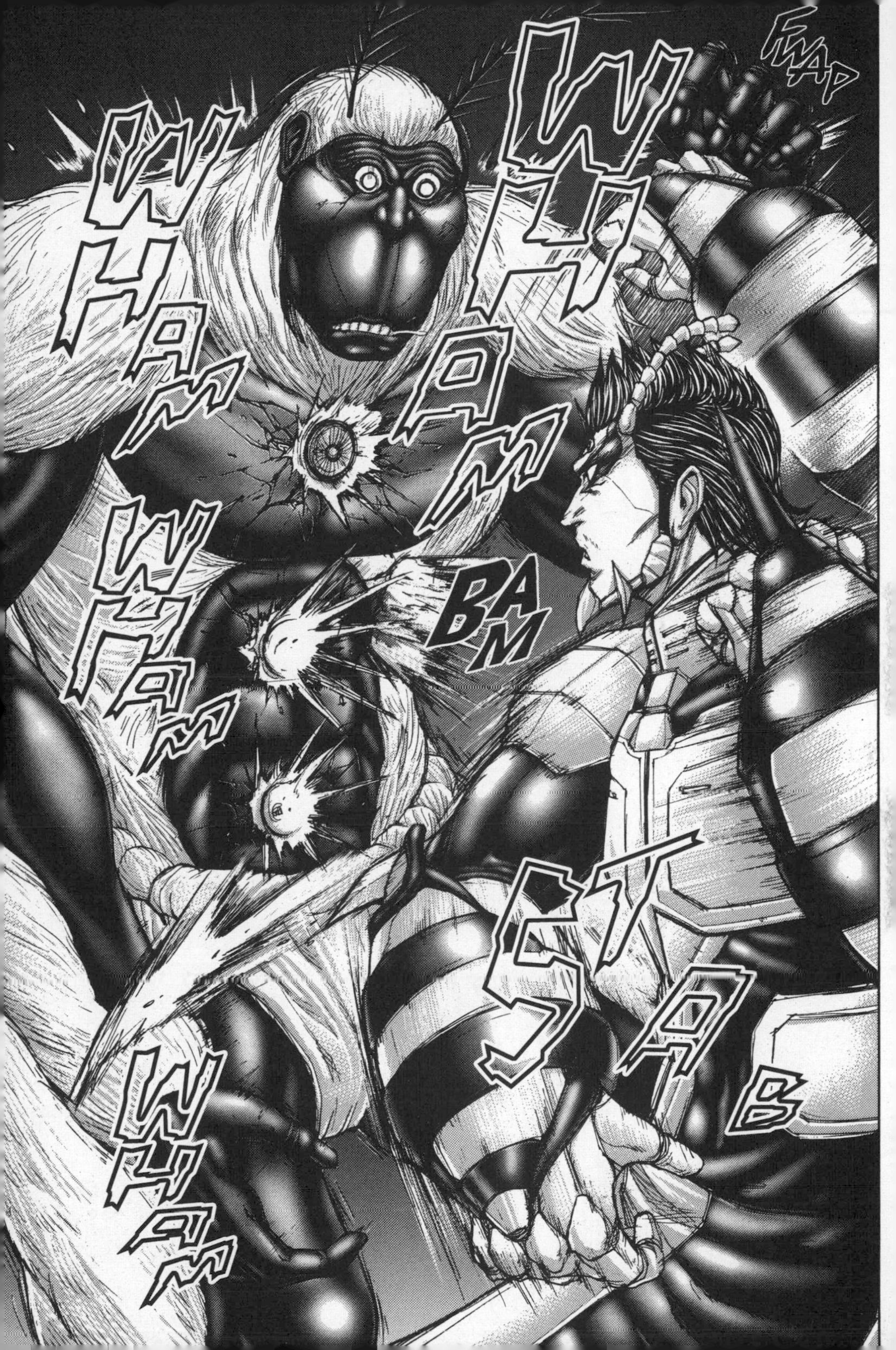
FWAP
WHAM
WHAM
WHAM
WHAM
BAM
STAB

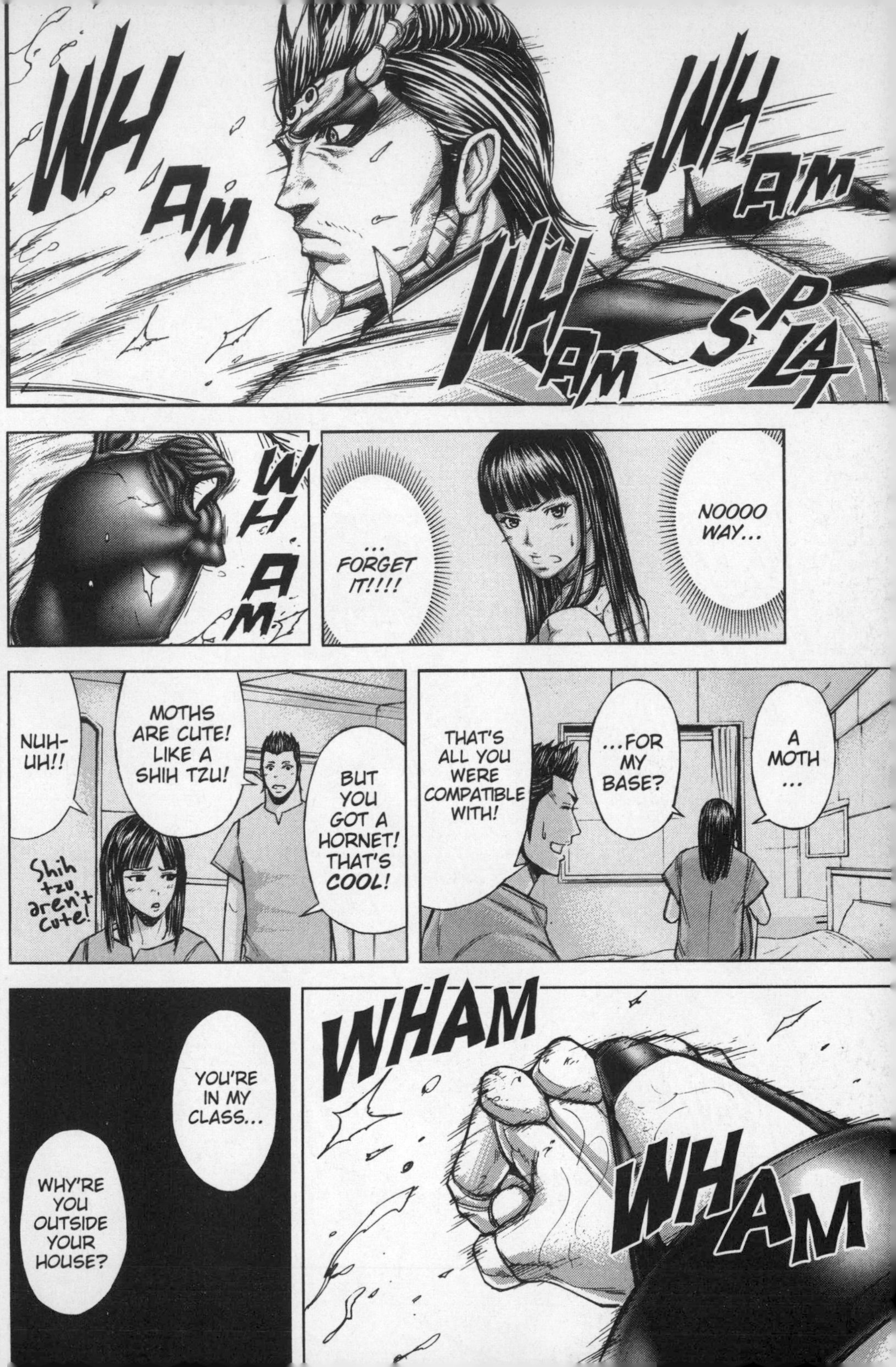
WHAM
SPLAT
WHAM
WHAM
NOOOO WAY...
... FORGET IT!!!!
WHAM
A MOTH ...
...FOR MY BASE?
THAT'S ALL YOU WERE COMPATIBLE WITH!
BUT YOU GOT A HORNET! THAT'S COOL!
MOTHS ARE CUTE! LIKE A SHIH TZU!
NUH-UH!!
Shih tzu aren't cute!
WHAM
WHAM
YOU'RE IN MY CLASS...
WHY'RE YOU OUTSIDE YOUR HOUSE?

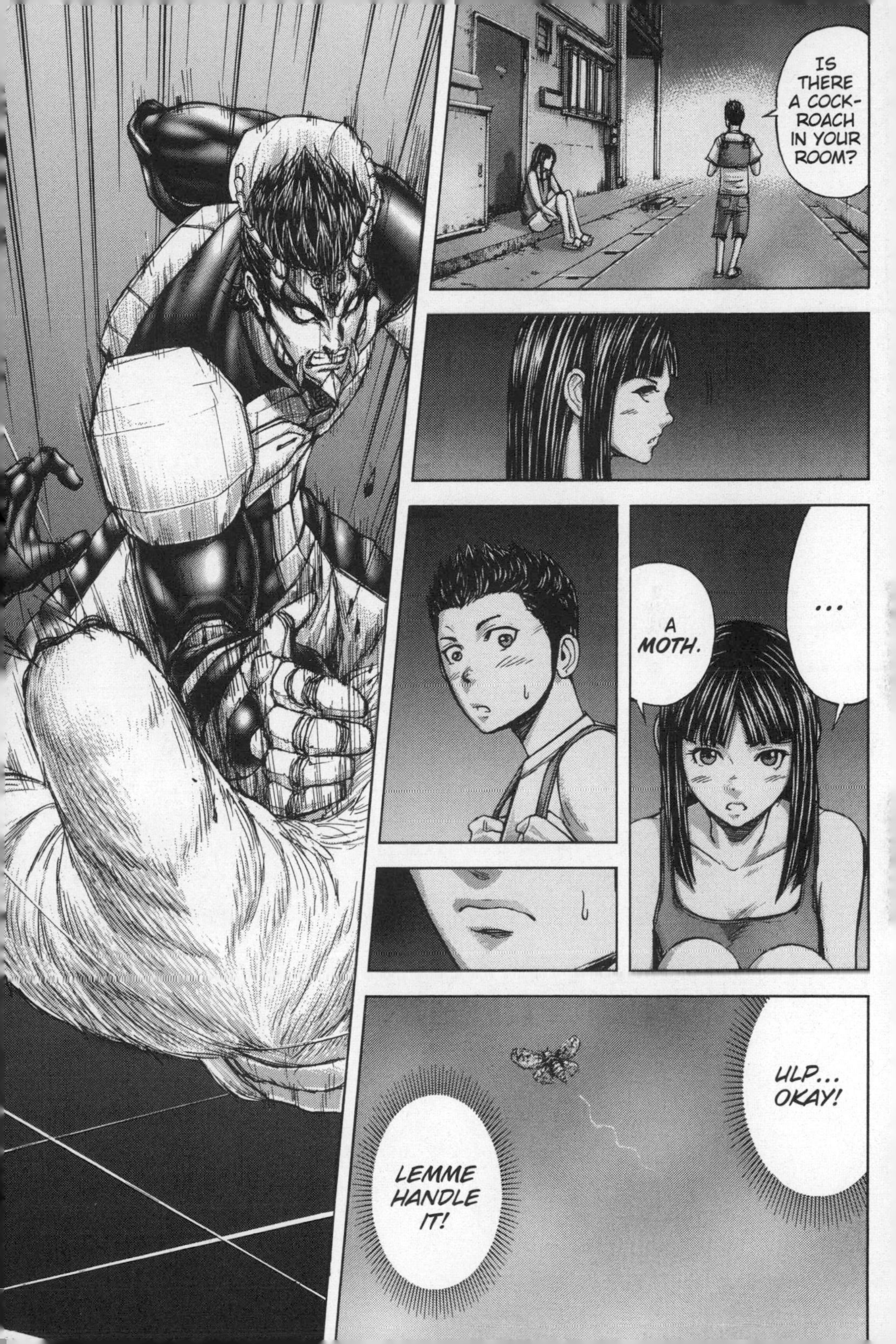
IS THERE A COCK-ROACH IN YOUR ROOM?
...
A MOTH.
ULP... OKAY!
LEMME HANDLE IT!

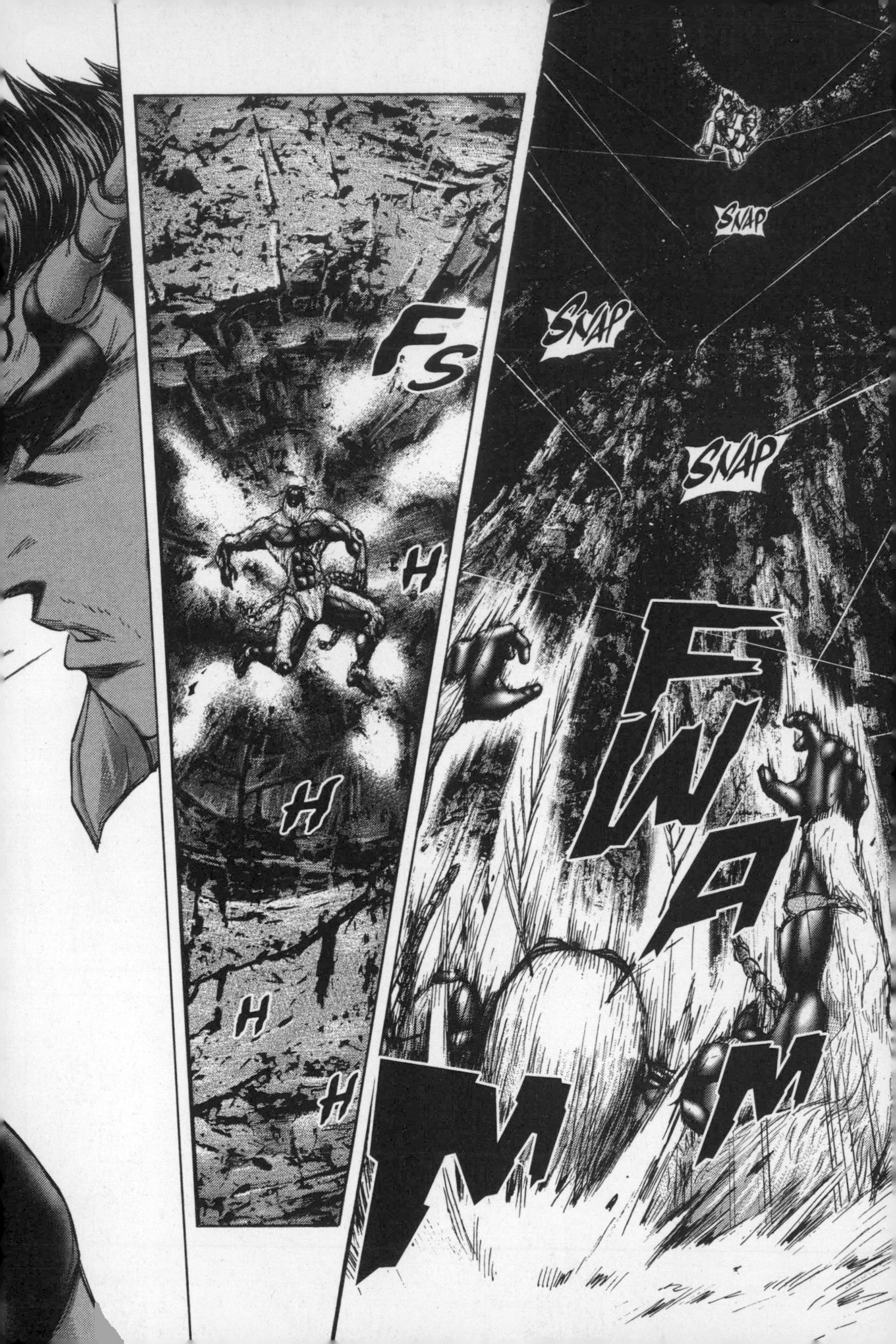
SNAP
SNAP
SNAP
FWAMM
Fs
H
H
H
H

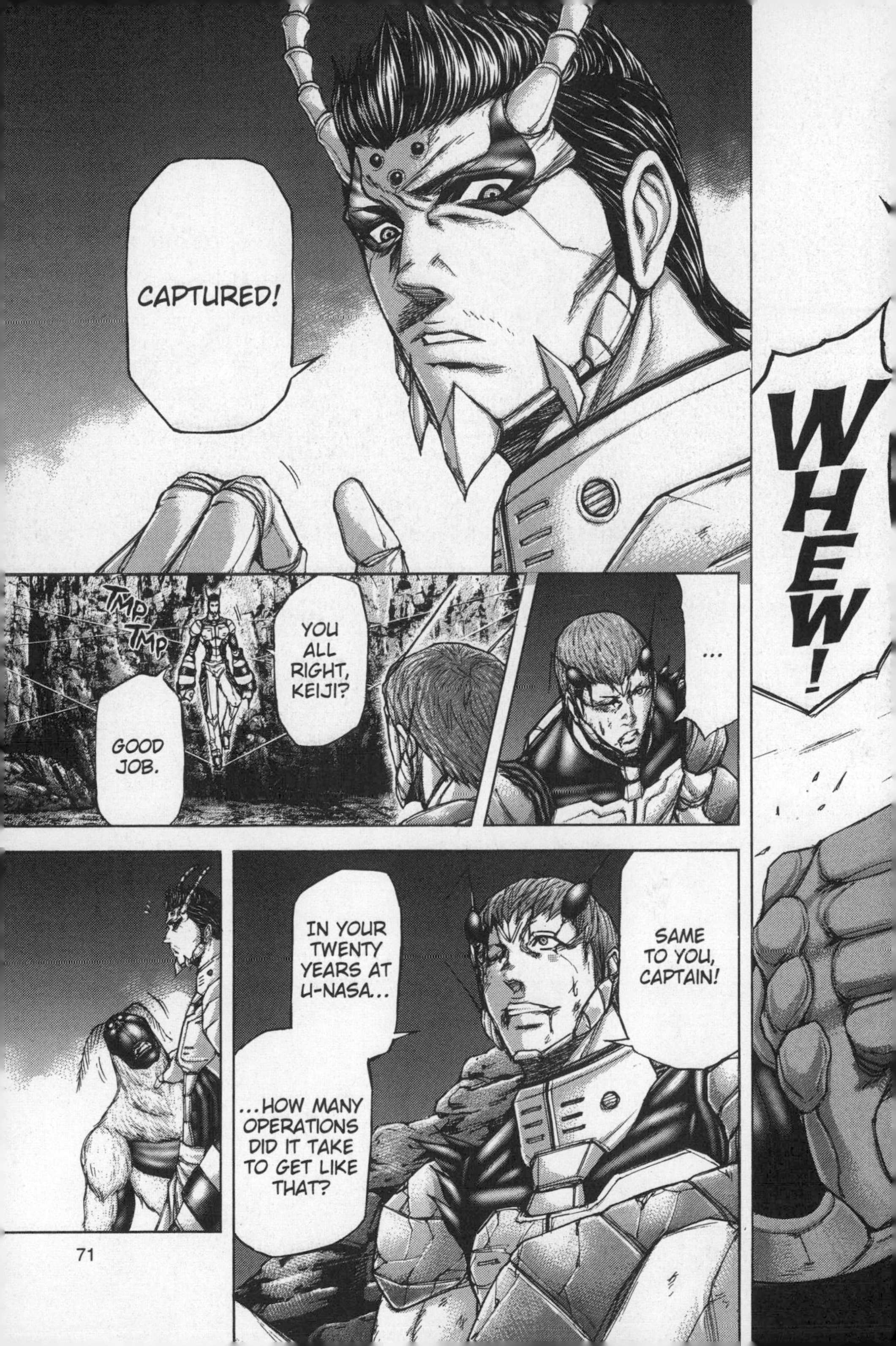
WHEW!
CAPTURED!
...
YOU ALL RIGHT, KEIJI?
TMP TMP
GOOD JOB.
SAME TO YOU, CAPTAIN!
IN YOUR TWENTY YEARS AT U-NASA...
...HOW MANY OPERATIONS DID IT TAKE TO GET LIKE THAT?

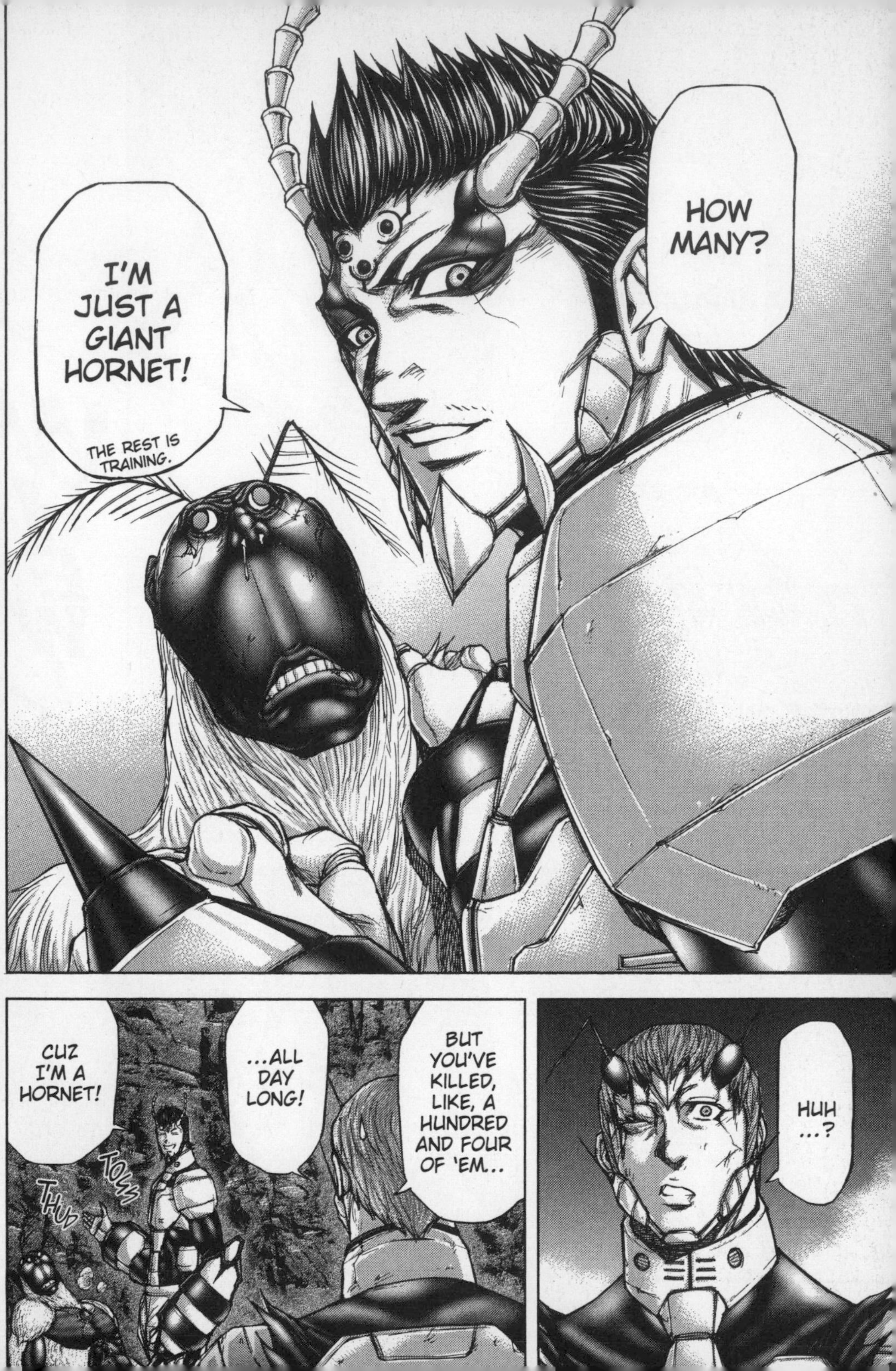
HOW MANY?
I'M JUST A GIANT HORNET!
THE REST IS TRAINING.
HUH ...?
BUT YOU'VE KILLED, LIKE, A HUNDRED AND FOUR OF 'EM...
...ALL DAY LONG!
CUZ I'M A HORNET!
TOSS
THUD

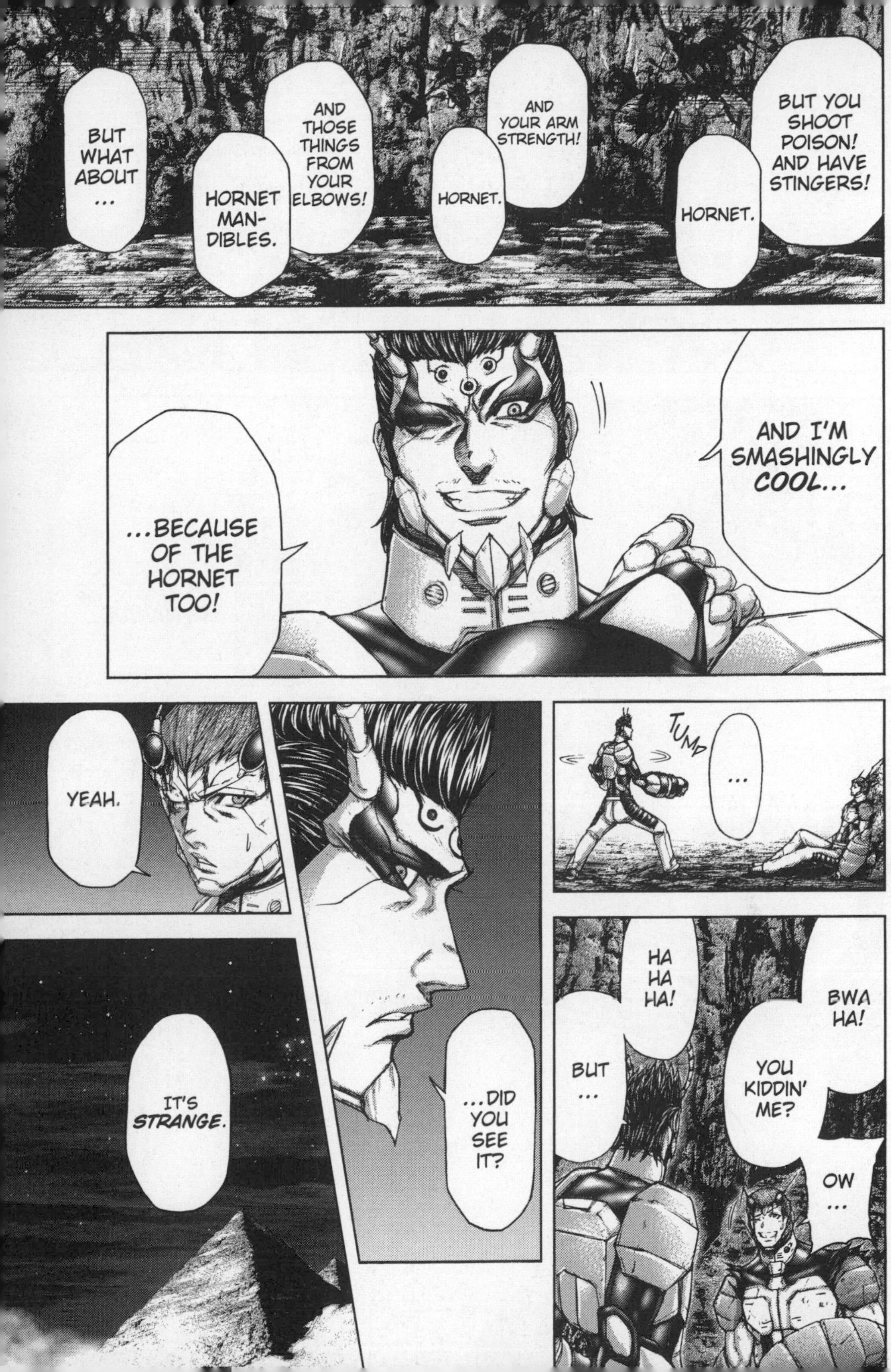
BUT YOU SHOOT POISON! AND HAVE STINGERS!
HORNET.
AND YOUR ARM STRENGTH!
HORNET.
AND THOSE THINGS FROM YOUR ELBOWS!
HORNET MAN-DIBLES.
BUT WHAT ABOUT ...
AND I'M SMASHINGLY COOL...
...BECAUSE OF THE HORNET TOO!
TUMP
...
BWA HA!
HA HA HA!
YOU KIDDIN' ME?
BUT ...
OW ...
...DID YOU SEE IT?
YEAH.
IT'S STRANGE.

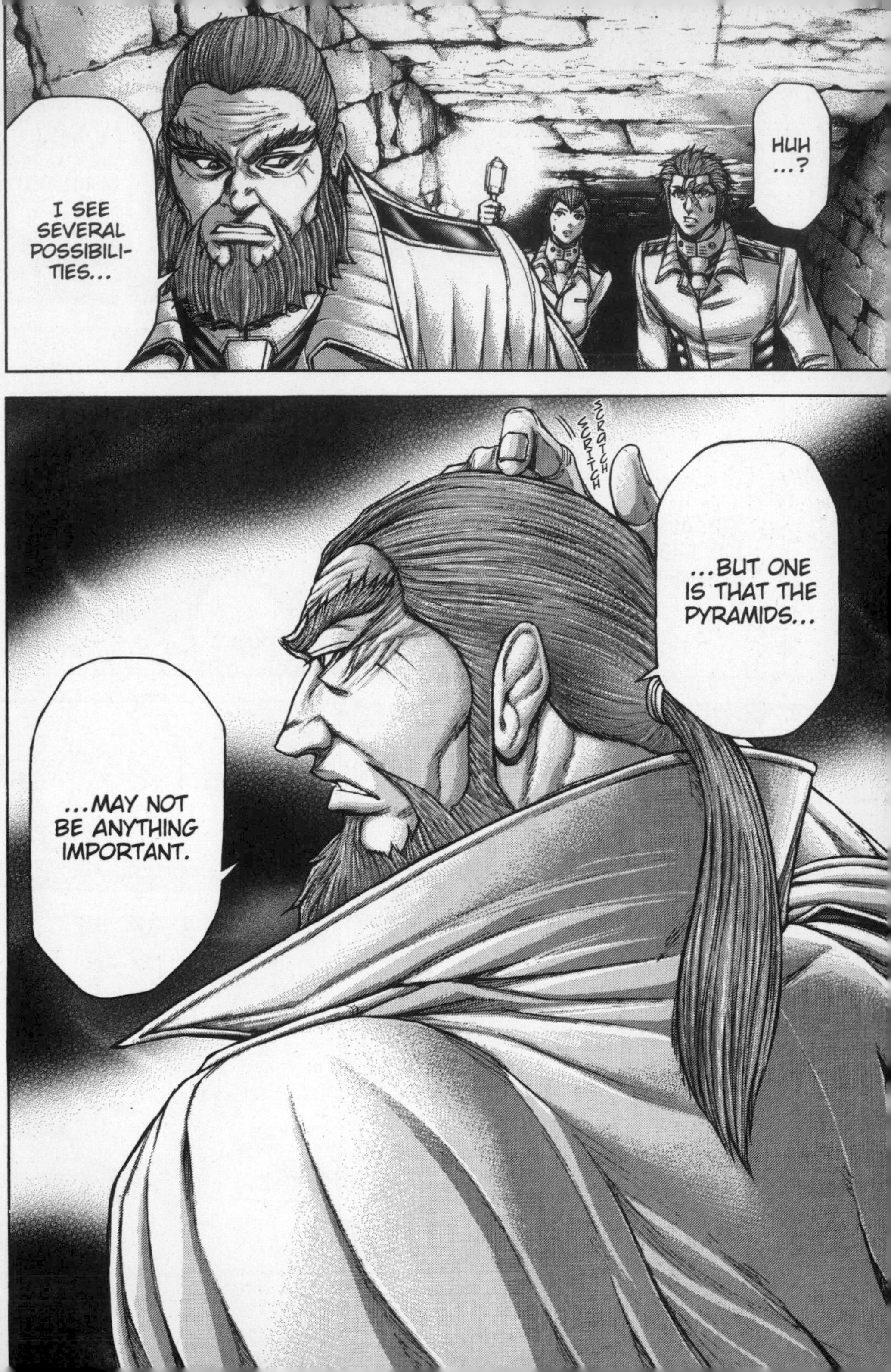
HUH ...?
I SEE SEVERAL POSSIBILI- TIES...
SCRATCH SCRITCH
...BUT ONE IS THAT THE PYRAMIDS...
...MAY NOT BE ANYTHING IMPORTANT.

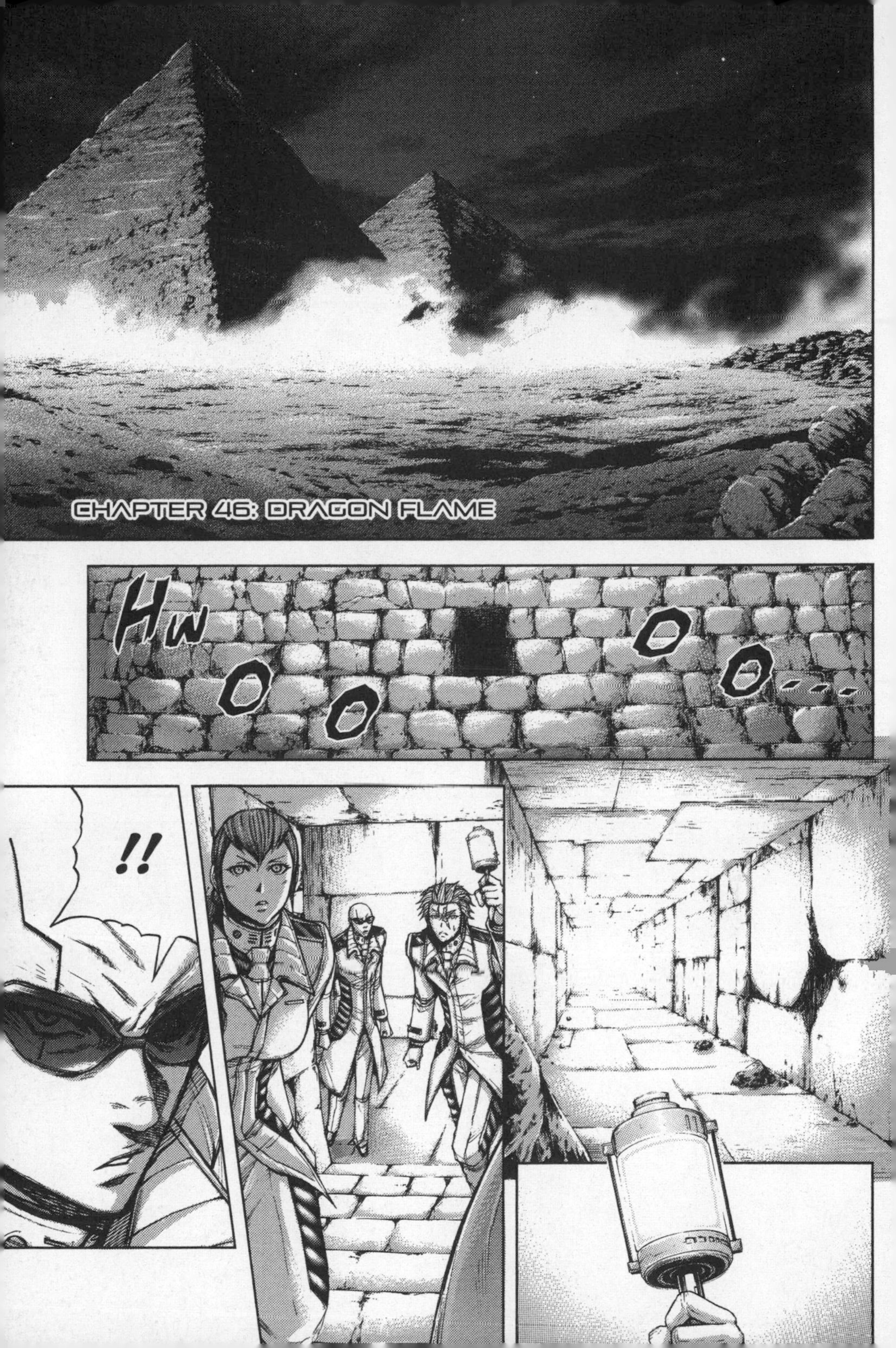
CHAPTER 46: DRAGON FLAME
HWOOOO...
!!

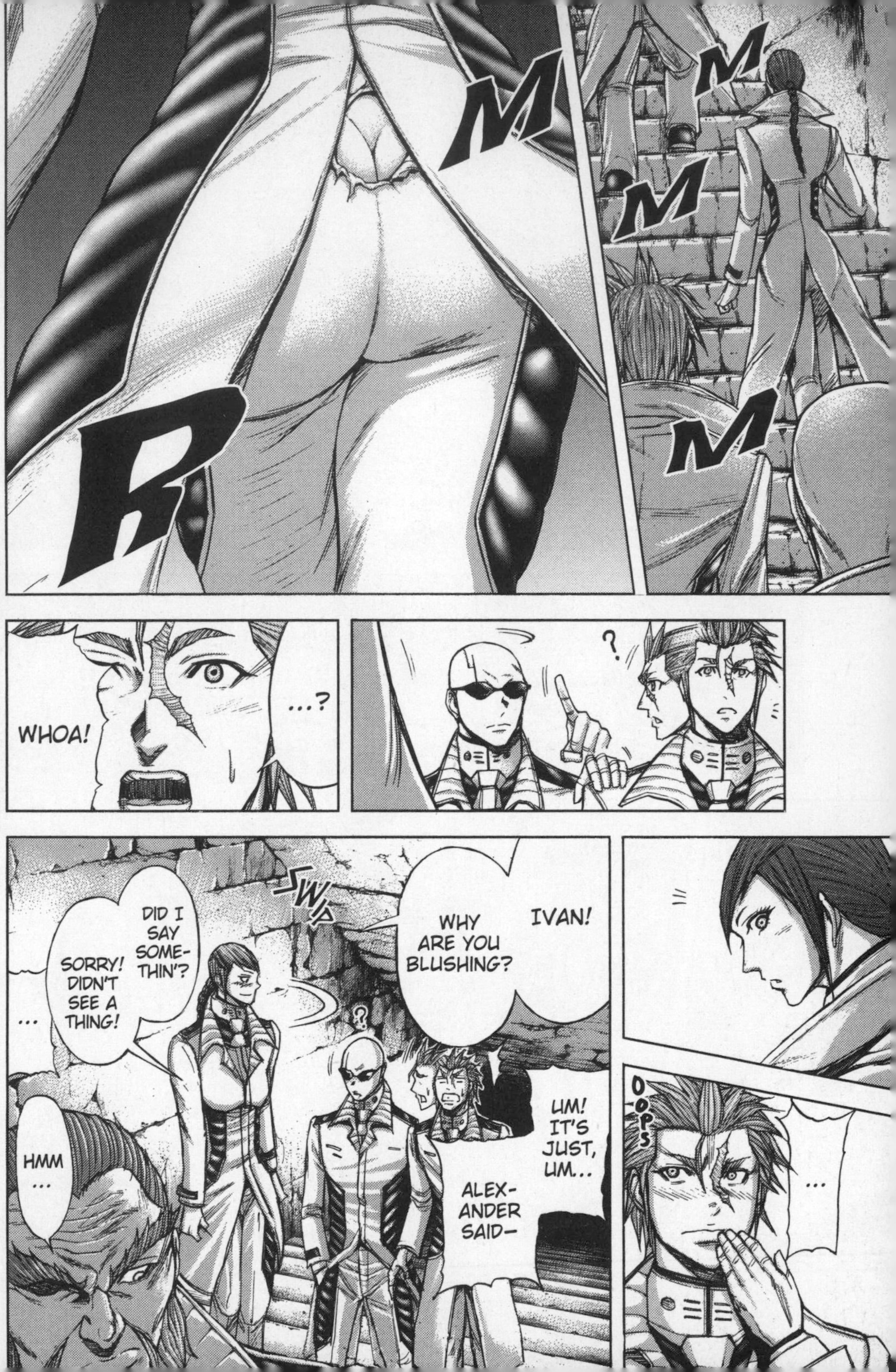
M
M
M
M
R
?
...?
WHOA!
IVAN!
WHY ARE YOU BLUSHING?
OOPS
...
UM! IT'S JUST, UM...
ALEX-ANDER SAID–
SWIP
DID I SAY SOME-THIN'?
SORRY! DIDN'T SEE A THING!
...
HMM ...

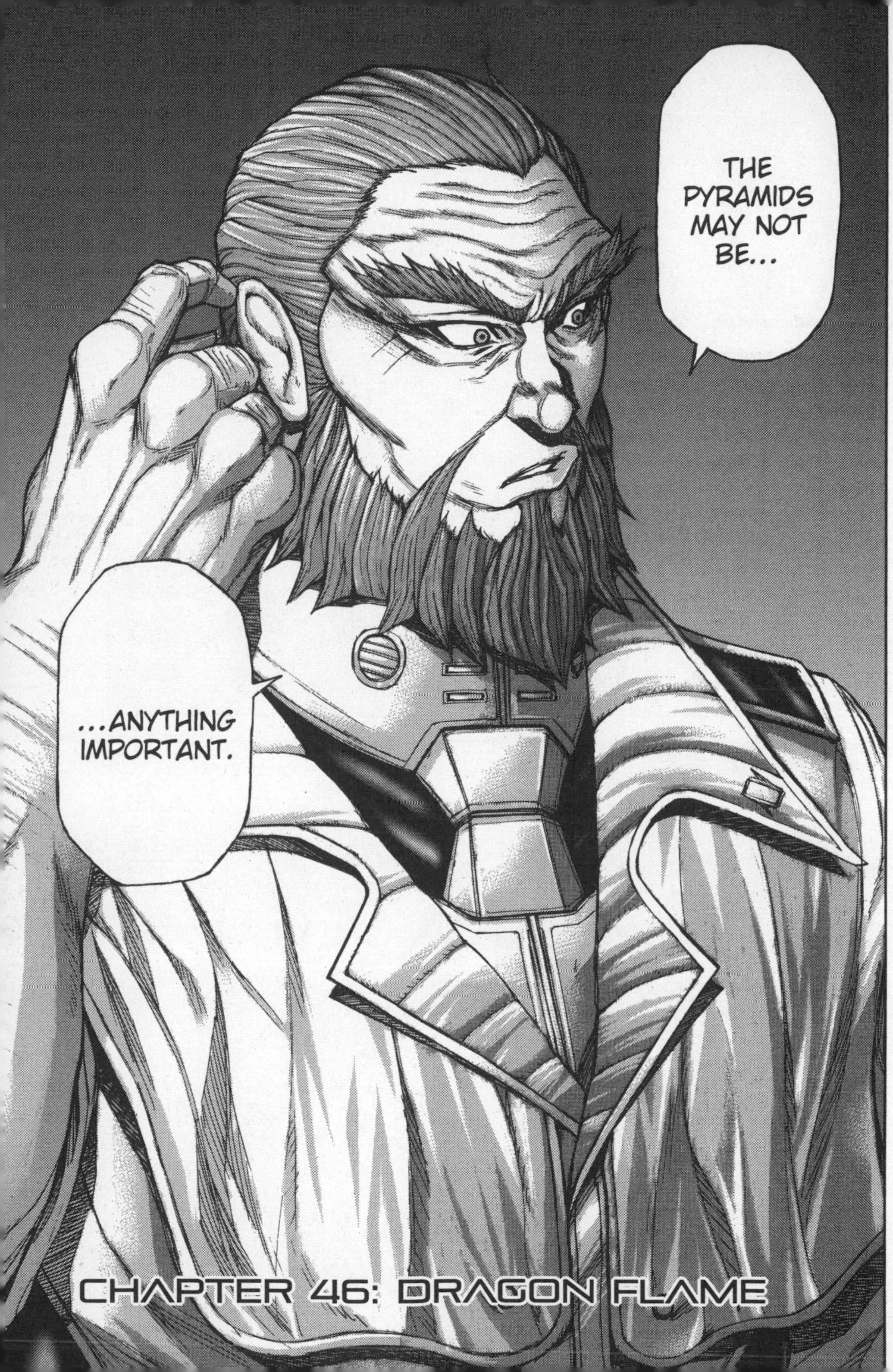
THE PYRAMIDS MAY NOT BE...
...ANYTHING IMPORTANT.
CHAPTER 46: DRAGON FLAME

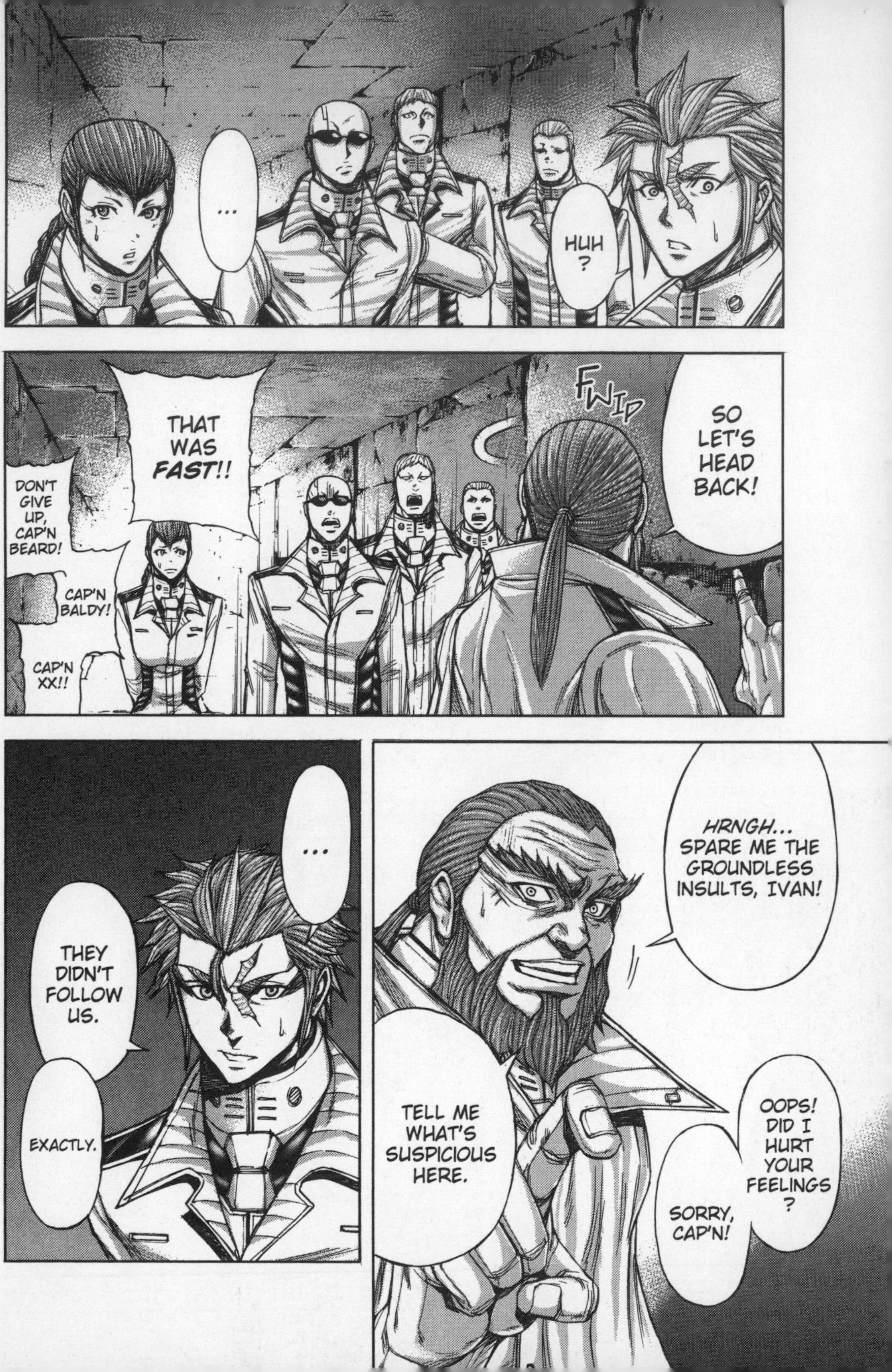
HUH ?
...
SO LET'S HEAD BACK!
FWIP
THAT WAS FAST!!
DON'T GIVE UP, CAP'N BEARD!
CAP'N BALDY!
CAP'N XX!!
HRNGH... SPARE ME THE GROUNDLESS INSULTS, IVAN!
OOPS! DID I HURT YOUR FEELINGS ?
TELL ME WHAT'S SUSPICIOUS HERE.
SORRY, CAP'N!
...
THEY DIDN'T FOLLOW US.
EXACTLY.

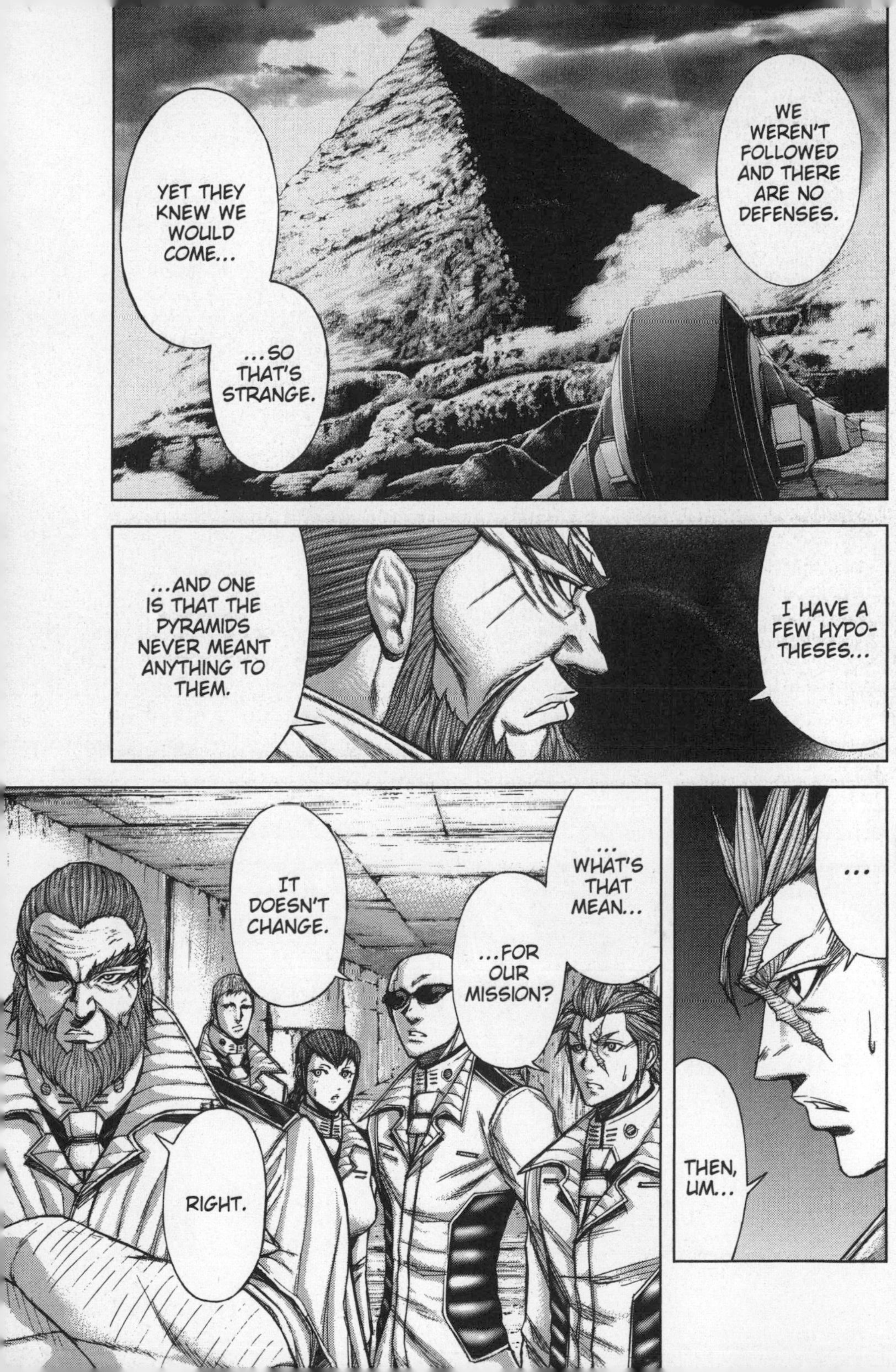
WE WEREN'T FOLLOWED AND THERE ARE NO DEFENSES.
YET THEY KNEW WE WOULD COME...
...SO THAT'S STRANGE.
I HAVE A FEW HYPO-THESES...
...AND ONE IS THAT THE PYRAMIDS NEVER MEANT ANYTHING TO THEM.
...
THEN, UM..
...WHAT'S THAT MEAN...
...FOR OUR MISSION?
IT DOESN'T CHANGE.
RIGHT.

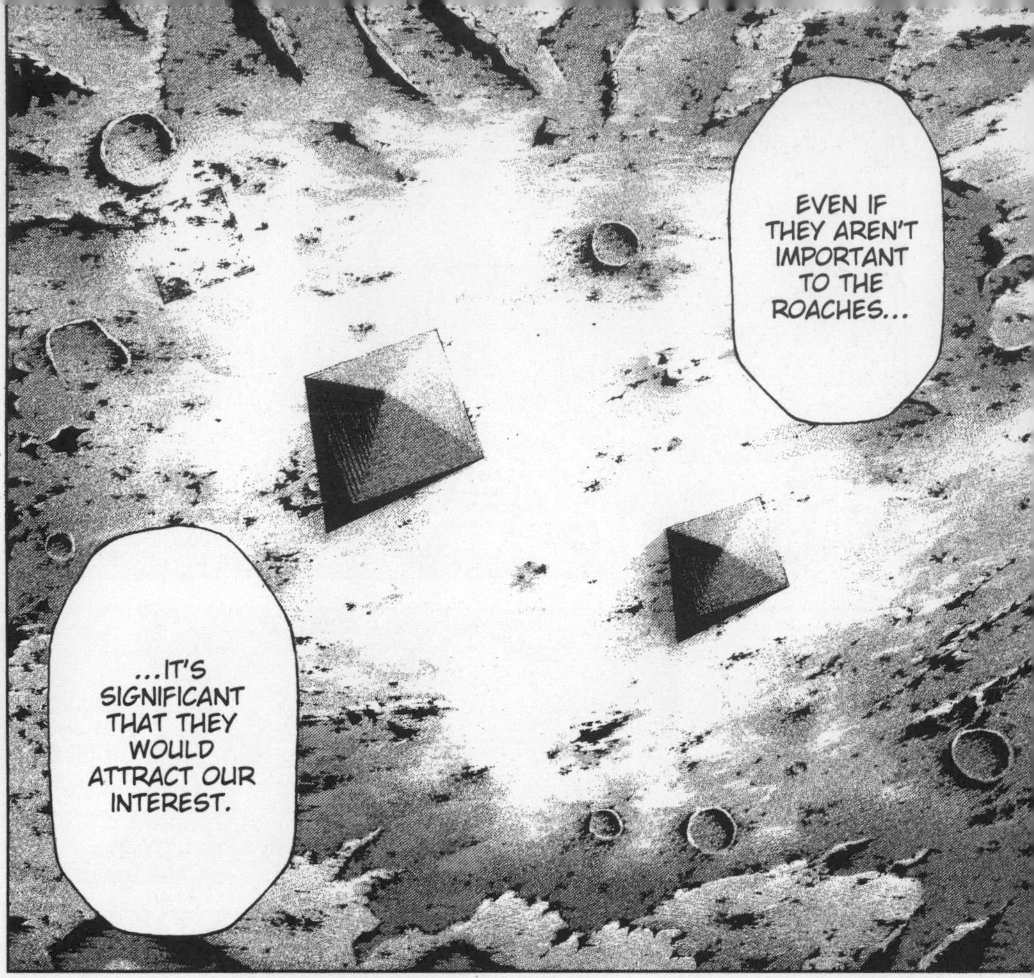
EVEN IF THEY AREN'T IMPORTANT TO THE ROACHES...
...IT'S SIGNIFICANT THAT THEY WOULD ATTRACT OUR INTEREST.

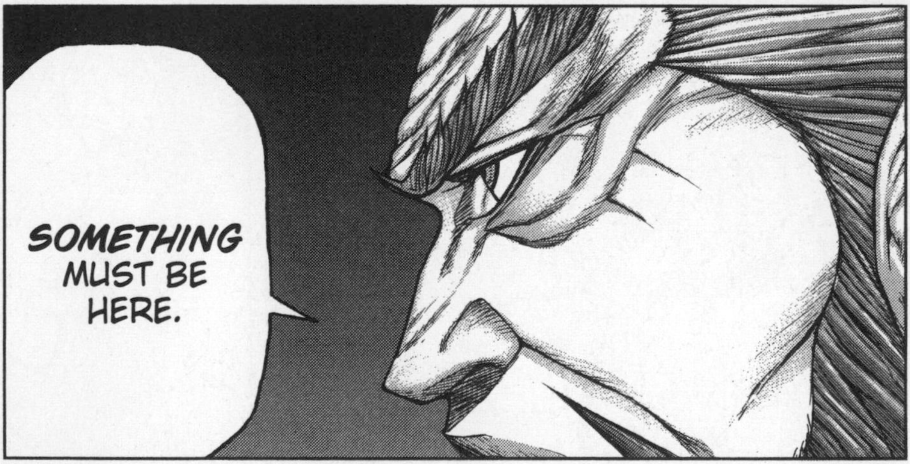
SOMETHING MUST BE HERE.

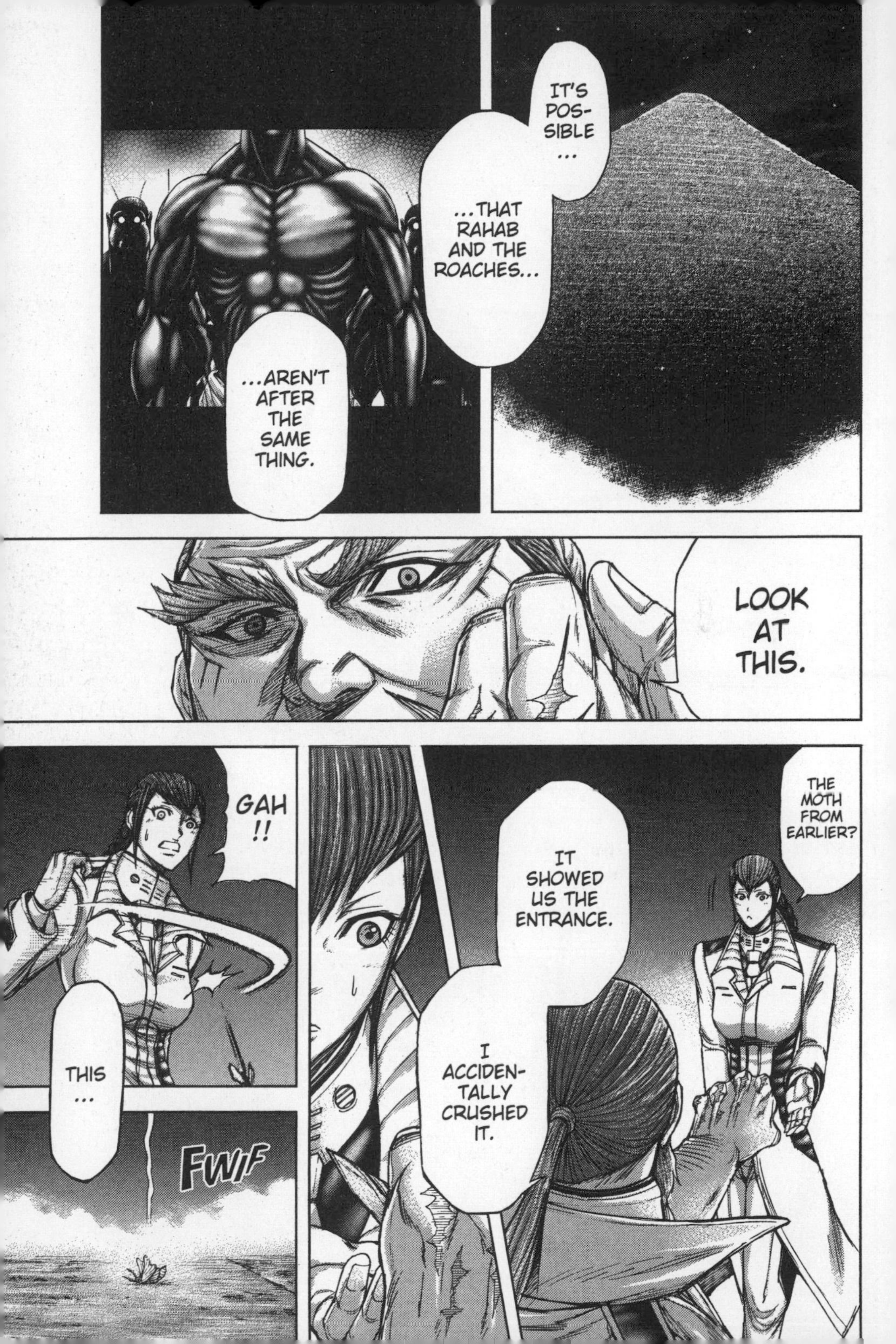
IT'S POS-SIBLE...
...THAT RAHAB AND THE ROACHES...
...AREN'T AFTER THE SAME THING.
LOOK AT THIS.
THE MOTH FROM EARLIER?
IT SHOWED US THE ENTRANCE.
I ACCIDEN-TALLY CRUSHED IT.
GAH!!
THIS...
FWIF

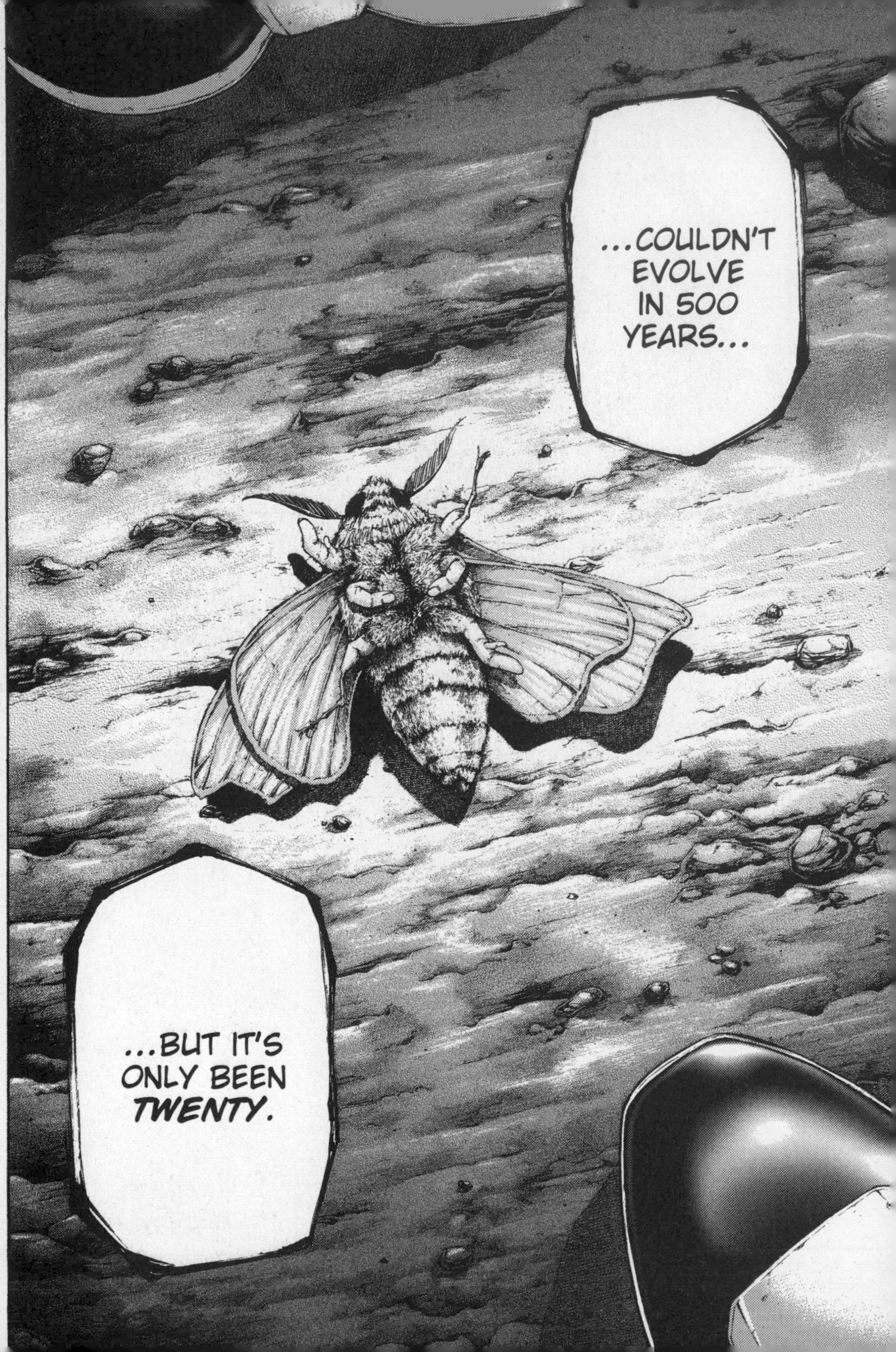
...COULDN'T EVOLVE IN 500 YEARS...
...BUT IT'S ONLY BEEN *TWENTY*.

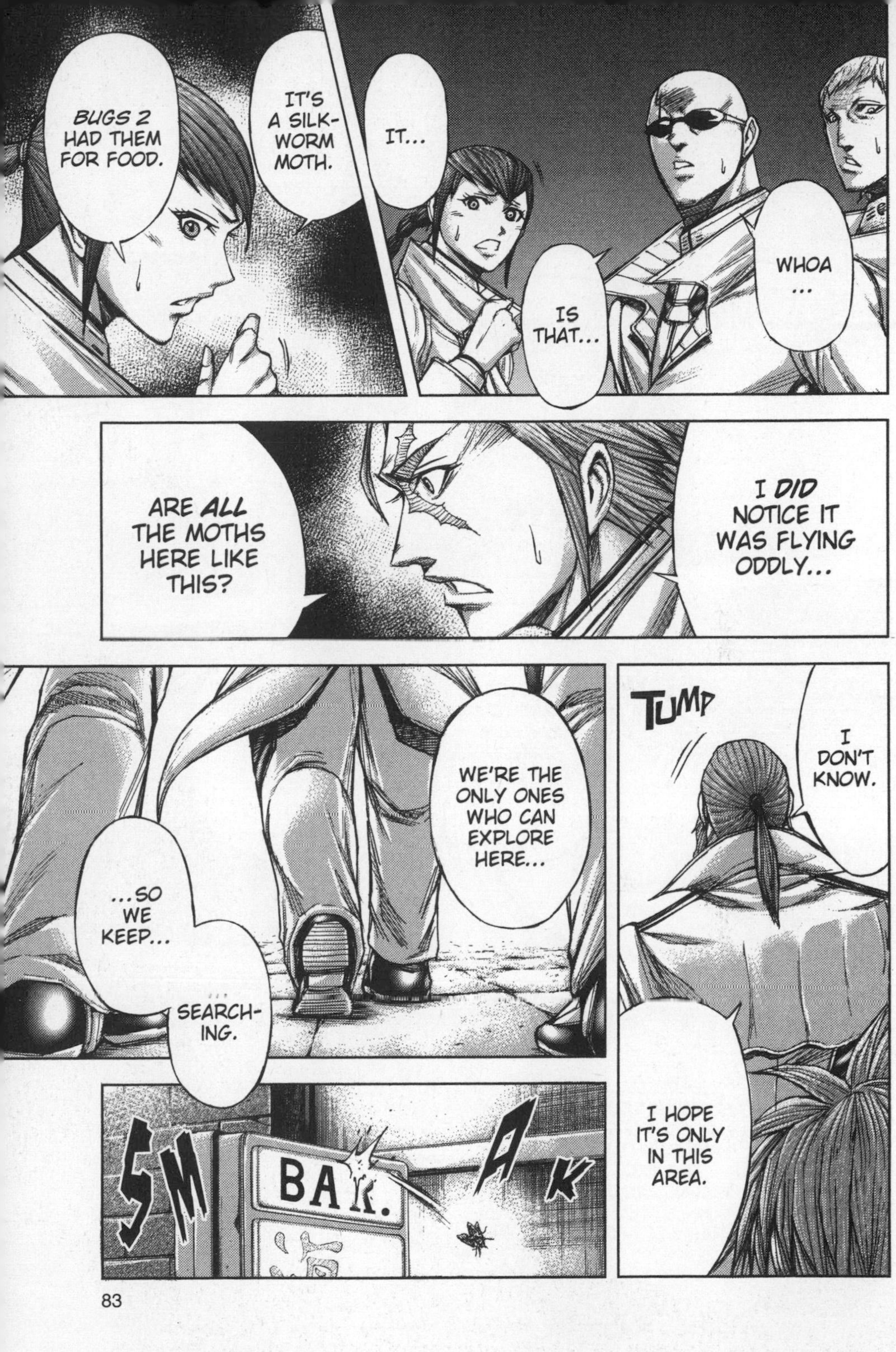
WHOA...
IS THAT...
IT...
IT'S A SILK-WORM MOTH.
BUGS 2 HAD THEM FOR FOOD.
I *DID* NOTICE IT WAS FLYING ODDLY...
ARE *ALL* THE MOTHS HERE LIKE THIS?
TUMP
I DON'T KNOW.
I HOPE IT'S ONLY IN THIS AREA.
WE'RE THE ONLY ONES WHO CAN EXPLORE HERE...
...SO WE KEEP...
...SEARCHING.
SMAK
BAK.

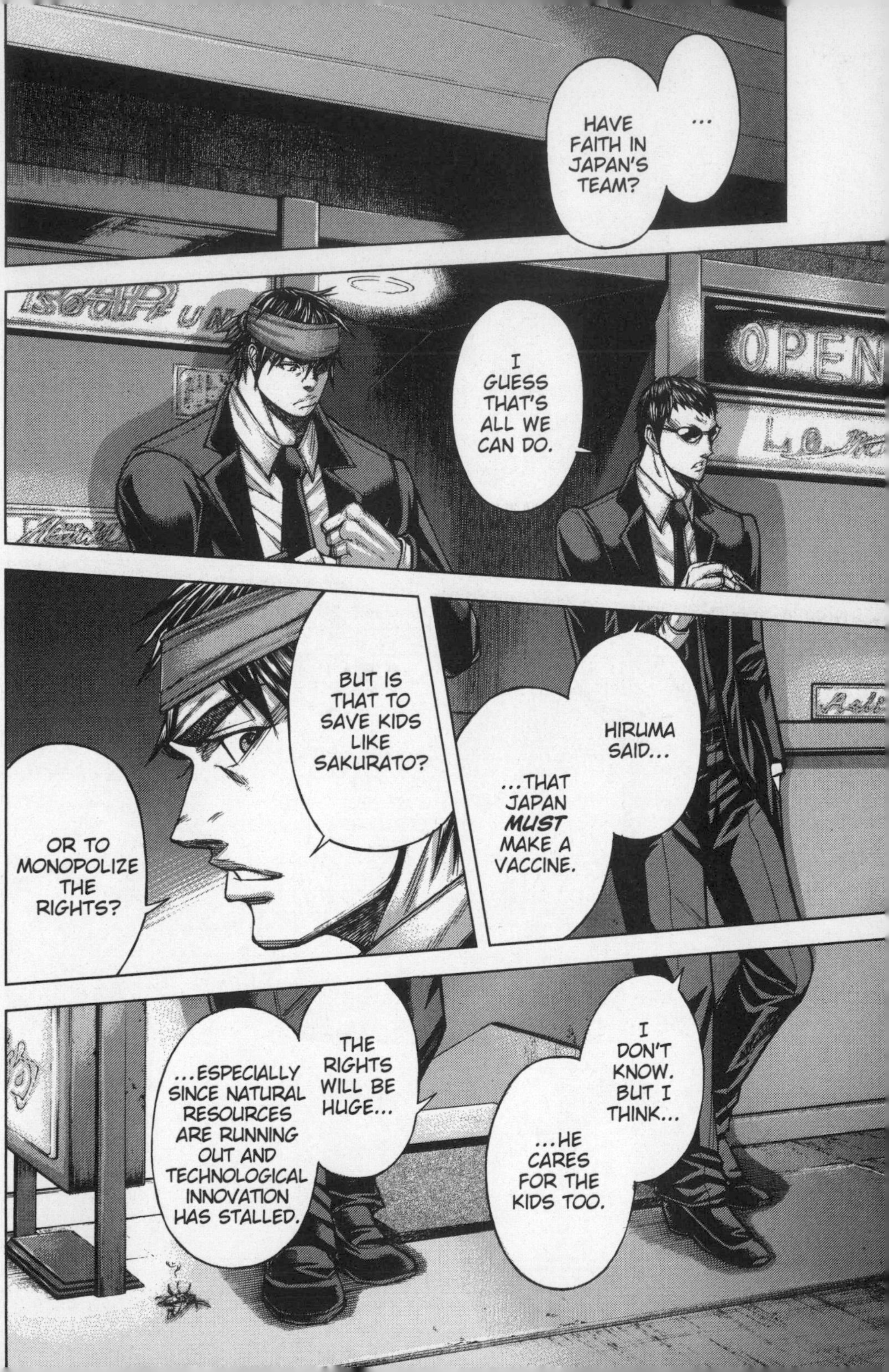

...
HAVE FAITH IN JAPAN'S TEAM?
OPEN
I GUESS THAT'S ALL WE CAN DO.
HIRUMA SAID...
...THAT JAPAN *MUST* MAKE A VACCINE.
BUT IS THAT TO SAVE KIDS LIKE SAKURATO?
OR TO MONOPOLIZE THE RIGHTS?
I DON'T KNOW. BUT I THINK...
...HE CARES FOR THE KIDS TOO.
THE RIGHTS WILL BE HUGE...
...ESPECIALLY SINCE NATURAL RESOURCES ARE RUNNING OUT AND TECHNOLOGICAL INNOVATION HAS STALLED.

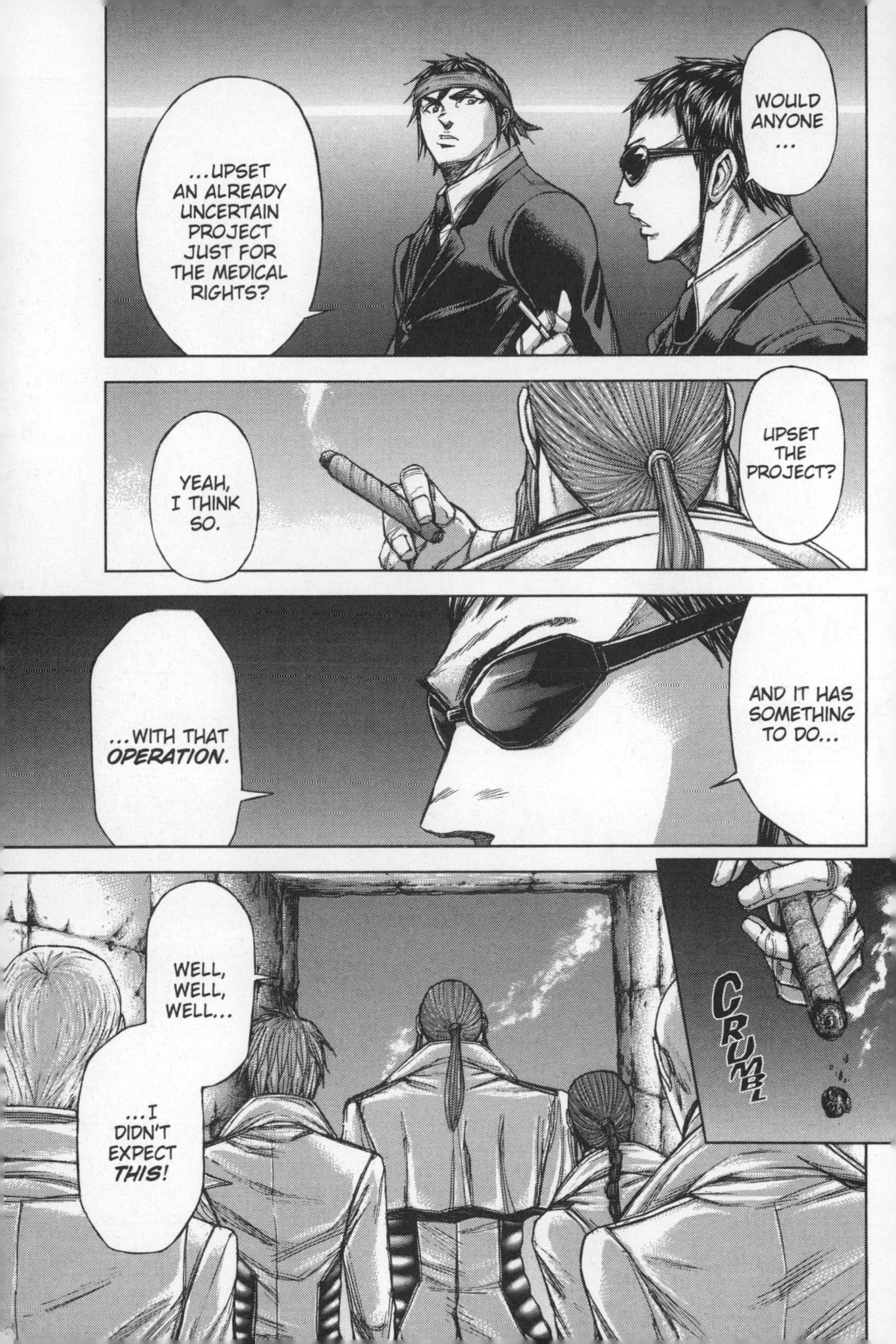
WOULD ANYONE ...
...UPSET AN ALREADY UNCERTAIN PROJECT JUST FOR THE MEDICAL RIGHTS?
UPSET THE PROJECT?
YEAH, I THINK SO.
AND IT HAS SOMETHING TO DO...
...WITH THAT *OPERATION*.
CRUMBL
WELL, WELL, WELL...
...I DIDN'T EXPECT *THIS*!

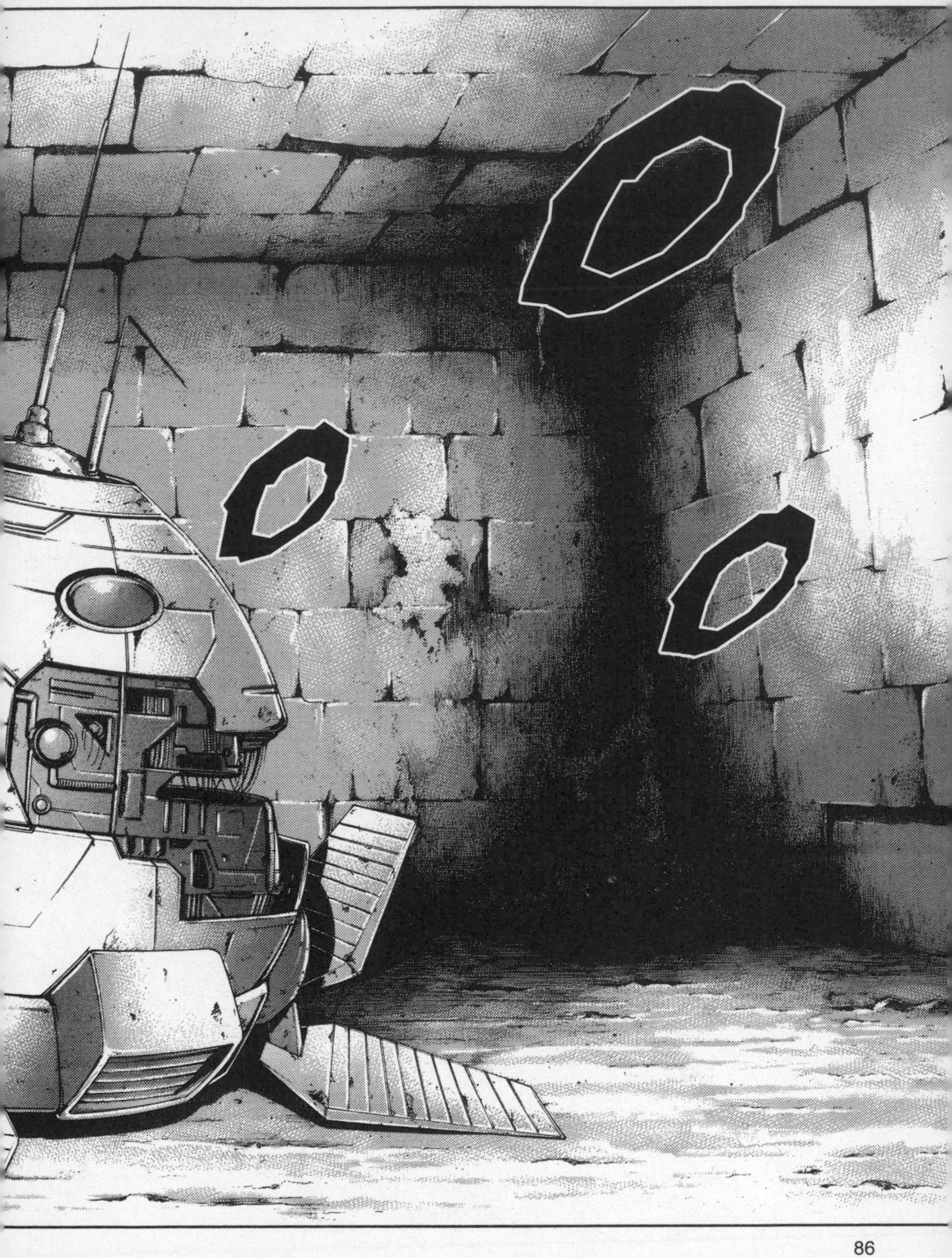

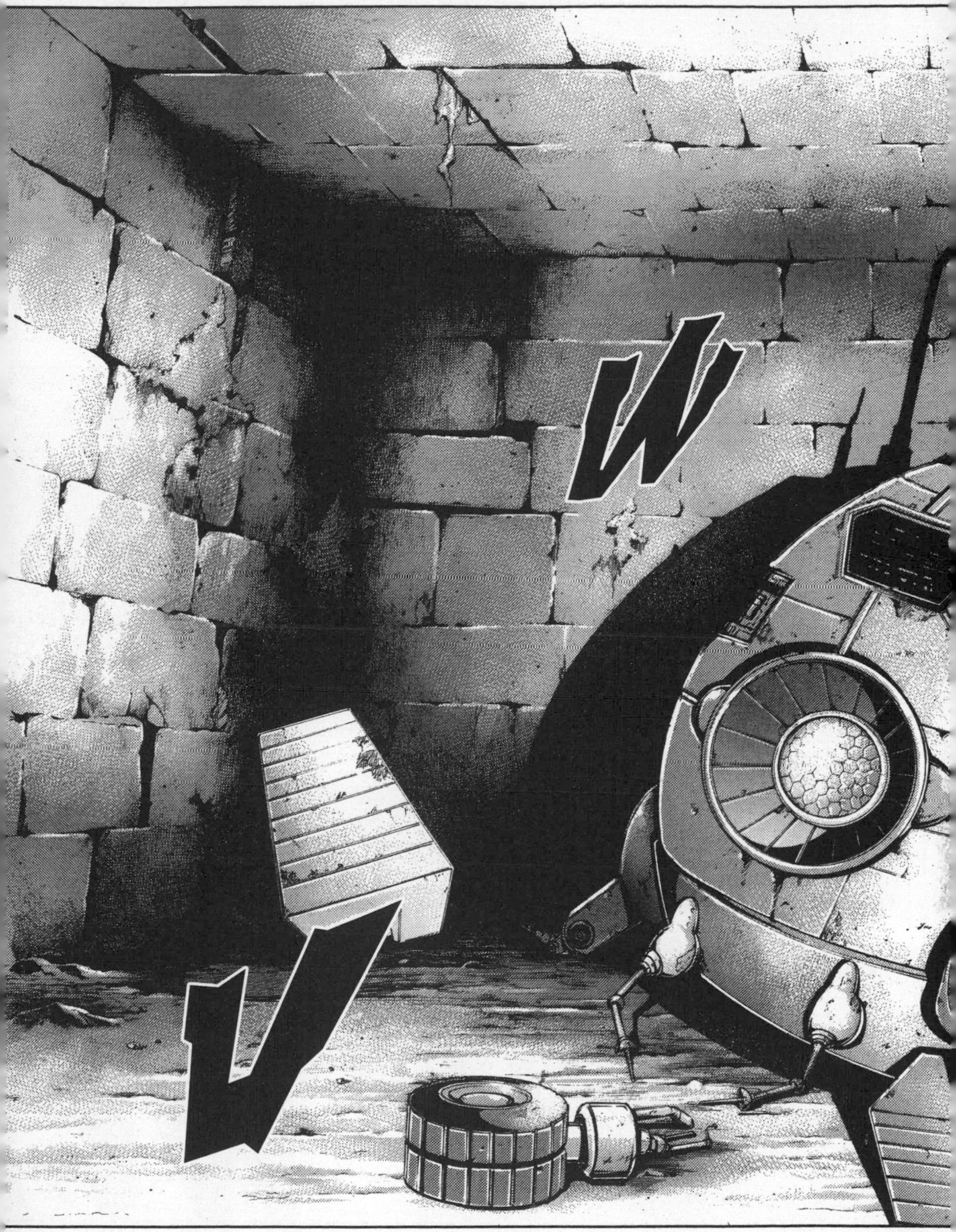
W
V

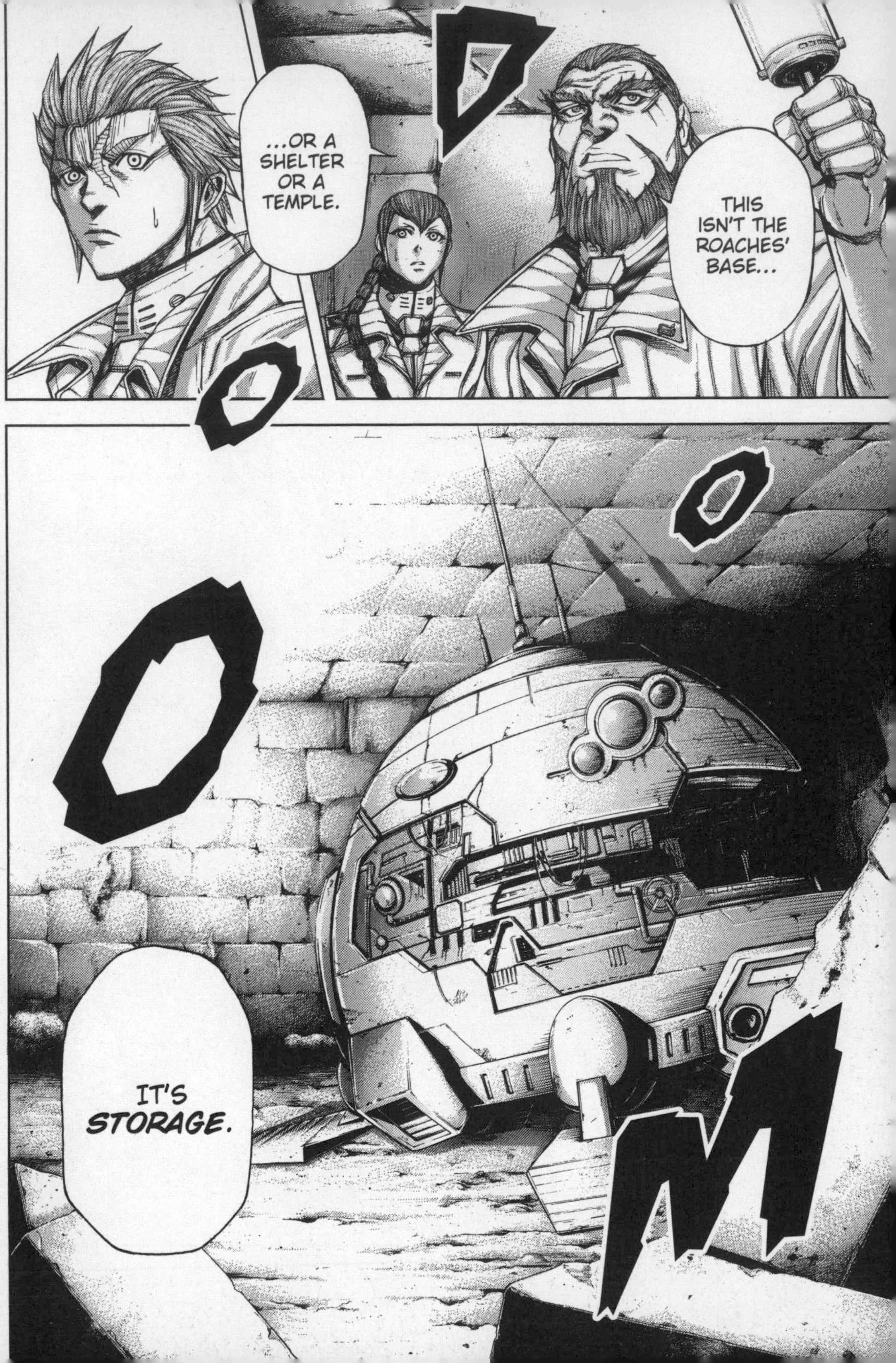
THIS ISN'T THE ROACHES' BASE...
...OR A SHELTER OR A TEMPLE.
DOOOM
IT'S STORAGE.

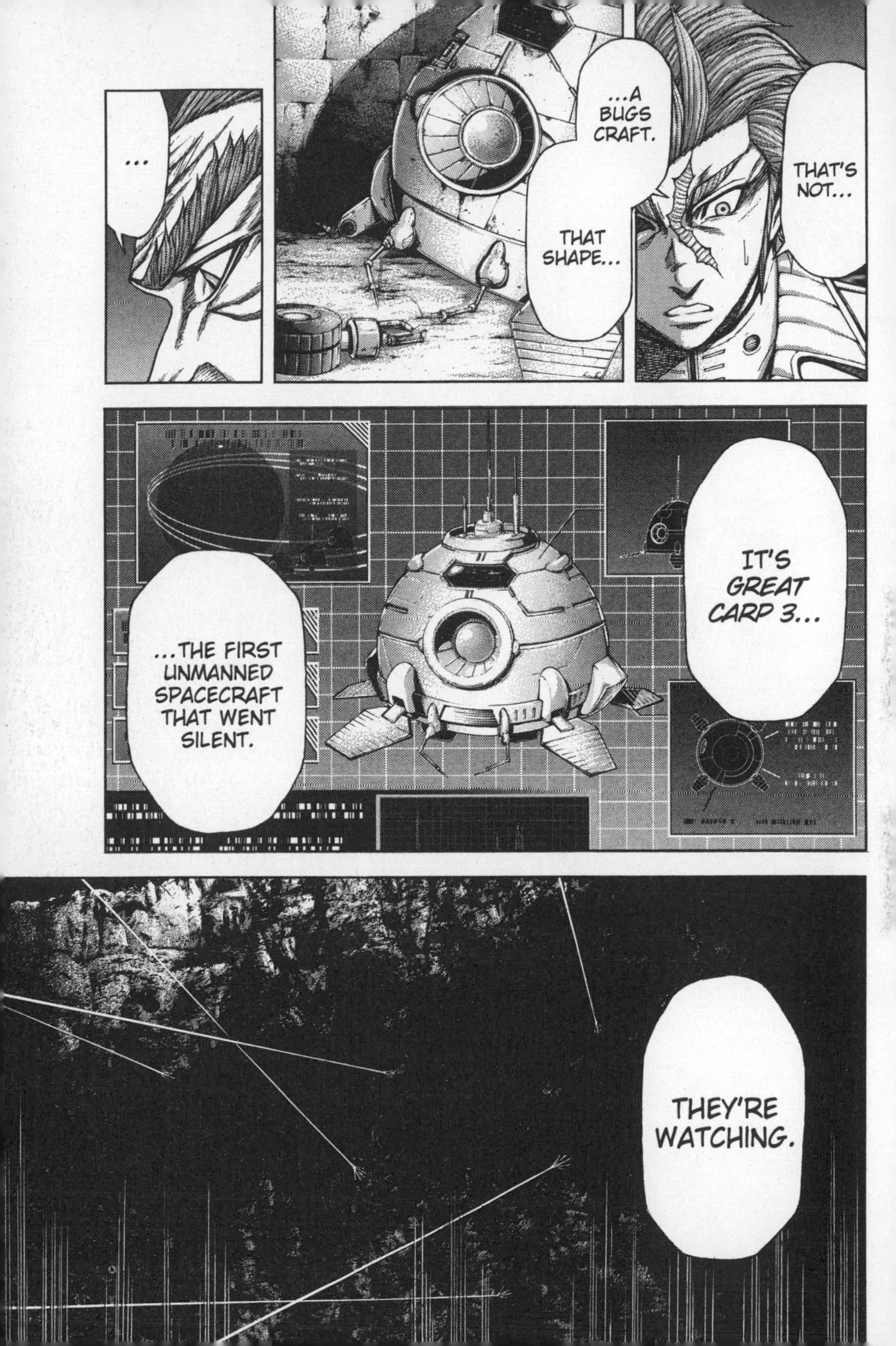
THAT'S NOT...
...A BUGS CRAFT.
THAT SHAPE...
...
IT'S GREAT CARP 3...
...THE FIRST UNMANNED SPACECRAFT THAT WENT SILENT.
THEY'RE WATCHING.

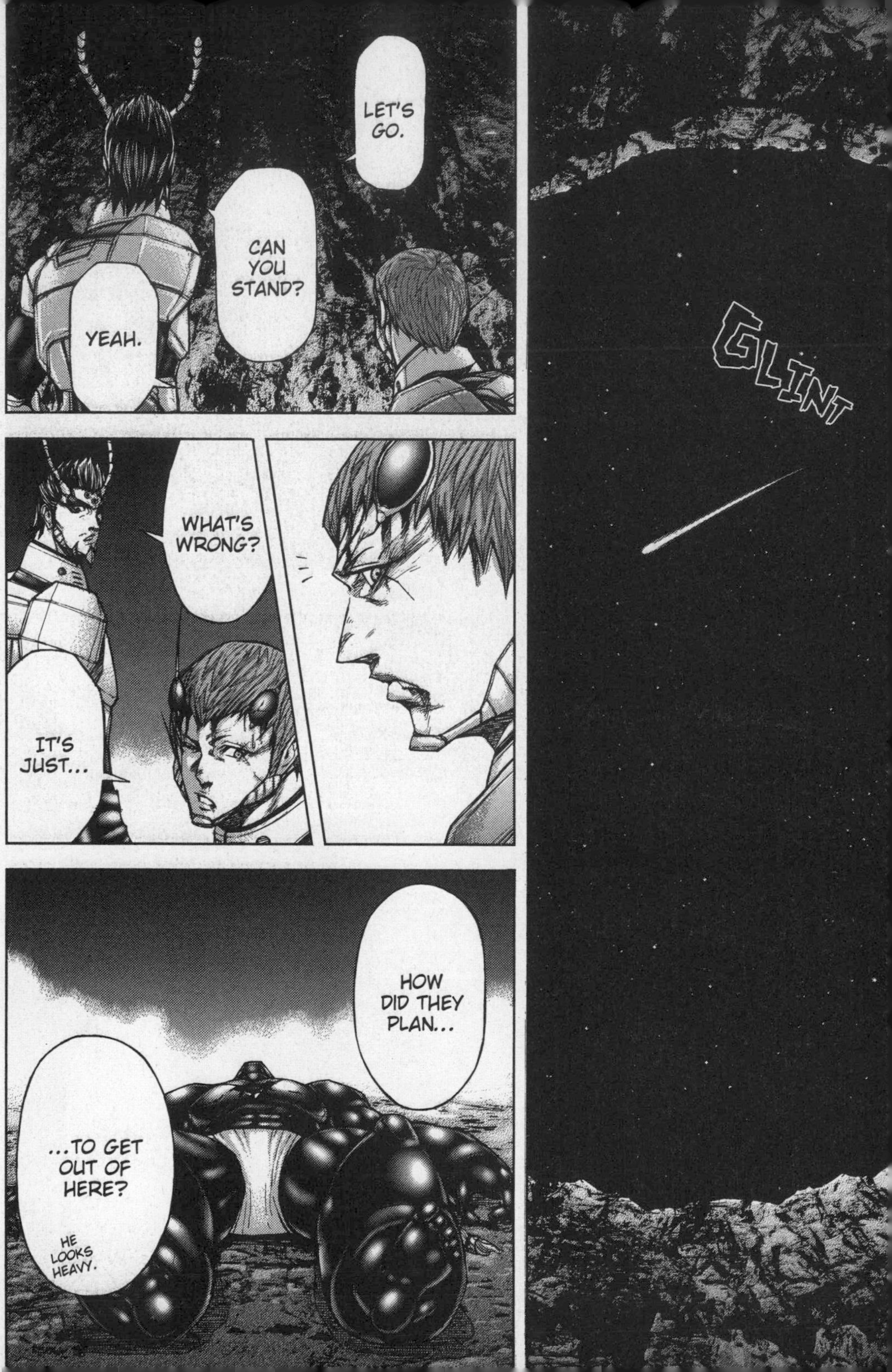
GLINT
LET'S GO.
CAN YOU STAND?
YEAH.
WHAT'S WRONG?
IT'S JUST...
HOW DID THEY PLAN...
...TO GET OUT OF HERE?
HE LOOKS HEAVY.

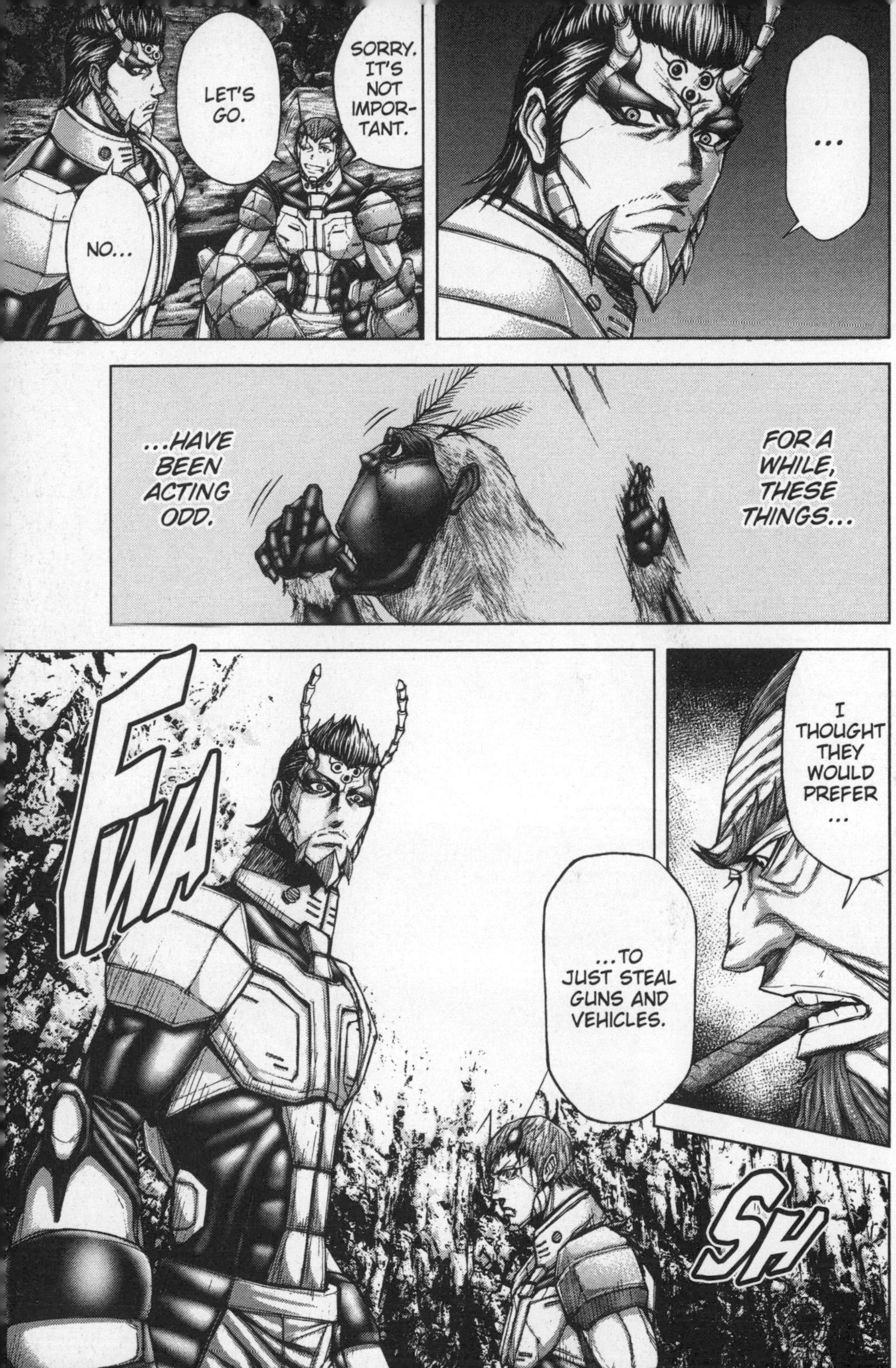
...
SORRY. IT'S NOT IMPORTANT.
LET'S GO.
NO...
FOR A WHILE, THESE THINGS...
...HAVE BEEN ACTING ODD.
I THOUGHT THEY WOULD PREFER ...
FWA
...TO JUST STEAL GUNS AND VEHICLES.
SH

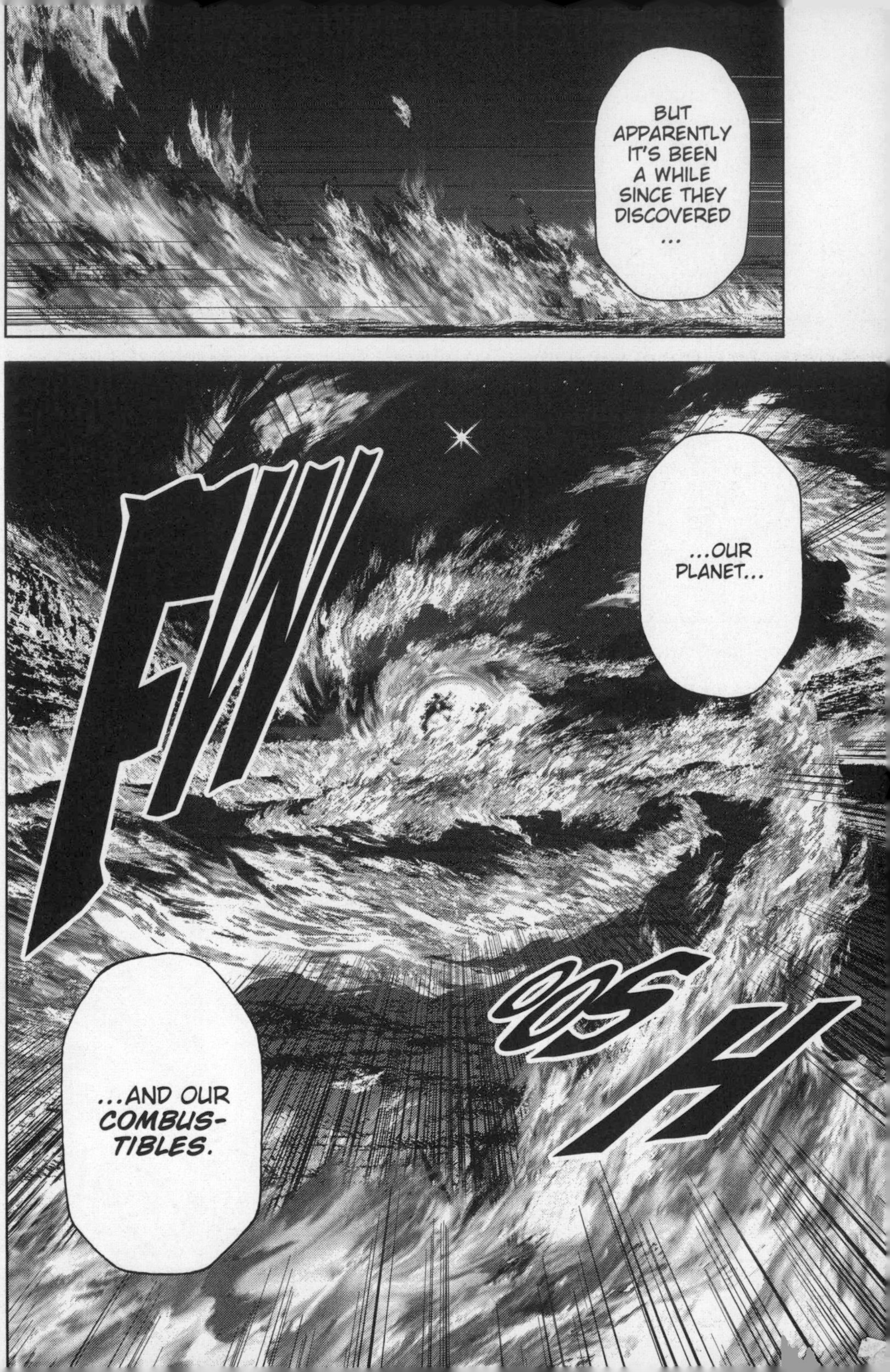
BUT APPARENTLY IT'S BEEN A WHILE SINCE THEY DISCOVERED ...
...OUR PLANET...
FWW
...AND OUR COMBUS-TIBLES.

UNRELEASED SCENE

At least finish your dessert!
What a waste...
MNCH
MNCH

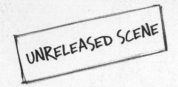

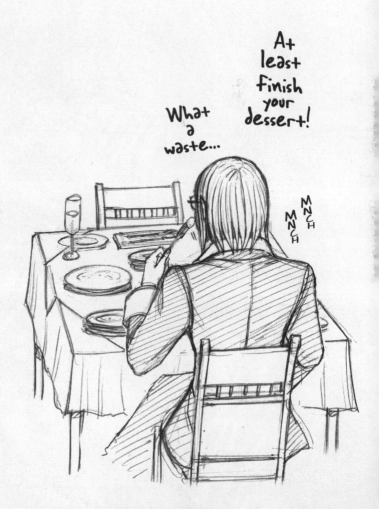

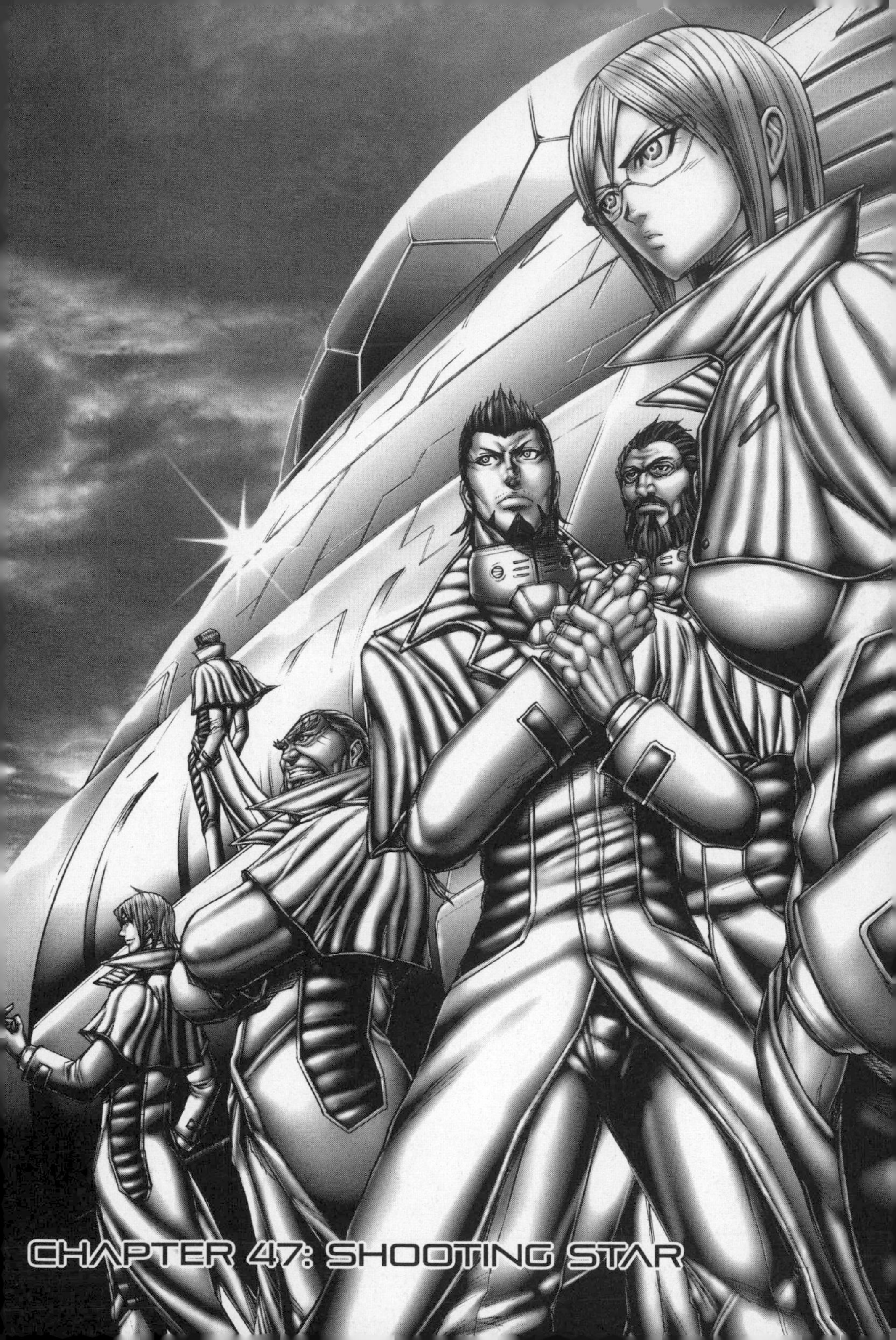
CHAPTER 47: SHOOTING STAR

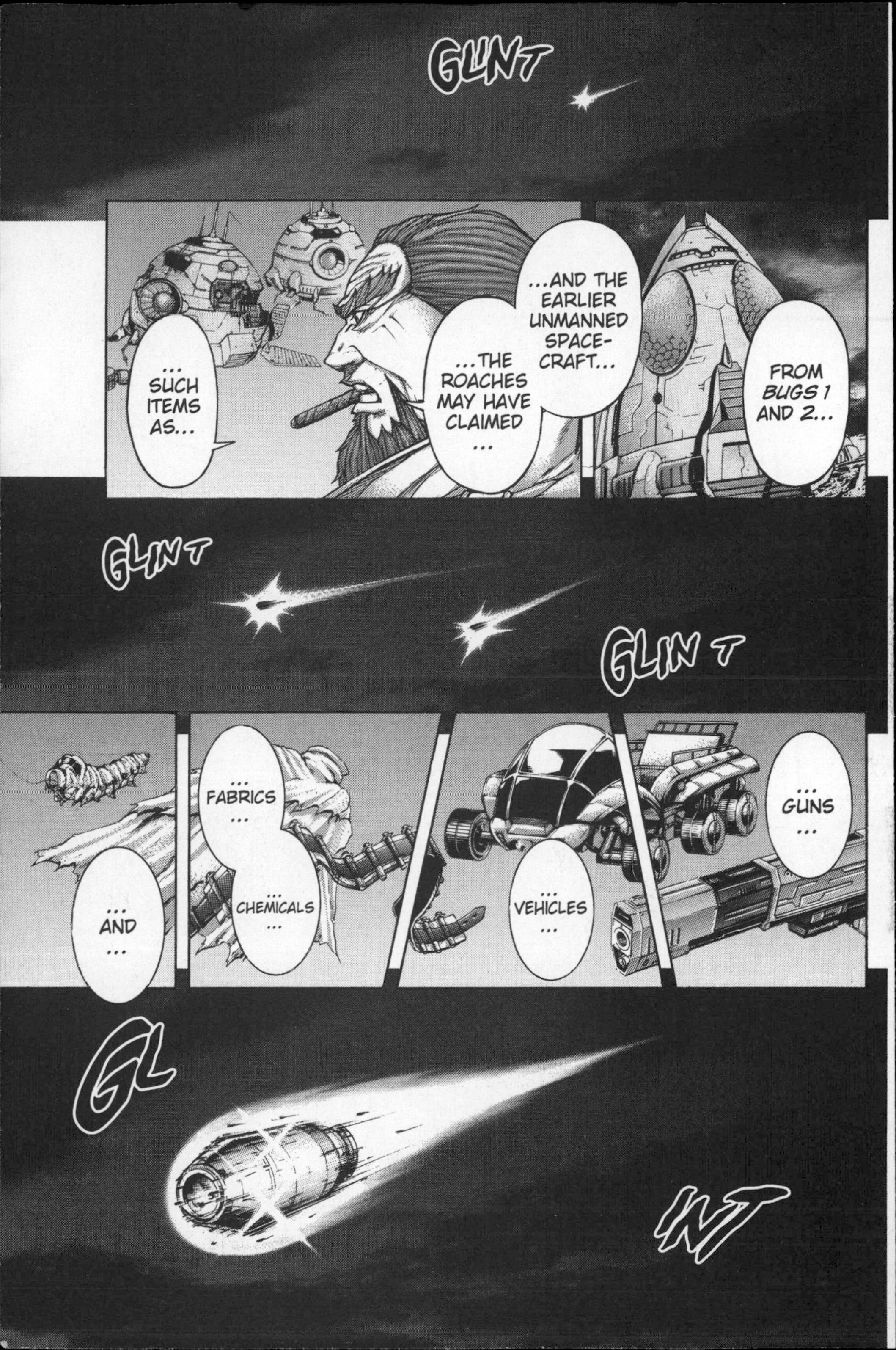
GLINT
FROM BUGS 1 AND 2...
...AND THE EARLIER UNMANNED SPACE-CRAFT...
...THE ROACHES MAY HAVE CLAIMED ...
... SUCH ITEMS AS...
GLINT
GLINT
... GUNS ...
... VEHICLES ...
... FABRICS ...
... CHEMICALS ...
... AND ...
GL
INT

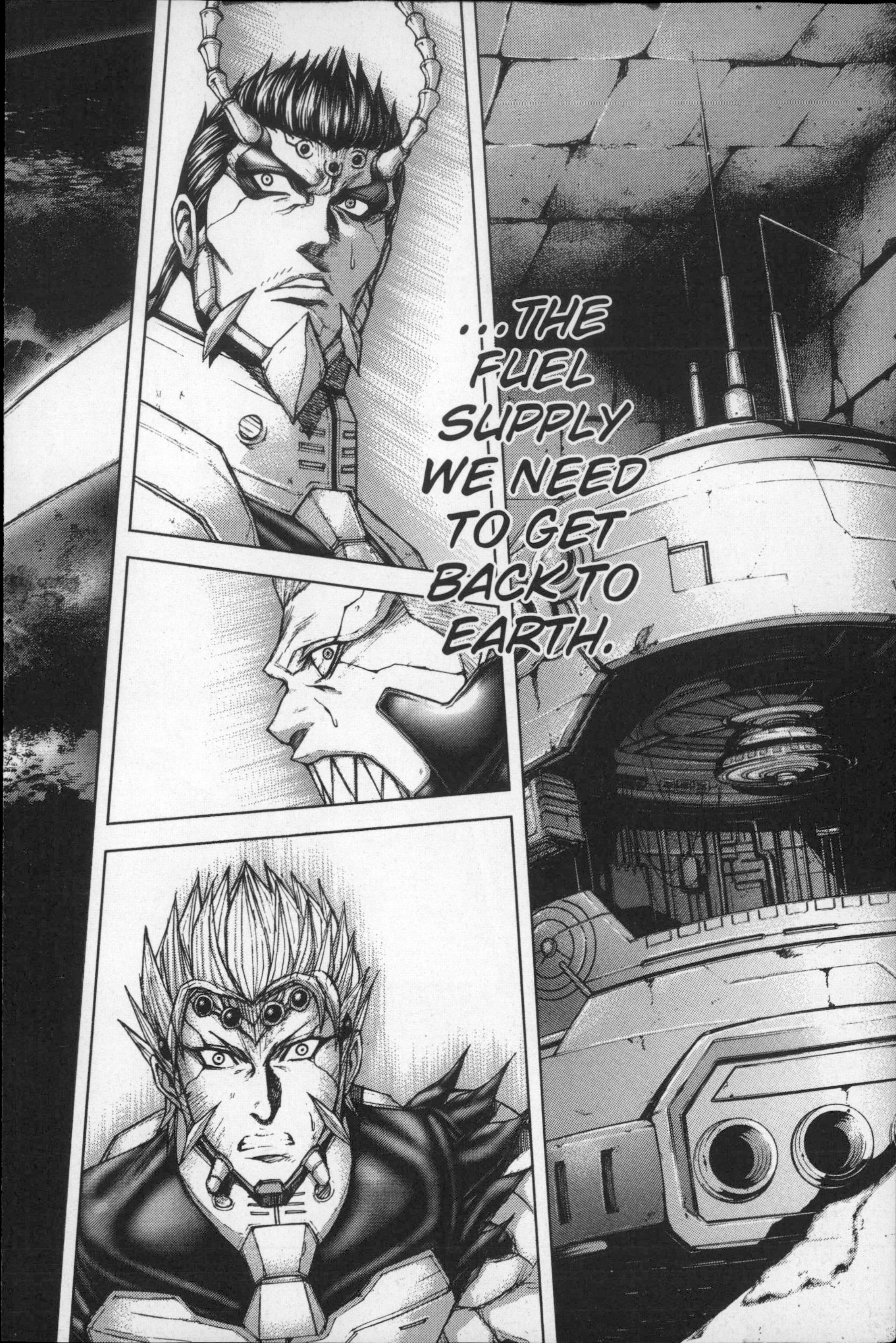
...THE FUEL SUPPLY WE NEED TO GET BACK TO EARTH.

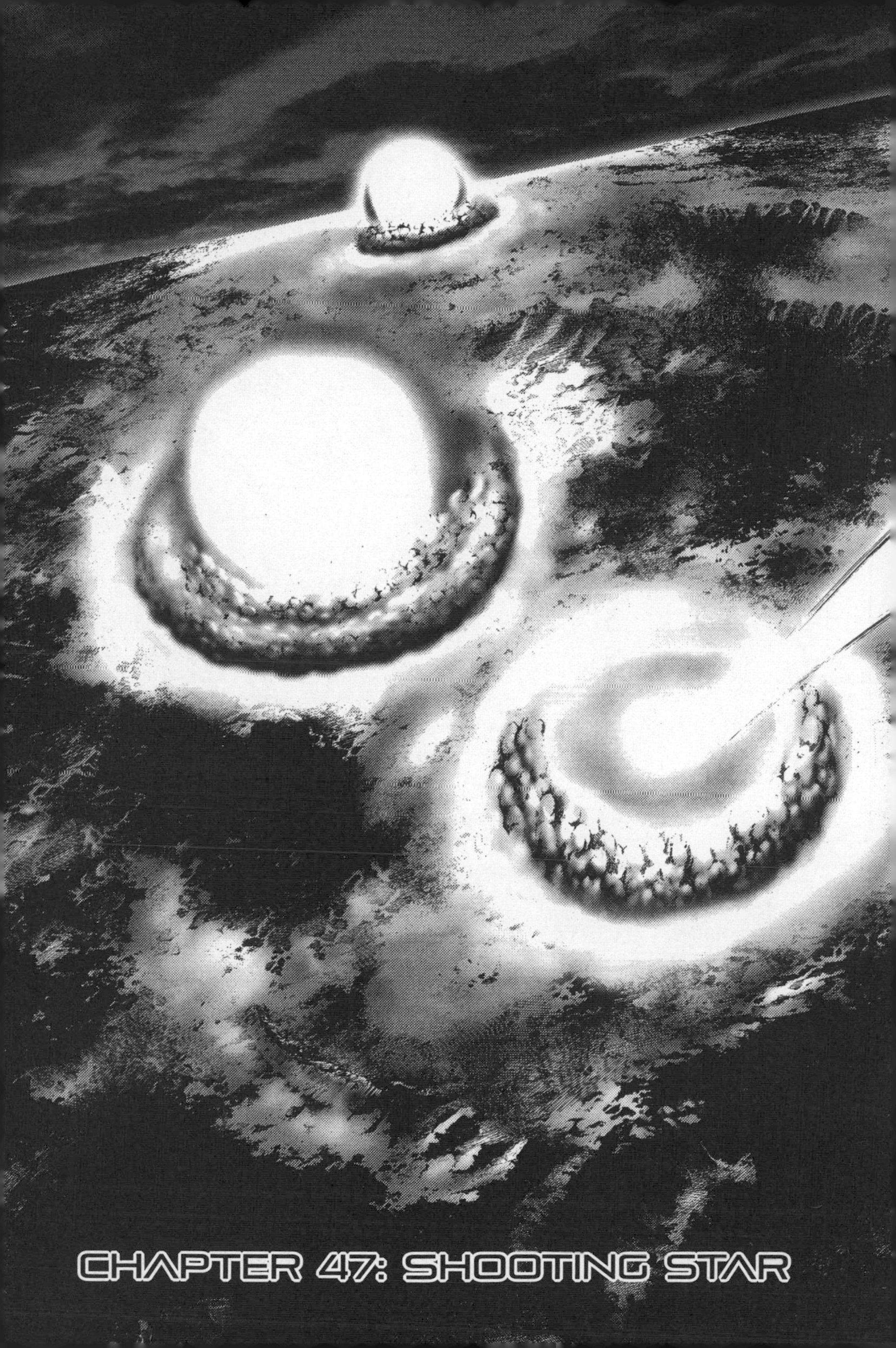
CHAPTER 47: SHOOTING STAR

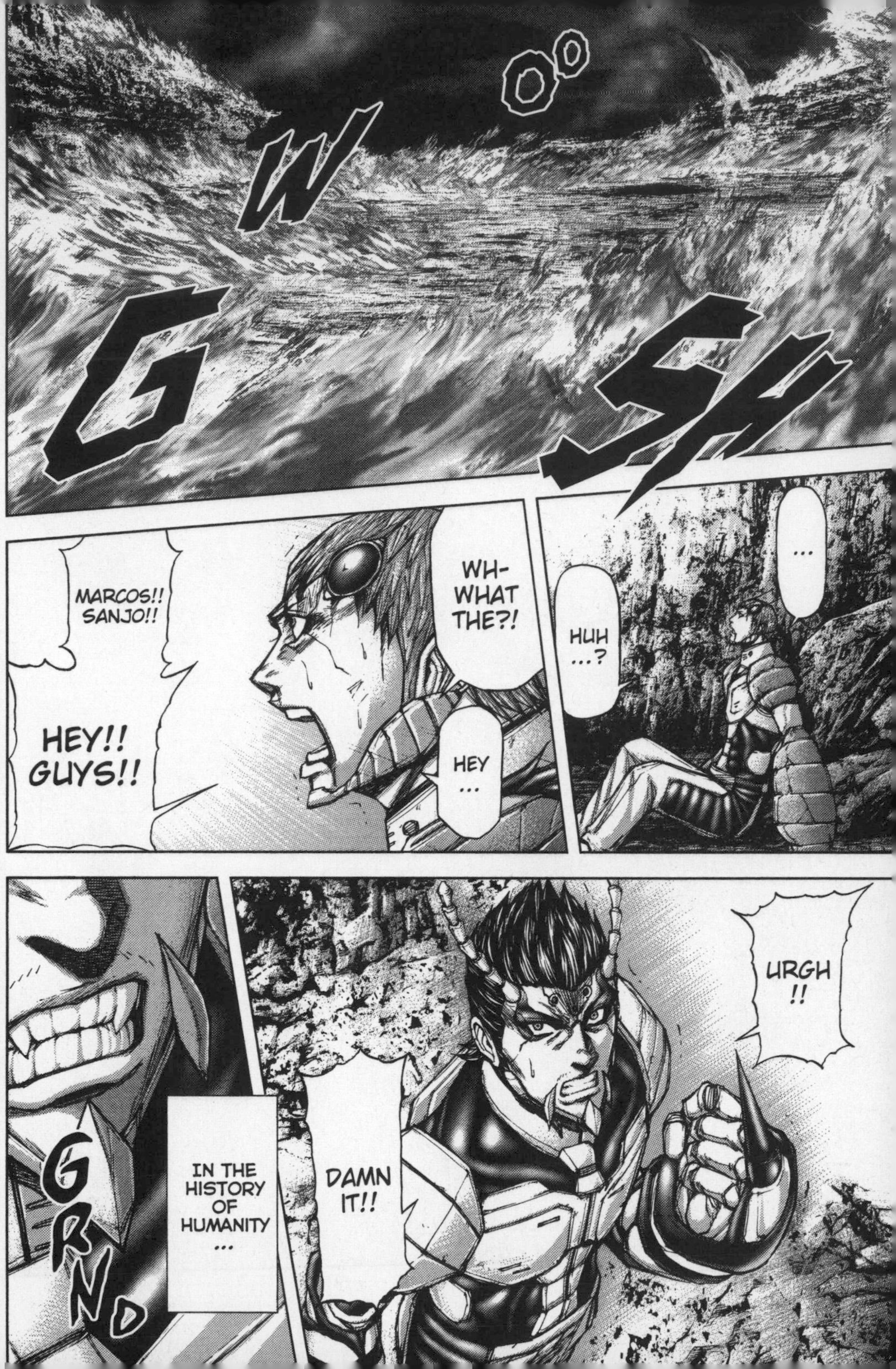
GWOOSH
...
HUH ...?
WH- WHAT THE?!
MARCOS!! SANJO!!
HEY ...
HEY!! GUYS!!
URGH !!
DAMN IT!!
IN THE HISTORY OF HUMANITY ...
GRND

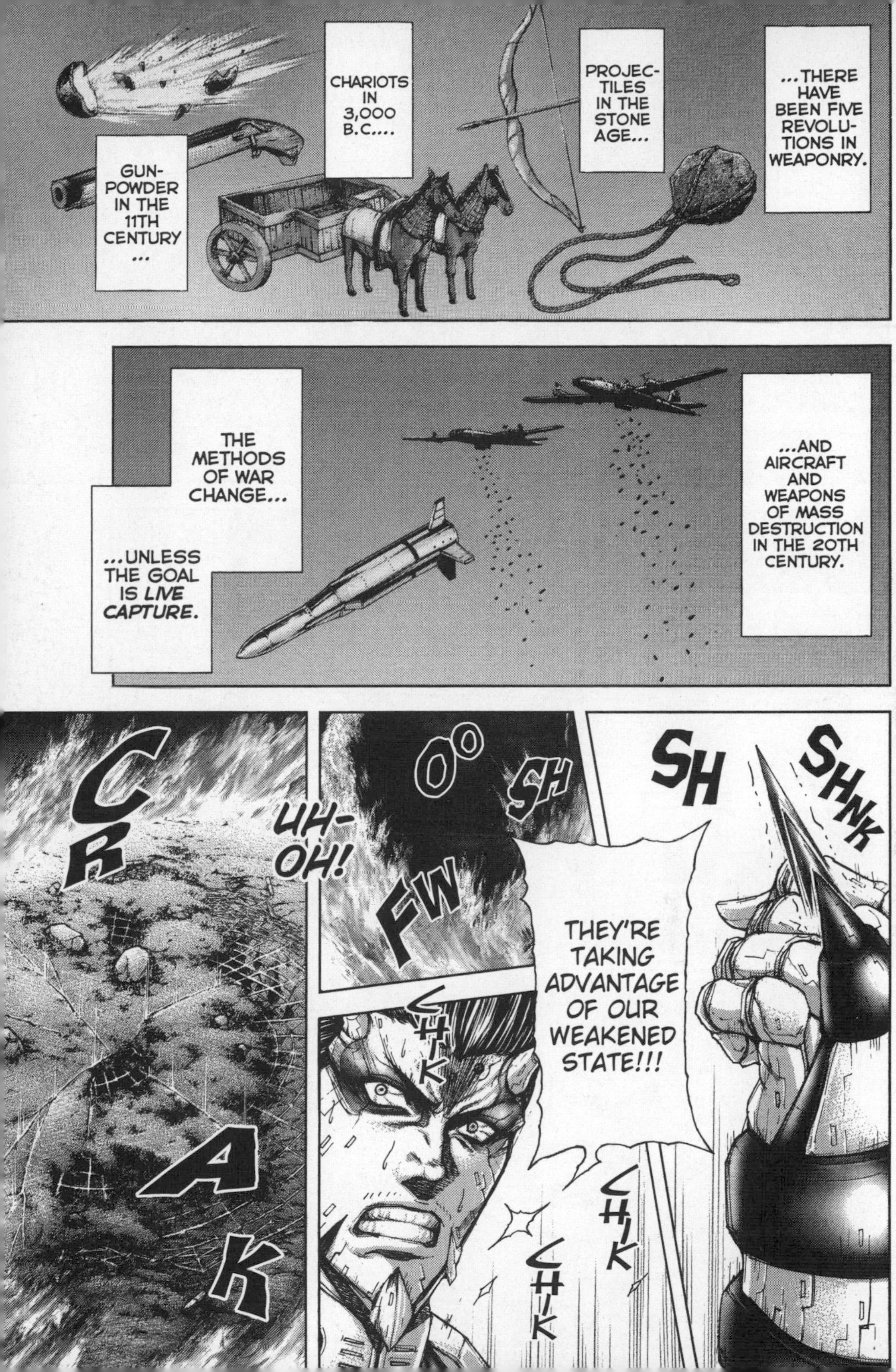
...THERE HAVE BEEN FIVE REVOLUTIONS IN WEAPONRY.
PROJECTILES IN THE STONE AGE...
CHARIOTS IN 3,000 B.C....
GUNPOWDER IN THE 11TH CENTURY...
...AND AIRCRAFT AND WEAPONS OF MASS DESTRUCTION IN THE 20TH CENTURY.
THE METHODS OF WAR CHANGE...
...UNLESS THE GOAL IS *LIVE CAPTURE*.
SHNK
SH
FWOOSH
UH-OH!
THEY'RE TAKING ADVANTAGE OF OUR WEAKENED STATE!!!
CHIK
CHIK
CHIK
CRAK

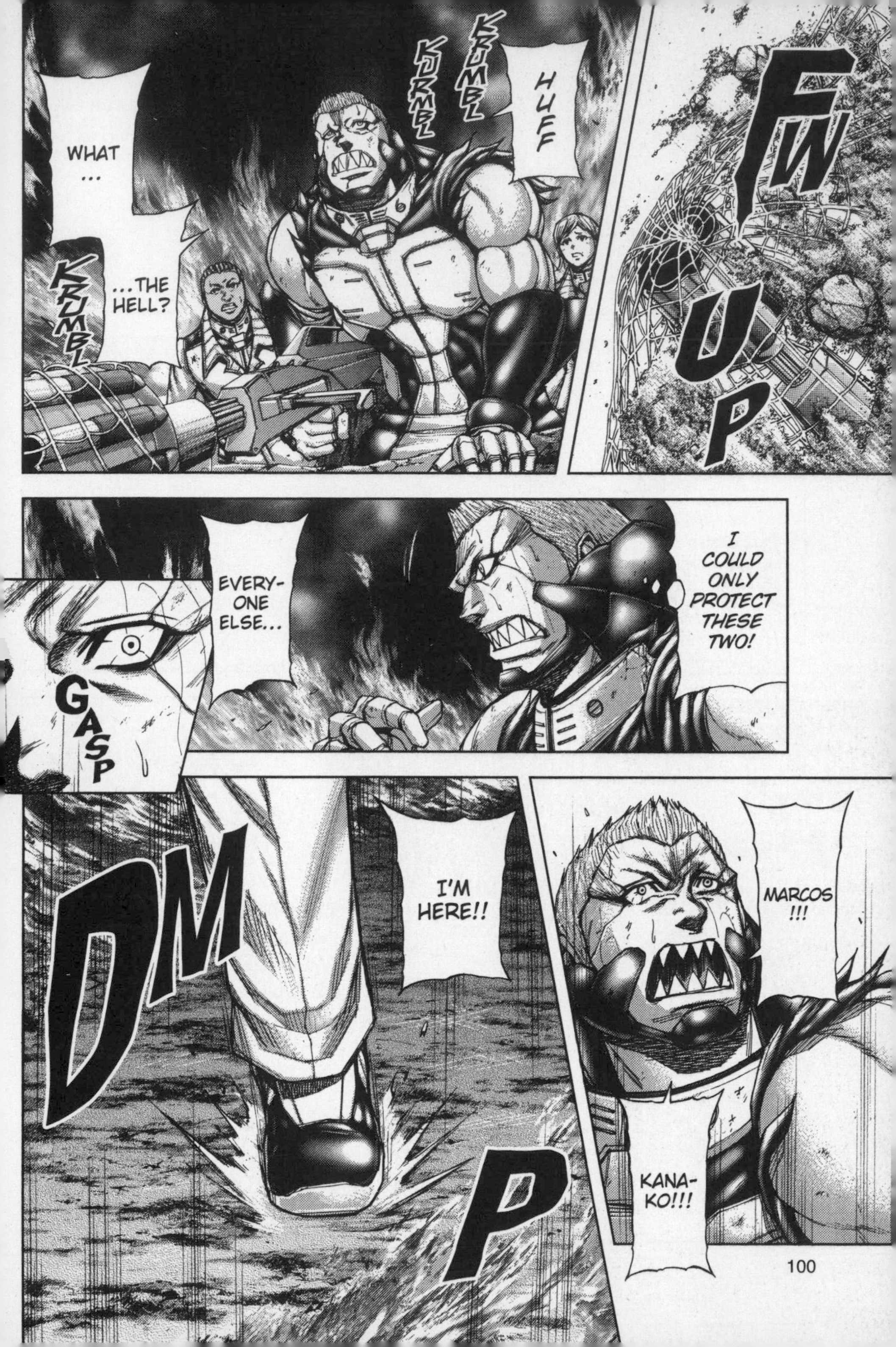
FWUP
HUFF
KRUMBL
KRUMBL
WHAT...
...THE HELL?
KRUMBL
I COULD ONLY PROTECT THESE TWO!
EVERY-ONE ELSE...
GASP
MARCOS!!!
KANA-KO!!!
I'M HERE!!
DMP

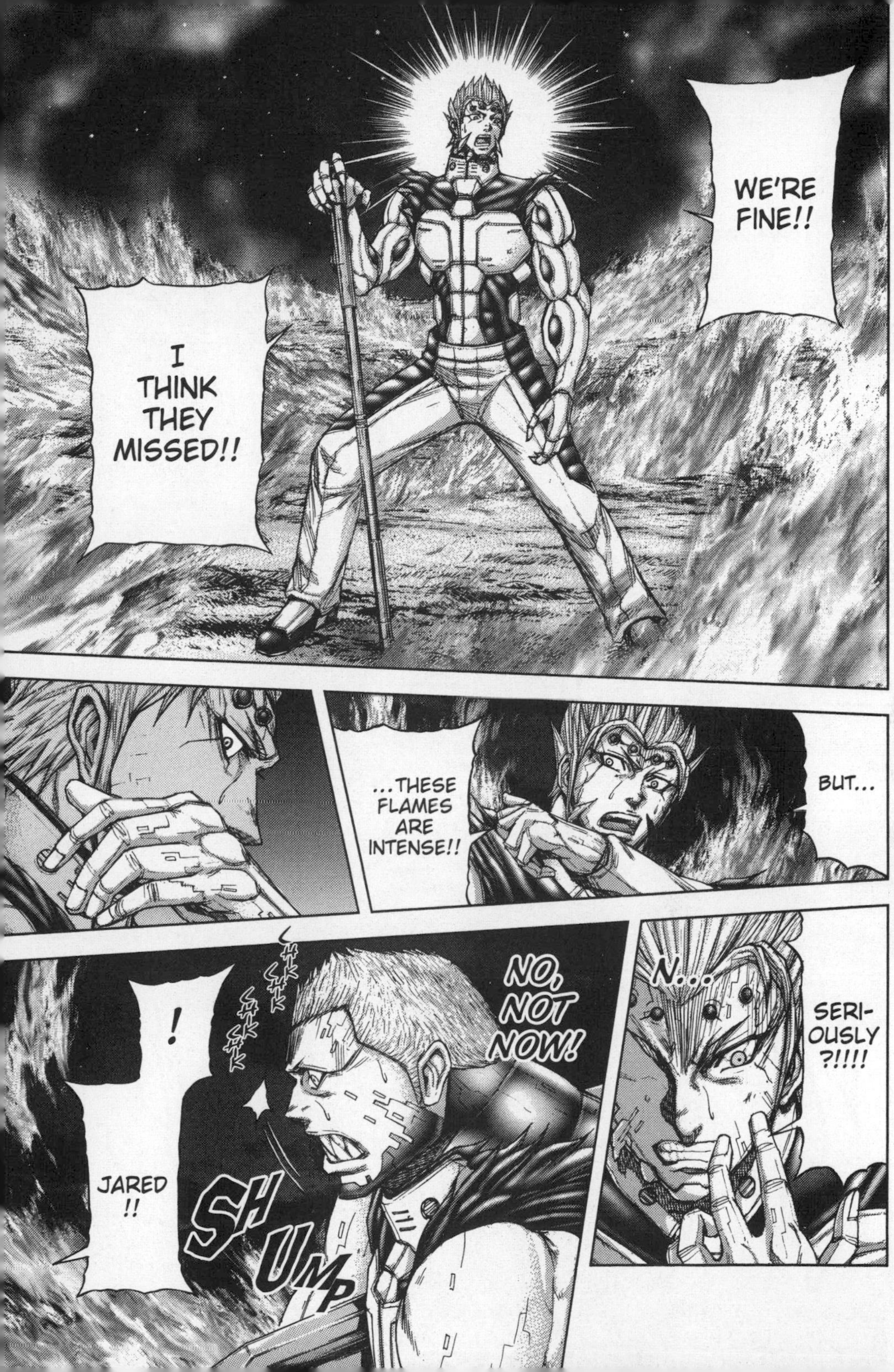
WE'RE FINE!!
I THINK THEY MISSED!!
BUT...
...THESE FLAMES ARE INTENSE!!
N...
SERI-OUSLY ?!!!!
NO, NOT NOW!
!
JARED !!
SHUMP

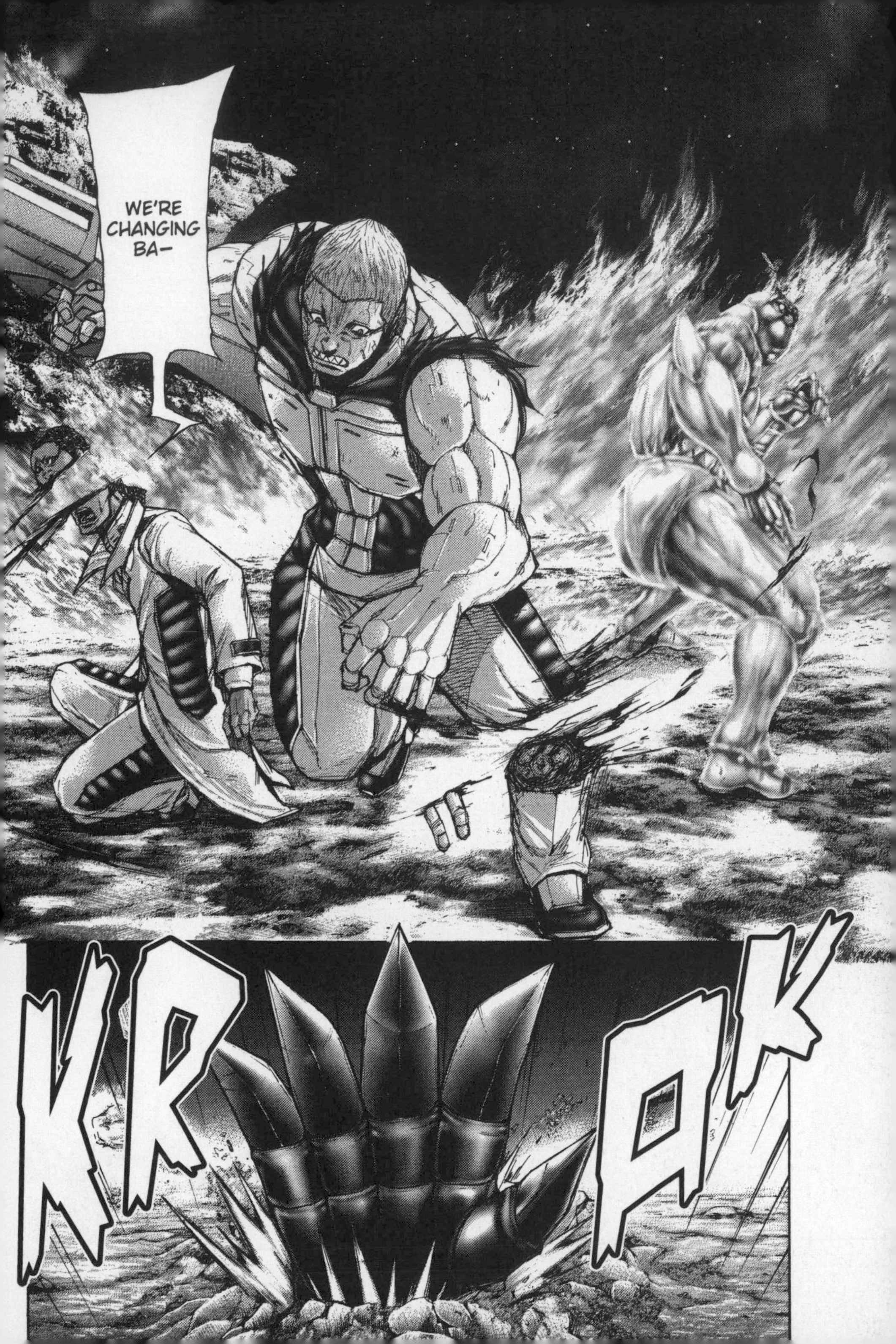
WE'RE CHANGING BA-
KRAK

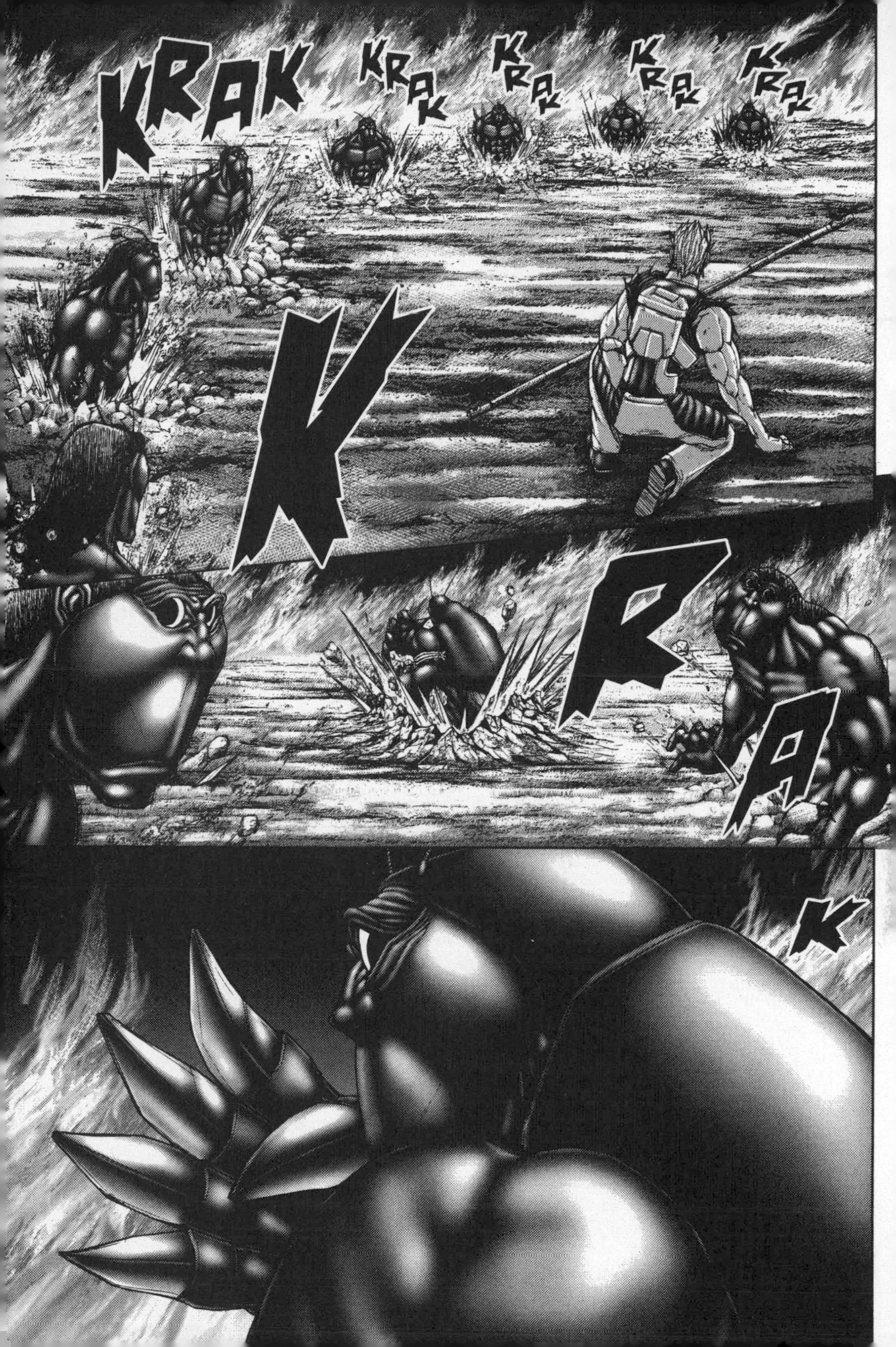
KRAK
KRAK
KRAK
KRAK
KRAK
KRAK
K

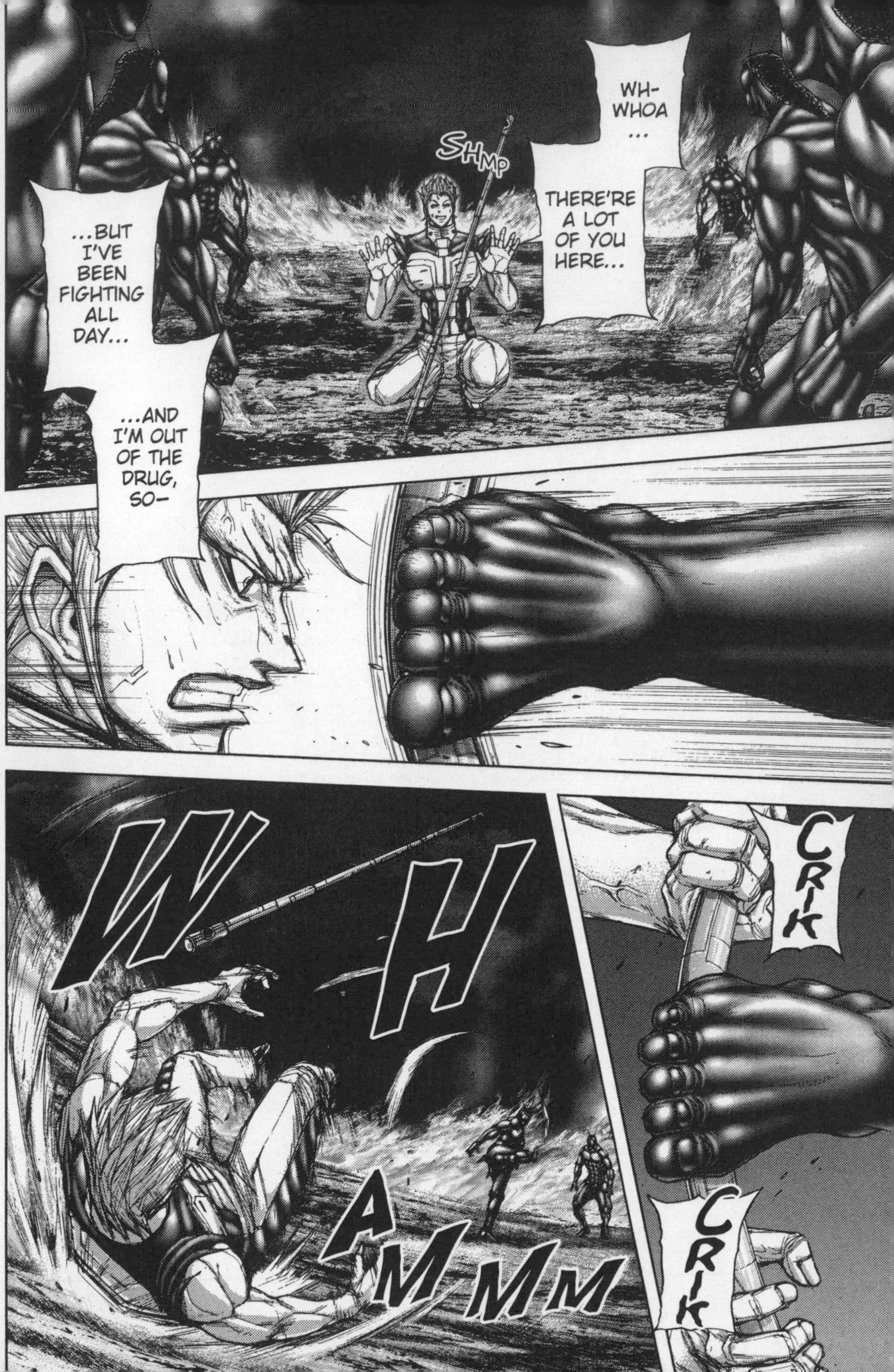
WH- WHOA ...
THERE'RE A LOT OF YOU HERE...
SHMP
...BUT I'VE BEEN FIGHTING ALL DAY...
...AND I'M OUT OF THE DRUG, SO–
CRIK
CRIK
WHAMMM

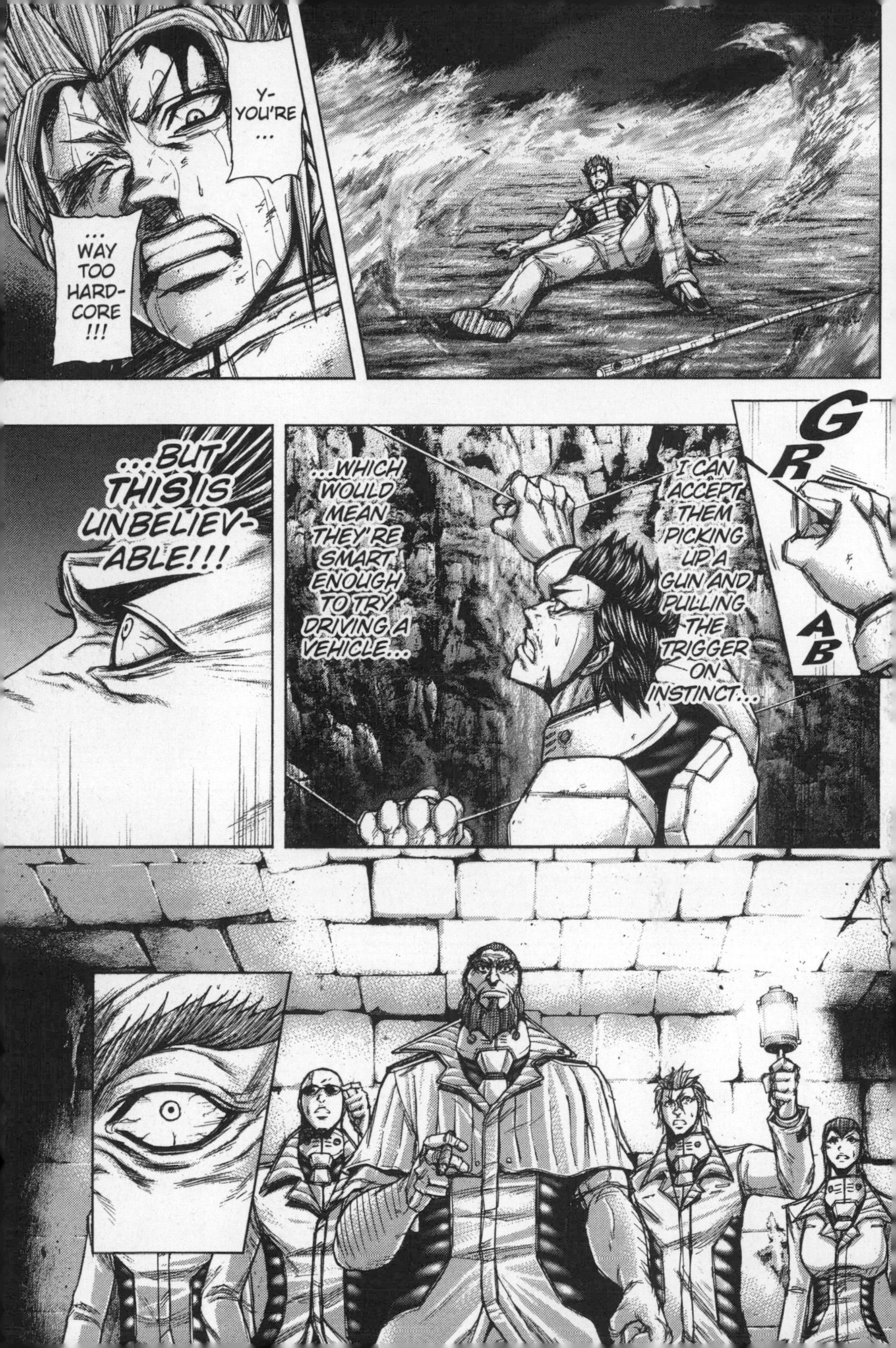
Y-YOU'RE ...
... WAY TOO HARD-CORE!!!
GRAB
I CAN ACCEPT THEM PICKING UP A GUN AND PULLING THE TRIGGER ON INSTINCT...
...WHICH WOULD MEAN THEY'RE SMART ENOUGH TO TRY DRIVING A VEHICLE...
...BUT THIS IS UNBELIEVABLE!!!

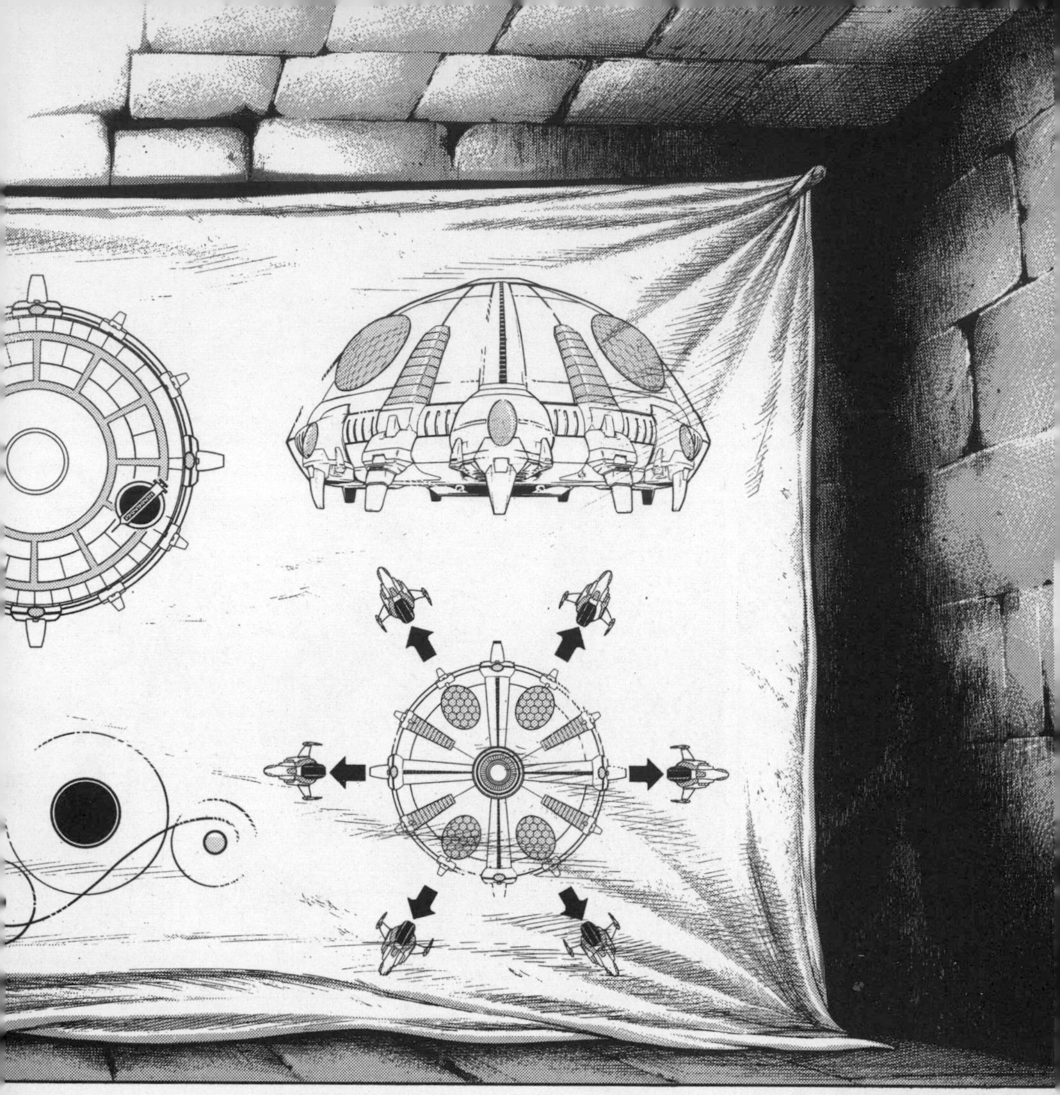

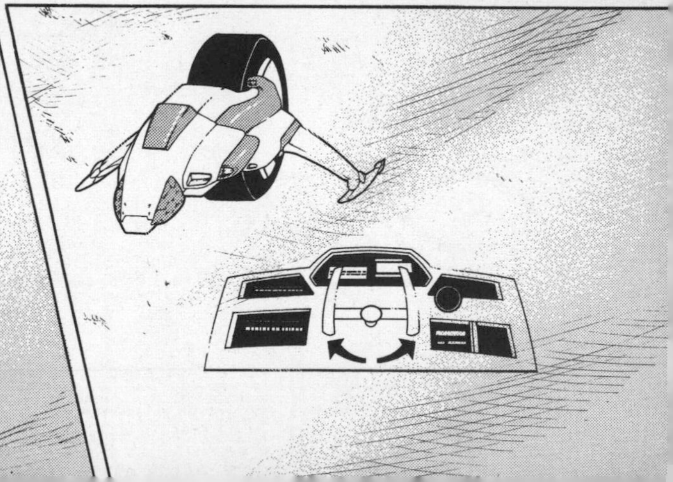

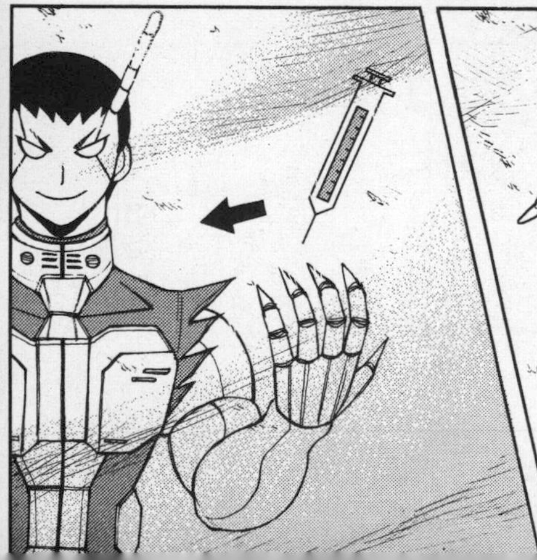

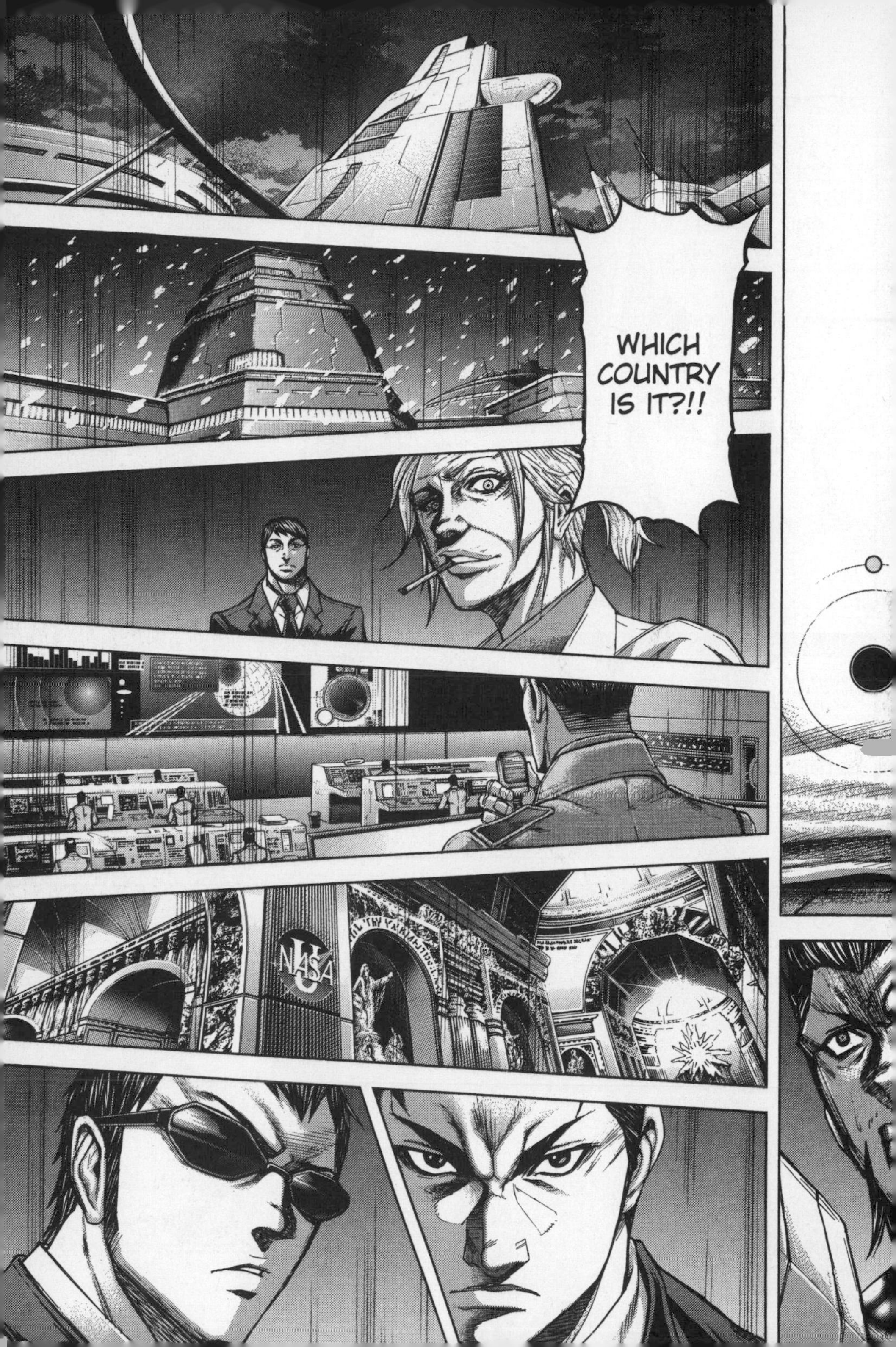
WHICH COUNTRY IS IT?!!

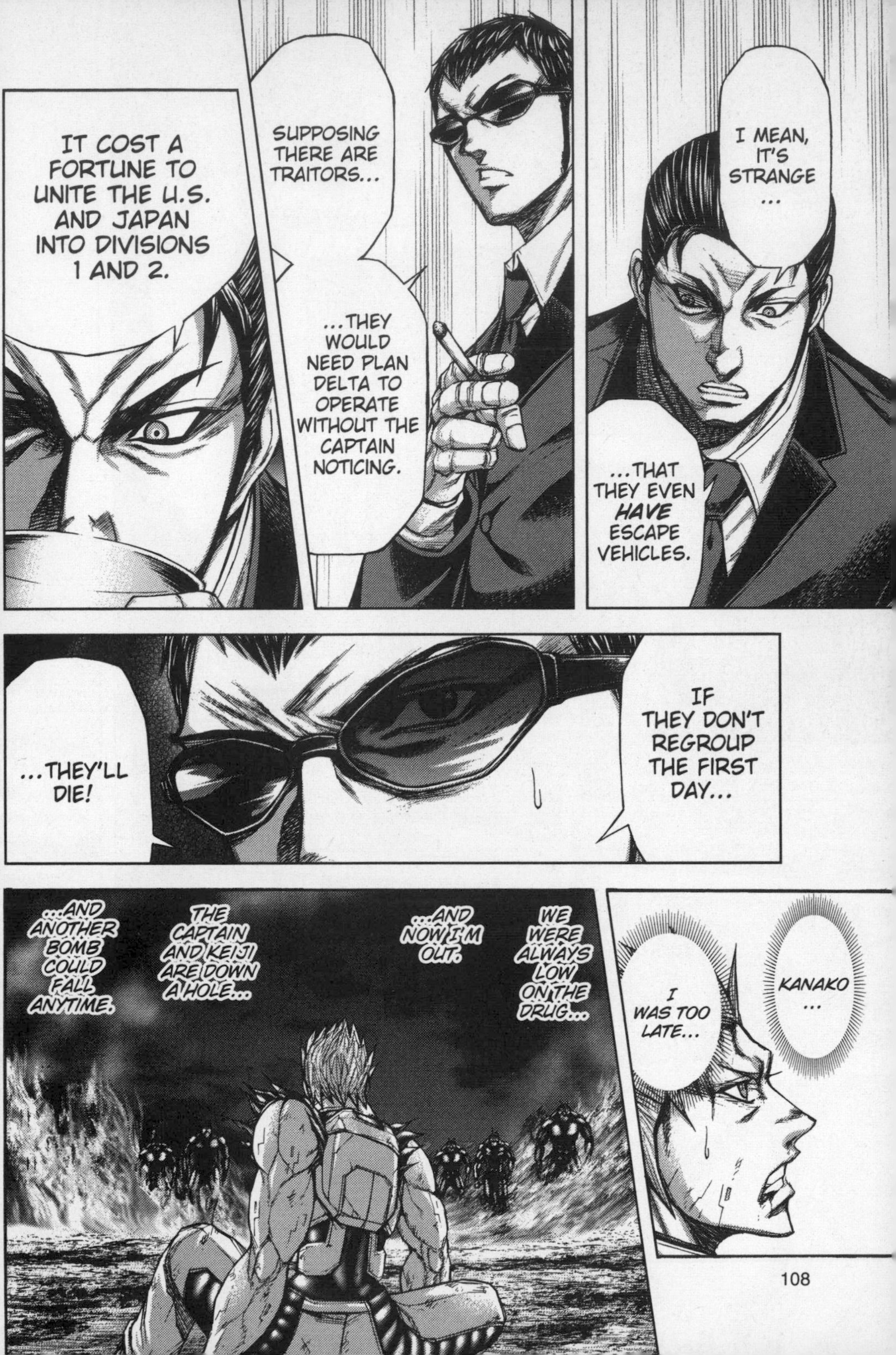
I MEAN, IT'S STRANGE ...
...THAT THEY EVEN **HAVE** ESCAPE VEHICLES.
SUPPOSING THERE ARE TRAITORS...
...THEY WOULD NEED PLAN DELTA TO OPERATE WITHOUT THE CAPTAIN NOTICING.
IT COST A FORTUNE TO UNITE THE U.S. AND JAPAN INTO DIVISIONS 1 AND 2.
IF THEY DON'T REGROUP THE FIRST DAY...
...THEY'LL DIE!
KANAKO ...
I WAS TOO LATE...
WE WERE ALWAYS LOW ON THE DRUG...
...AND NOW I'M OUT.
THE CAPTAIN AND KEIJI ARE DOWN A HOLE...
...AND ANOTHER BOMB COULD FALL ANYTIME.

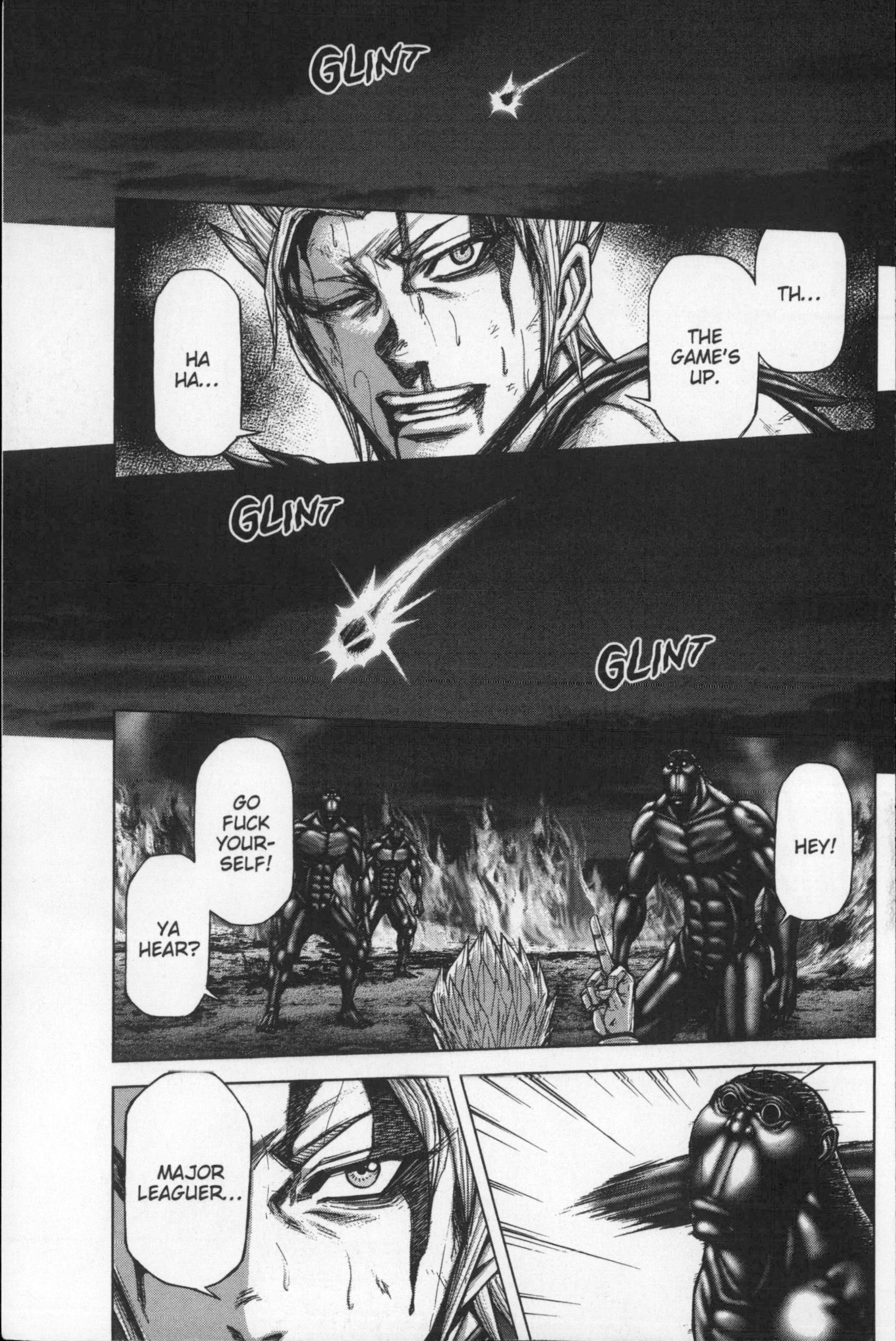
GLINT
TH...
THE GAME'S UP.
HA HA...
GLINT
GLINT
HEY!
GO FUCK YOUR-SELF!
YA HEAR?
MAJOR LEAGUER...

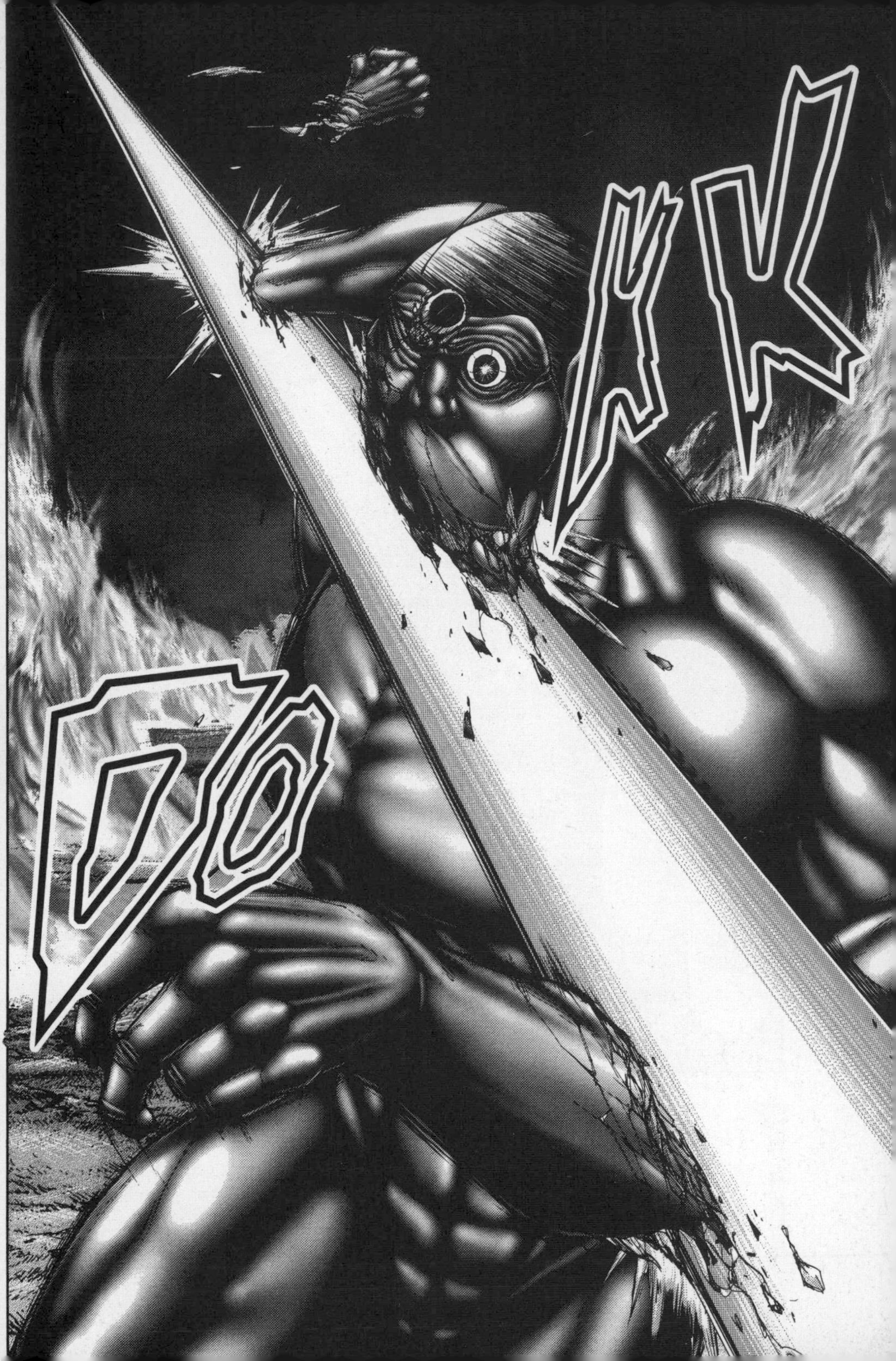
DO
AK

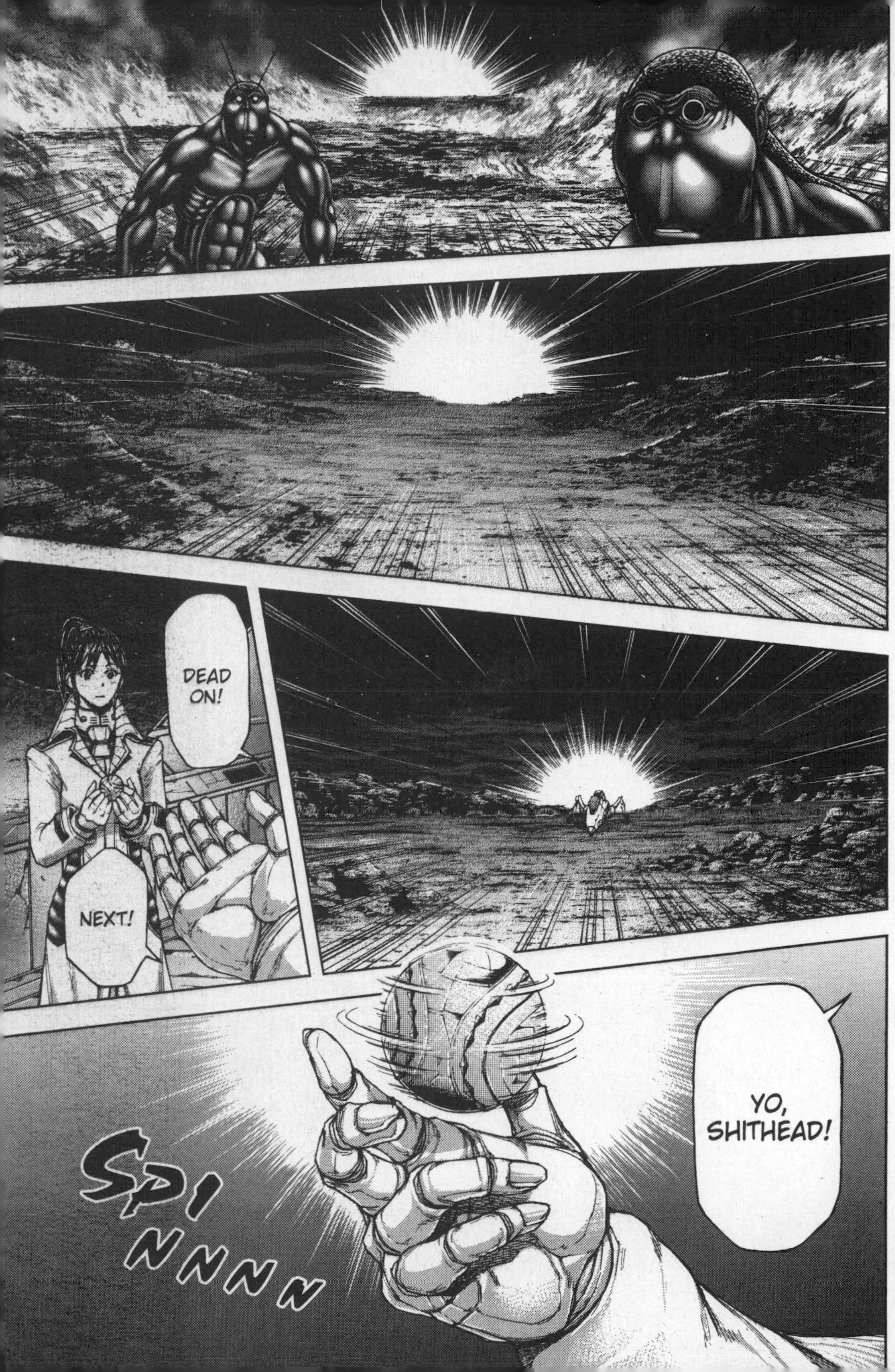
DEAD ON!
NEXT!
YO, SHITHEAD!
SPINNNNN

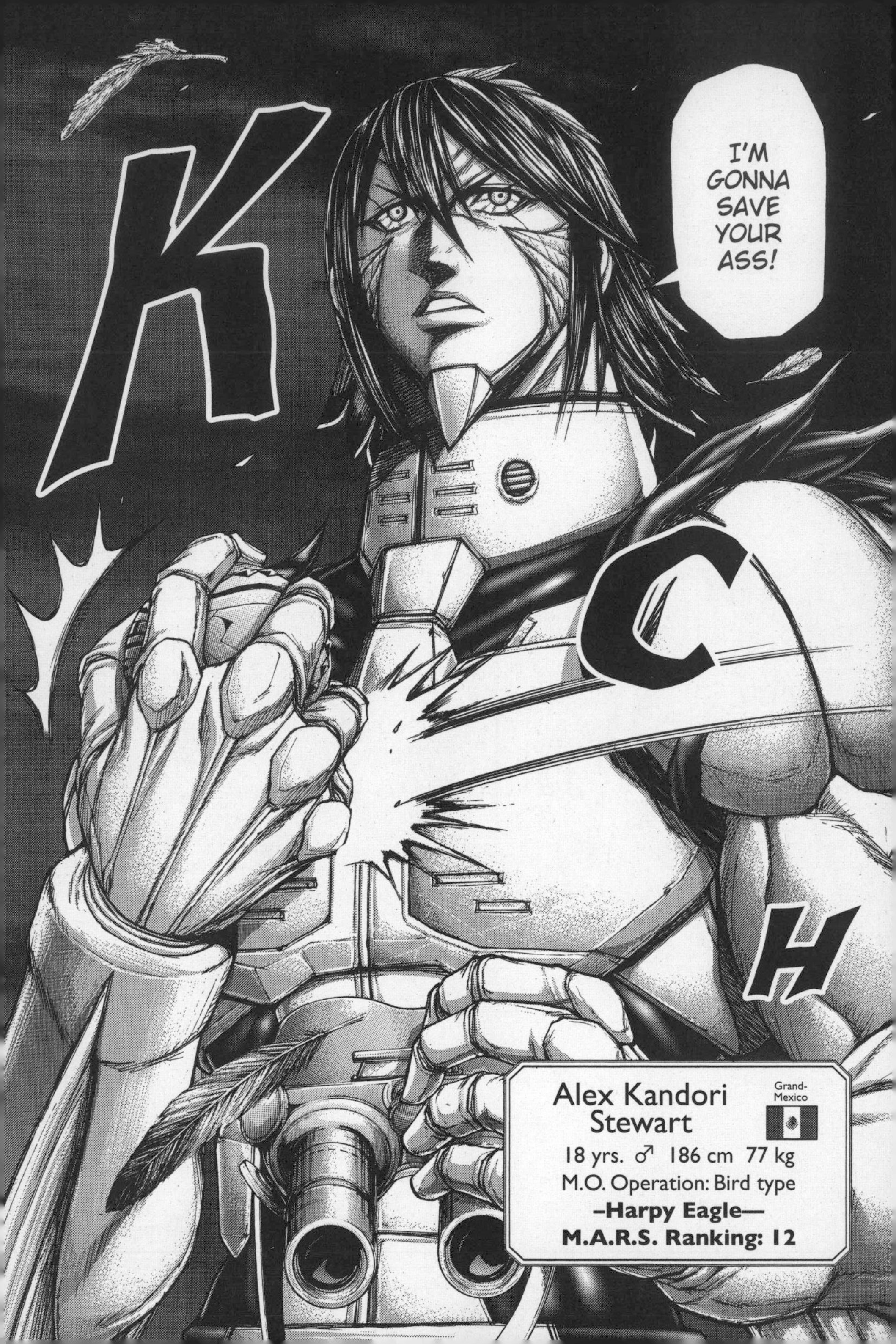
I'M GONNA SAVE YOUR ASS!
K
C
H
Alex Kandori Stewart
Grand-Mexico
18 yrs. ♂ 186 cm 77 kg
M.O. Operation: Bird type
–Harpy Eagle—
M.A.R.S. Ranking: 12

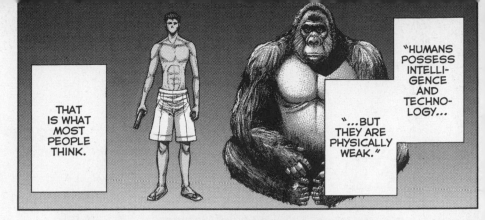

"HUMANS POSSESS INTELLIGENCE AND TECHNOLOGY...
"...BUT THEY ARE PHYSICALLY WEAK."
THAT IS WHAT MOST PEOPLE THINK.
EVOLUTION WEAKENED THEIR FIVE SENSES AND PHYSICAL BUILD.
THEIR CLAWS RETRACTED TO USE TOOLS...
...AND SHARP TEETH BECAME UNNECESSARY...
...SO THEY REGRESSED.
CHAPTER 48: PITCHERS
BUT...
...IN ADDITION TO THEIR WELL-DEVELOPED CEREBRAL CORTEX...
...HUMANS HAVE EVOLVED A PHYSICAL ABILITY FOR USE IN BATTLE.

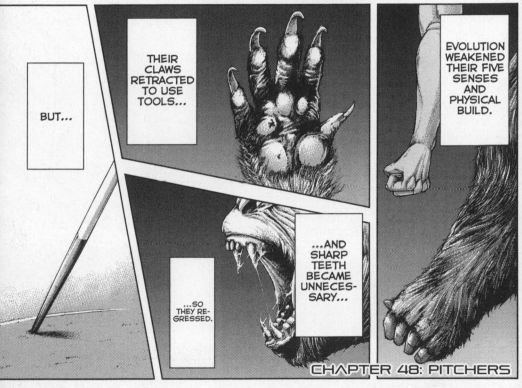

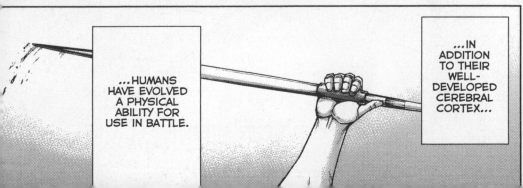

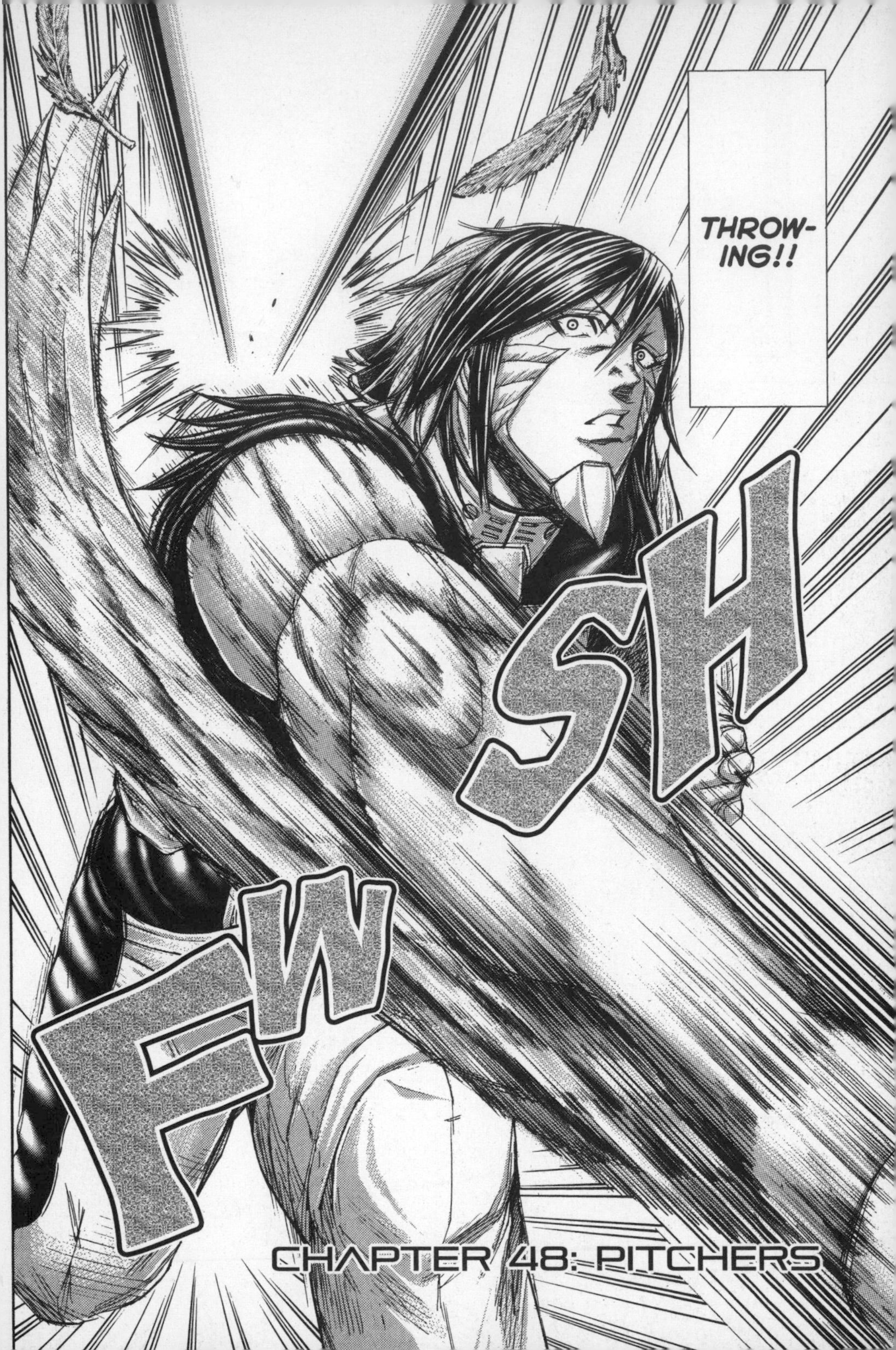
THROW-
ING!!
FWSH
CHAPTER 48: PITCHERS

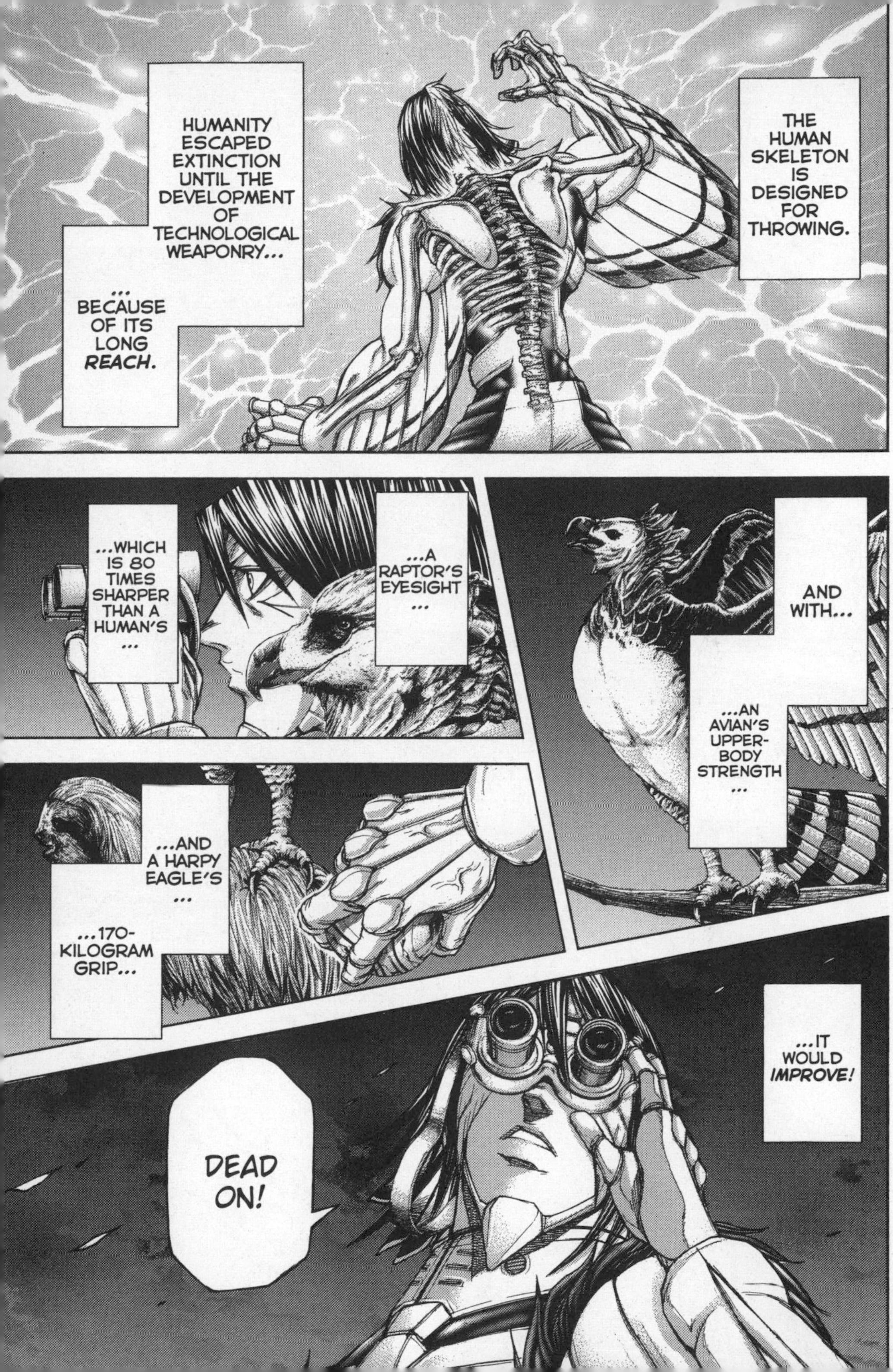
THE HUMAN SKELETON IS DESIGNED FOR THROWING.
HUMANITY ESCAPED EXTINCTION UNTIL THE DEVELOPMENT OF TECHNOLOGICAL WEAPONRY...
...BECAUSE OF ITS LONG *REACH*.
AND WITH...
...AN AVIAN'S UPPER-BODY STRENGTH...
...A RAPTOR'S EYESIGHT...
...WHICH IS 80 TIMES SHARPER THAN A HUMAN'S...
...AND A HARPY EAGLE'S...
...170-KILOGRAM GRIP...
...IT WOULD *IMPROVE!*
DEAD ON!

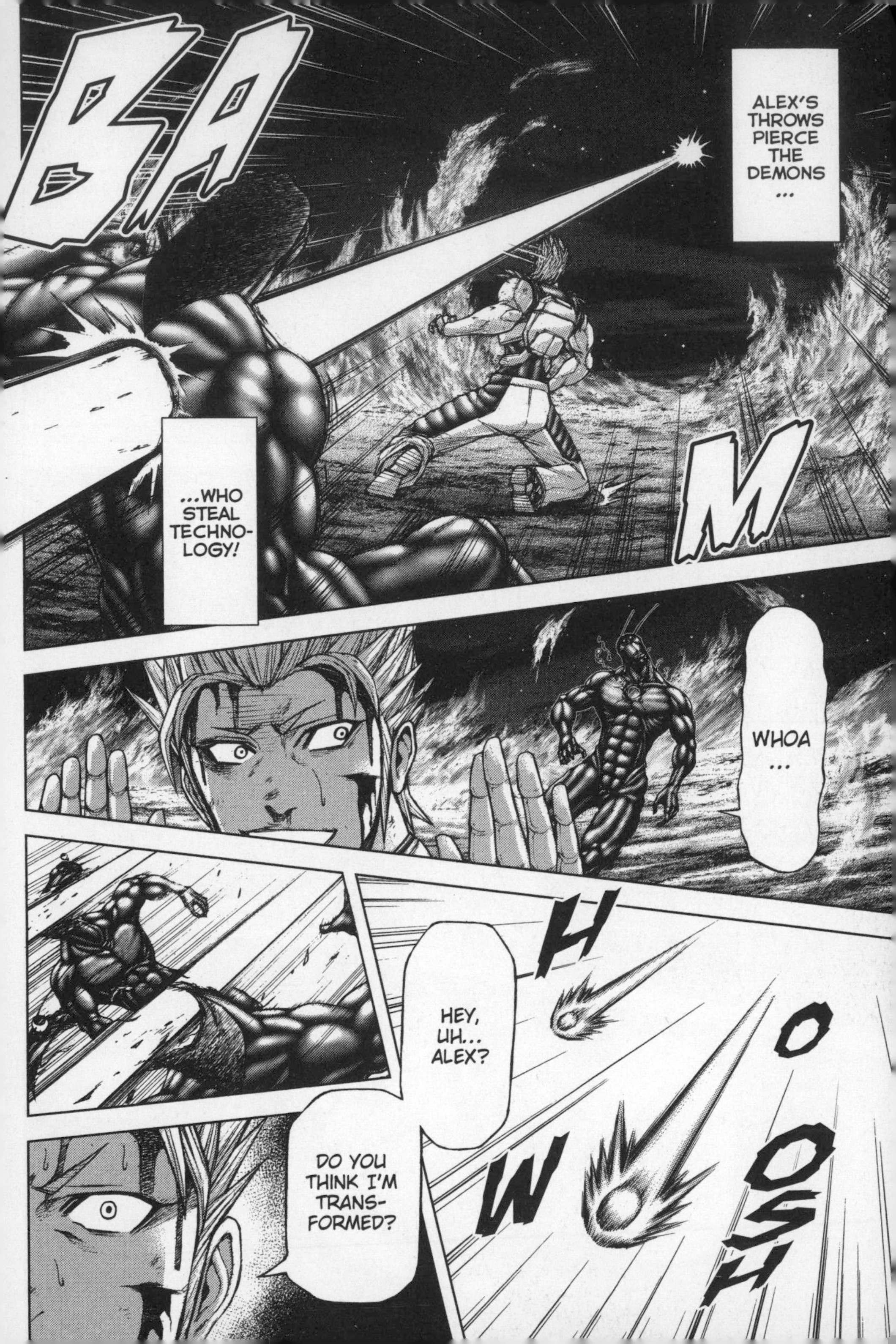
ALEX'S THROWS PIERCE THE DEMONS...
BA
M
...WHO STEAL TECHNO-LOGY!
WHOA...
H
HEY, UH... ALEX?
OOSH
W
DO YOU THINK I'M TRANS-FORMED?

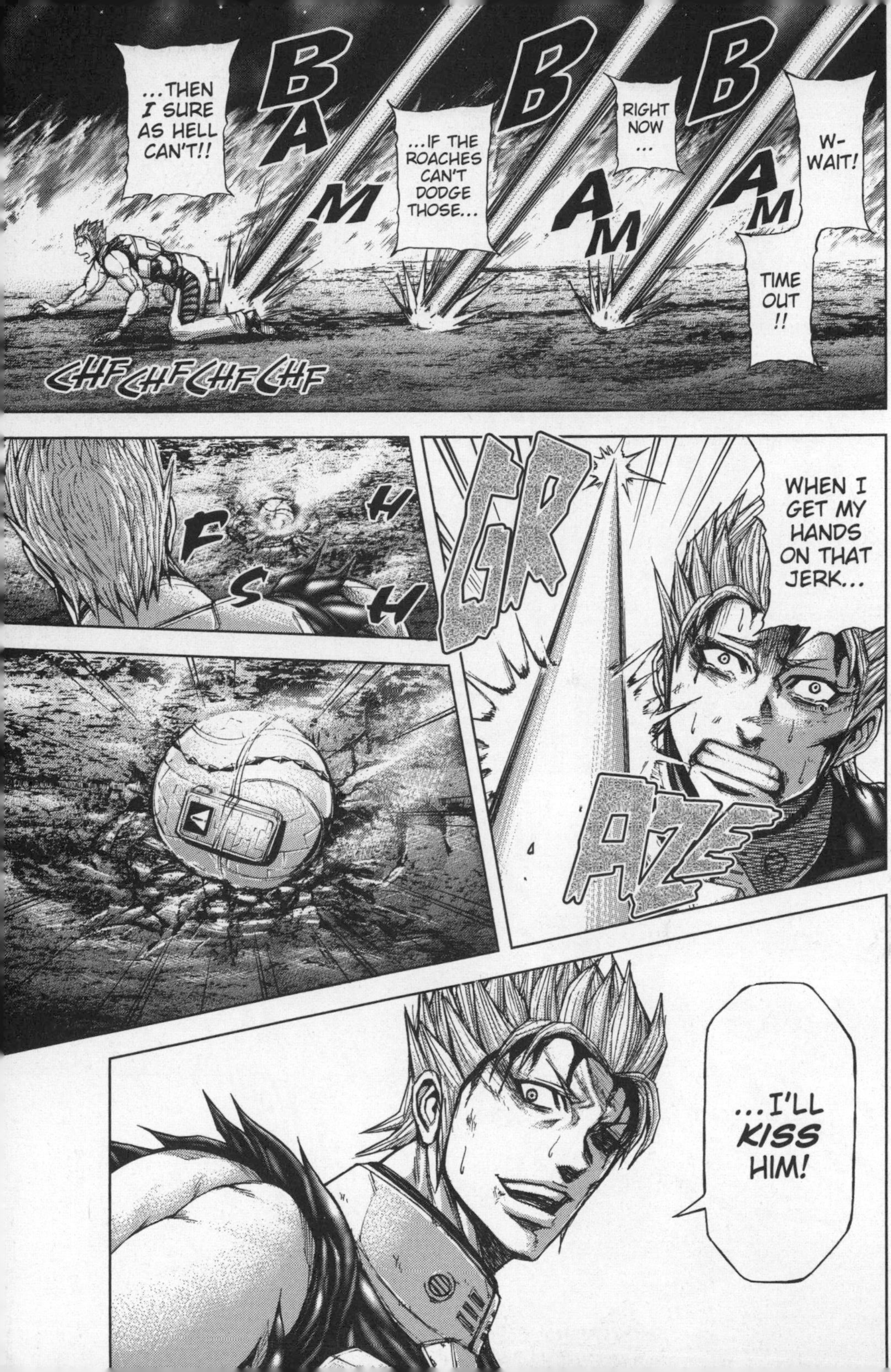
W-
WAIT!
TIME OUT!!
BAM
RIGHT NOW...
BAM
...IF THE ROACHES CAN'T DODGE THOSE...
BAM
...THEN I SURE AS HELL CAN'T!!
CHF CHF CHF CHF
WHEN I GET MY HANDS ON THAT JERK...
GRAZE
FSHHH
...I'LL KISS HIM!

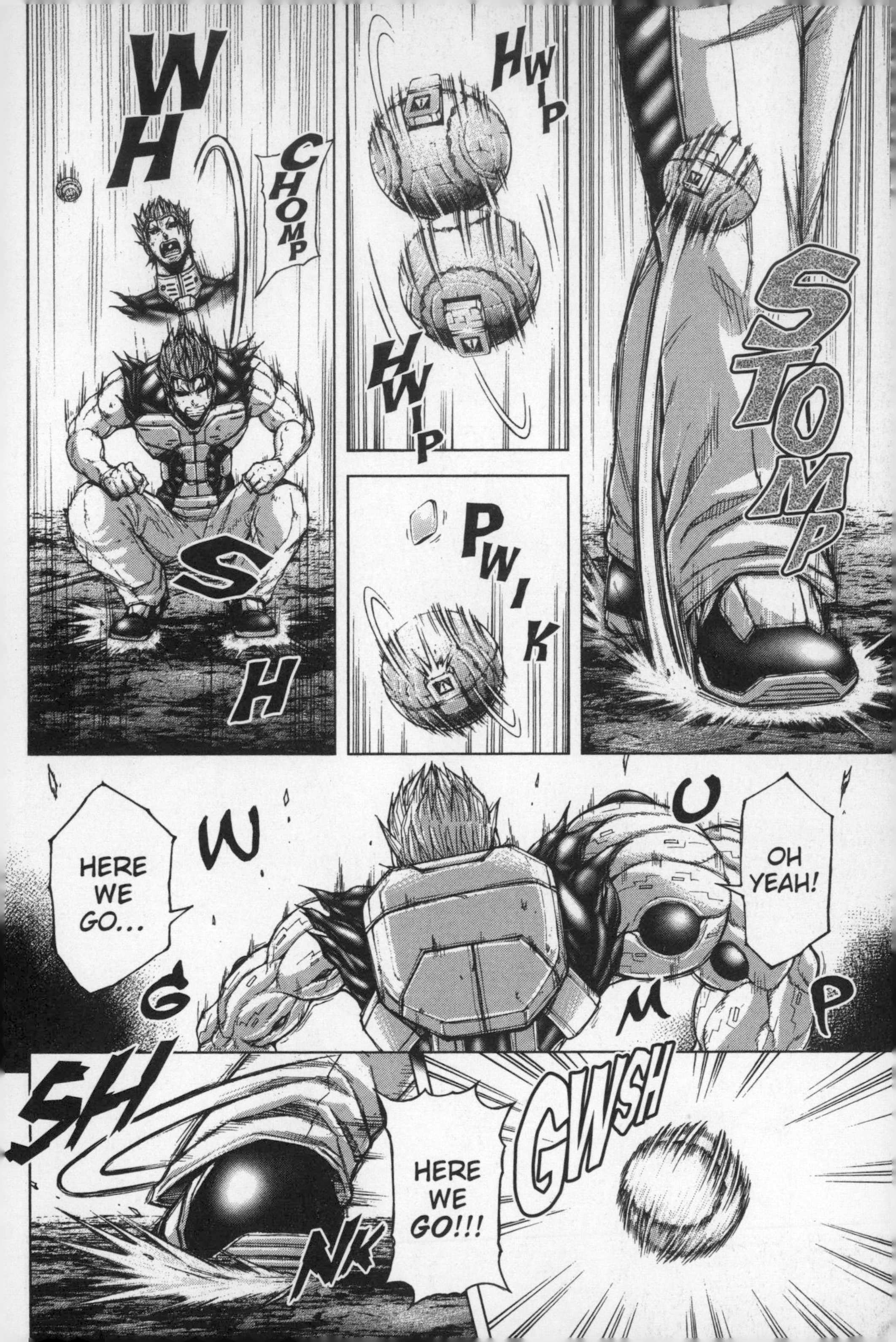
STOMP
HWIP
HWIP
PWIK
CHOMP
WH
SH
OH YEAH!
U
M
P
W
HERE WE GO...
G
GWSH
HERE WE GO!!!
SH
NK

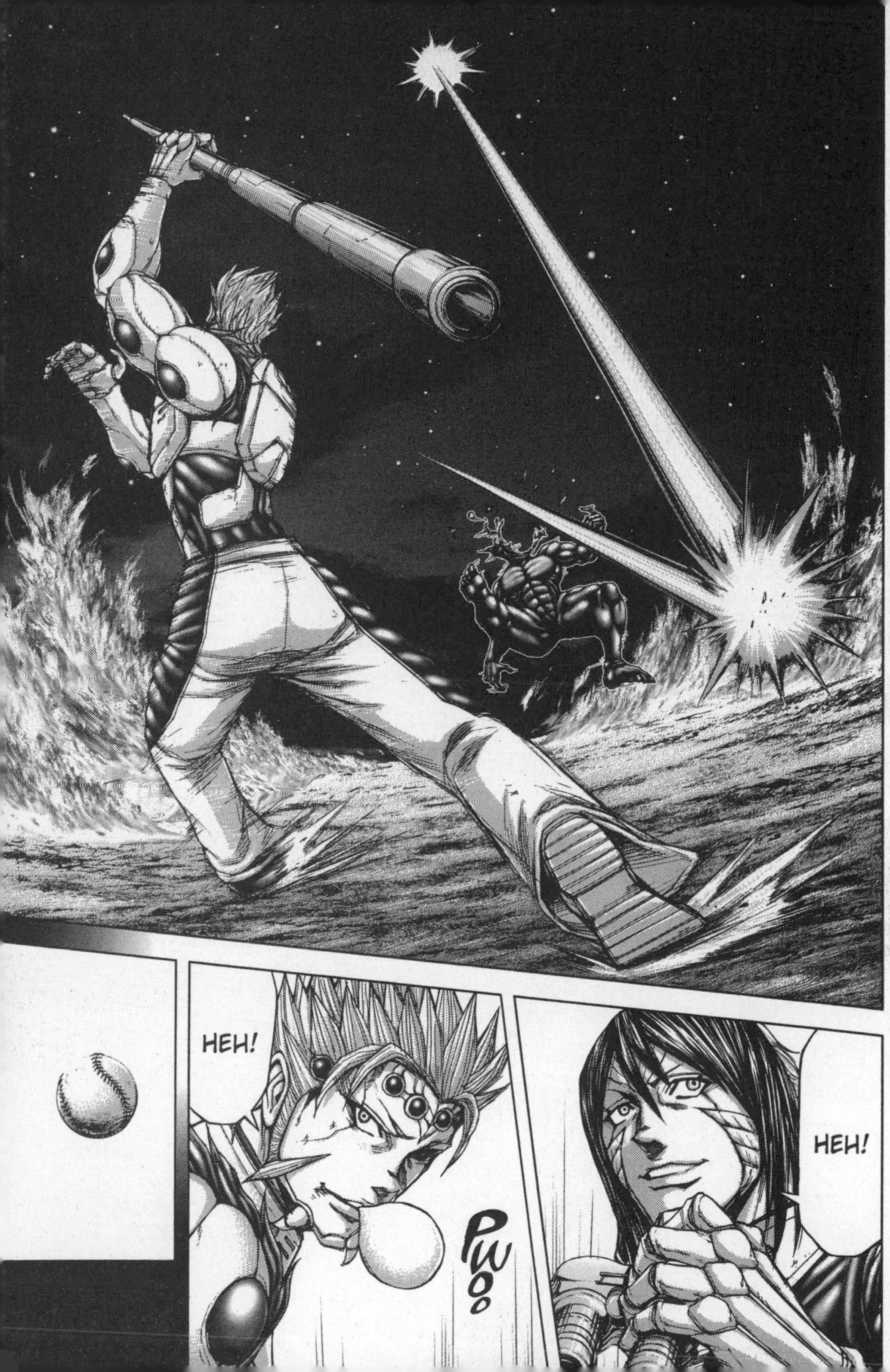

HEH!
HEH!
PWOO

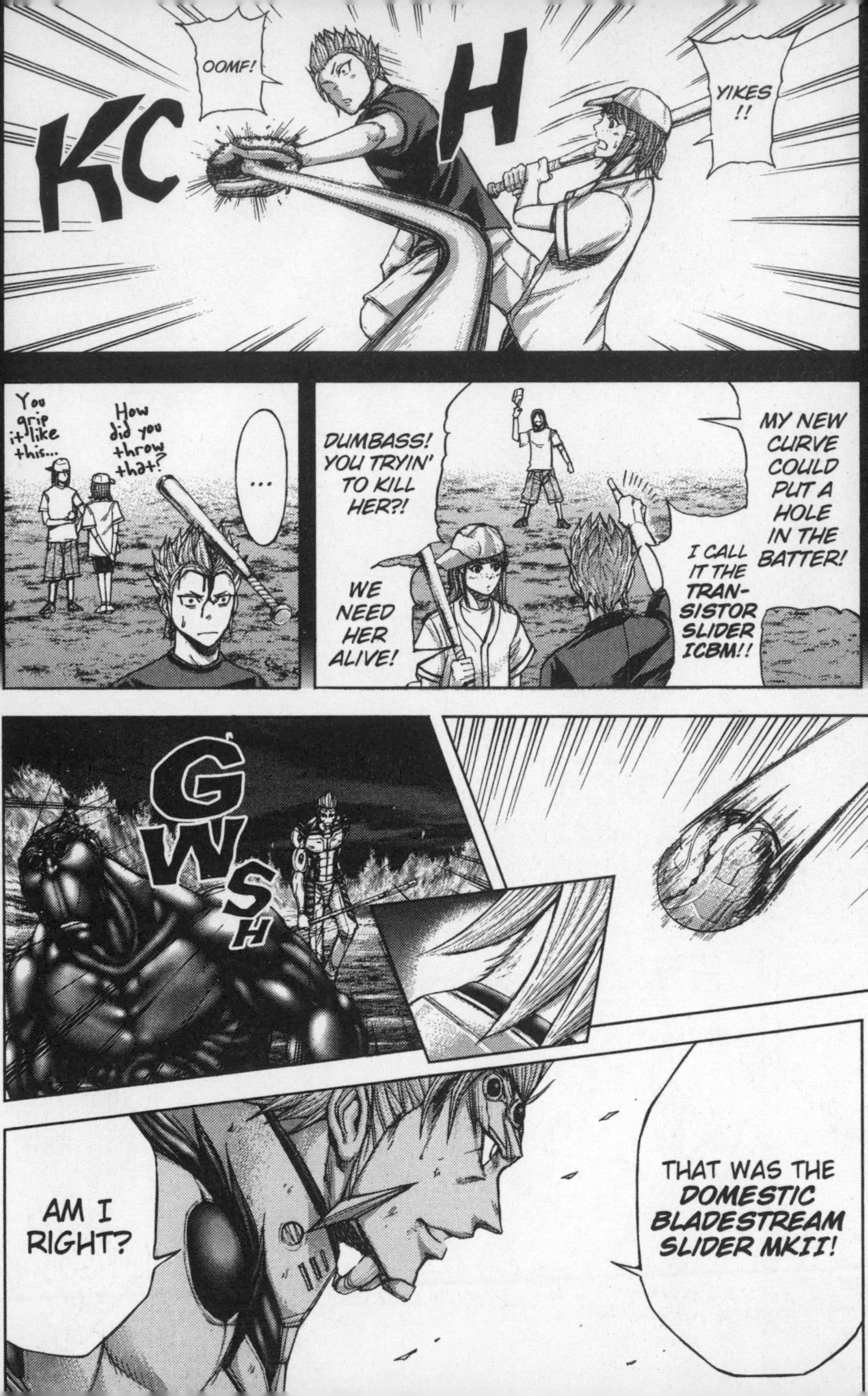
YIKES !!
OOMF!
KCH
MY NEW CURVE COULD PUT A HOLE IN THE BATTER!
I CALL IT THE TRAN-SISTOR SLIDER ICBM!!
DUMBASS! YOU TRYIN' TO KILL HER?!
WE NEED HER ALIVE!
...
How did you throw that?
You grip it like this...
GWSH
THAT WAS THE DOMESTIC BLADESTREAM SLIDER MKII!
AM I RIGHT?

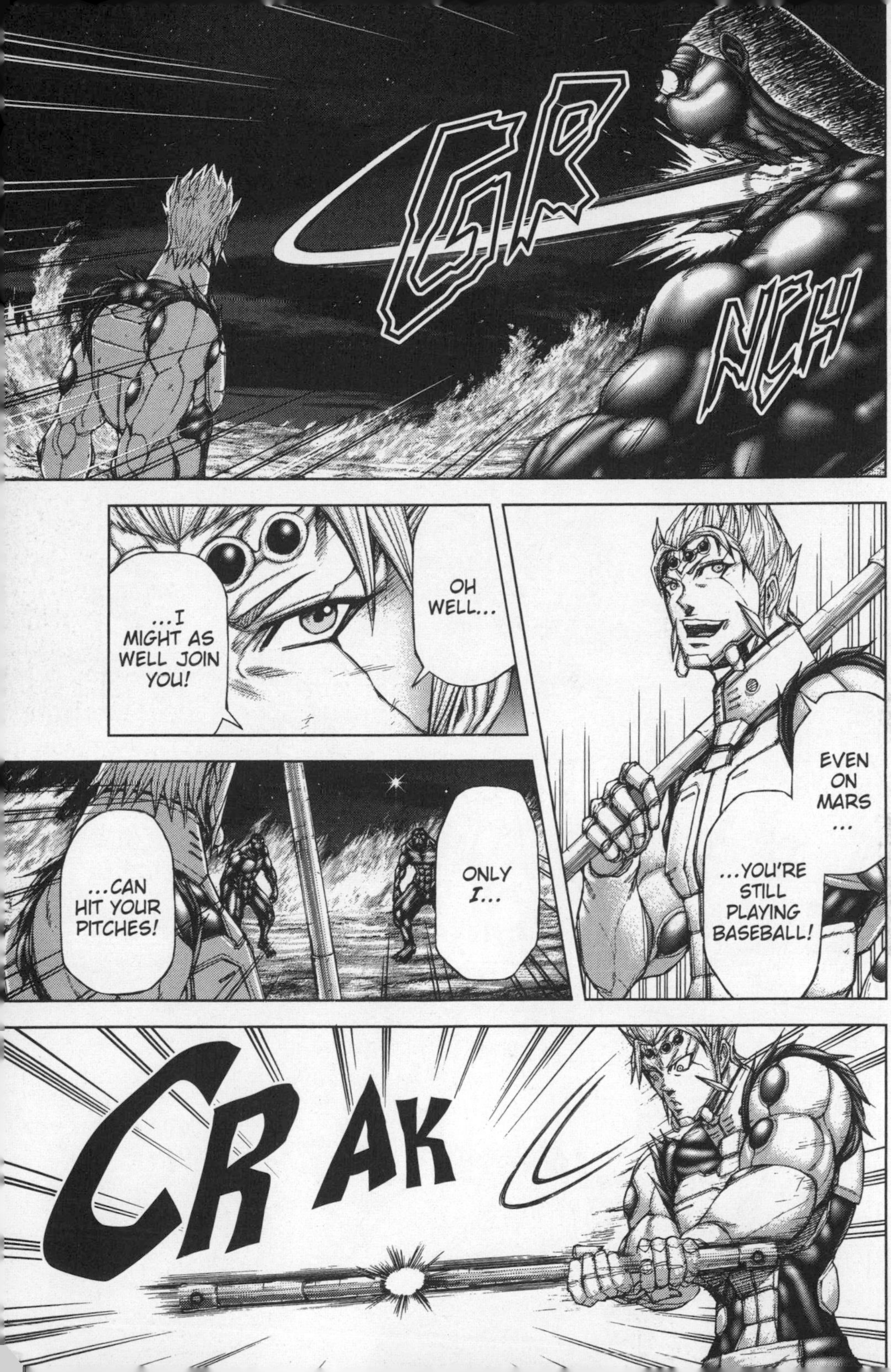
GRNCH
EVEN ON MARS...
...YOU'RE STILL PLAYING BASEBALL!
OH WELL...
...I MIGHT AS WELL JOIN YOU!
ONLY I...
...CAN HIT YOUR PITCHES!
CRAK

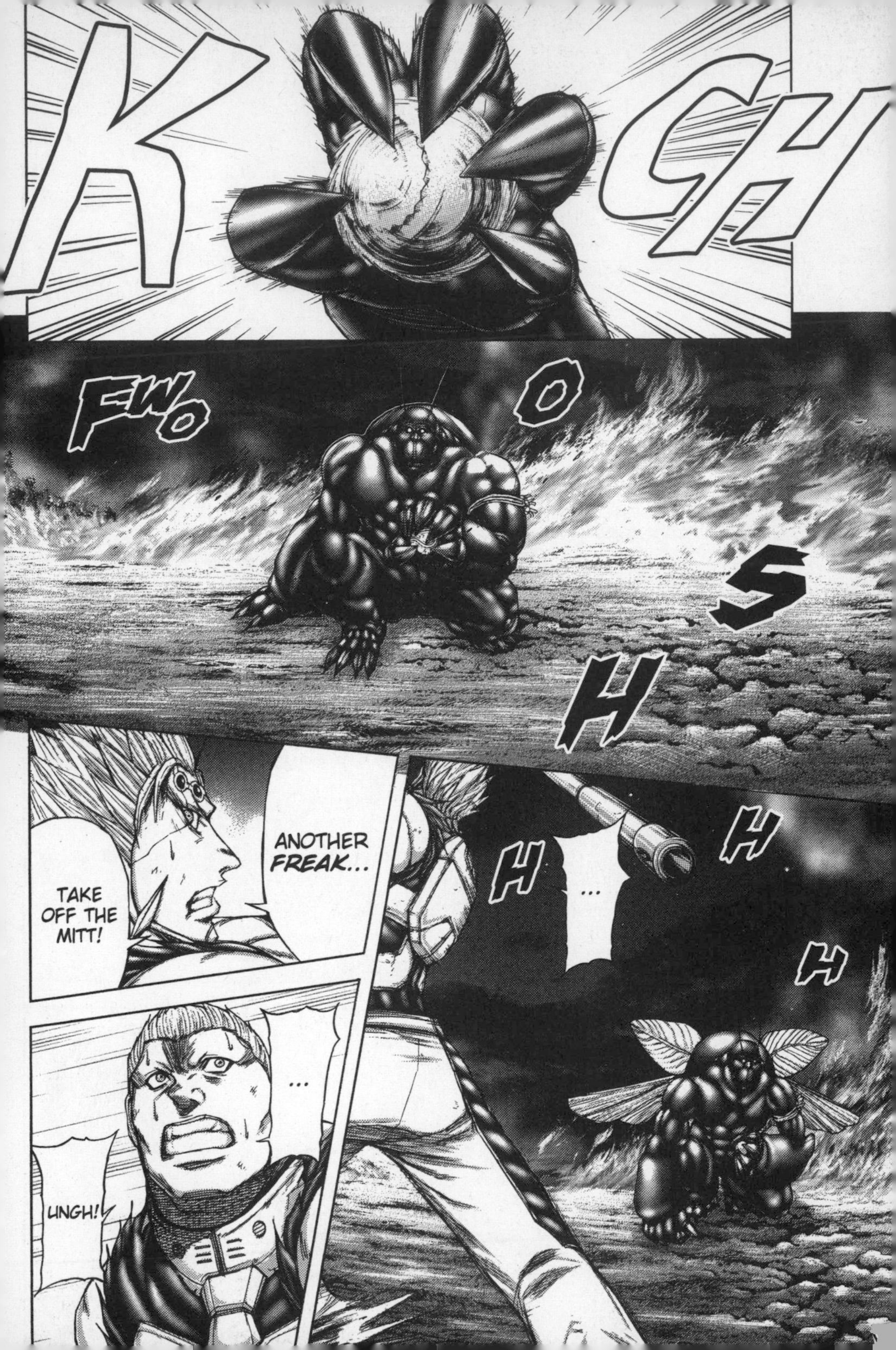
K
CH
FWO
O
S
H
H
H
H
H
...
ANOTHER FREAK...
TAKE OFF THE MITT!
...
UNGH!

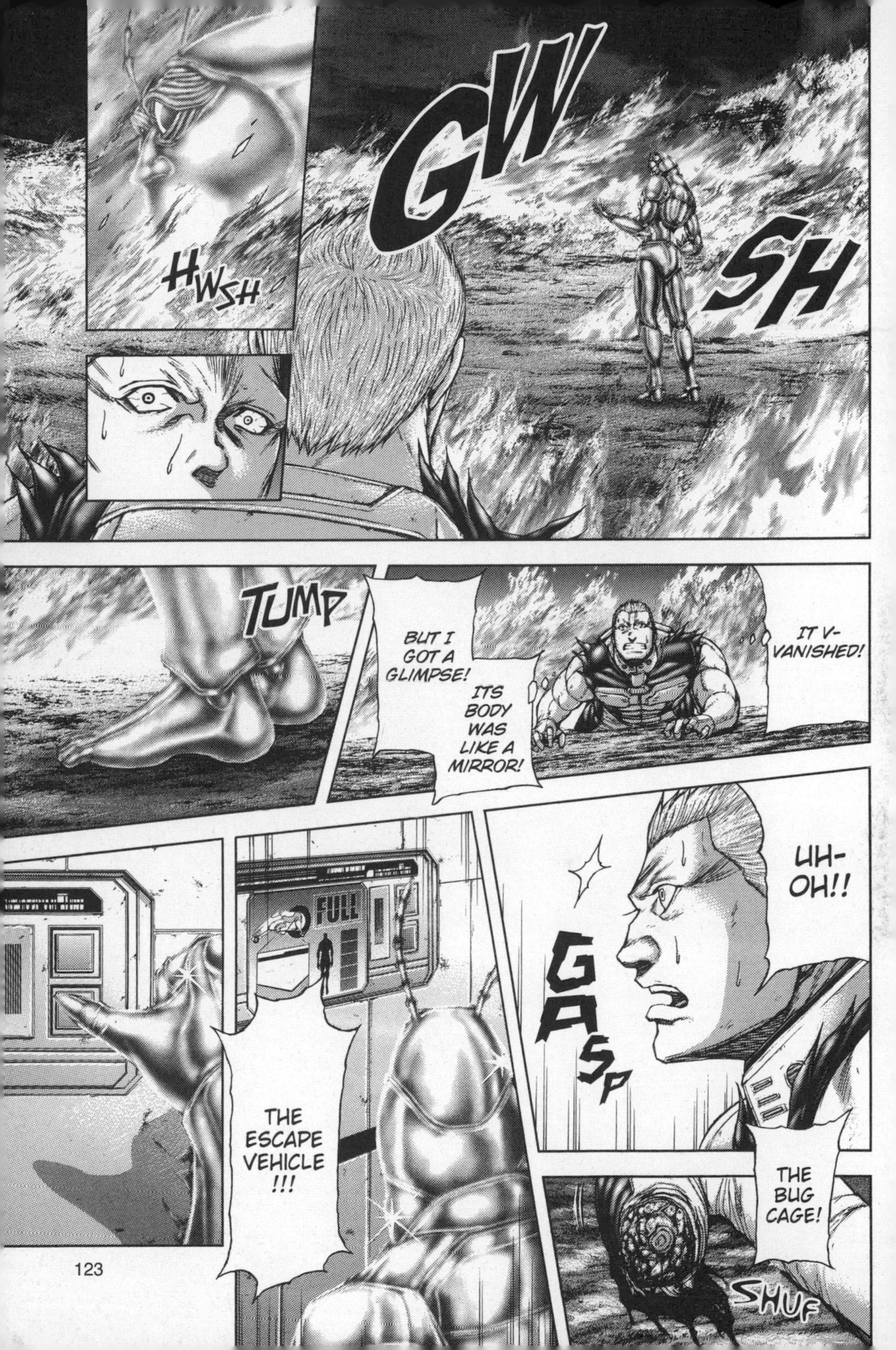
GW
SH
HWSH
IT V-VANISHED!
BUT I GOT A GLIMPSE!
ITS BODY WAS LIKE A MIRROR!
TUMP
UH-OH!!
GASP
THE BUG CAGE!
SHUF
FULL
THE ESCAPE VEHICLE!!!

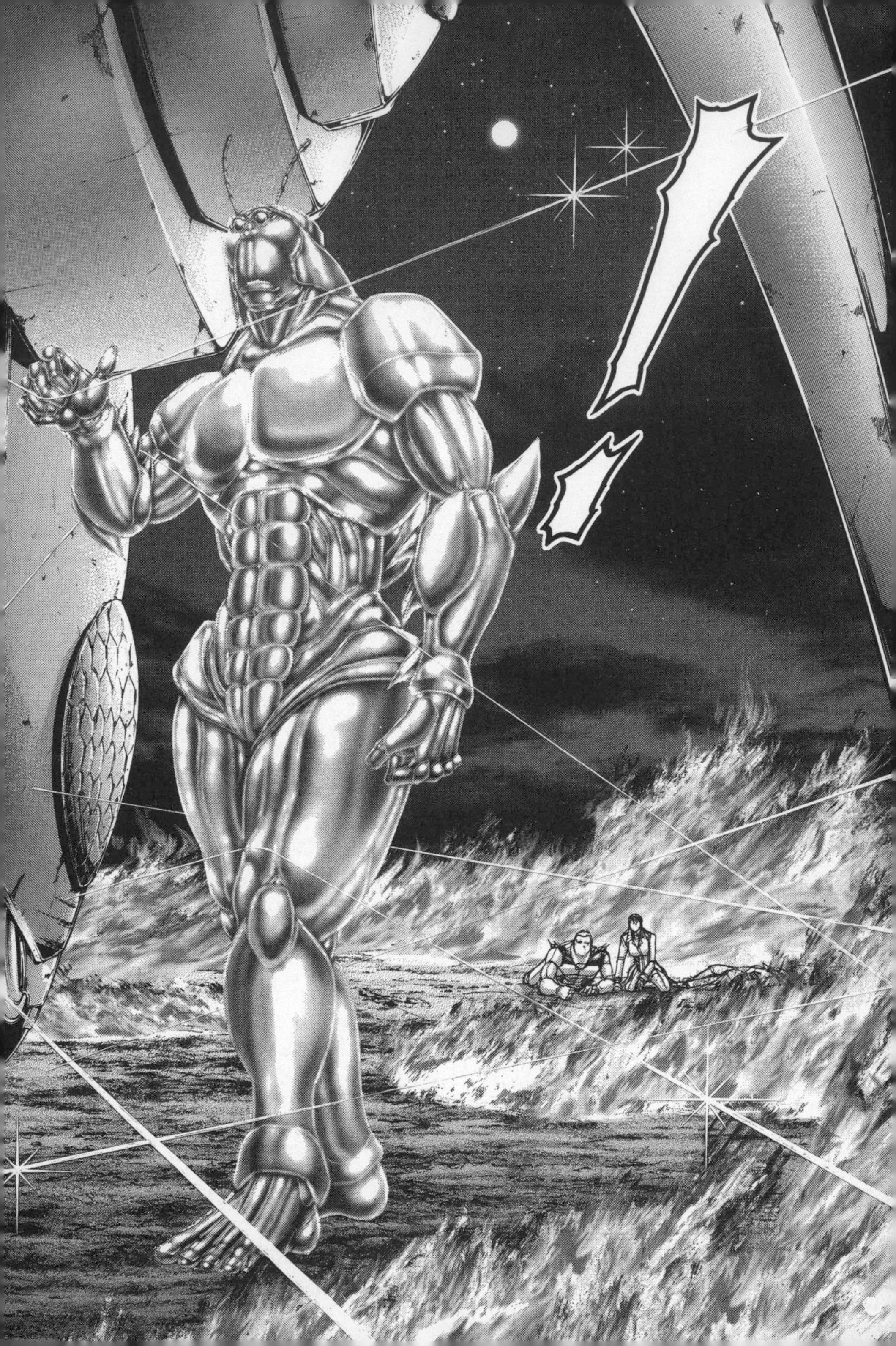

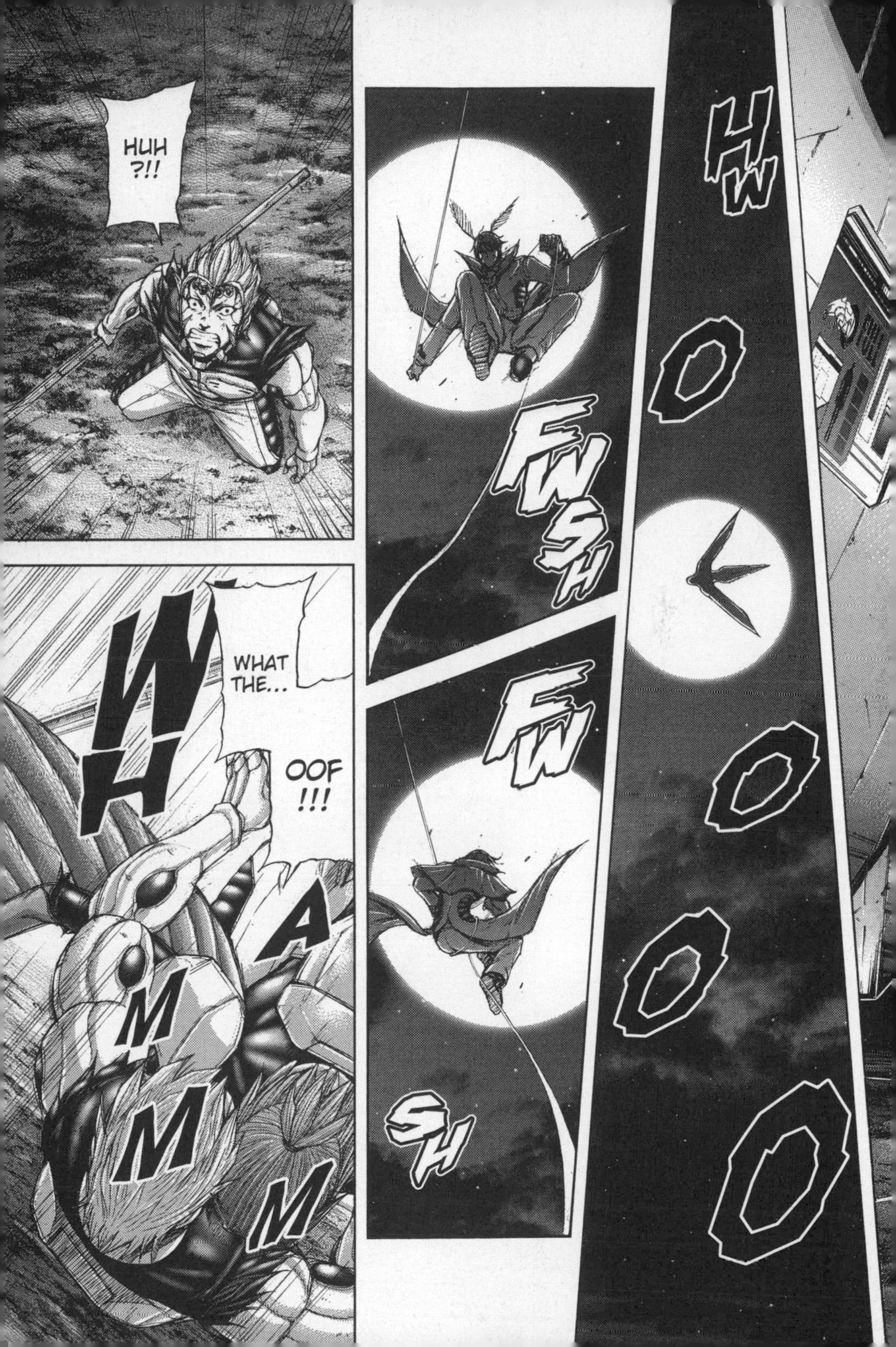
HWOOOO
FWSH
FWSH
HUH ?!!
WHAMMM
WHAT THE...
OOF !!!

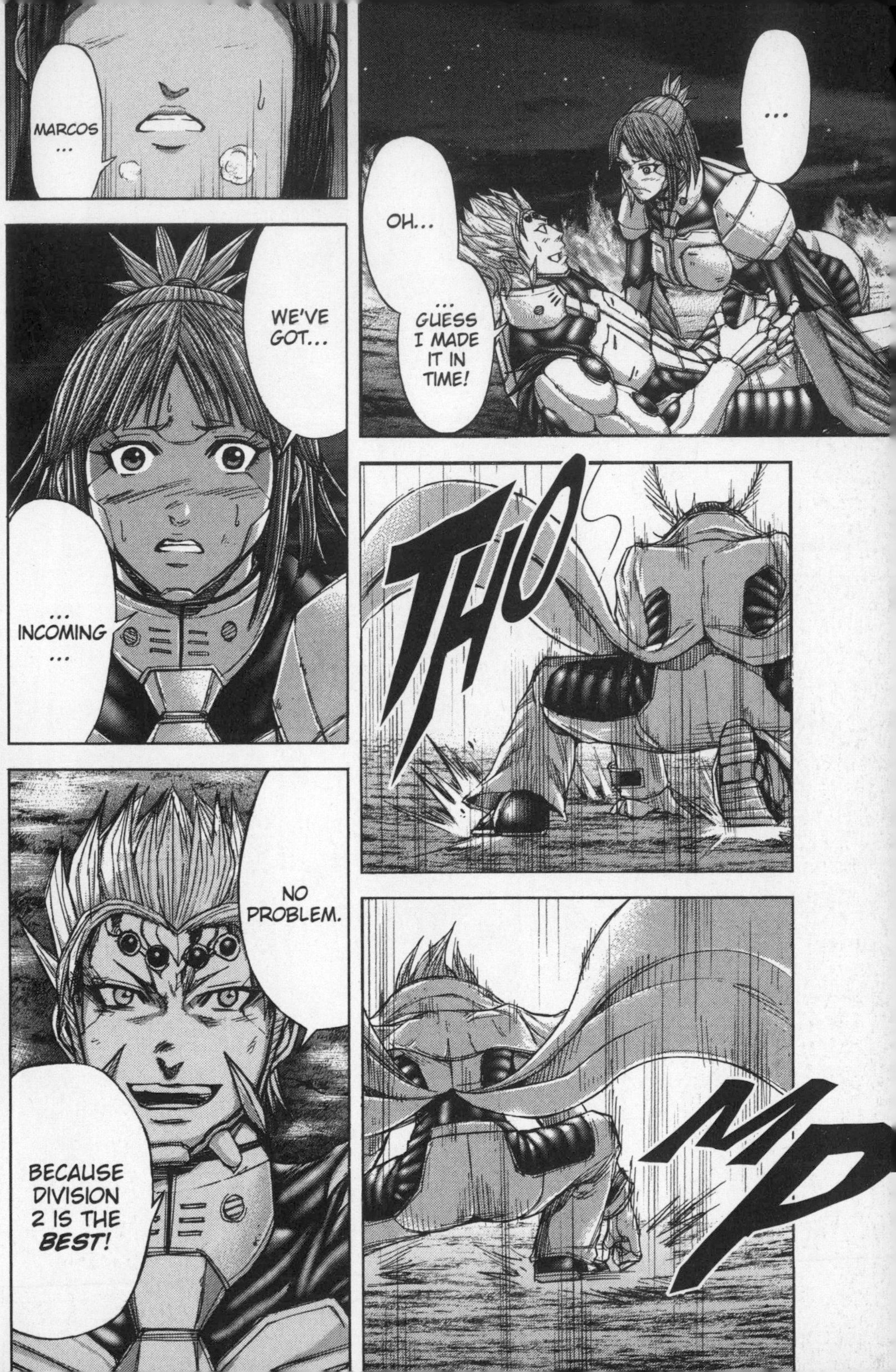
...
OH...
... GUESS I MADE IT IN TIME!
MARCOS ...
THO
WE'VE GOT...
... INCOMING ...
MP
NO PROBLEM.
BECAUSE DIVISION 2 IS THE BEST!

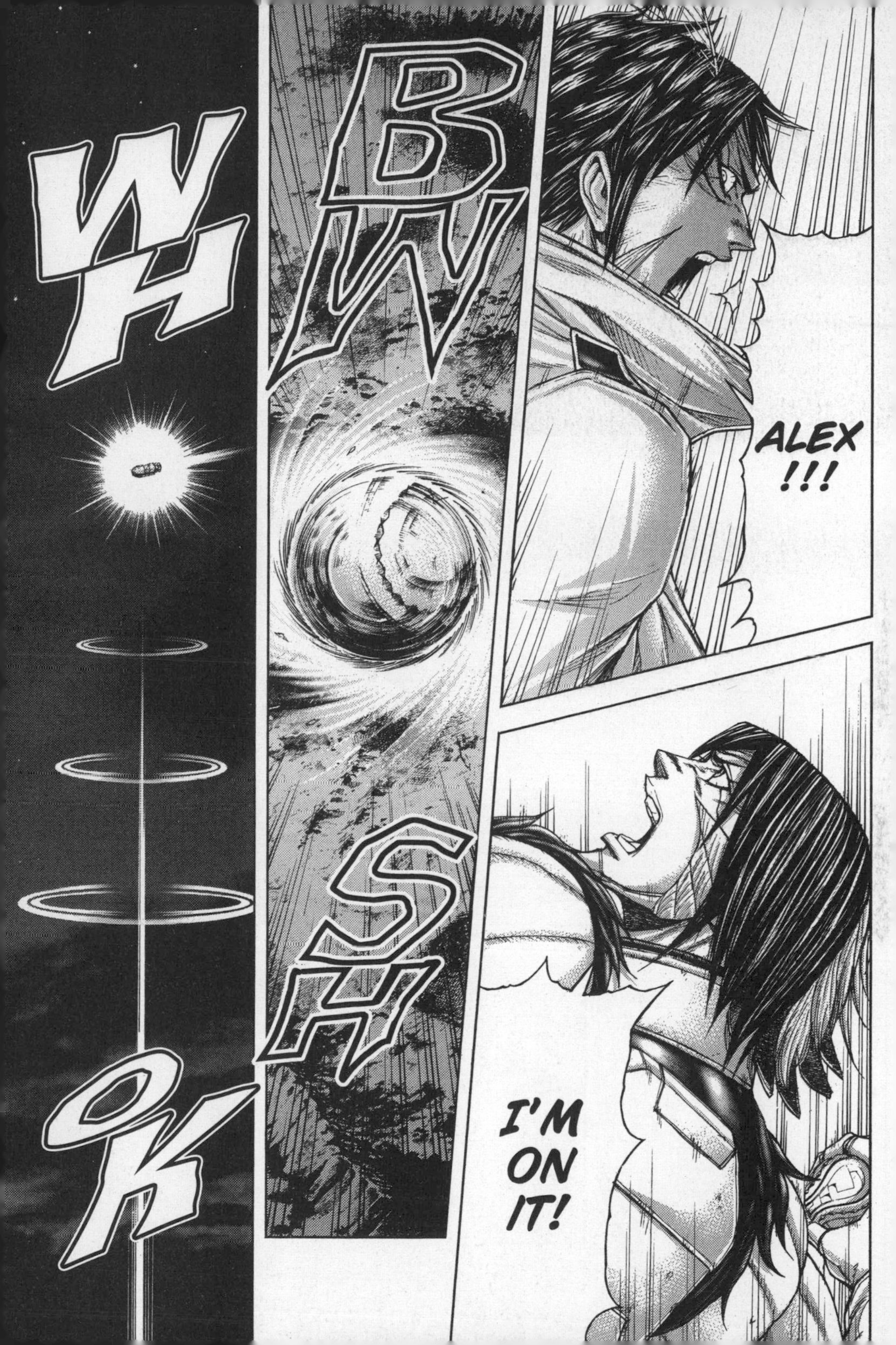
ALEX !!!
I'M ON IT!
BWSH
WHOK

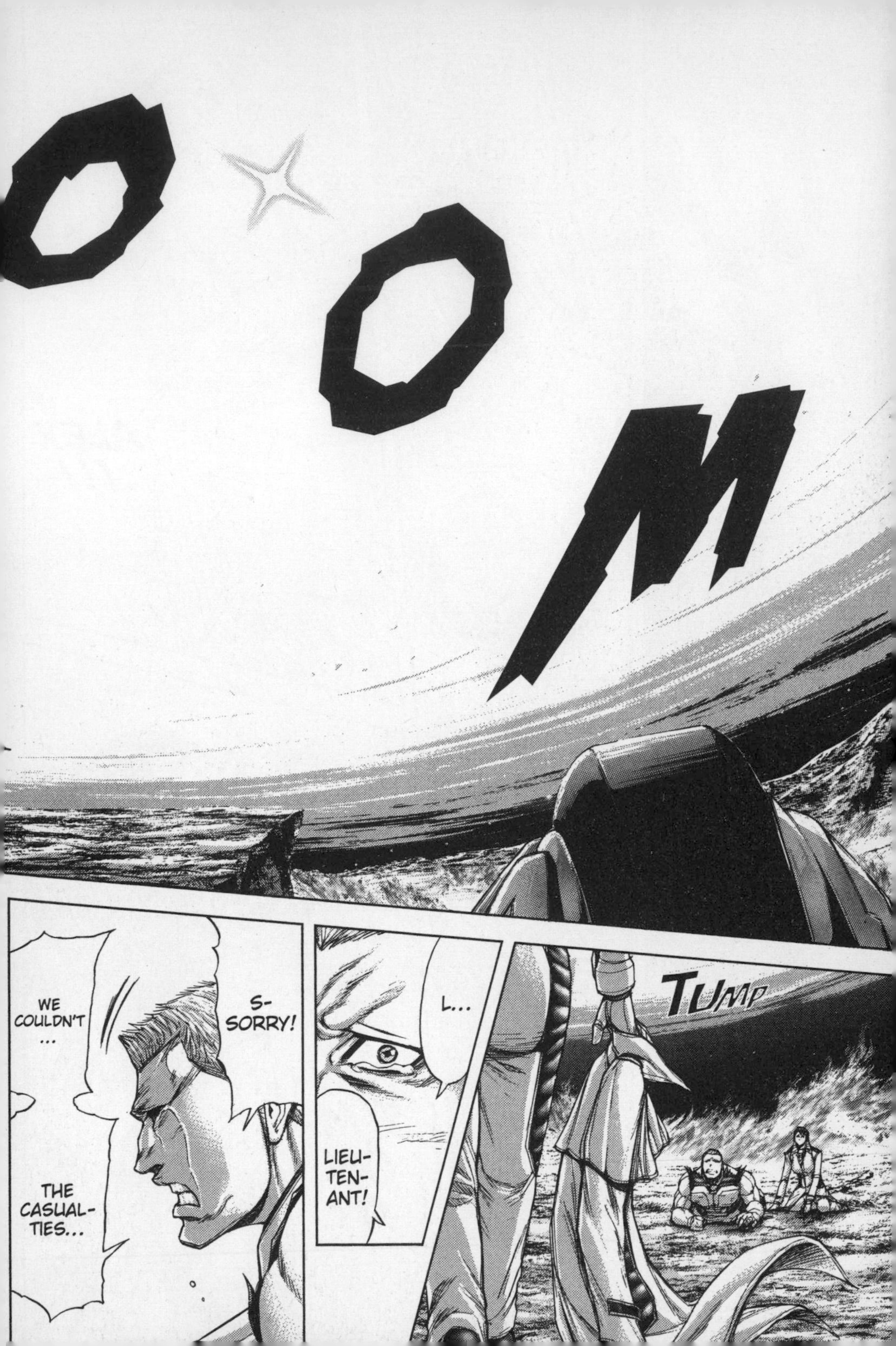

OOM
TUMP
L...
LIEU-TEN-ANT!
S-SORRY!
WE COULDN'T ...
THE CASUAL-TIES...

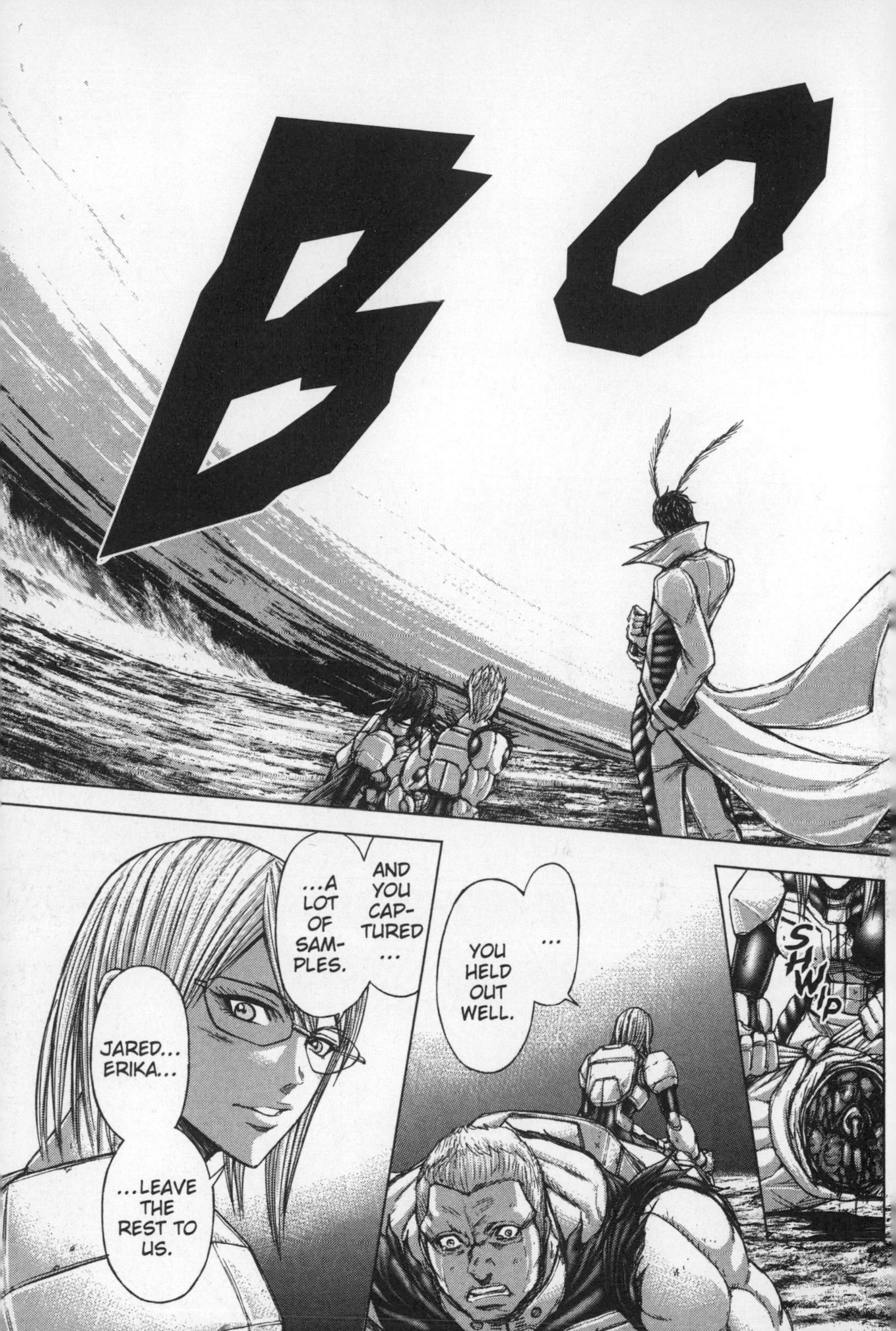
BO
SHWIP
... YOU HELD OUT WELL.
AND YOU CAPTURED ...
...A LOT OF SAMPLES.
JARED... ERIKA...
...LEAVE THE REST TO US.

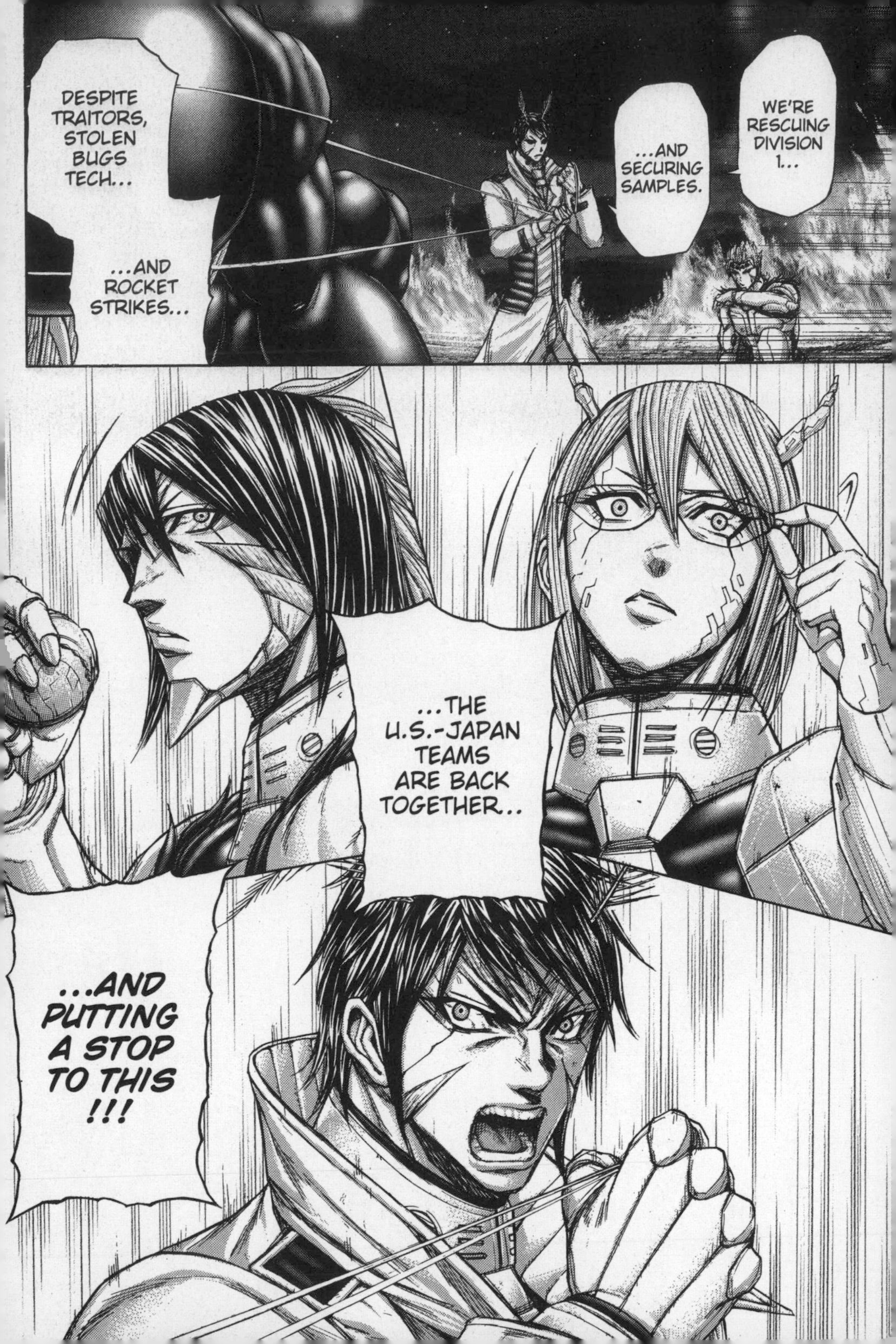
WE'RE RESCUING DIVISION 1...
...AND SECURING SAMPLES.
DESPITE TRAITORS, STOLEN BUGS TECH...
...AND ROCKET STRIKES...
...THE U.S.-JAPAN TEAMS ARE BACK TOGETHER...
...AND PUTTING A STOP TO THIS!!!

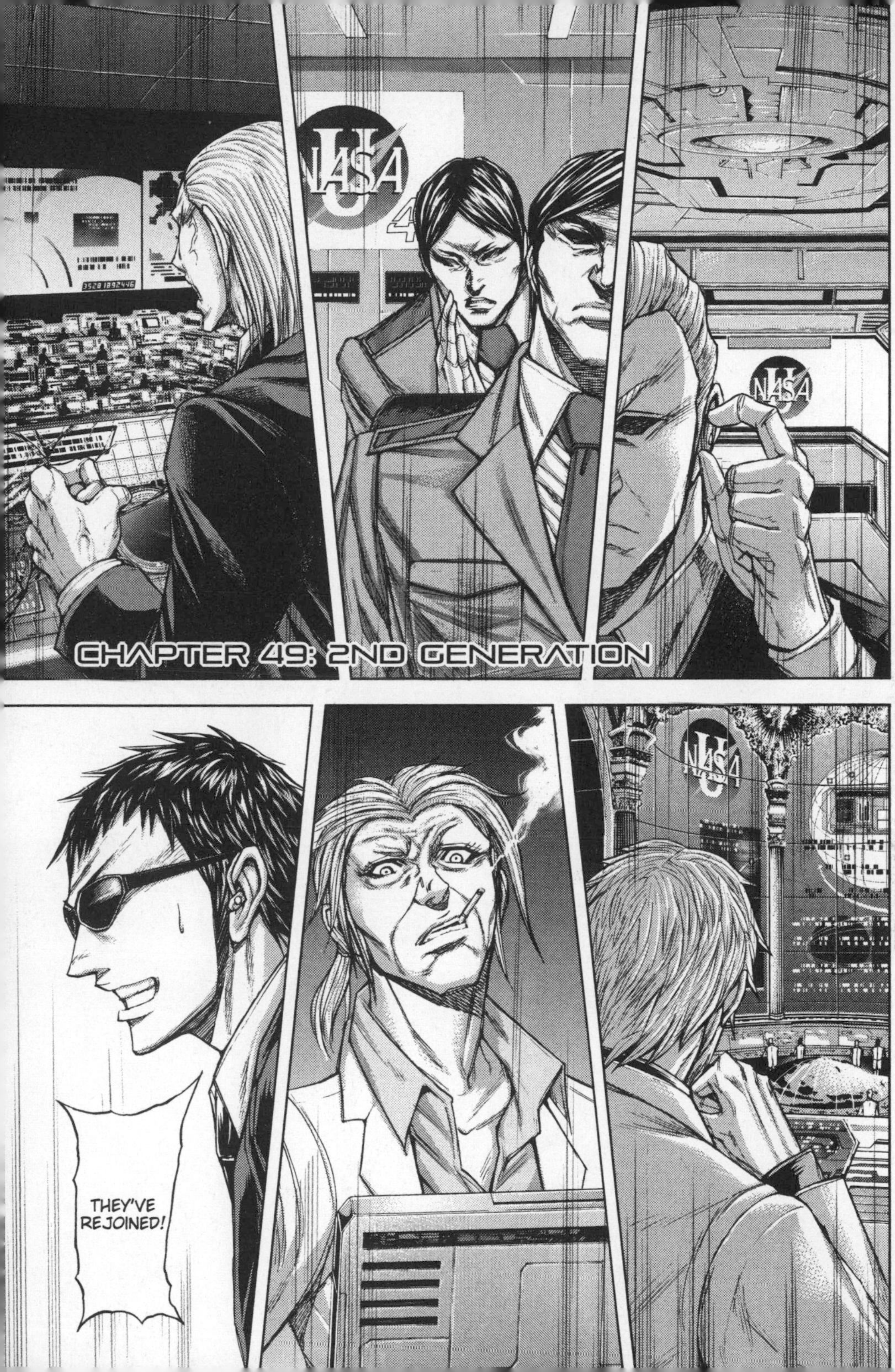
CHAPTER 49: 2ND GENERATION
THEY'VE REJOINED!

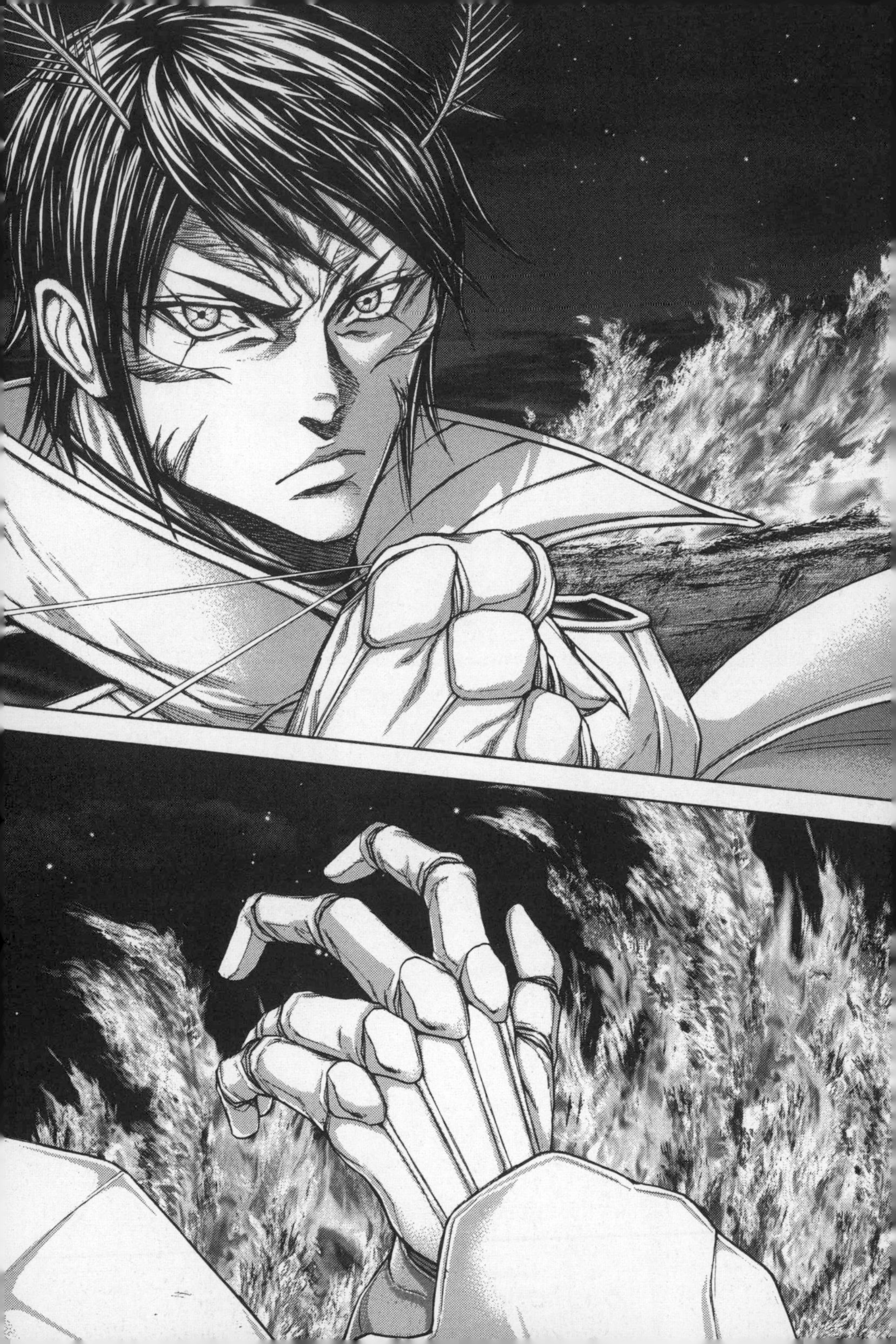

CHAPTER 49: 2ND GENERATION

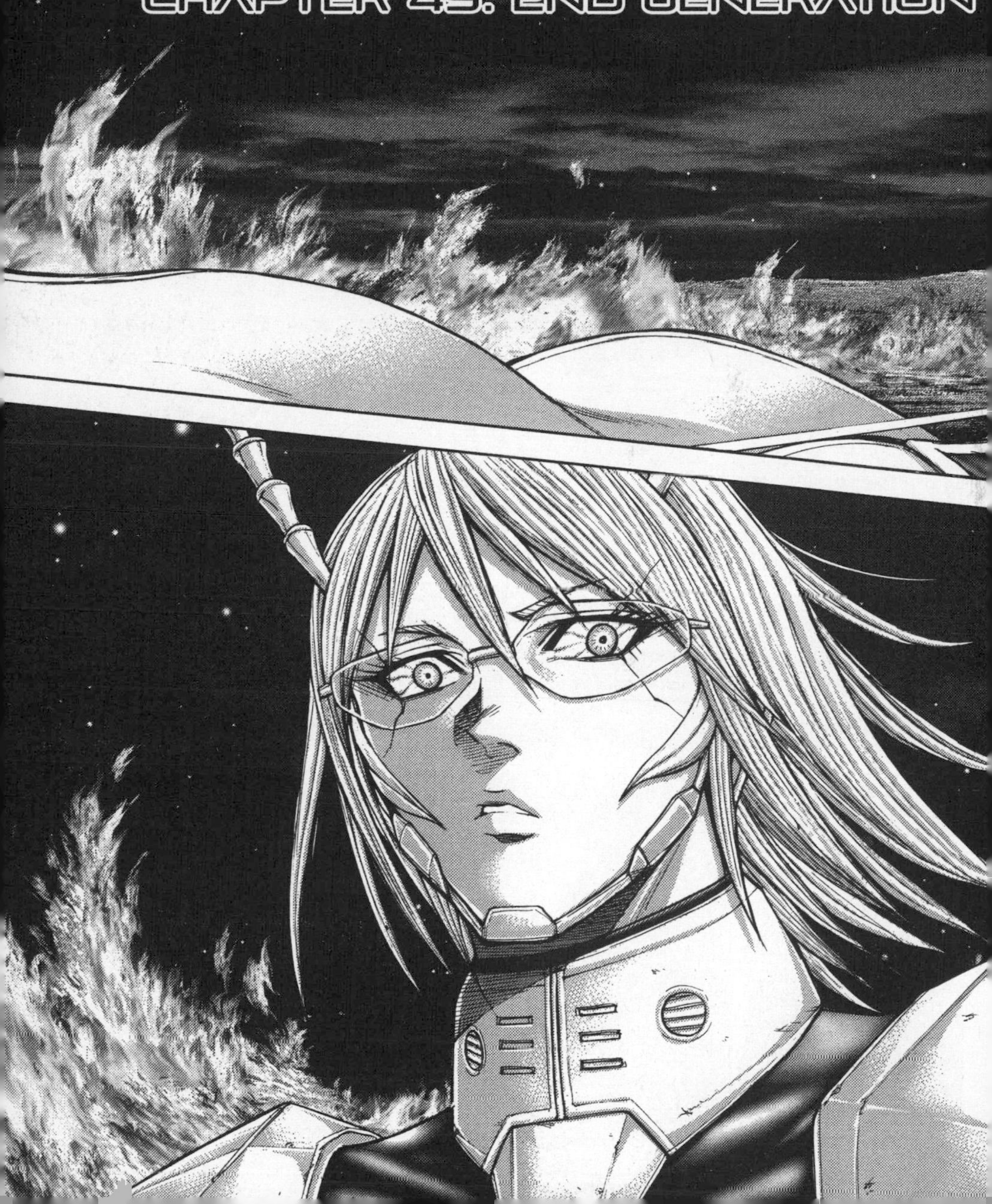

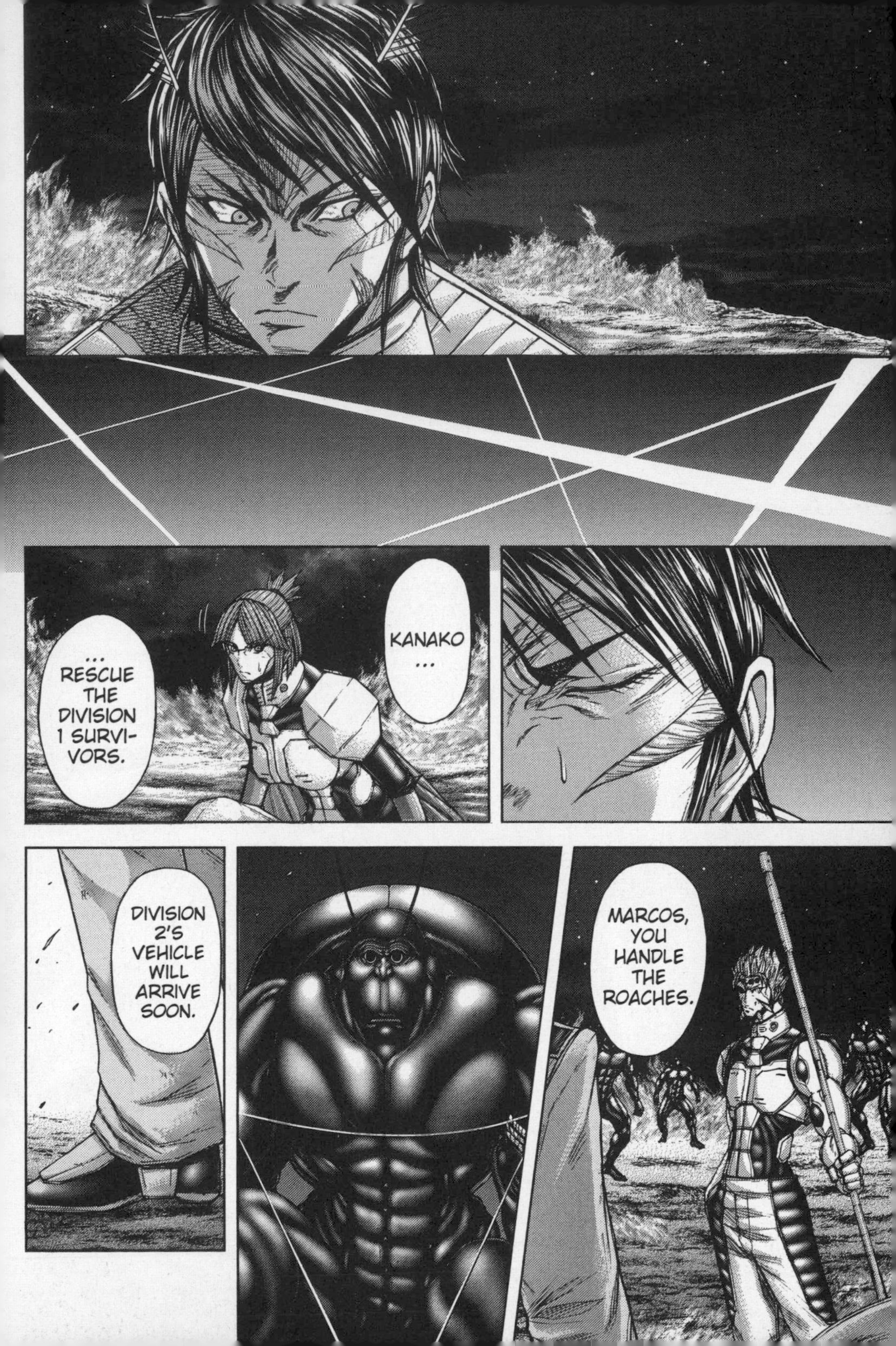
KANAKO ...
... RESCUE THE DIVISION 1 SURVIVORS.
MARCOS, YOU HANDLE THE ROACHES.
DIVISION 2'S VEHICLE WILL ARRIVE SOON.

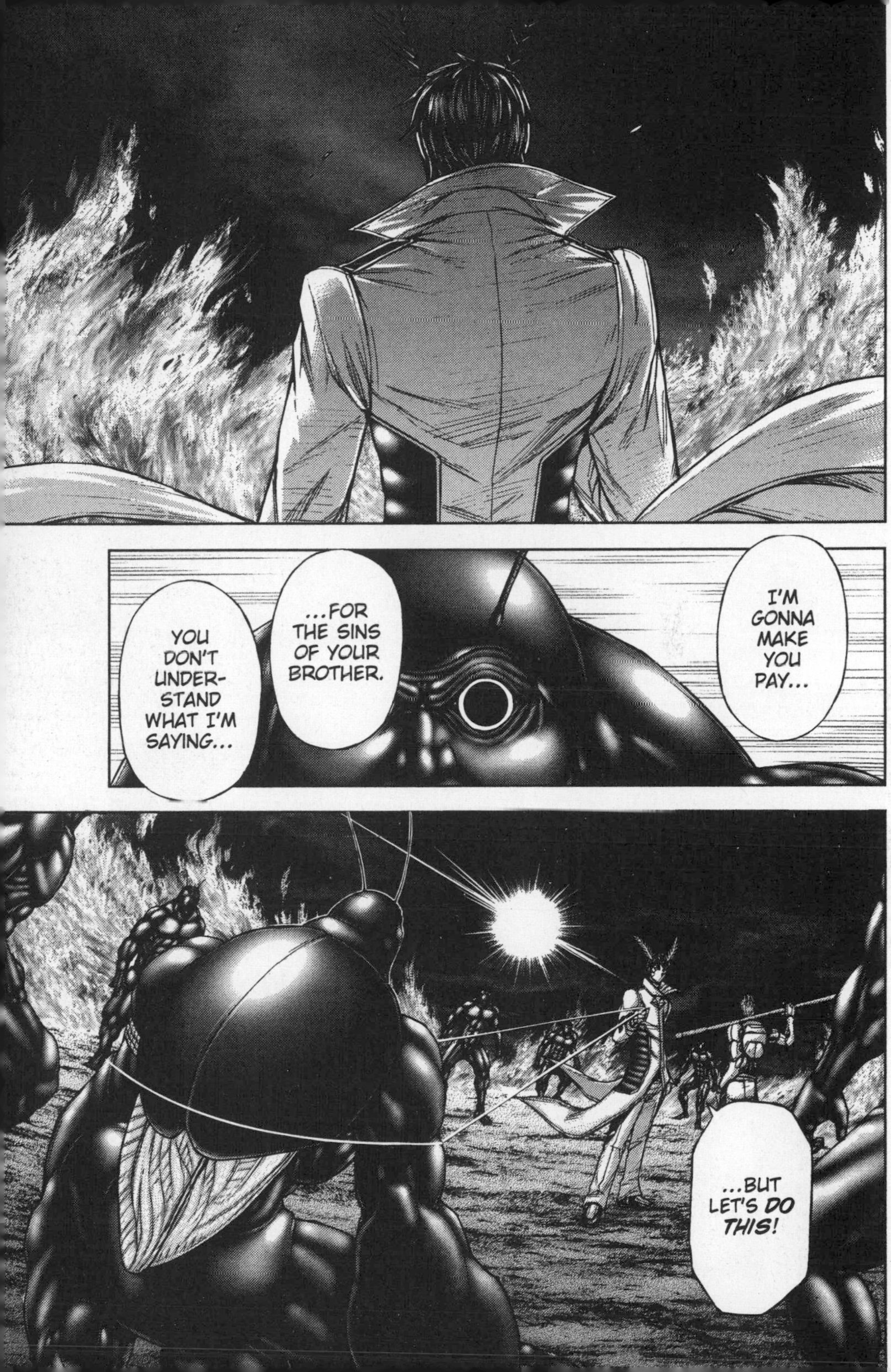
I'M GONNA MAKE YOU PAY...
...FOR THE SINS OF YOUR BROTHER.
YOU DON'T UNDER-STAND WHAT I'M SAYING...
...BUT LET'S *DO THIS!*

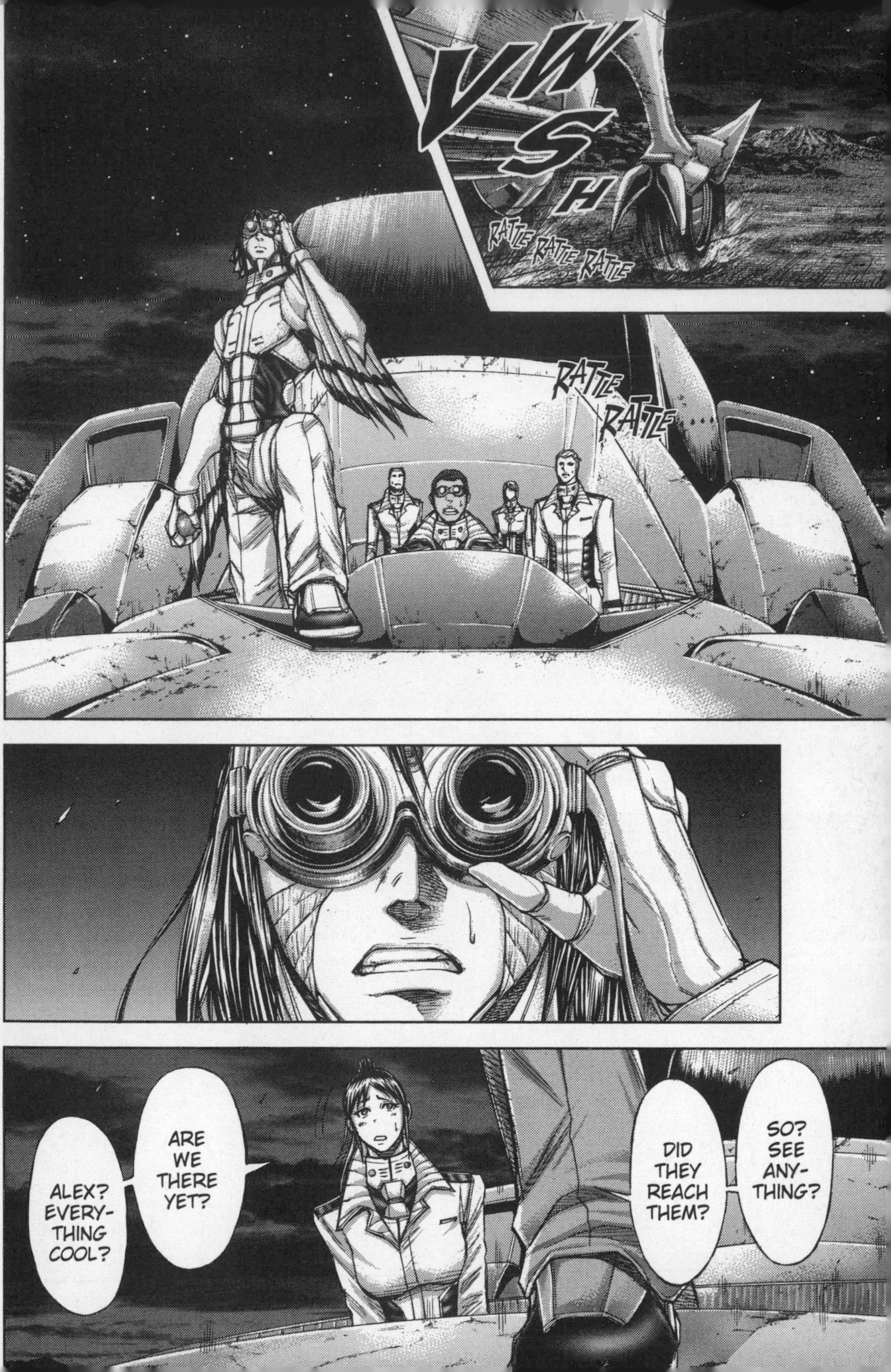
VWSH
RATTLE RATTLE RATTLE
RATTLE RATTLE
SO? SEE ANYTHING?
DID THEY REACH THEM?
ARE WE THERE YET?
ALEX? EVERYTHING COOL?

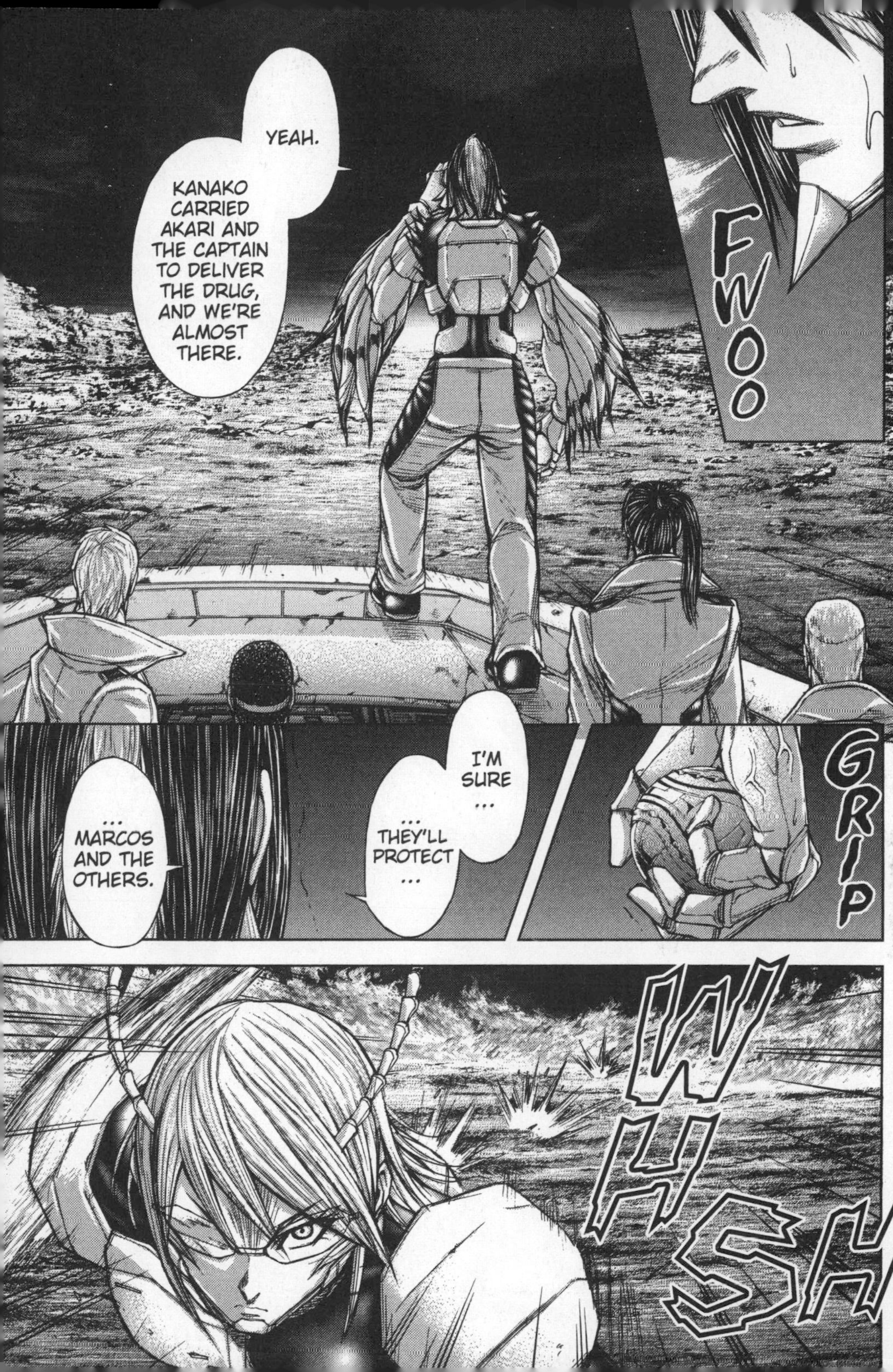
FWOO
YEAH.
KANAKO CARRIED AKARI AND THE CAPTAIN TO DELIVER THE DRUG, AND WE'RE ALMOST THERE.
GRIP
I'M SURE ...
... THEY'LL PROTECT ...
... MARCOS AND THE OTHERS.
WHSH

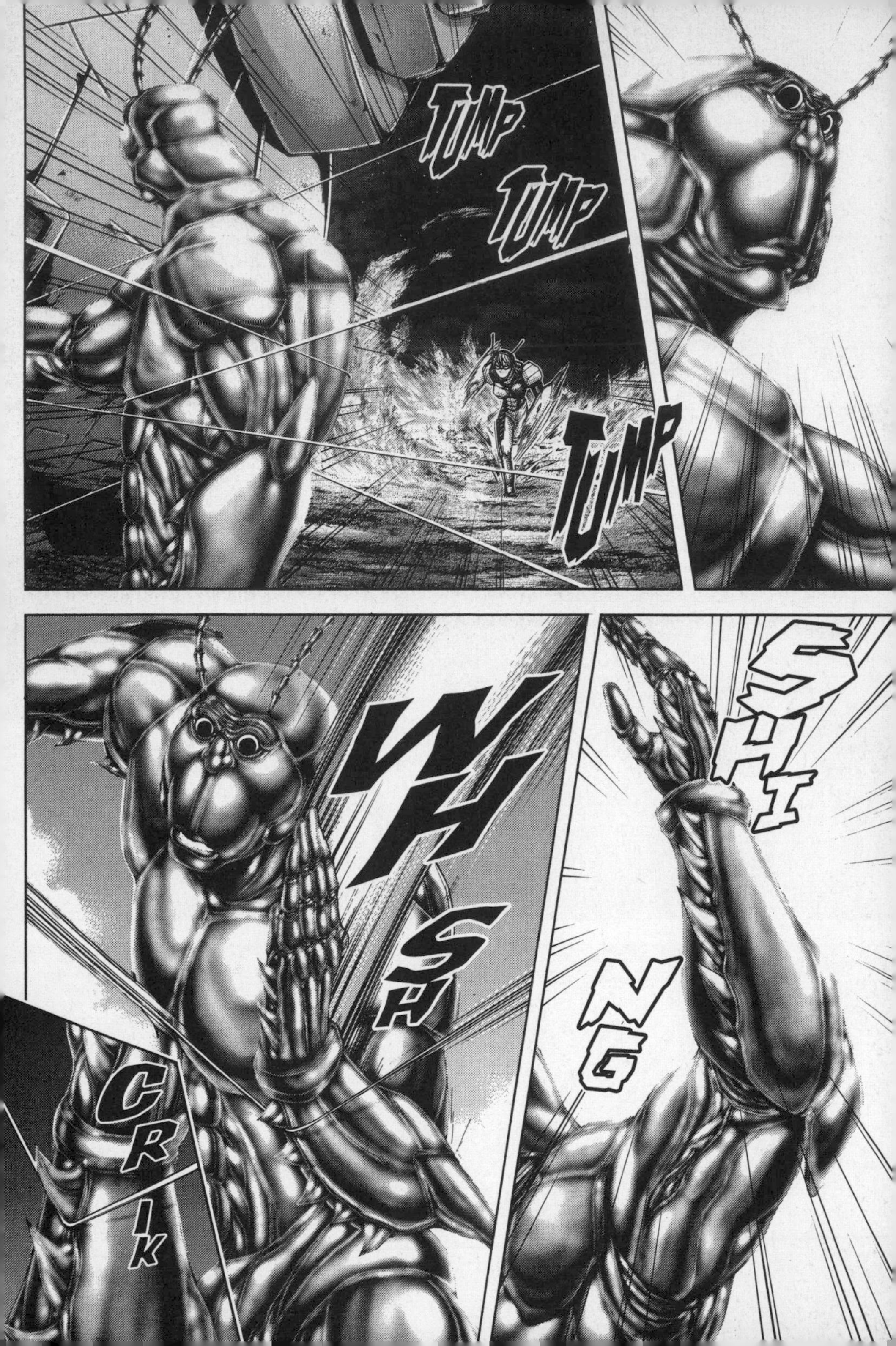
TUMP
TUMP
TUMP
SHING
WHSH
CRIK

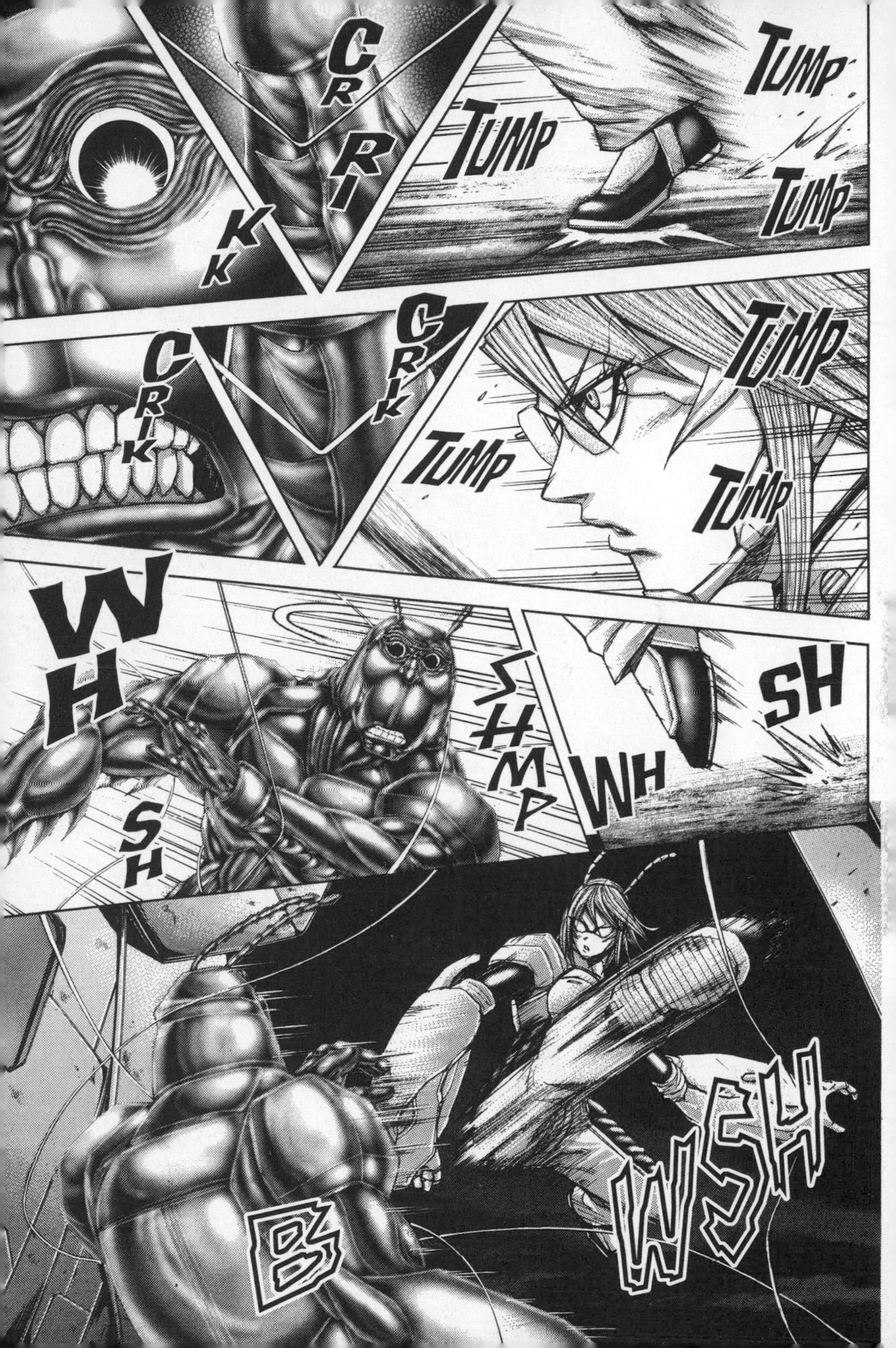
TUMP
TUMP
TUMP
CRRIKK
TUMP
TUMP
TUMP
CRIK
CRIK
WHSH
SHMP
WHSH
WSH

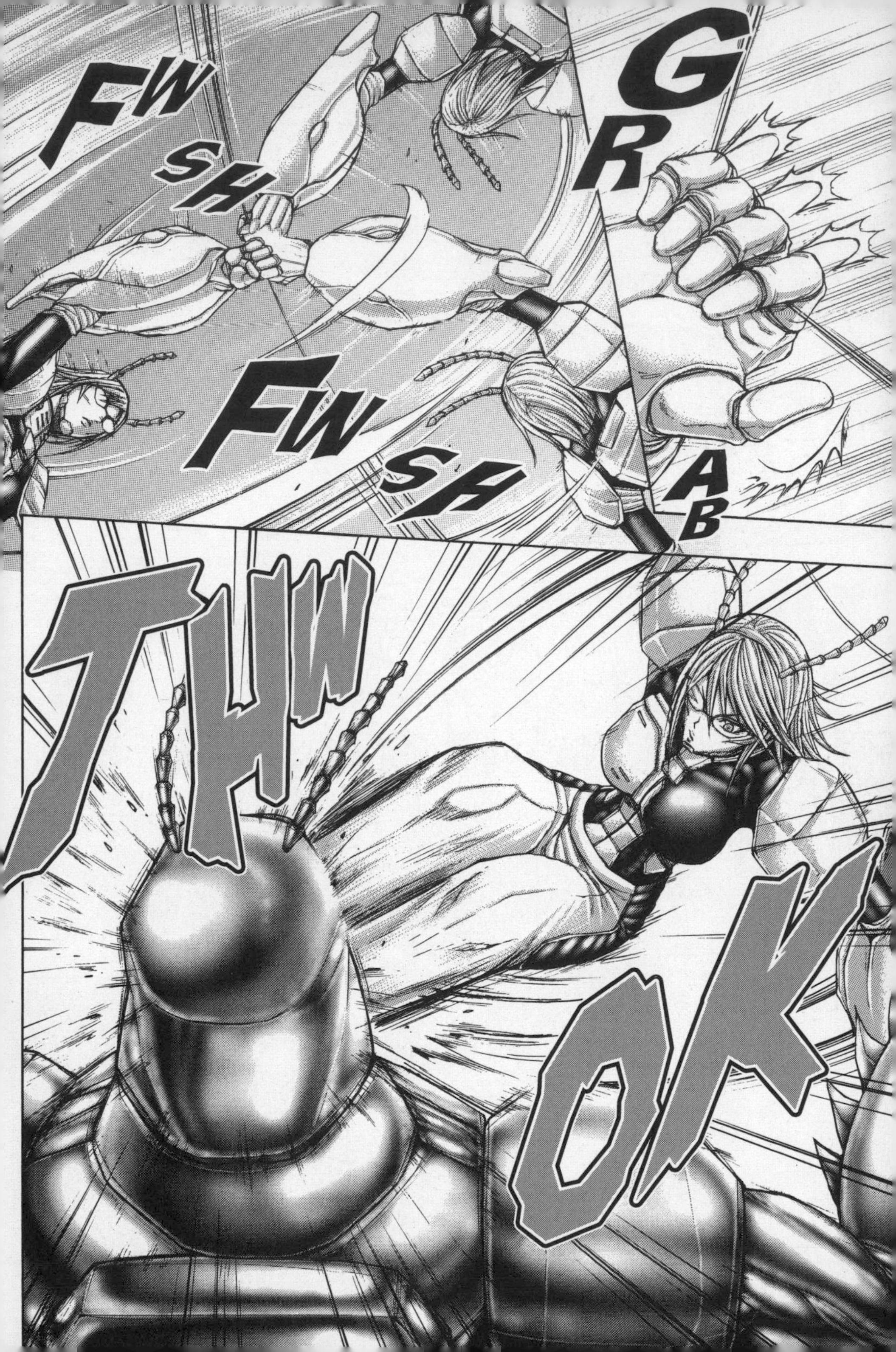
GRAB
FWSH
FWSH
THWOK

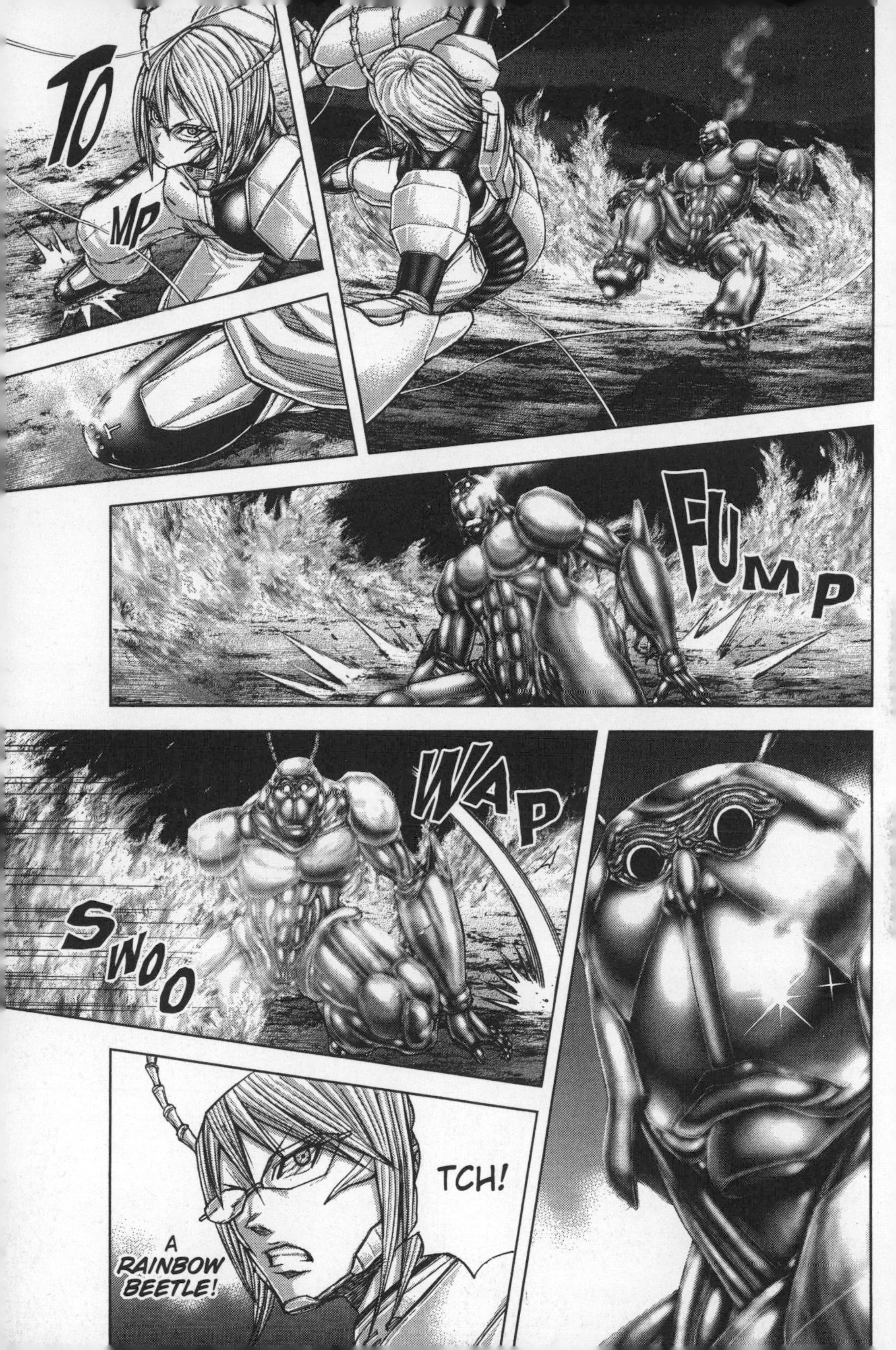
TO
MP
FUMP
WAP
SWOO
TCH!
A RAINBOW BEETLE!

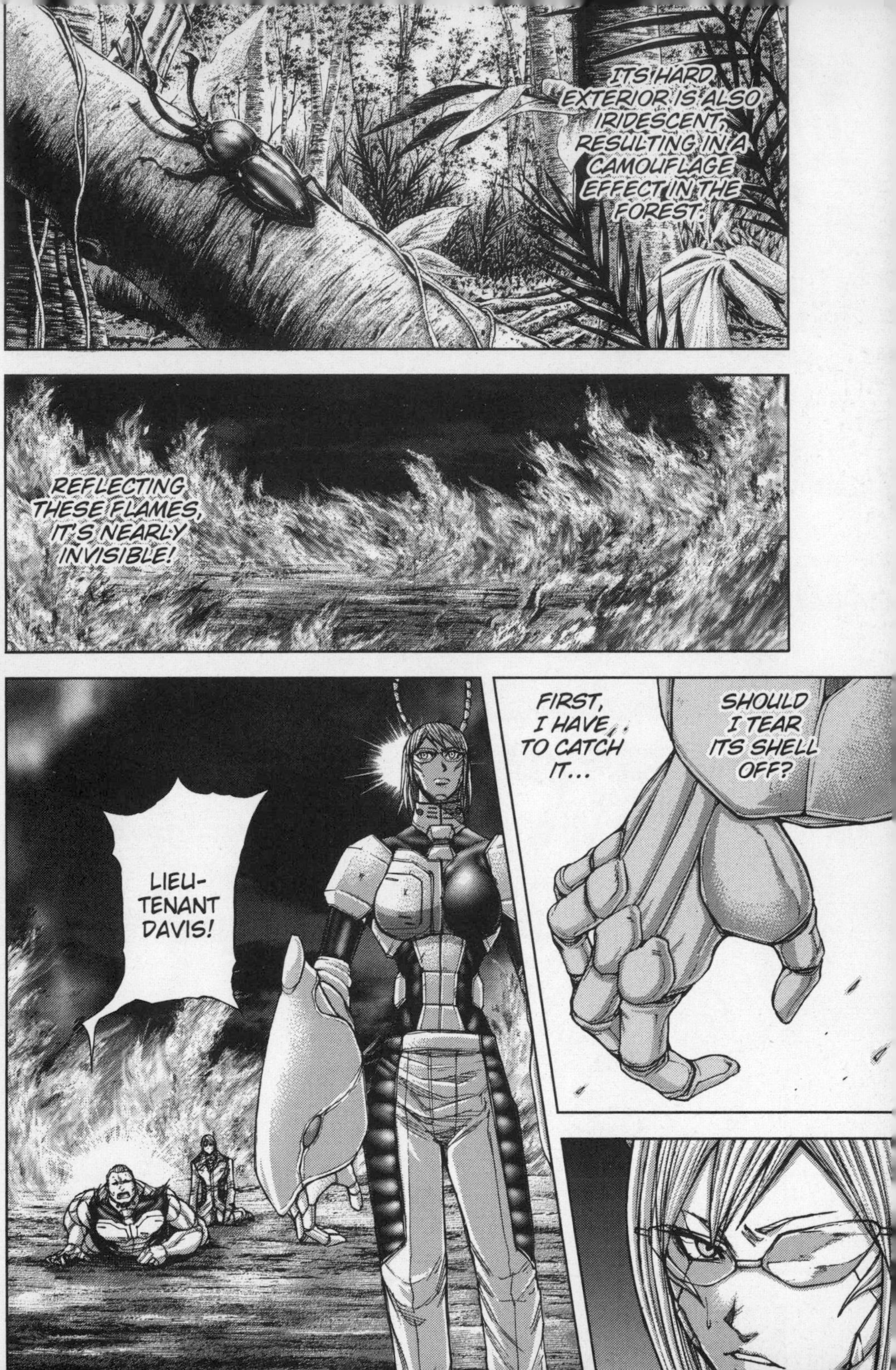
ITS HARD EXTERIOR IS ALSO IRIDESCENT, RESULTING IN A CAMOUFLAGE EFFECT IN THE FOREST.
REFLECTING THESE FLAMES, IT'S NEARLY INVISIBLE!
SHOULD I TEAR ITS SHELL OFF?
FIRST, I HAVE TO CATCH IT...
LIEU-TENANT DAVIS!

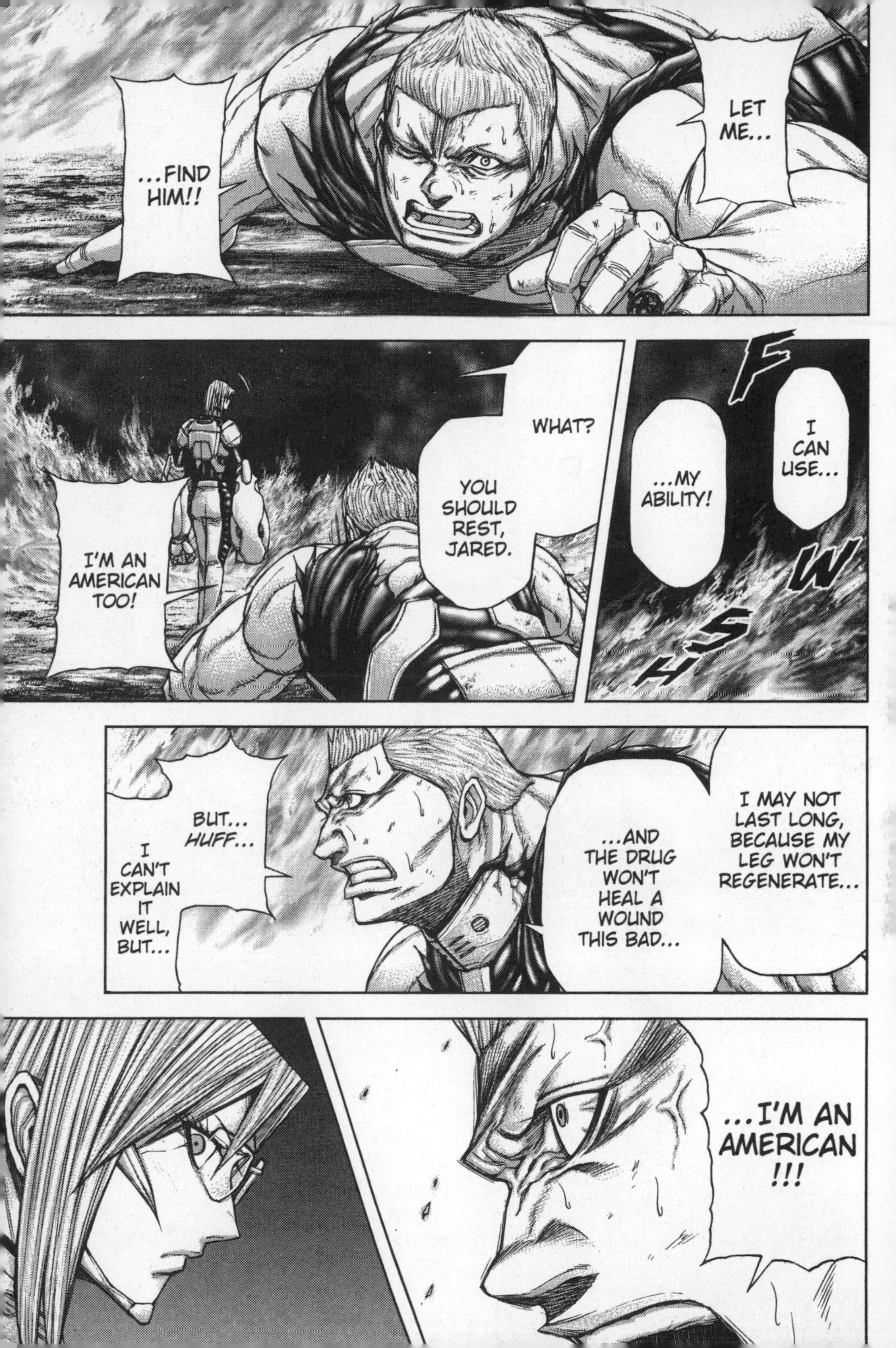
LET ME...
...FIND HIM!!
I CAN USE...
...MY ABILITY!
FWSH
WHAT?
YOU SHOULD REST, JARED.
I'M AN AMERICAN TOO!
I MAY NOT LAST LONG, BECAUSE MY LEG WON'T REGENERATE...
...AND THE DRUG WON'T HEAL A WOUND THIS BAD...
BUT... *HUFF*...
I CAN'T EXPLAIN IT WELL, BUT...
...I'M AN AMERICAN!!!

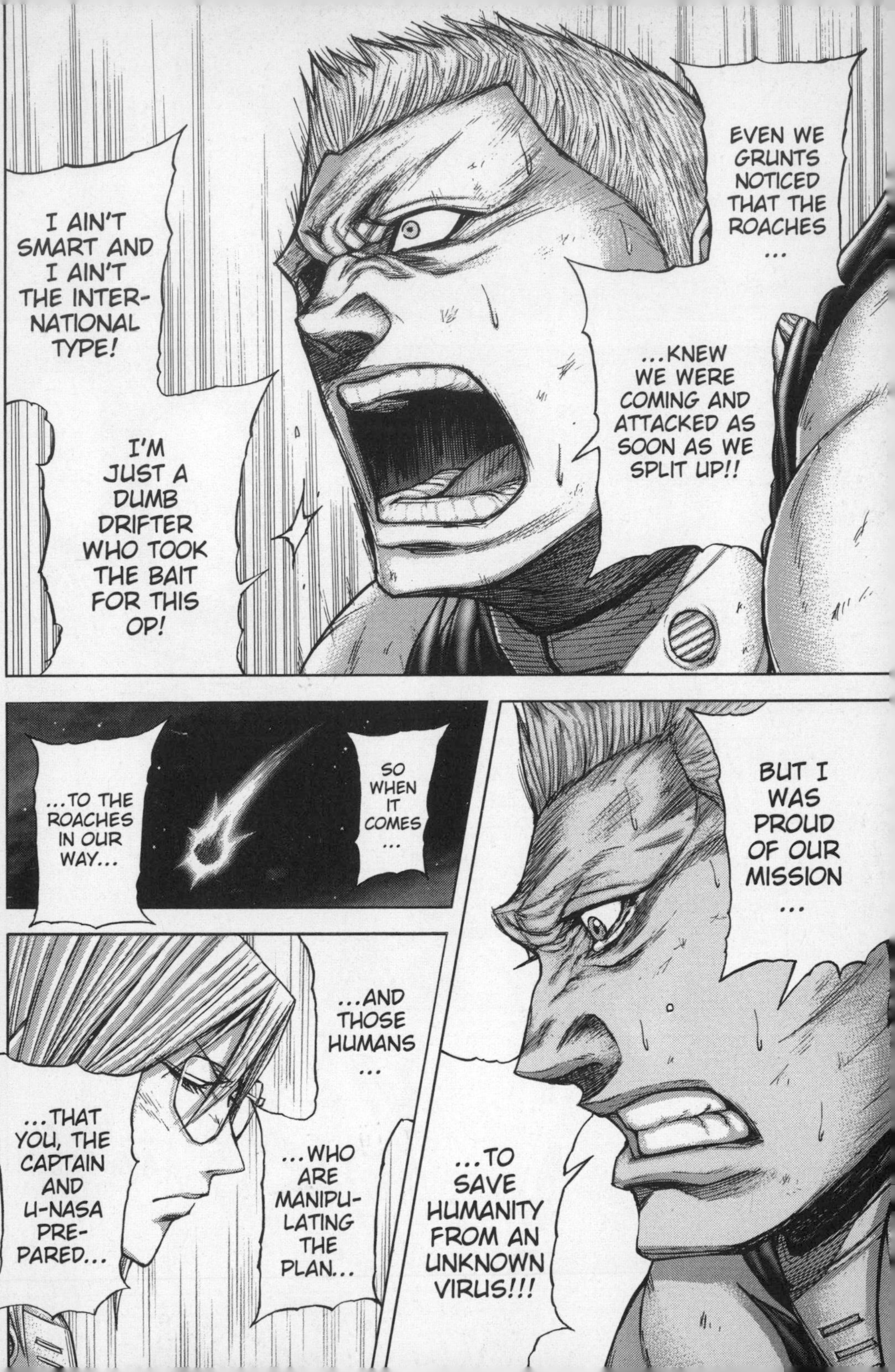
EVEN WE GRUNTS NOTICED THAT THE ROACHES ...
...KNEW WE WERE COMING AND ATTACKED AS SOON AS WE SPLIT UP!!
I AIN'T SMART AND I AIN'T THE INTER-NATIONAL TYPE!
I'M JUST A DUMB DRIFTER WHO TOOK THE BAIT FOR THIS OP!
BUT I WAS PROUD OF OUR MISSION ...
...TO SAVE HUMANITY FROM AN UNKNOWN VIRUS!!!
SO WHEN IT COMES ...
...TO THE ROACHES IN OUR WAY...
...AND THOSE HUMANS ...
...WHO ARE MANIPU-LATING THE PLAN...
...THAT YOU, THE CAPTAIN AND U-NASA PRE-PARED...

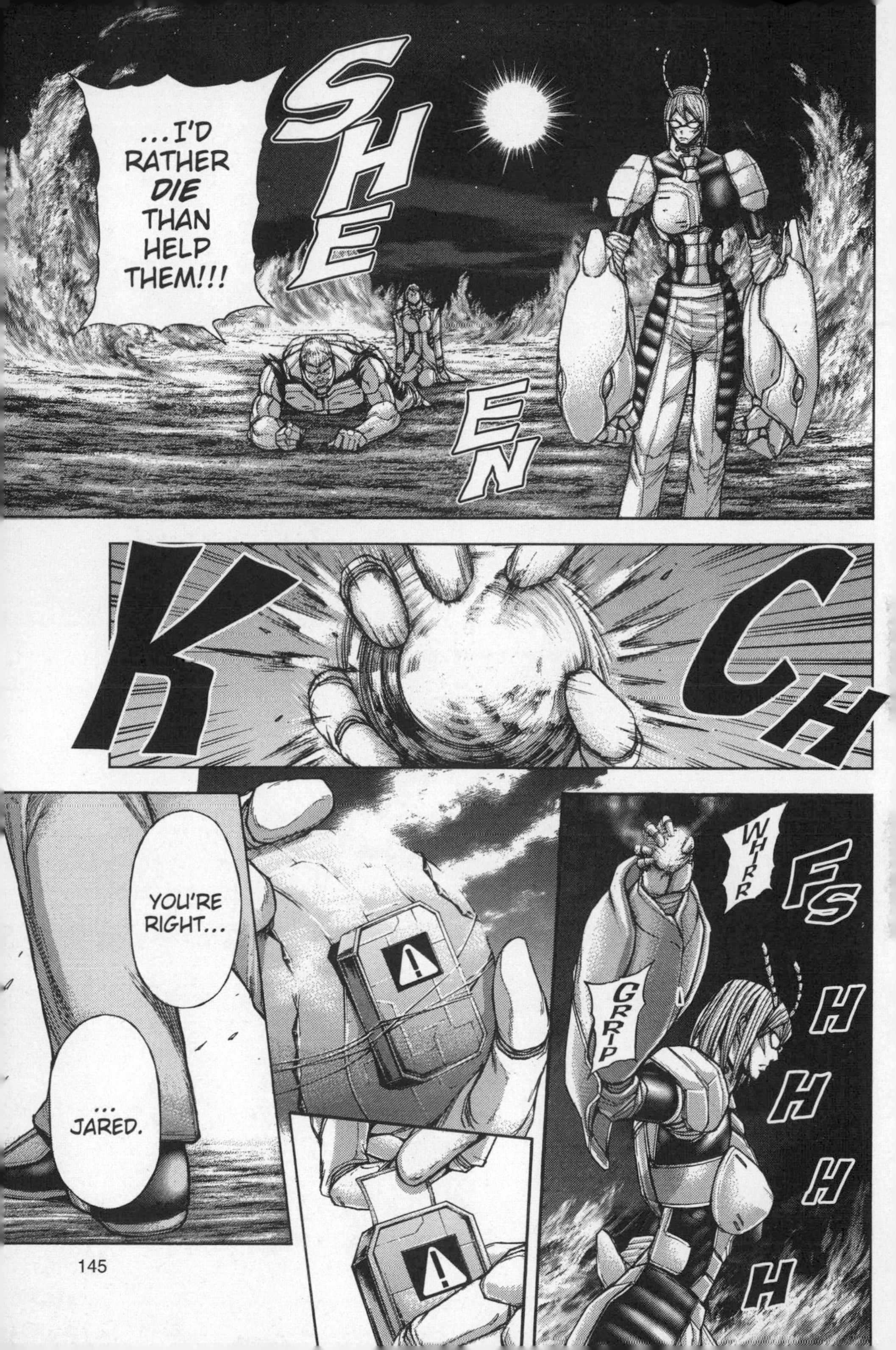
SHEEN
...I'D RATHER DIE THAN HELP THEM!!!
KCH
WHIRR
FSHHHHHH
GRRIP
YOU'RE RIGHT...
...JARED.

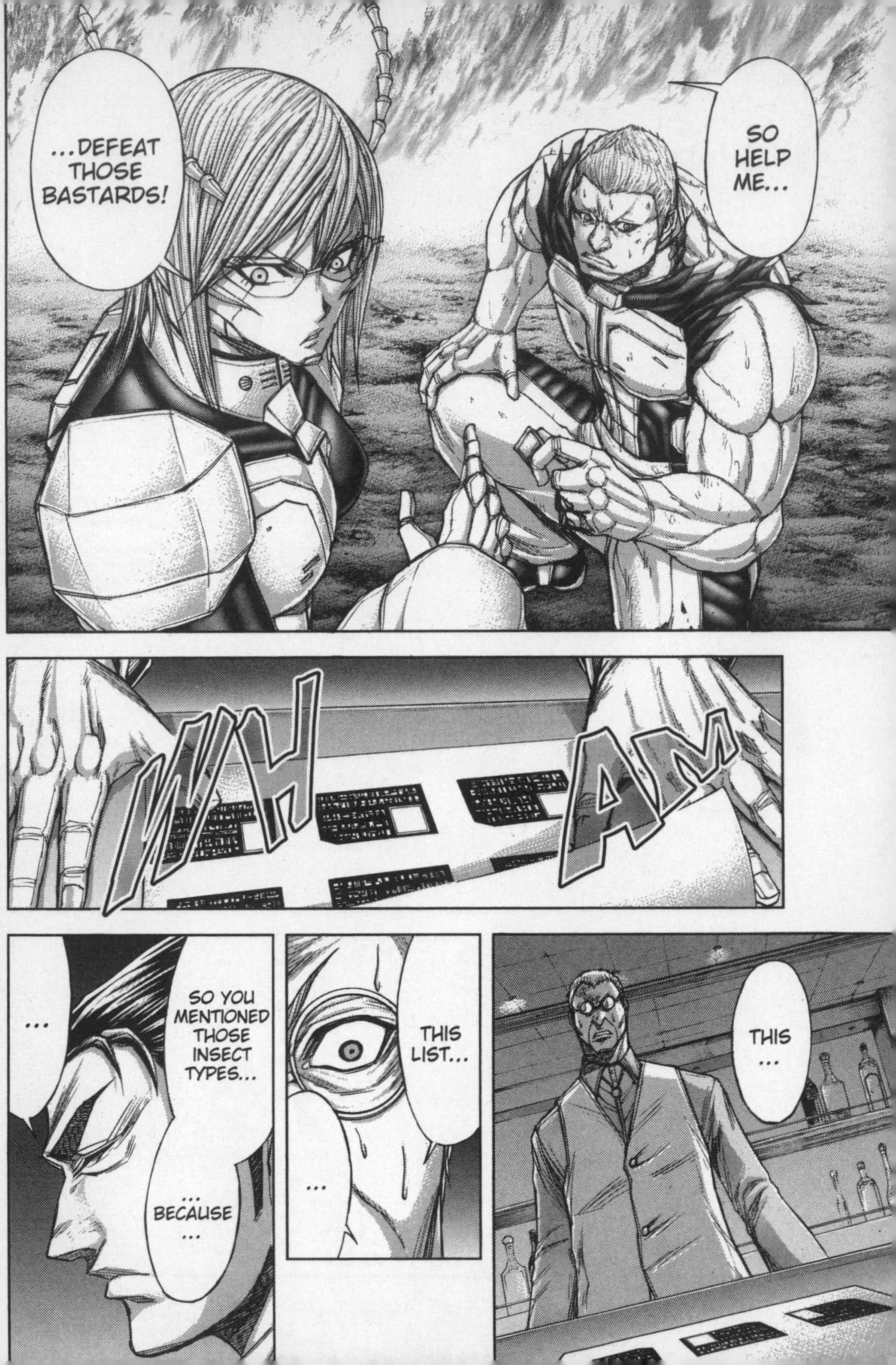
SO HELP ME...
...DEFEAT THOSE BASTARDS!
WHAM
THIS ...
THIS LIST...
...
SO YOU MENTIONED THOSE INSECT TYPES...
...
... BECAUSE ...

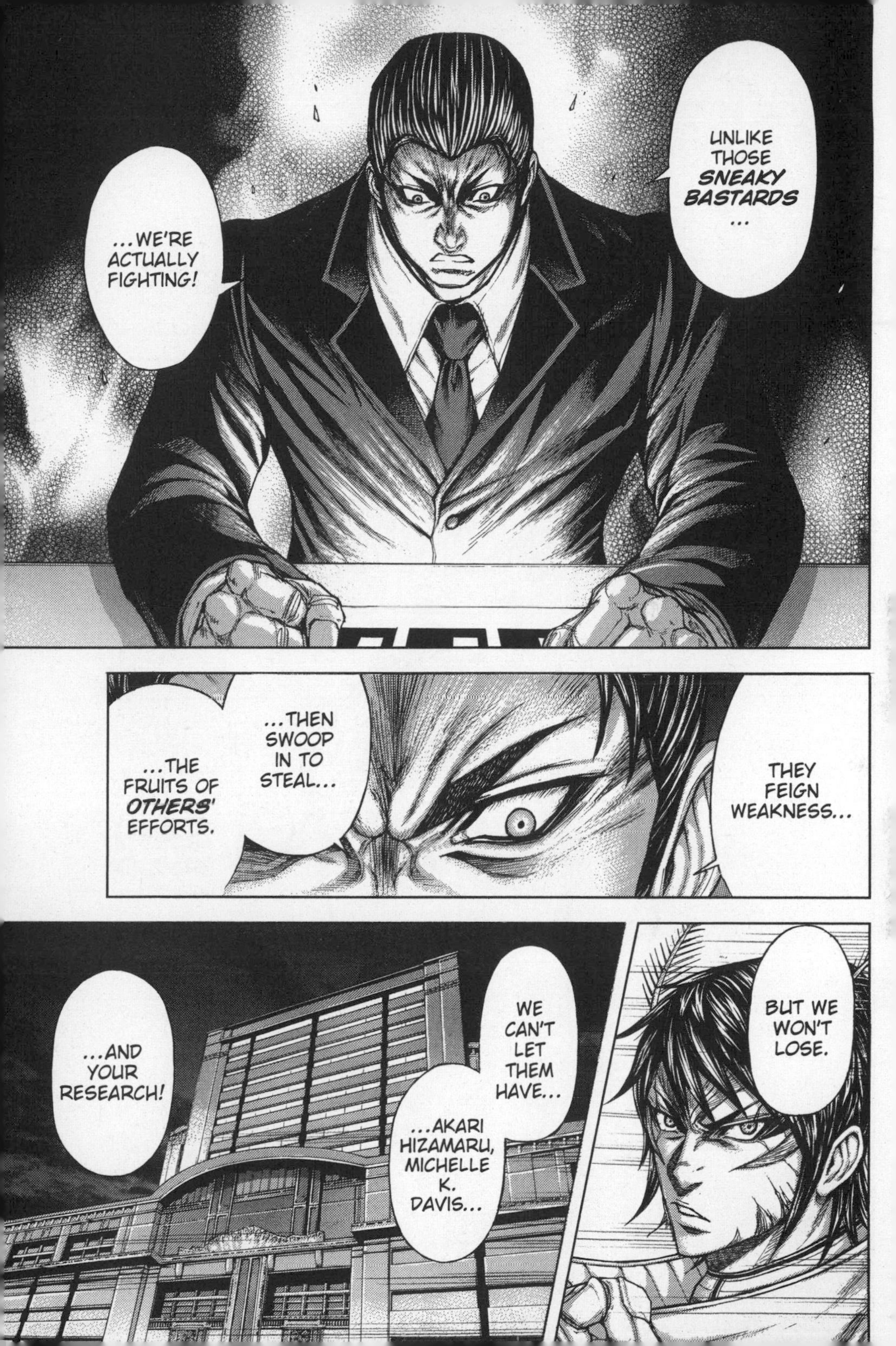
UNLIKE THOSE SNEAKY BASTARDS...
...WE'RE ACTUALLY FIGHTING!
THEY FEIGN WEAKNESS...
...THEN SWOOP IN TO STEAL...
...THE FRUITS OF OTHERS' EFFORTS.
BUT WE WON'T LOSE.
WE CAN'T LET THEM HAVE...
...AKARI HIZAMARU, MICHELLE K. DAVIS...
...AND YOUR RESEARCH!

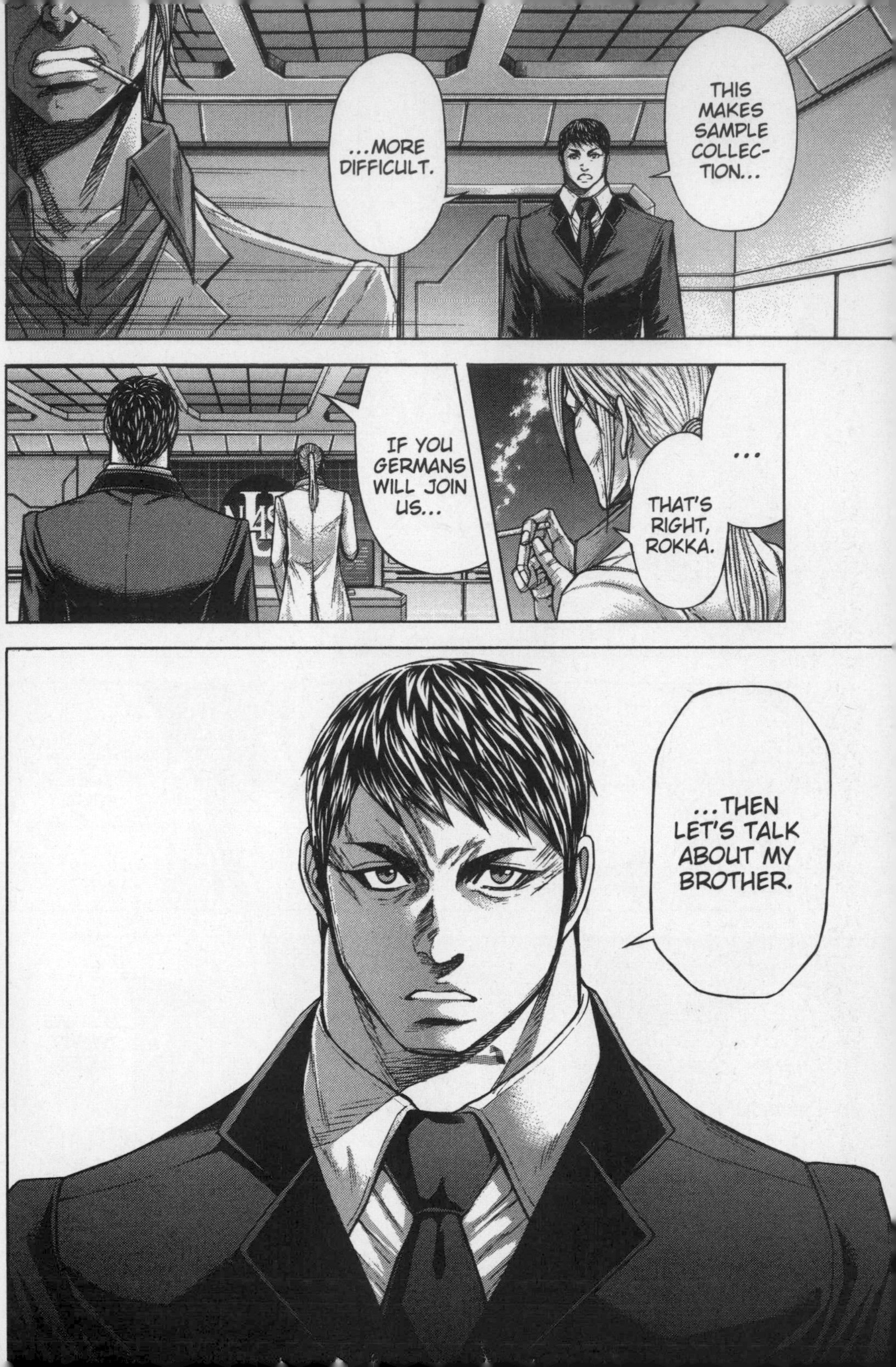
THIS MAKES SAMPLE COLLECTION...
...MORE DIFFICULT.
...
THAT'S RIGHT, ROKKA.
IF YOU GERMANS WILL JOIN US...
...THEN LET'S TALK ABOUT MY BROTHER.

TERRA FORMARS
Character

Kanako Sanjo ♀

Japan 19 yrs. 160 cm 42kg

M.A.R.S. Ranking: 15

Operation Base: Spine-tailed Swift

Favorite Foods: Soymilk, yoghurt
Dislikes: Family restaurant managers who
only hire the type of girl they like
Eye Color: Black Blood Type: A
DOB: February 9 (Aquarius)

Her father was a famous soccer athlete and her mother an entertainer. Kanako was thought to have a bright future in track and field, but everything changed when her father was arrested for drug possession. When her mother became involved in a disreputable business, the two quarreled and Kanako left her.

Pursued by her family's ballooning debts and their collectors, she joined the Mars mission in order to raise a large amount of money all at once and cut all ties. A Cup, but it sits high.

Keiji Onizuka ♂

Japan 24 yrs. 175 cm 61kg

M.A.R.S. Ranking: 8

Operation Base: Peacock Mantis Shrimp

Favorite Food: Sashimi (esp. shrimp)
Dislikes: People who carry their umbrella horizontally
Eye Color: Black Blood Type: O
DOB: June 23 (Scorpio)

As a child, he spent a lot of time at home watching all kinds of movies with his mother.

He found it easy to lose weight, so after dominating the lightweight division, he aimed for the super featherweight championship but had to quit due to retinal detachment in his eye. The surgery was difficult, but it prevented progression of the disease. Nonetheless, complete restoration to reclaim his boxing license would have cost even more money.

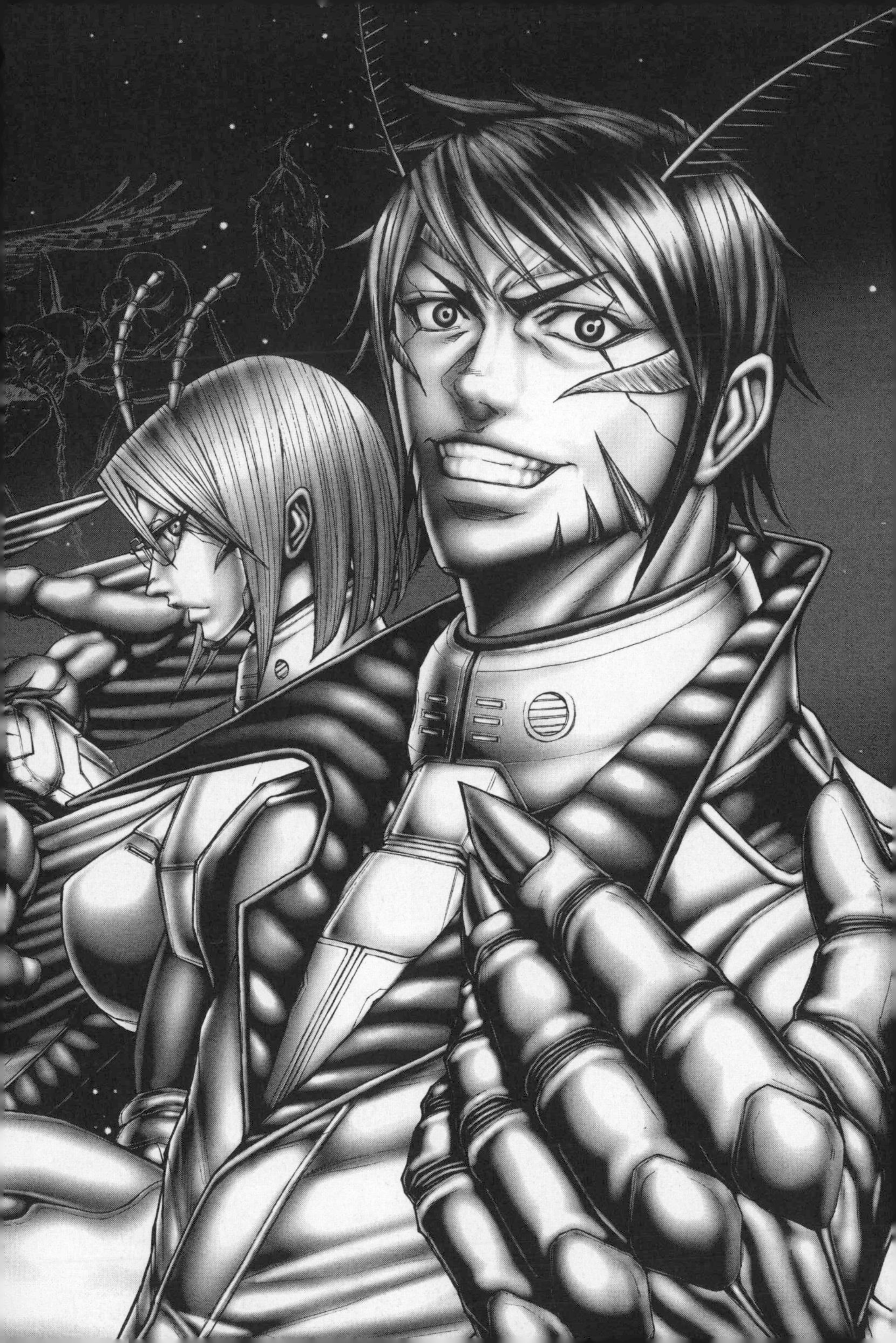

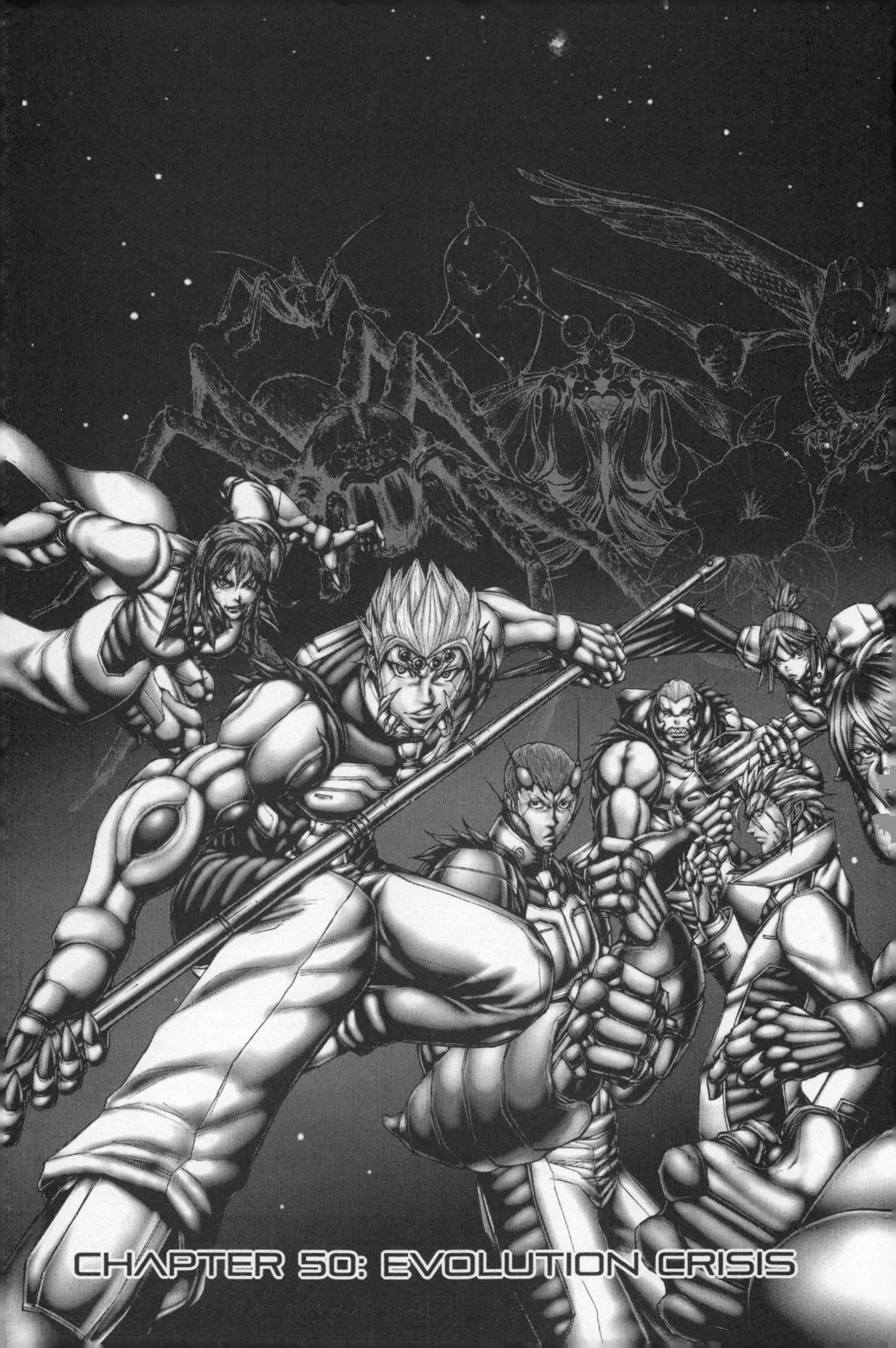
CHAPTER 50: EVOLUTION CRISIS

TERRA
FORMARS

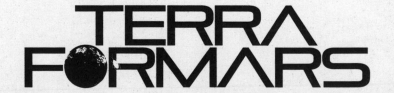

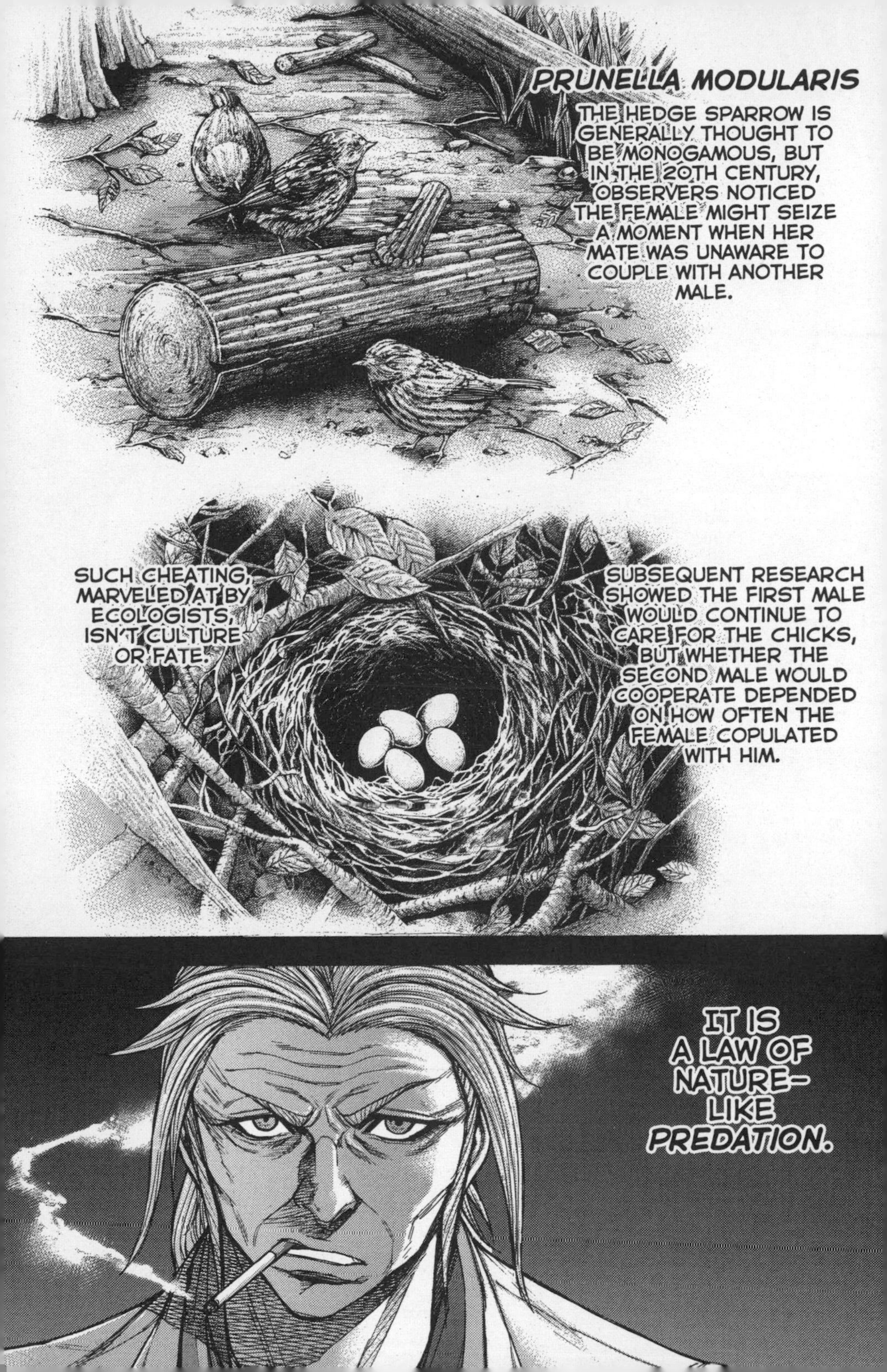
PRUNELLA MODULARIS
THE HEDGE SPARROW IS GENERALLY THOUGHT TO BE MONOGAMOUS, BUT IN THE 20TH CENTURY, OBSERVERS NOTICED THE FEMALE MIGHT SEIZE A MOMENT WHEN HER MATE WAS UNAWARE TO COUPLE WITH ANOTHER MALE.
SUBSEQUENT RESEARCH SHOWED THE FIRST MALE WOULD CONTINUE TO CARE FOR THE CHICKS, BUT WHETHER THE SECOND MALE WOULD COOPERATE DEPENDED ON HOW OFTEN THE FEMALE COPULATED WITH HIM.
SUCH CHEATING, MARVELED AT BY ECOLOGISTS, ISN'T CULTURE OR FATE.
IT IS A LAW OF NATURE– LIKE PREDATION.

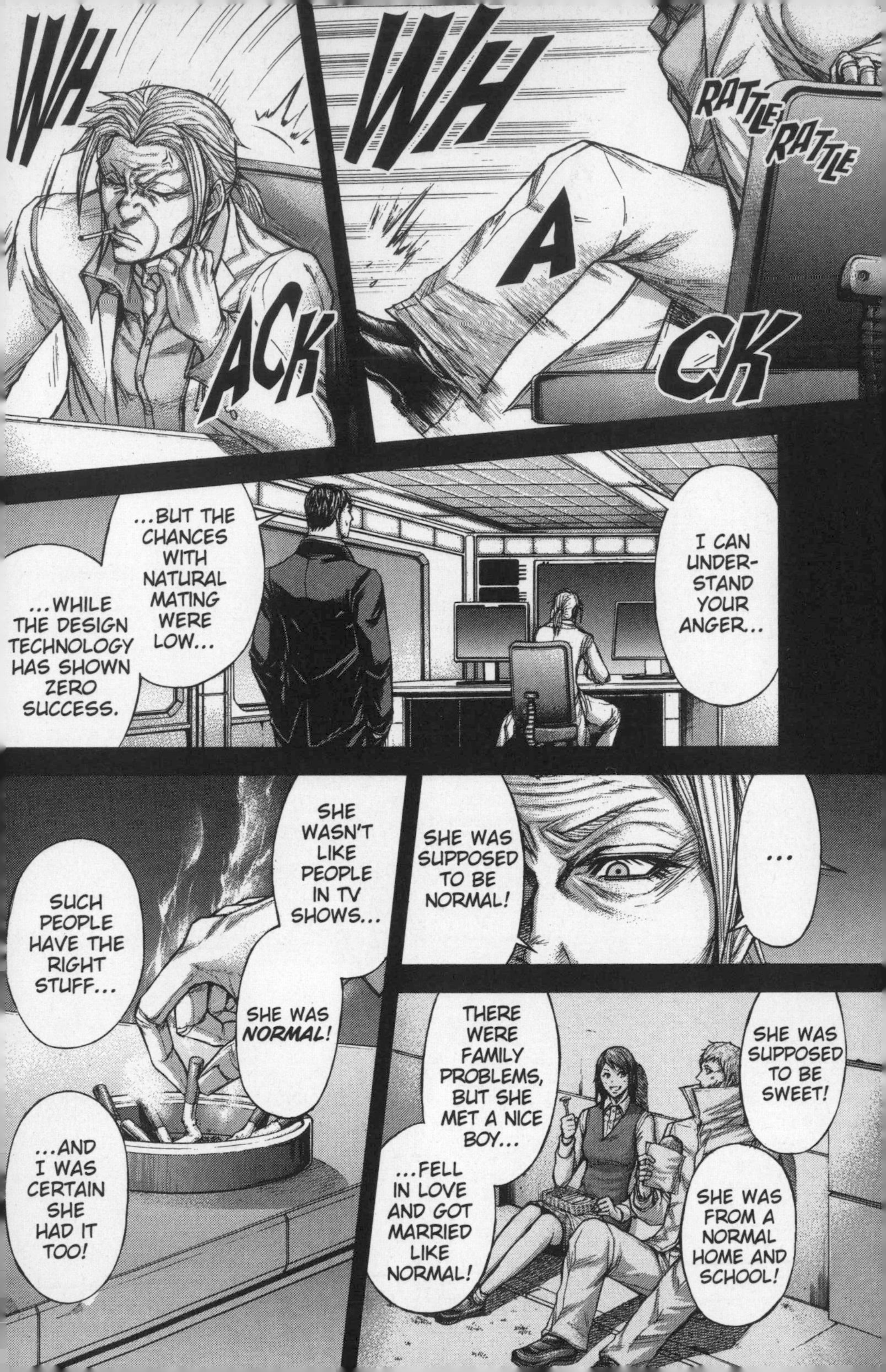
WH
A
CK
RATTLE RATTLE
WH
ACK
I CAN UNDERSTAND YOUR ANGER...
...BUT THE CHANCES WITH NATURAL MATING WERE LOW...
...WHILE THE DESIGN TECHNOLOGY HAS SHOWN ZERO SUCCESS.
...
SHE WAS SUPPOSED TO BE NORMAL!
SHE WAS SUPPOSED TO BE SWEET!
THERE WERE FAMILY PROBLEMS, BUT SHE MET A NICE BOY...
SHE WAS FROM A NORMAL HOME AND SCHOOL!
...FELL IN LOVE AND GOT MARRIED LIKE NORMAL!
SHE WASN'T LIKE PEOPLE IN TV SHOWS...
SUCH PEOPLE HAVE THE RIGHT STUFF...
SHE WAS *NORMAL*!
...AND I WAS CERTAIN SHE HAD IT TOO!

THE NECESSARY ELEMENT THAT CREATED *THE FIRST!*

CHAPTER 50: EVOLUTION CRISIS

JARED ...

...DO IT!

L-LIEU-TENANT?

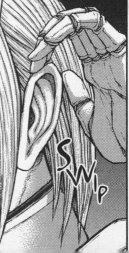

SWIP

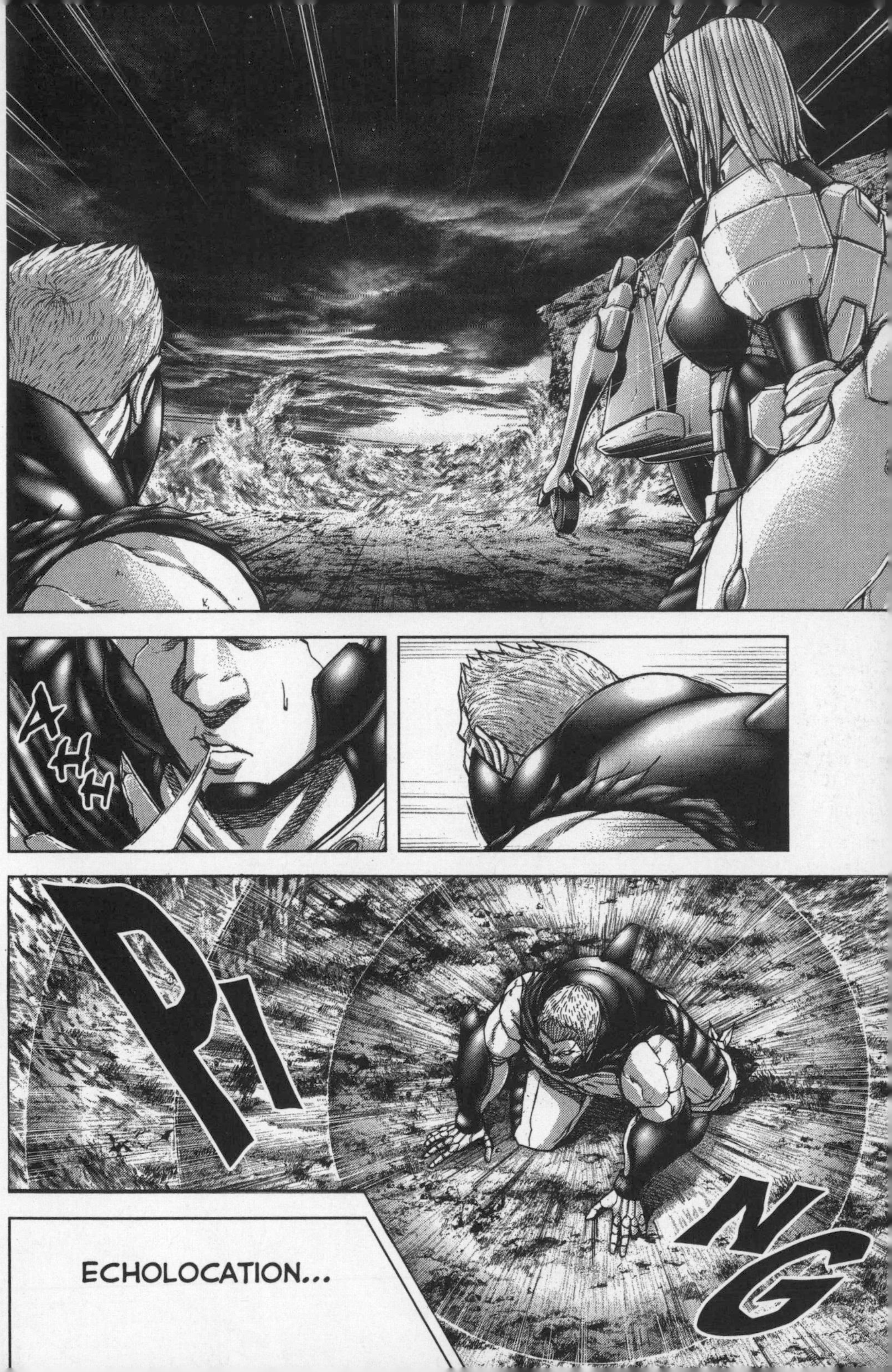
AHHH
PING
ECHOLOCATION...

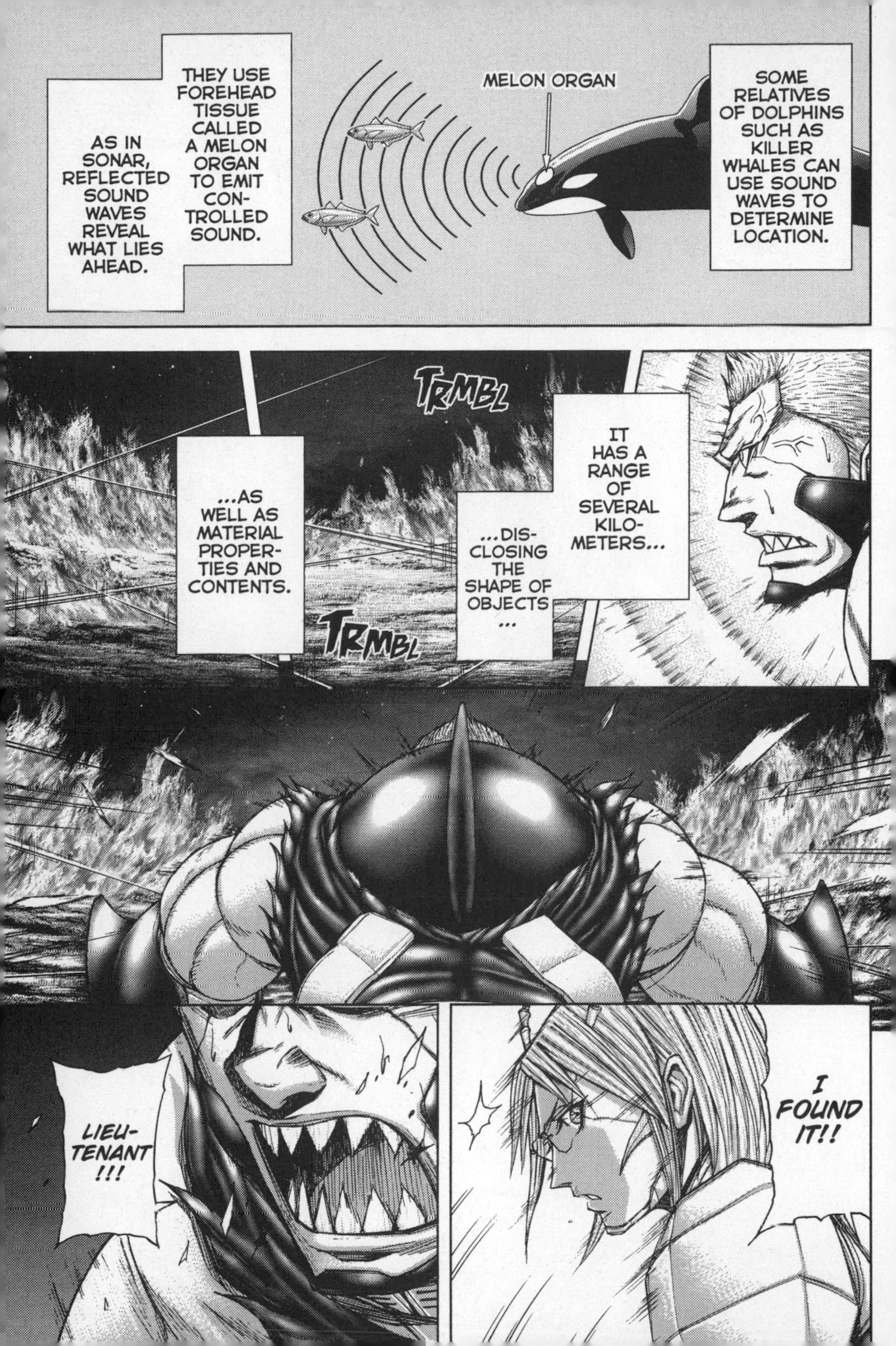

SOME RELATIVES OF DOLPHINS SUCH AS KILLER WHALES CAN USE SOUND WAVES TO DETERMINE LOCATION.
MELON ORGAN
THEY USE FOREHEAD TISSUE CALLED A MELON ORGAN TO EMIT CONTROLLED SOUND.
AS IN SONAR, REFLECTED SOUND WAVES REVEAL WHAT LIES AHEAD.
IT HAS A RANGE OF SEVERAL KILOMETERS...
TRMBL
...DISCLOSING THE SHAPE OF OBJECTS...
...AS WELL AS MATERIAL PROPERTIES AND CONTENTS.
TRMBL
I FOUND IT!!
LIEUTENANT!!!

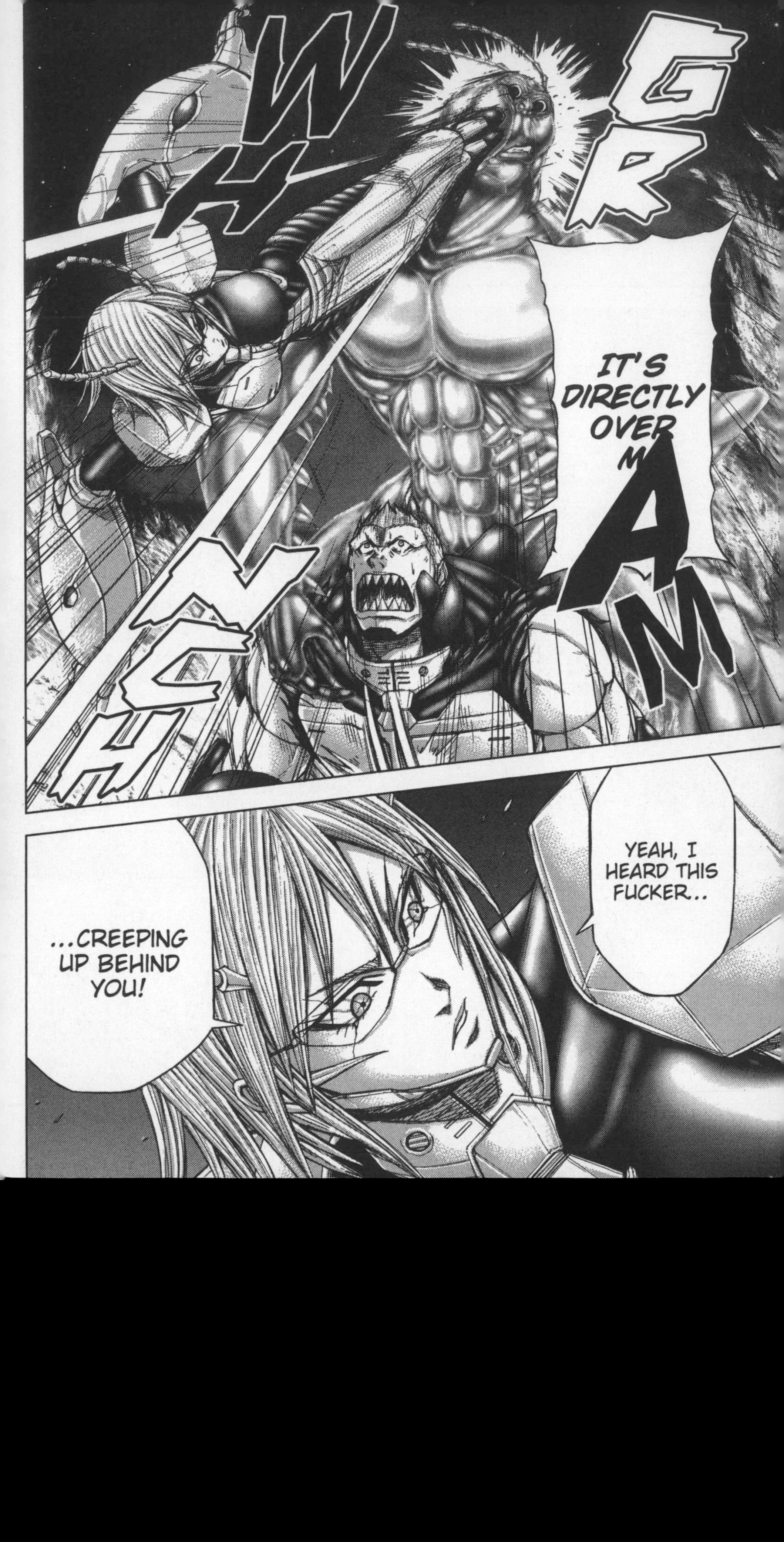
GR
IT'S DIRECTLY OVER M
WH
AM
NCH
YEAH, I HEARD THIS FUCKER...
...CREEPING UP BEHIND YOU!

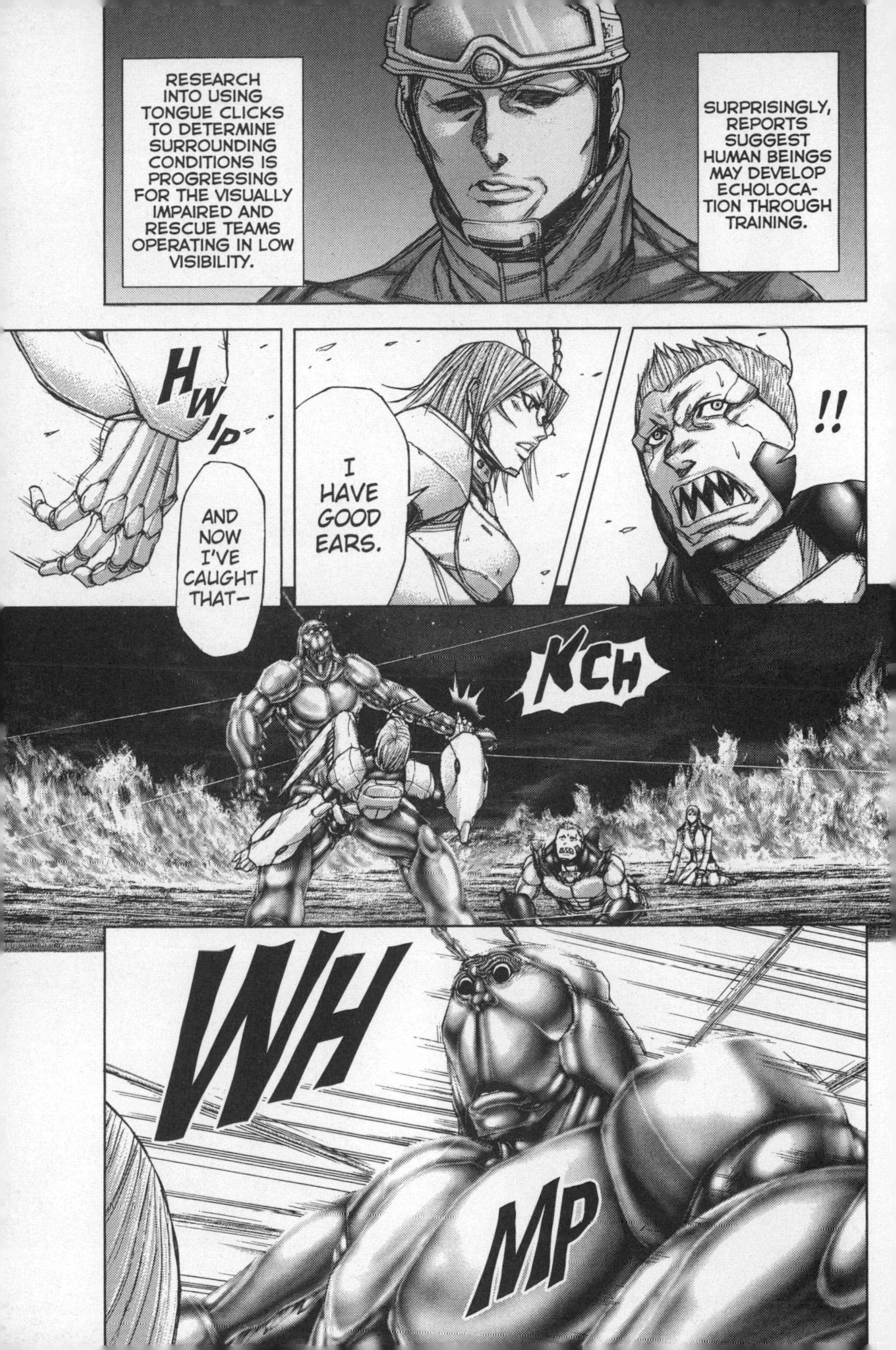
SURPRISINGLY, REPORTS SUGGEST HUMAN BEINGS MAY DEVELOP ECHOLOCATION THROUGH TRAINING.
RESEARCH INTO USING TONGUE CLICKS TO DETERMINE SURROUNDING CONDITIONS IS PROGRESSING FOR THE VISUALLY IMPAIRED AND RESCUE TEAMS OPERATING IN LOW VISIBILITY.
!!
I HAVE GOOD EARS.
HWIP
AND NOW I'VE CAUGHT THAT—
KCH
WHMP

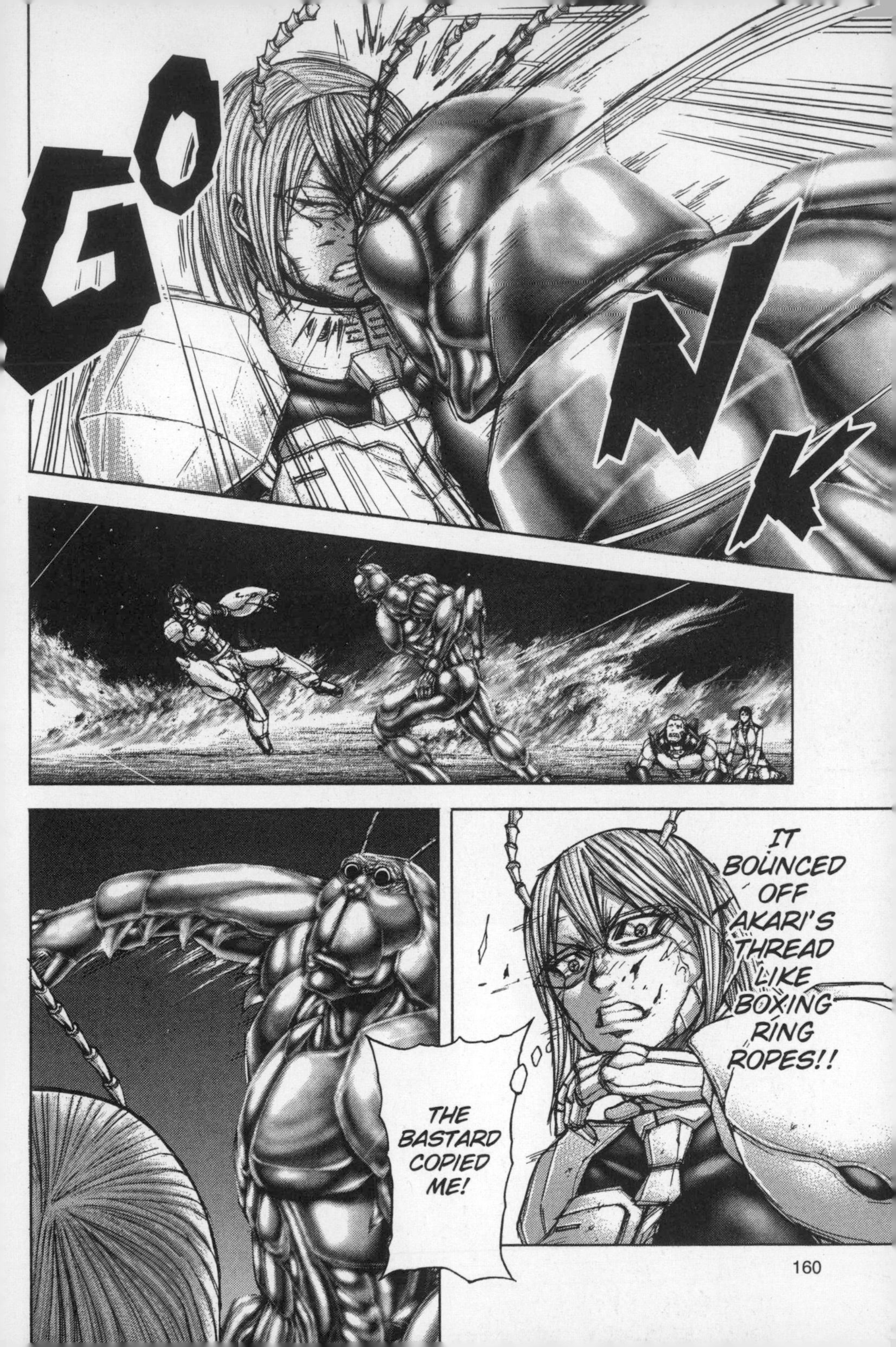
GONK
IT BOUNCED OFF AKARI'S THREAD LIKE BOXING RING ROPES!!
THE BASTARD COPIED ME!

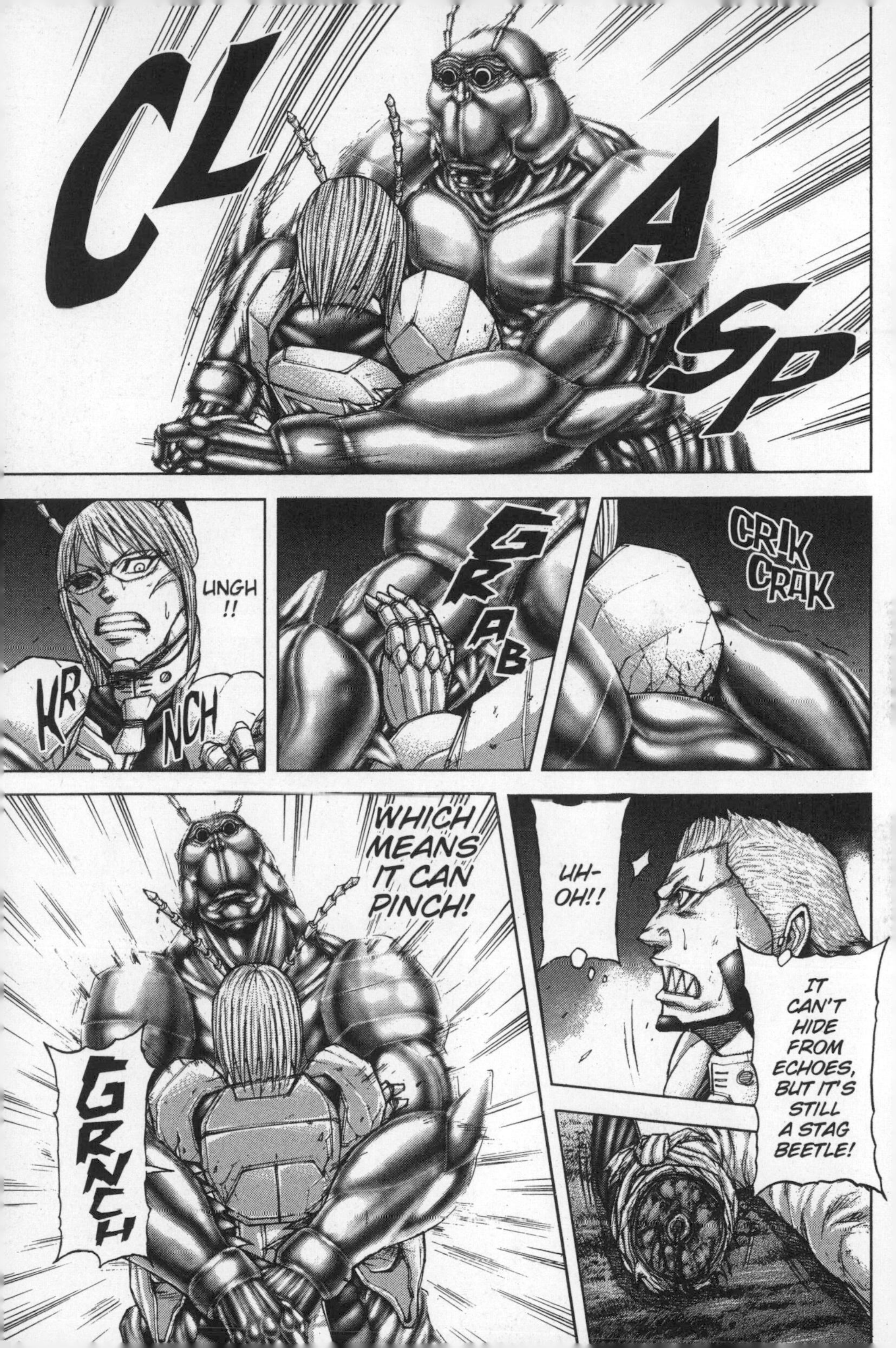
CLASP
CRIK CRAK
GRAB
UNGH!!
KRNCH
UH-OH!!
IT CAN'T HIDE FROM ECHOES, BUT IT'S STILL A STAG BEETLE!
WHICH MEANS IT CAN PINCH!
GRNCH

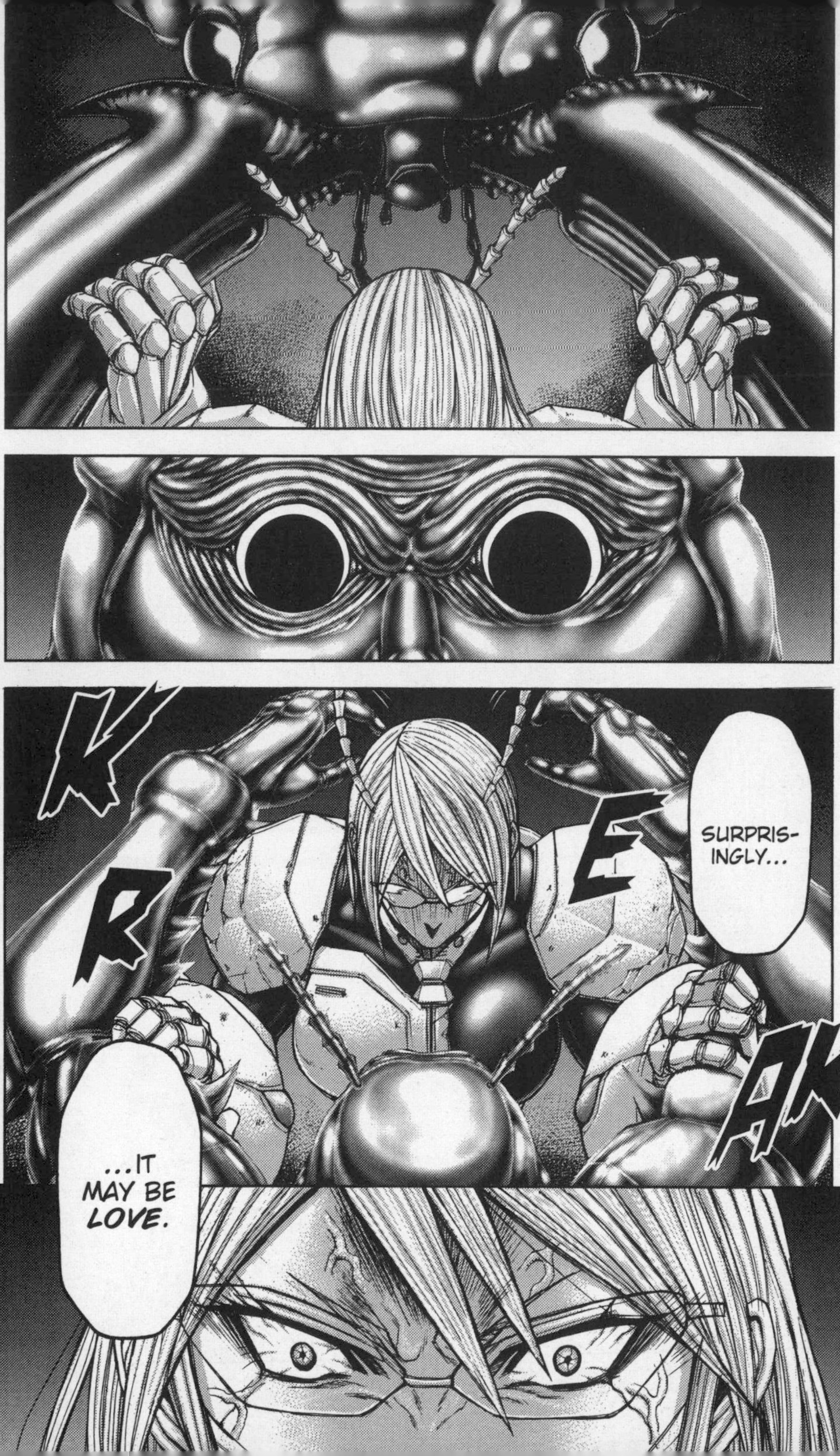
KREAK
SURPRIS-INGLY...
...IT MAY BE LOVE.

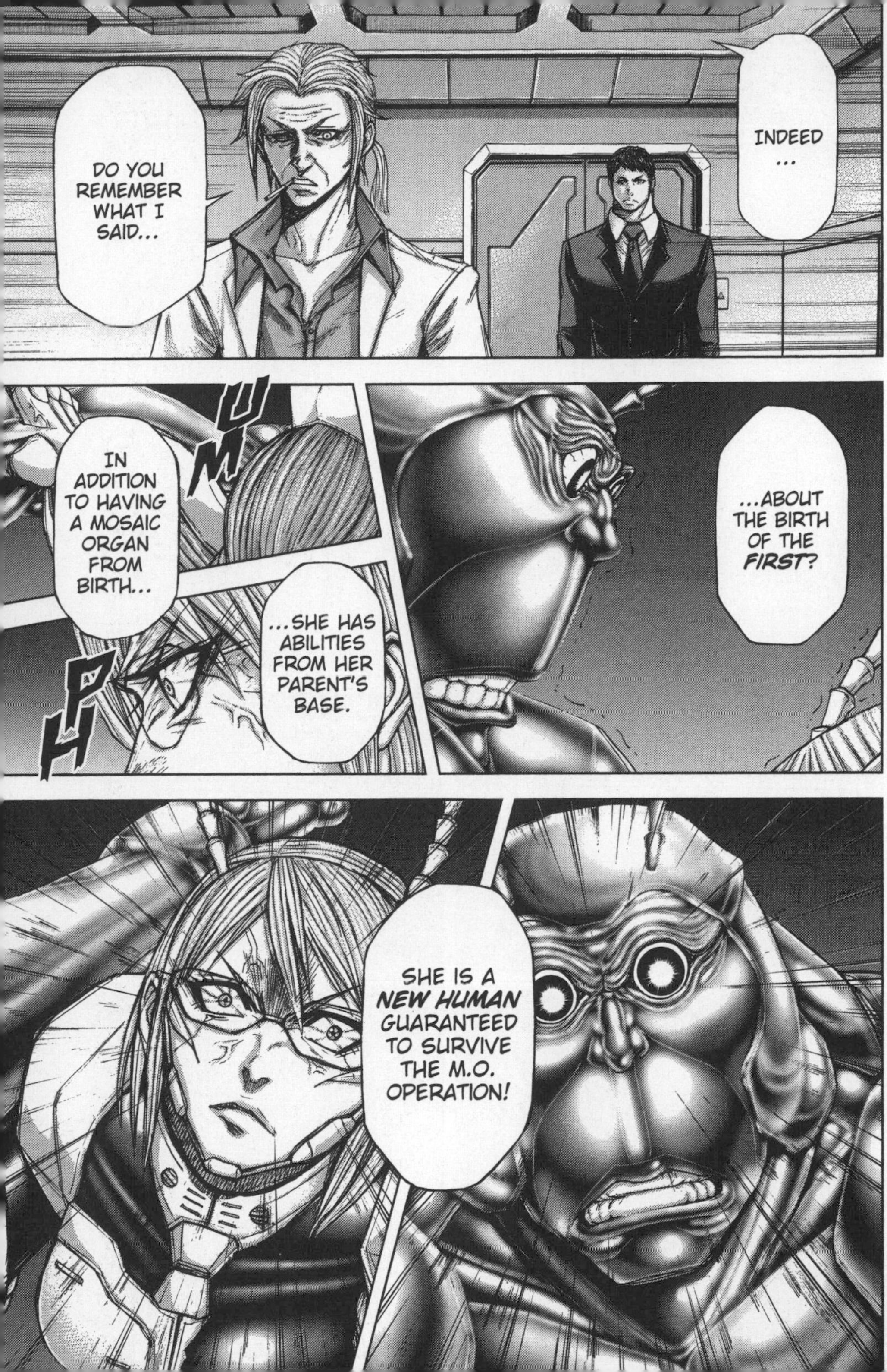
INDEED ...
DO YOU REMEMBER WHAT I SAID...
...ABOUT THE BIRTH OF THE *FIRST*?
IN ADDITION TO HAVING A MOSAIC ORGAN FROM BIRTH...
...SHE HAS ABILITIES FROM HER PARENT'S BASE.
SHE IS A ***NEW HUMAN*** GUARANTEED TO SURVIVE THE M.O. OPERATION!

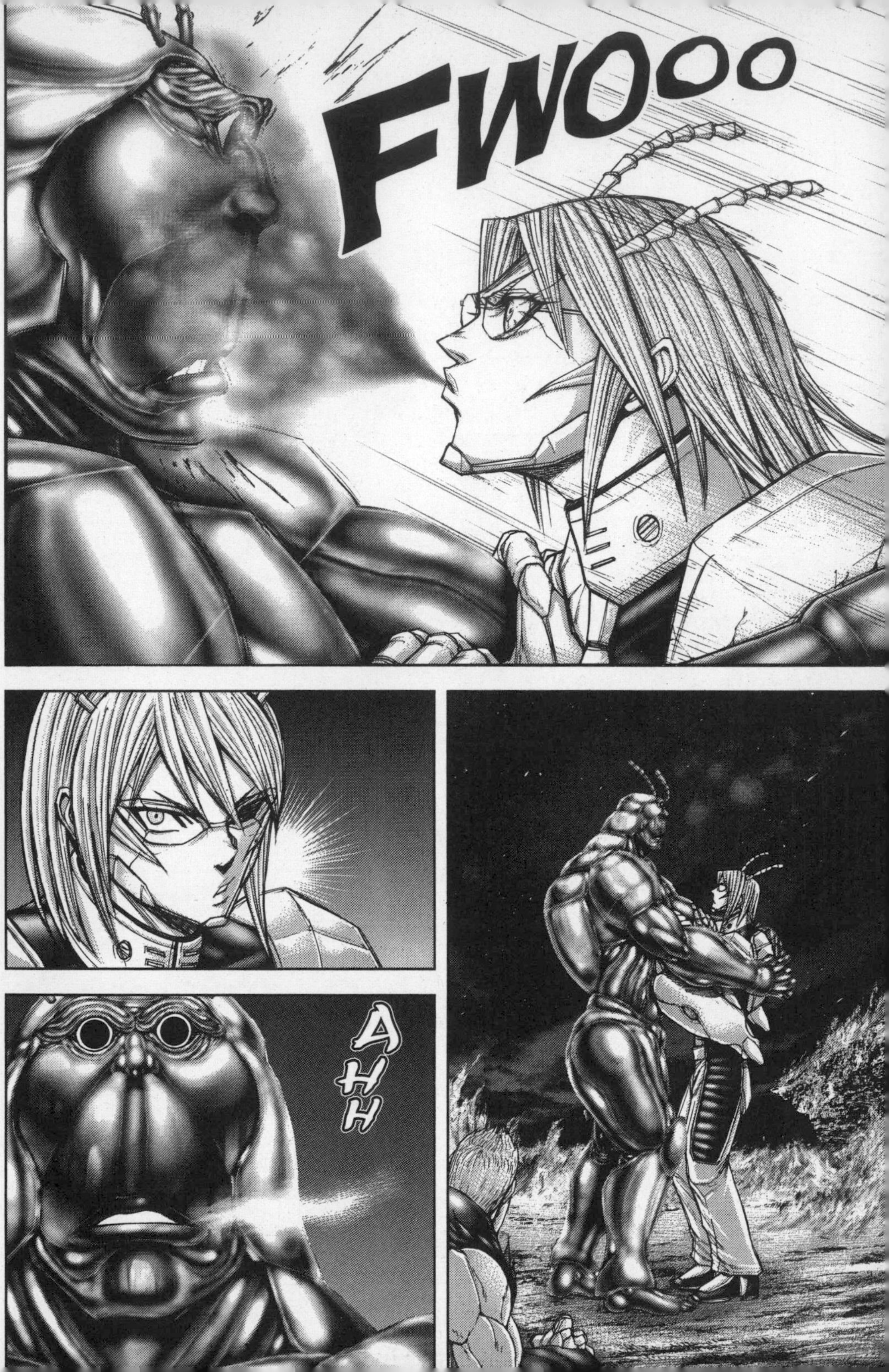
FWOOO
AHH

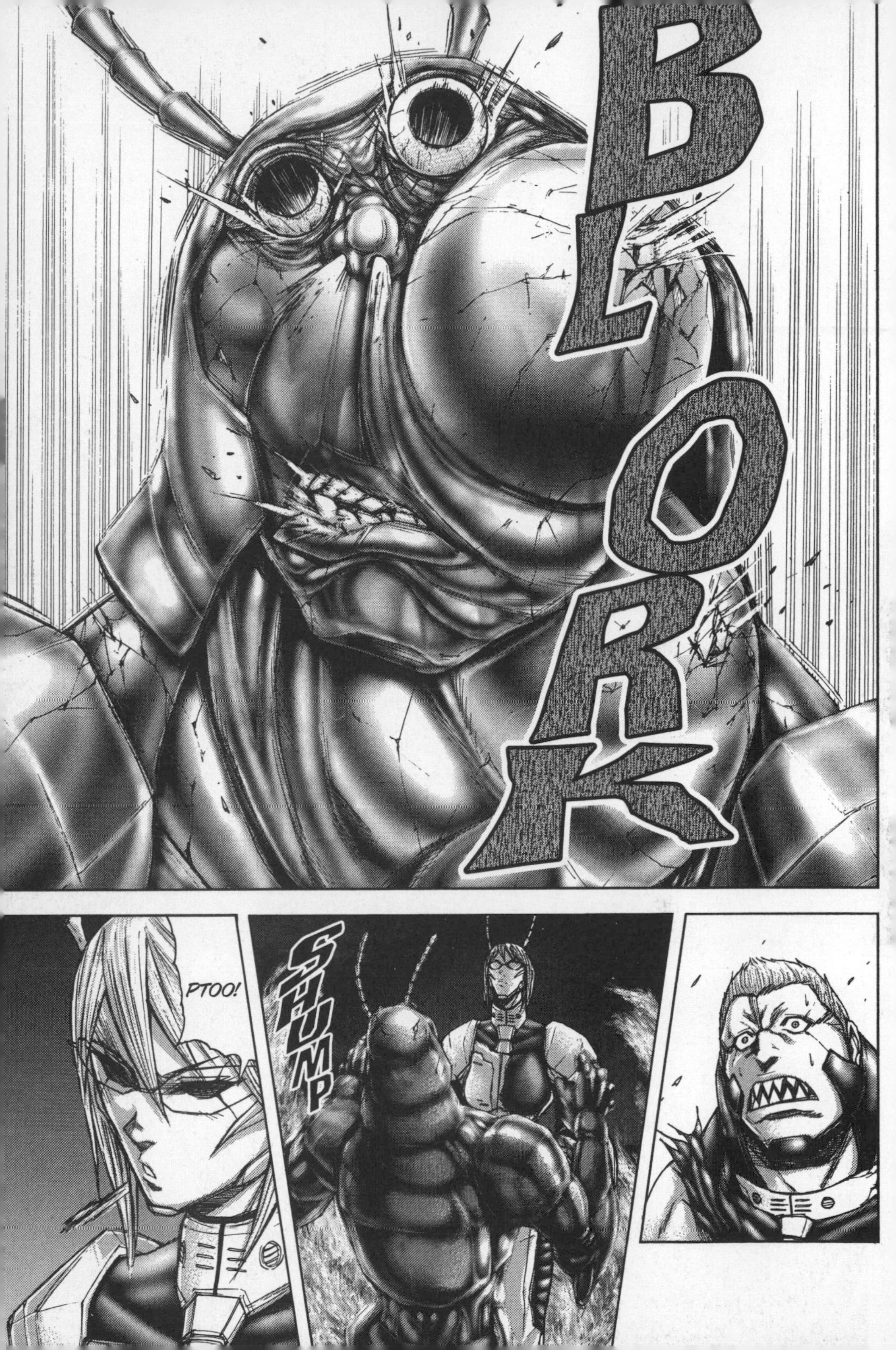
BLORK
SHUMP
PTOO!

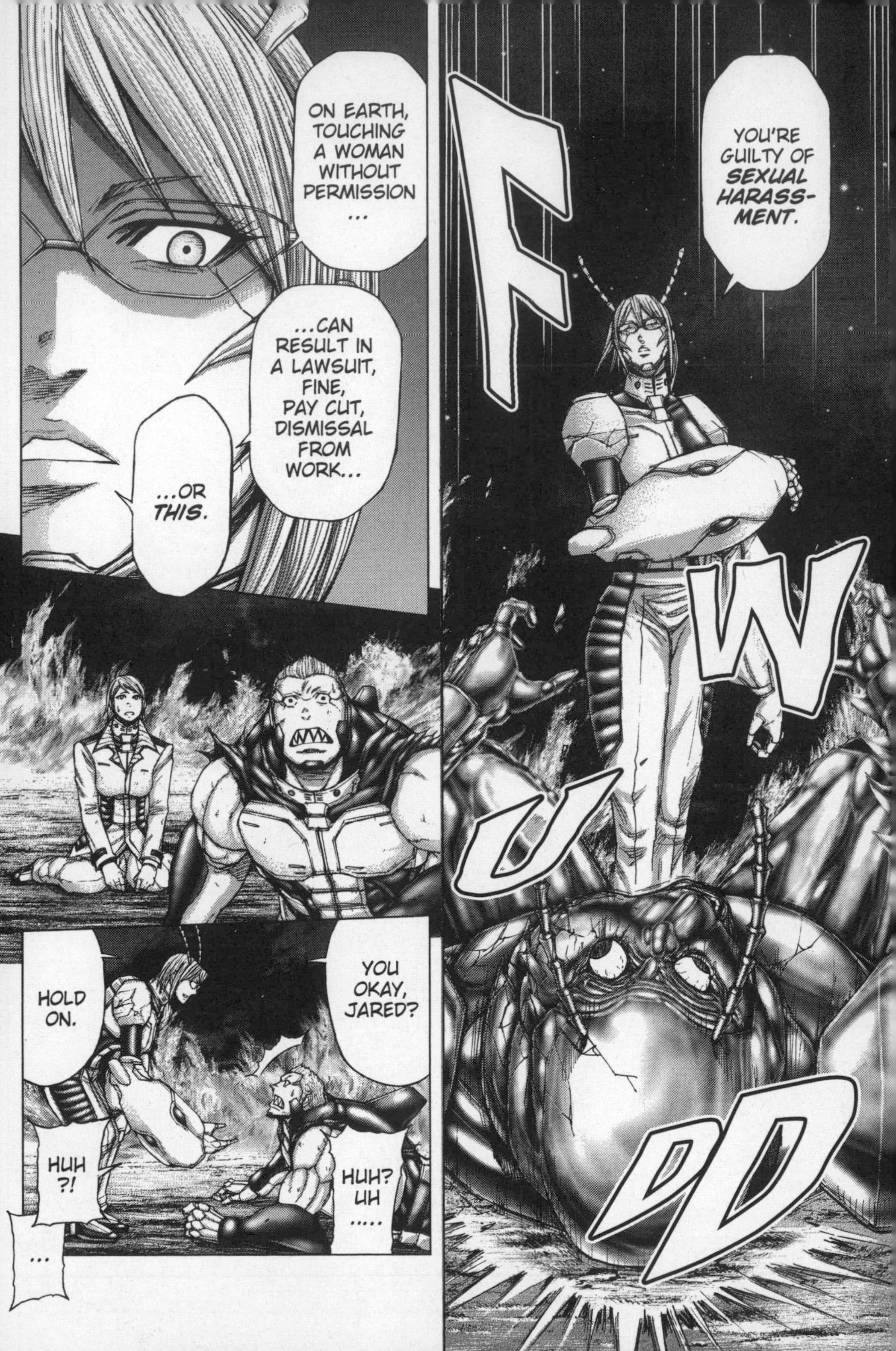
YOU'RE GUILTY OF *SEXUAL HARASSMENT*.
FWUDD
ON EARTH, TOUCHING A WOMAN WITHOUT PERMISSION ...
...CAN RESULT IN A LAWSUIT, FINE, PAY CUT, DISMISSAL FROM WORK...
...OR *THIS*.
YOU OKAY, JARED?
HOLD ON.
HUH? UH .....
HUH ?!
...

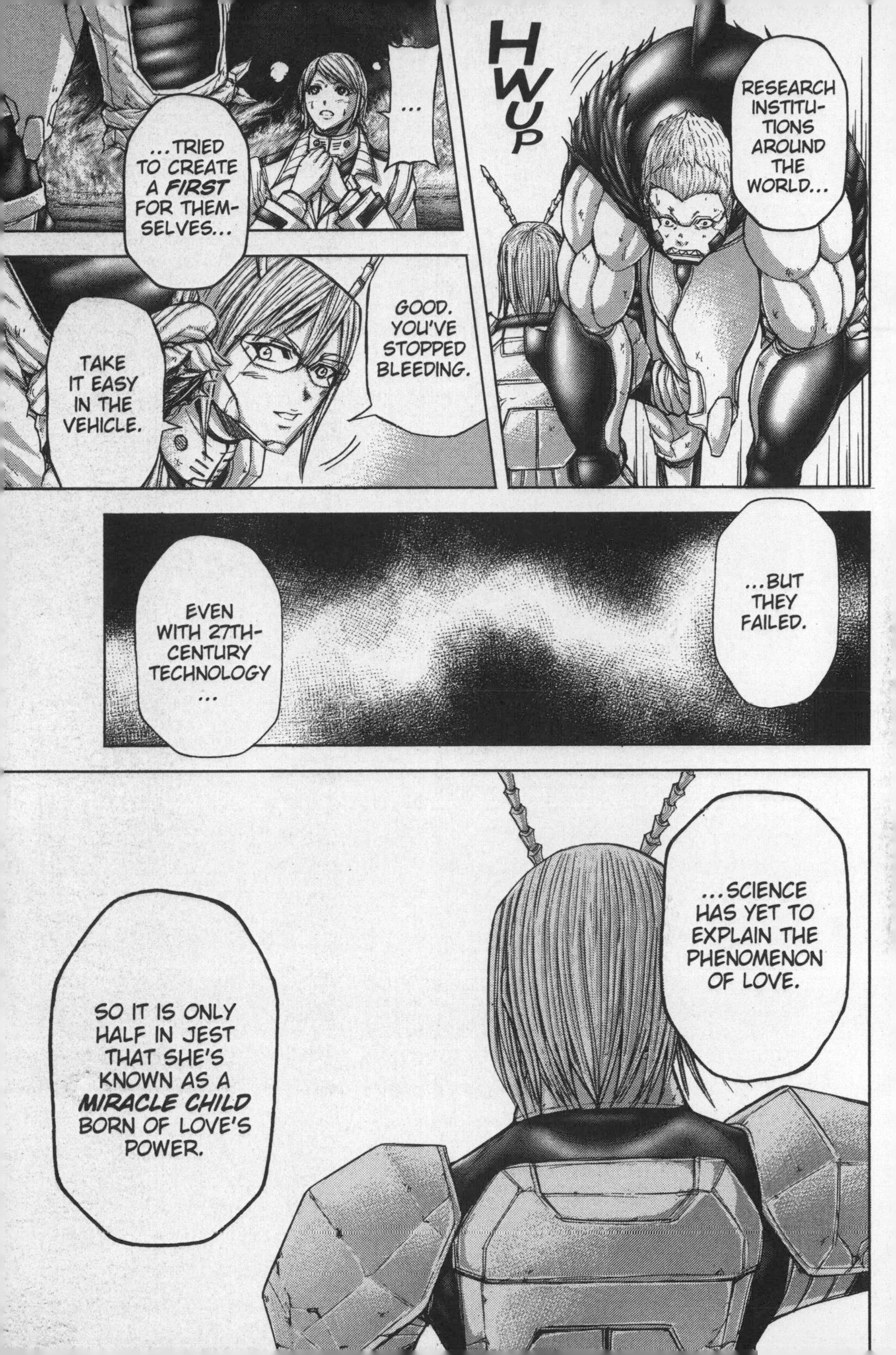
HWUP
RESEARCH INSTITUTIONS AROUND THE WORLD...
...
...TRIED TO CREATE A *FIRST* FOR THEMSELVES...
GOOD. YOU'VE STOPPED BLEEDING.
TAKE IT EASY IN THE VEHICLE.
...BUT THEY FAILED.
EVEN WITH 27TH-CENTURY TECHNOLOGY...
...SCIENCE HAS YET TO EXPLAIN THE PHENOMENON OF LOVE.
SO IT IS ONLY HALF IN JEST THAT SHE'S KNOWN AS A ***MIRACLE CHILD*** BORN OF LOVE'S POWER.

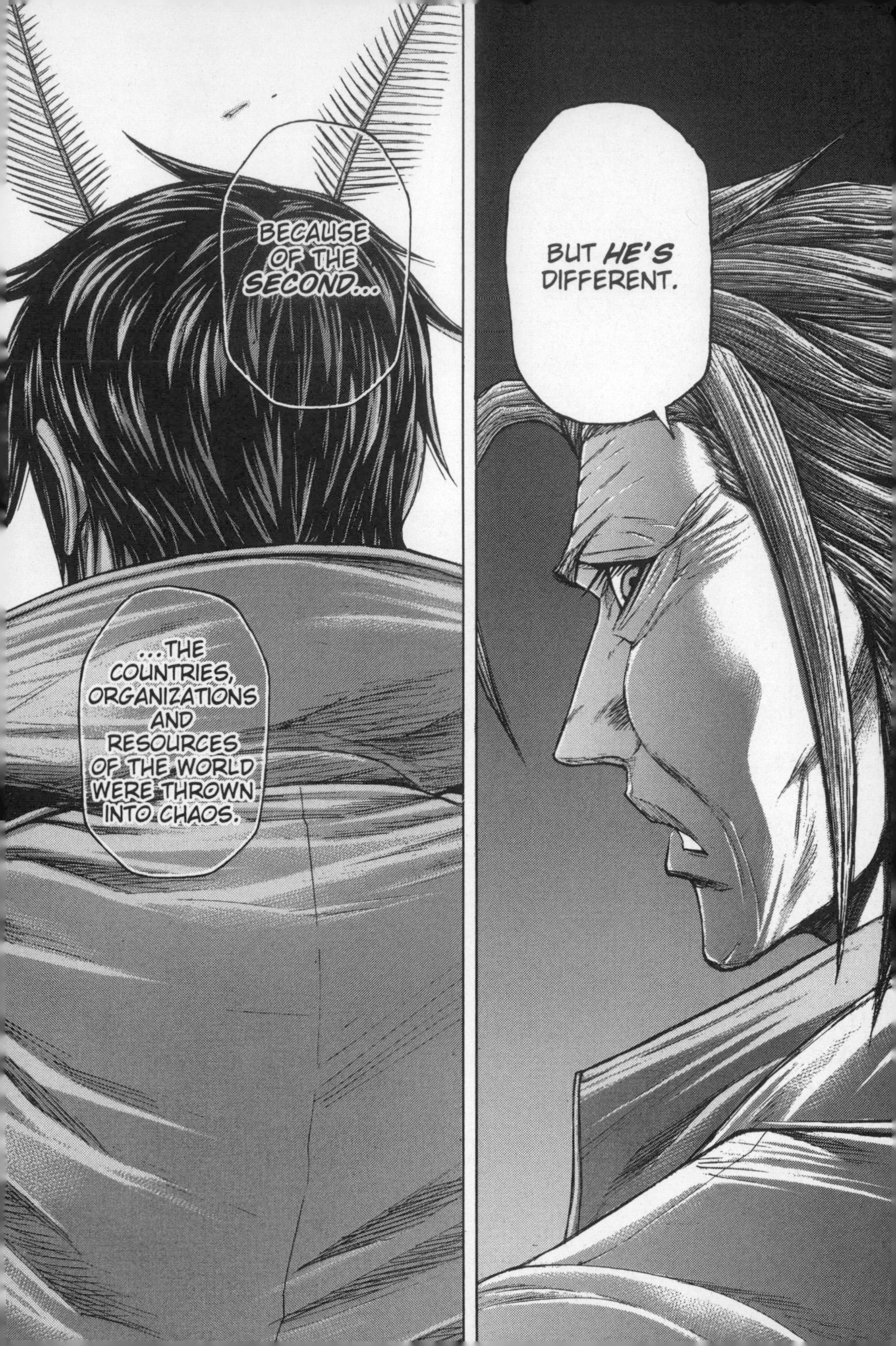
BUT HE'S DIFFERENT.
BECAUSE OF THE SECOND...
...THE COUNTRIES, ORGANIZATIONS AND RESOURCES OF THE WORLD WERE THROWN INTO CHAOS.

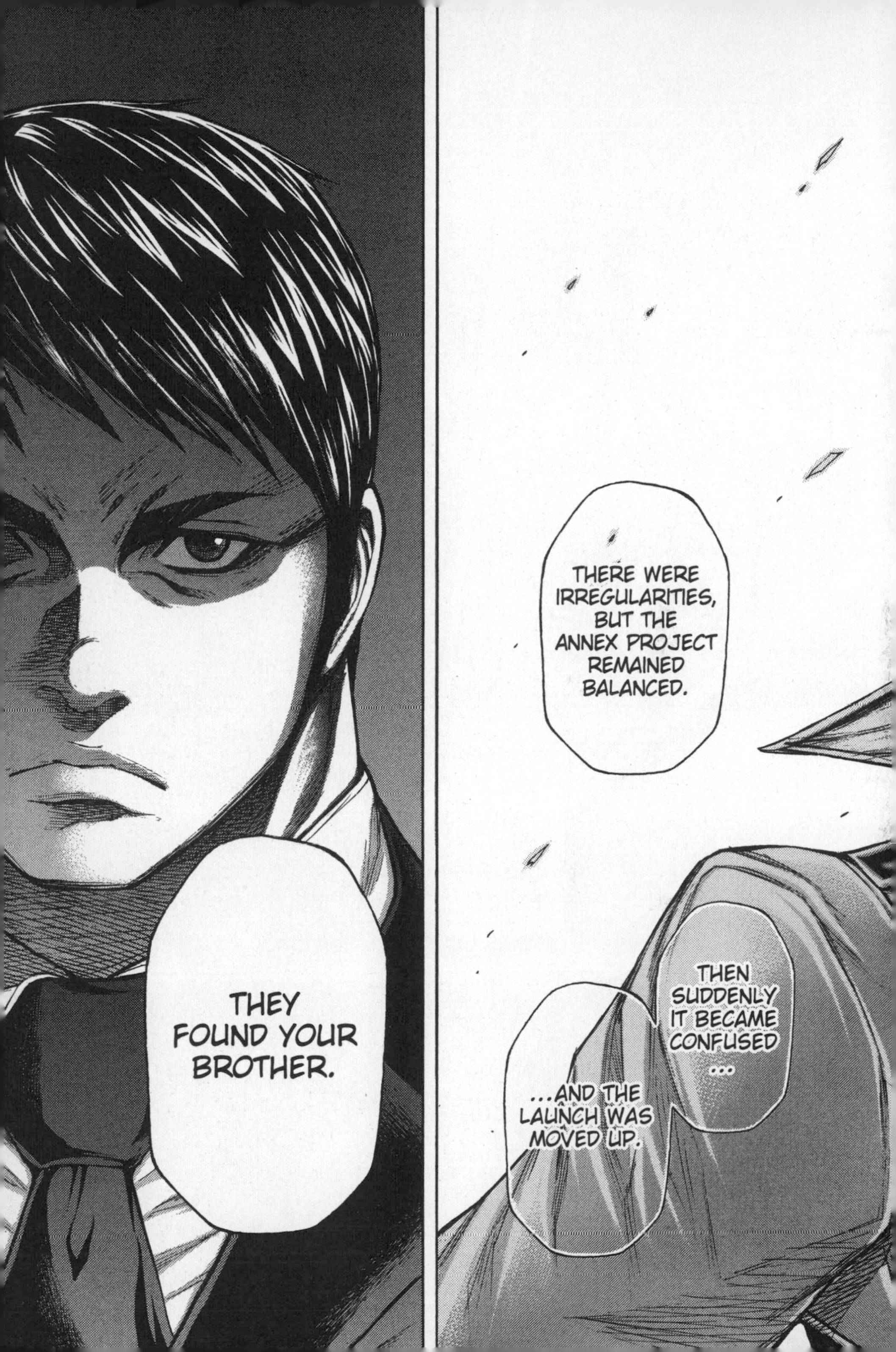
THERE WERE IRREGULARITIES, BUT THE ANNEX PROJECT REMAINED BALANCED.
THEN SUDDENLY IT BECAME CONFUSED...
...AND THE LAUNCH WAS MOVED UP.
THEY FOUND YOUR BROTHER.

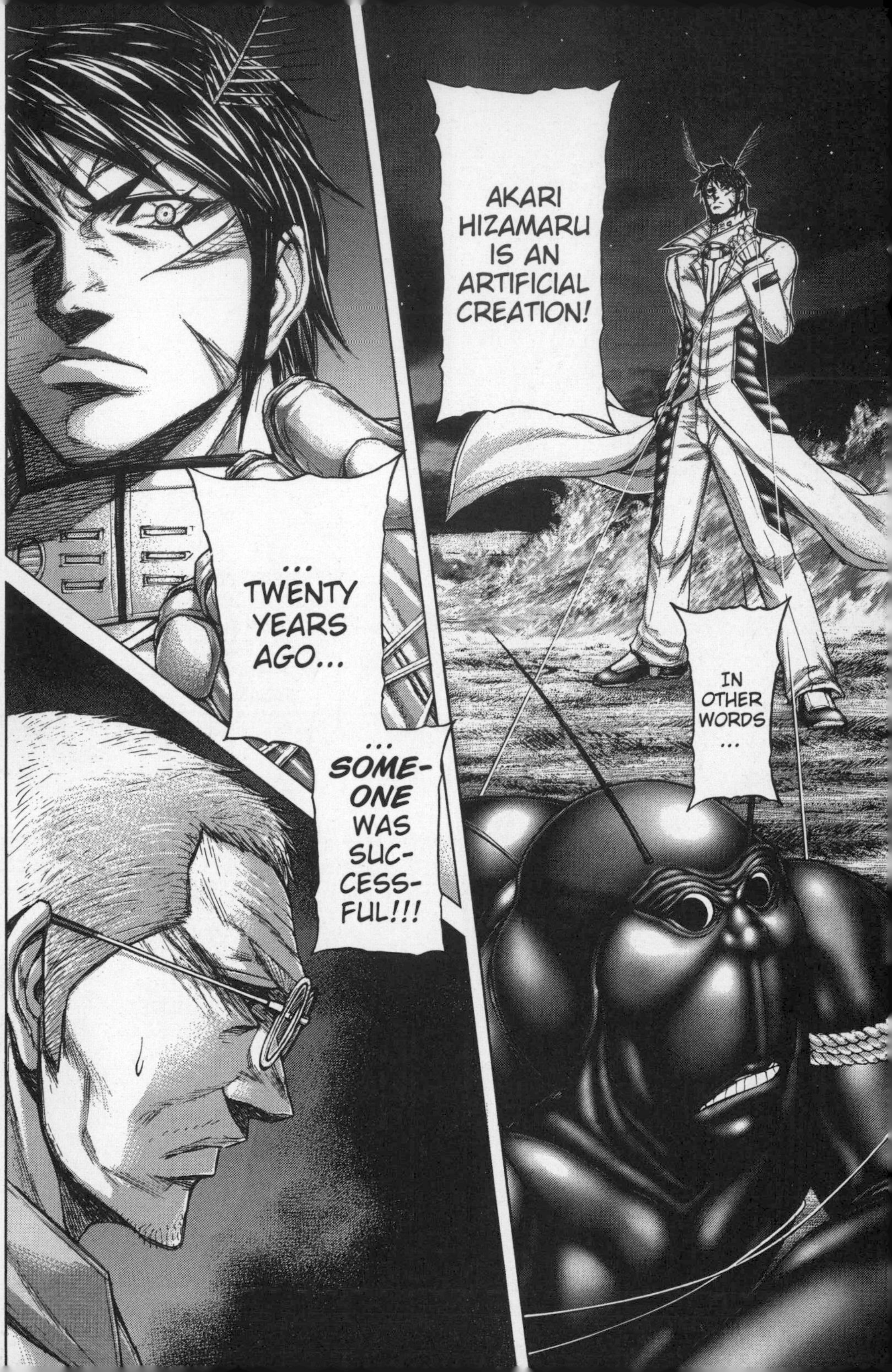
AKARI HIZAMARU IS AN ARTIFICIAL CREATION!
IN OTHER WORDS ...
... TWENTY YEARS AGO...
... SOME-ONE WAS SUC-CESS-FUL!!!

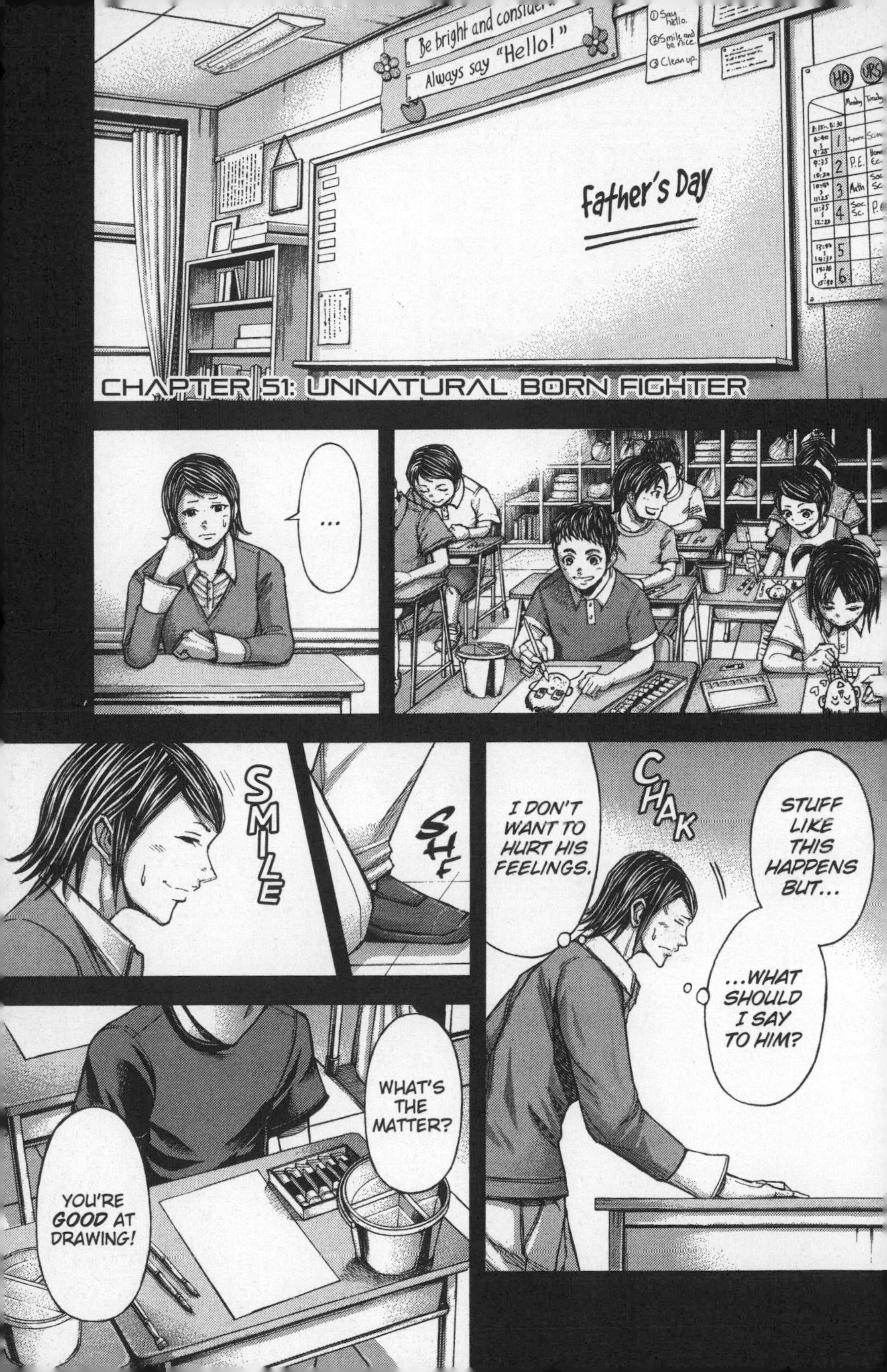
Be bright and consid
Always say "Hello!"
① Say hello.
② Smile and be nice.
③ Clean up.
Father's Day
CHAPTER 51: UNNATURAL BORN FIGHTER
...
CHAK
STUFF LIKE THIS HAPPENS BUT...
I DON'T WANT TO HURT HIS FEELINGS.
...WHAT SHOULD I SAY TO HIM?
SHF
SMILE
WHAT'S THE MATTER?
YOU'RE GOOD AT DRAWING!

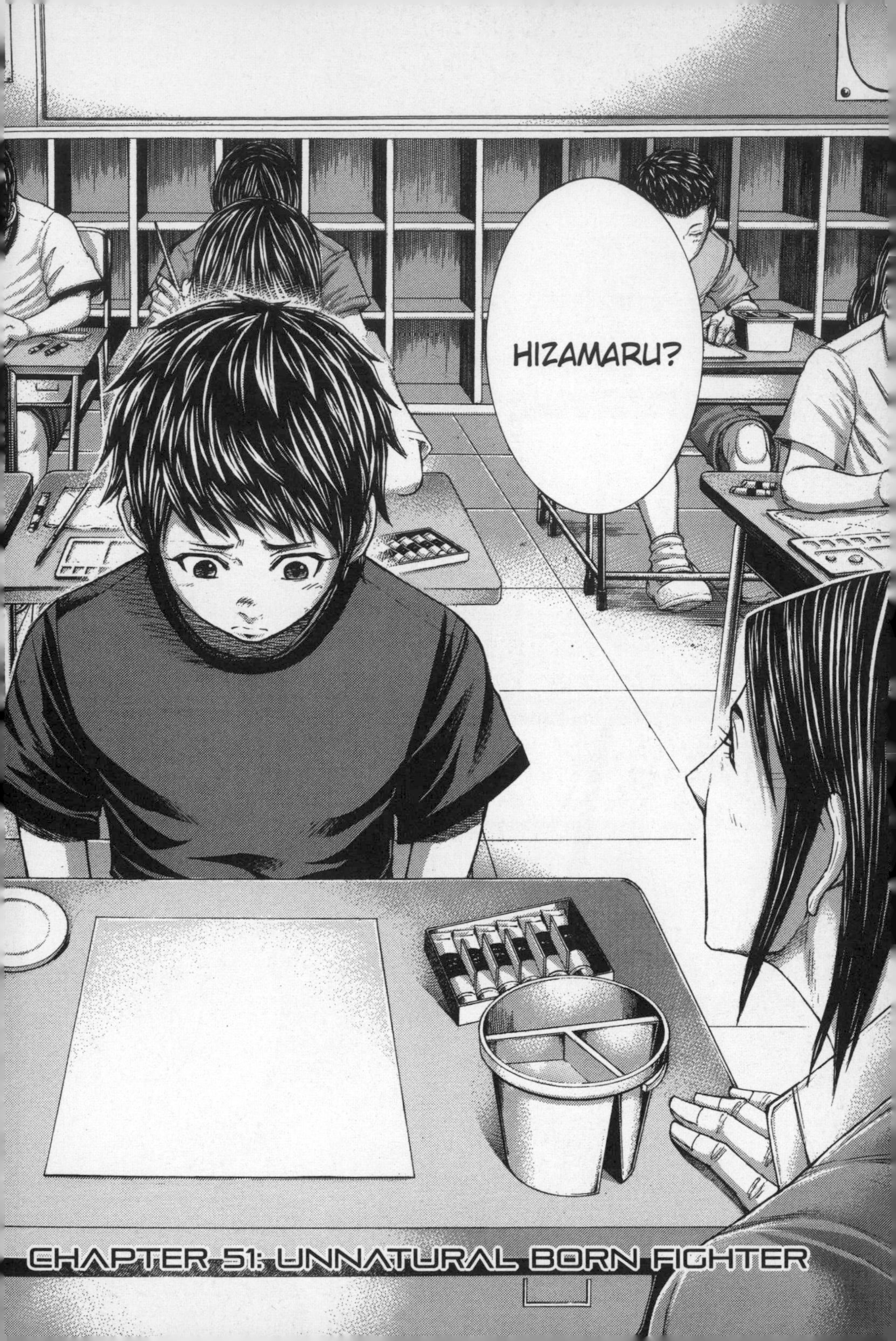
HIZAMARU?
CHAPTER 51: UNNATURAL BORN FIGHTER

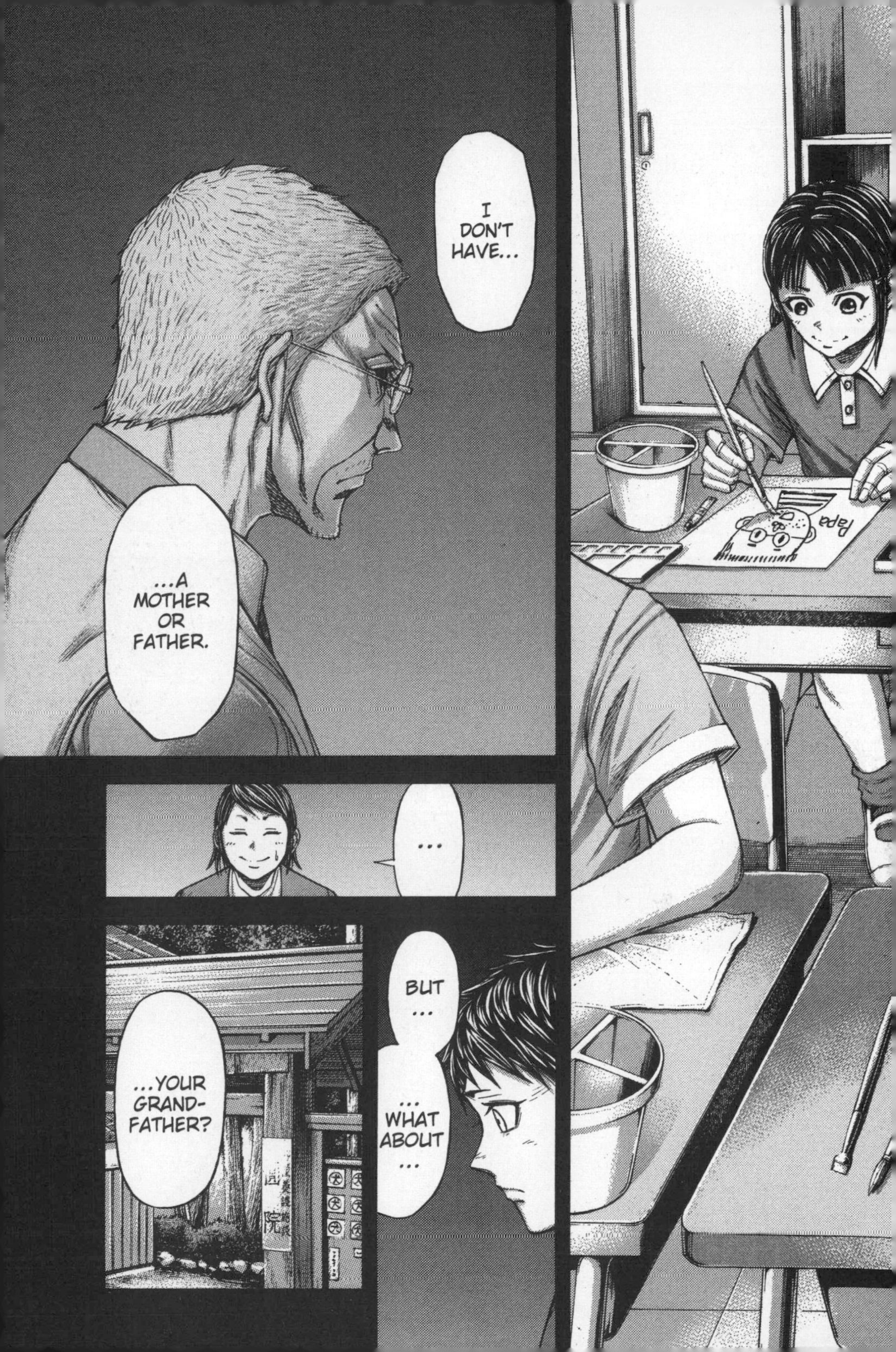
Papa
I DON'T HAVE...
...A MOTHER OR FATHER.
...
BUT ...
... WHAT ABOUT ...
...YOUR GRAND-FATHER?

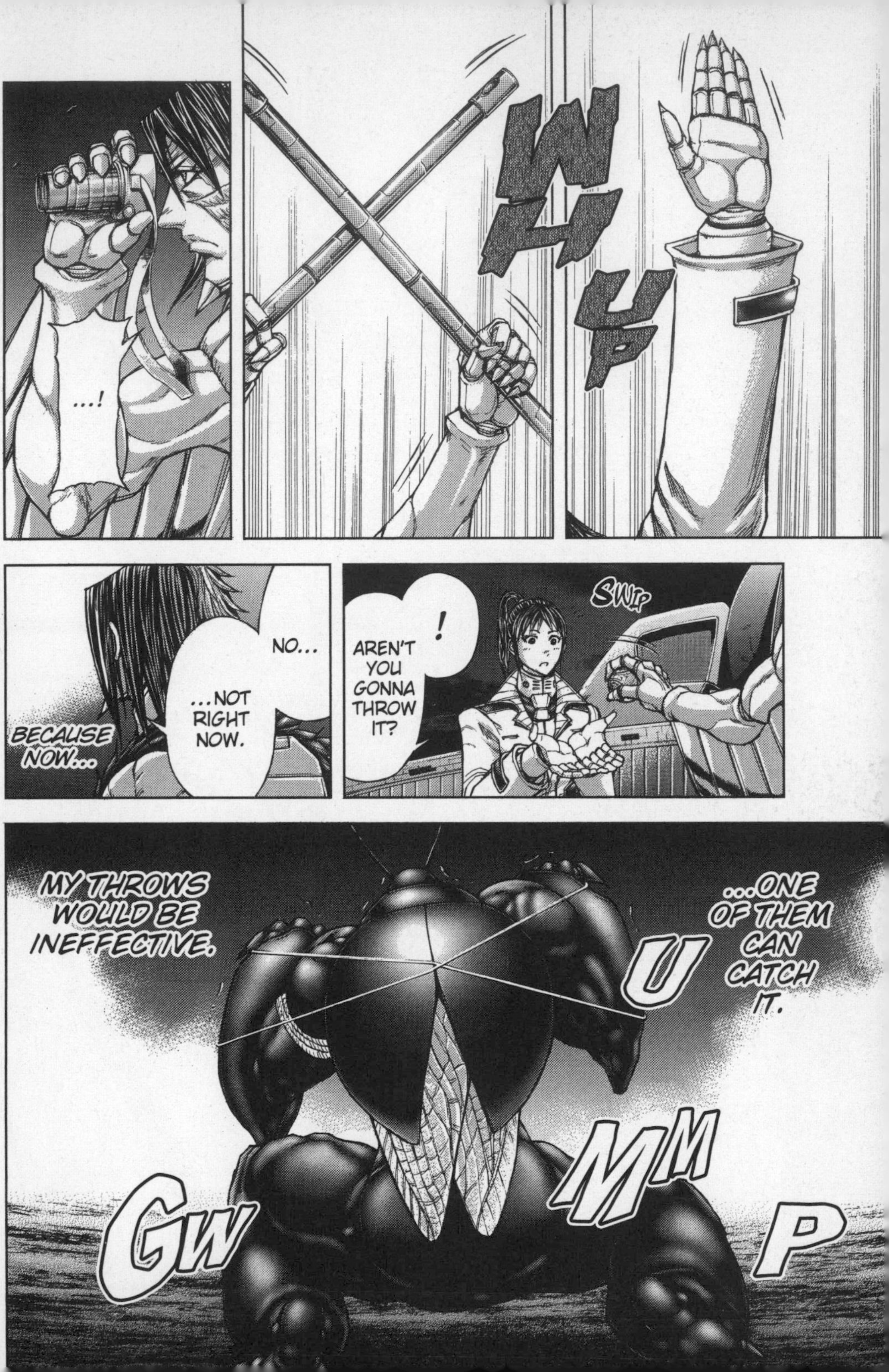
WHIP
...!
SWIP
!
AREN'T YOU GONNA THROW IT?
NO...
...NOT RIGHT NOW.
BECAUSE NOW...
...ONE OF THEM CAN CATCH IT.
MY THROWS WOULD BE INEFFECTIVE.
U
MM
P
GW

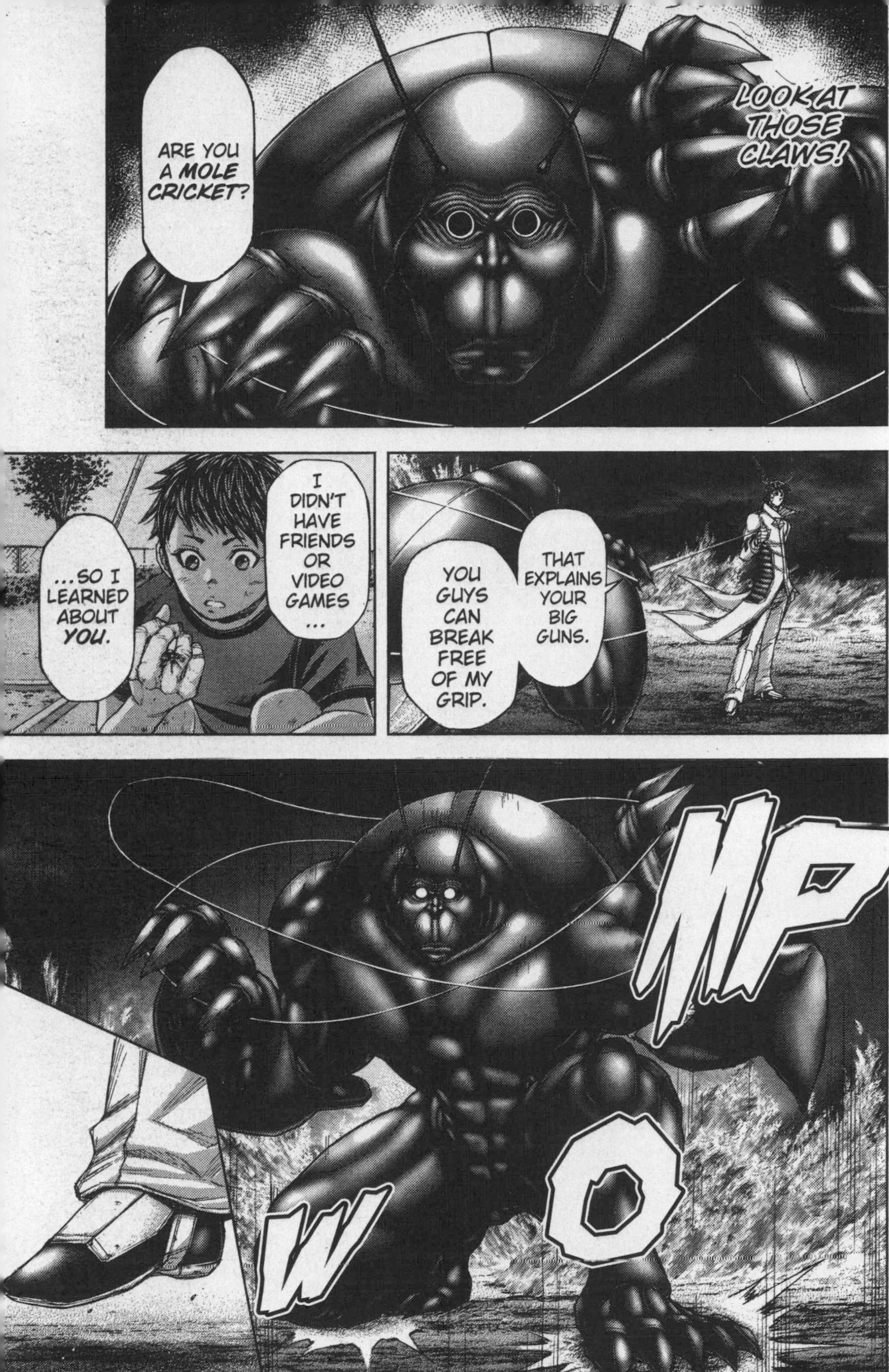
LOOK AT THOSE CLAWS!
ARE YOU A MOLE CRICKET?
THAT EXPLAINS YOUR BIG GUNS.
YOU GUYS CAN BREAK FREE OF MY GRIP.
I DIDN'T HAVE FRIENDS OR VIDEO GAMES...
...SO I LEARNED ABOUT YOU.
WOMP

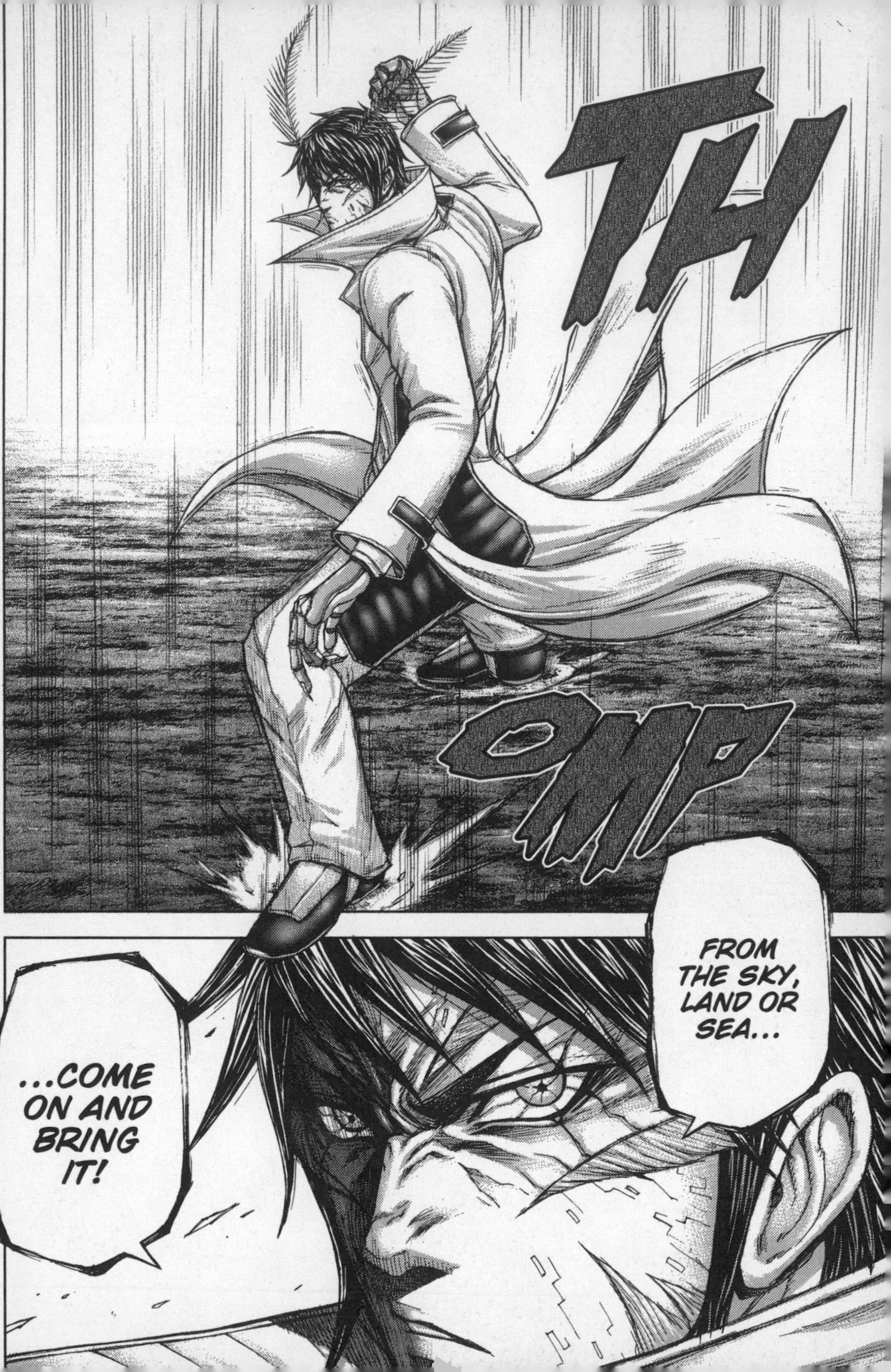
THOMP
FROM THE SKY, LAND OR SEA...
...COME ON AND BRING IT!

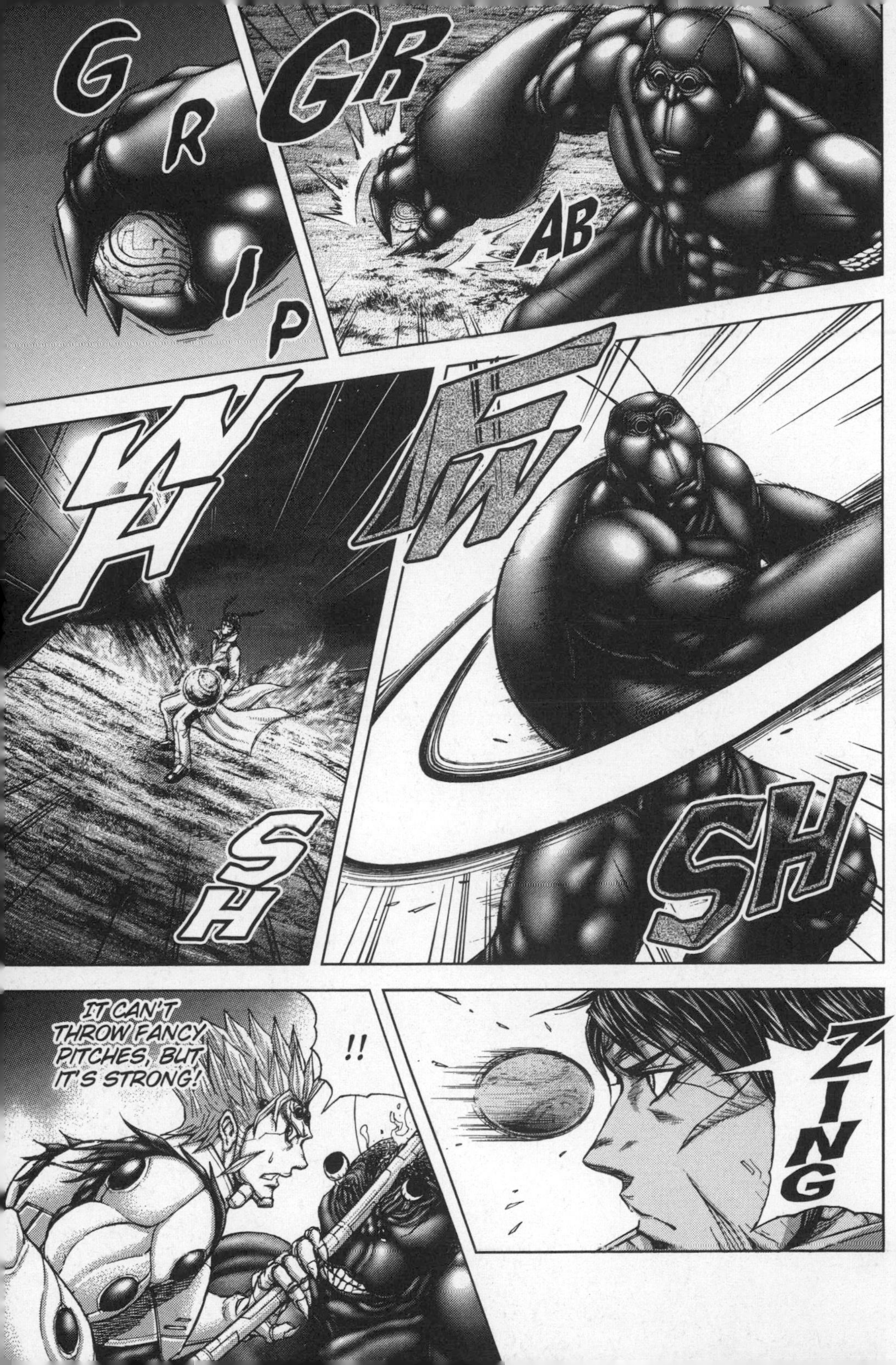
GRAB
GRIP
WSH
WHSH
ZING
IT CAN'T THROW FANCY PITCHES, BUT IT'S STRONG!
!!

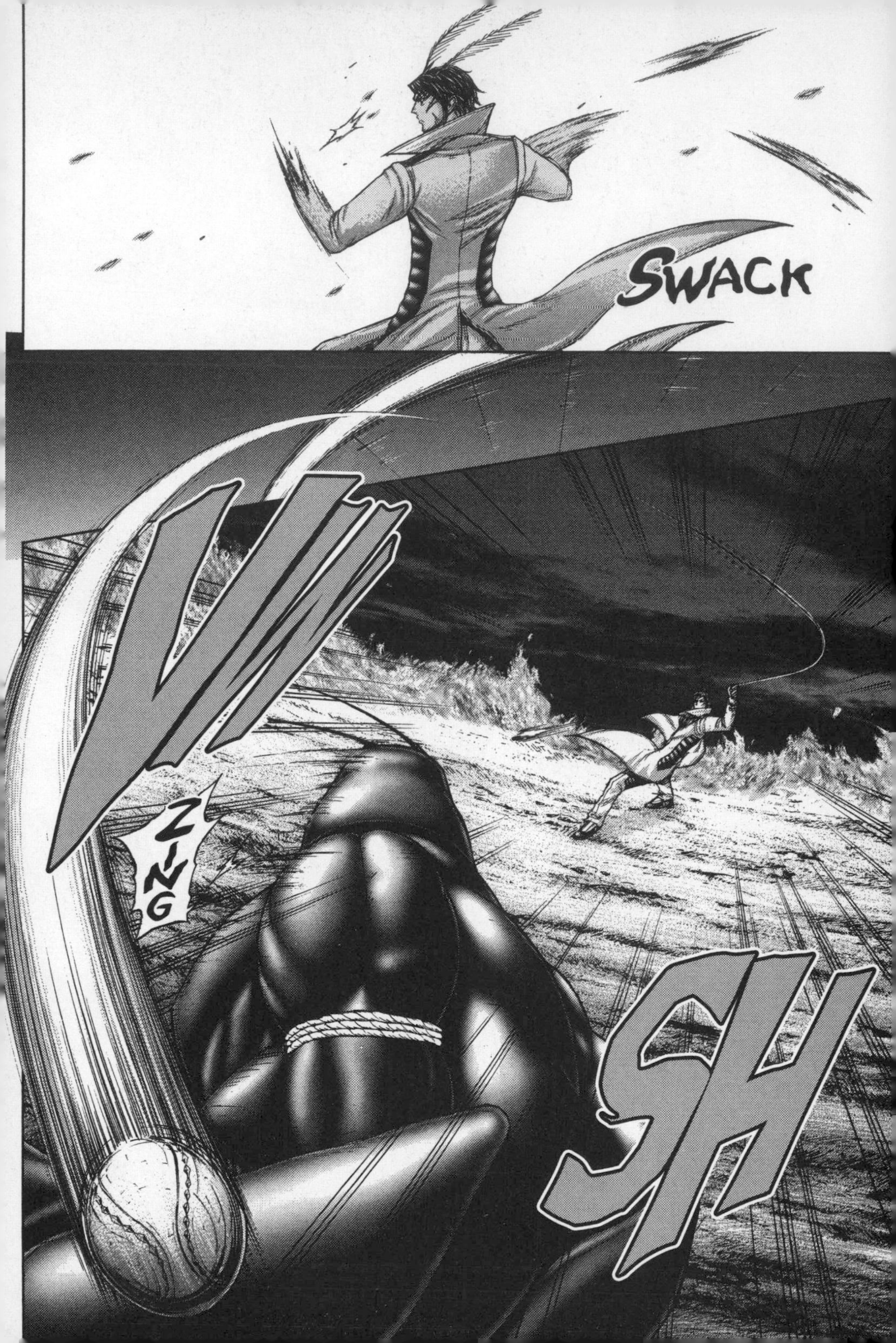
SWACK
VI
ZING
SH

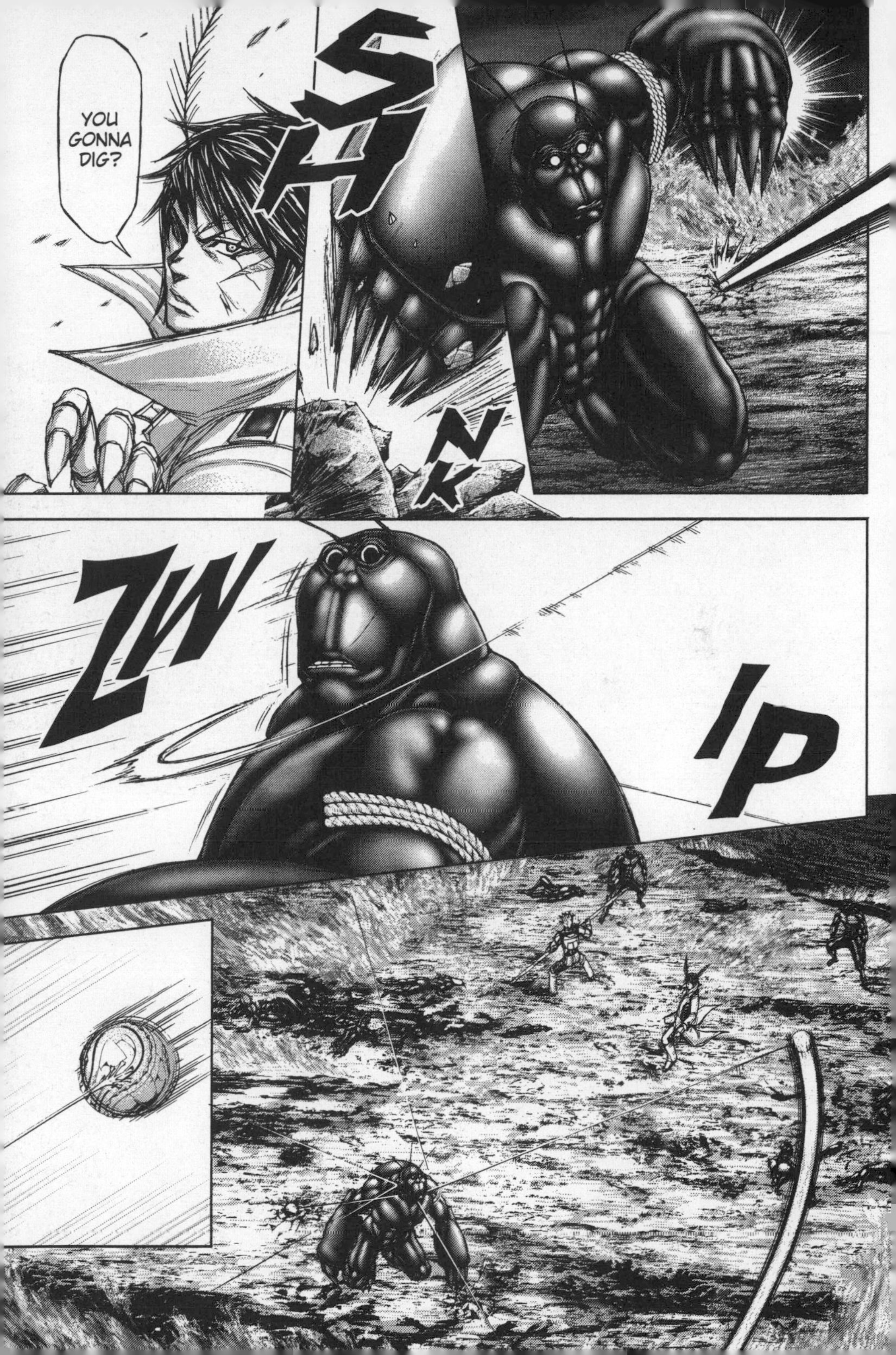
SHNK
YOU GONNA DIG?
ZWIP

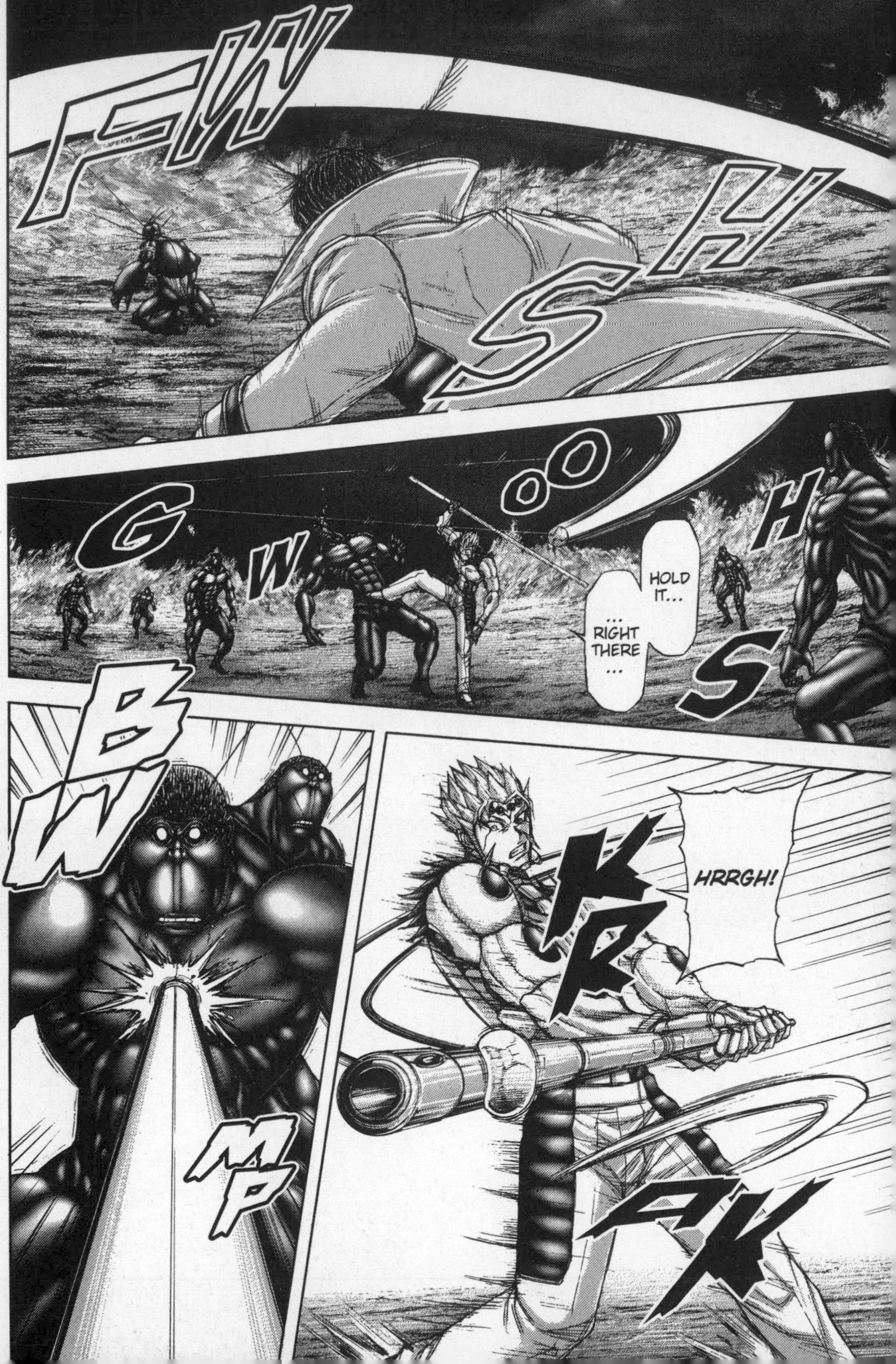
FWSH
GWOOSH
HOLD IT...
...RIGHT THERE...
KRAK
HRRGH!
BWMP

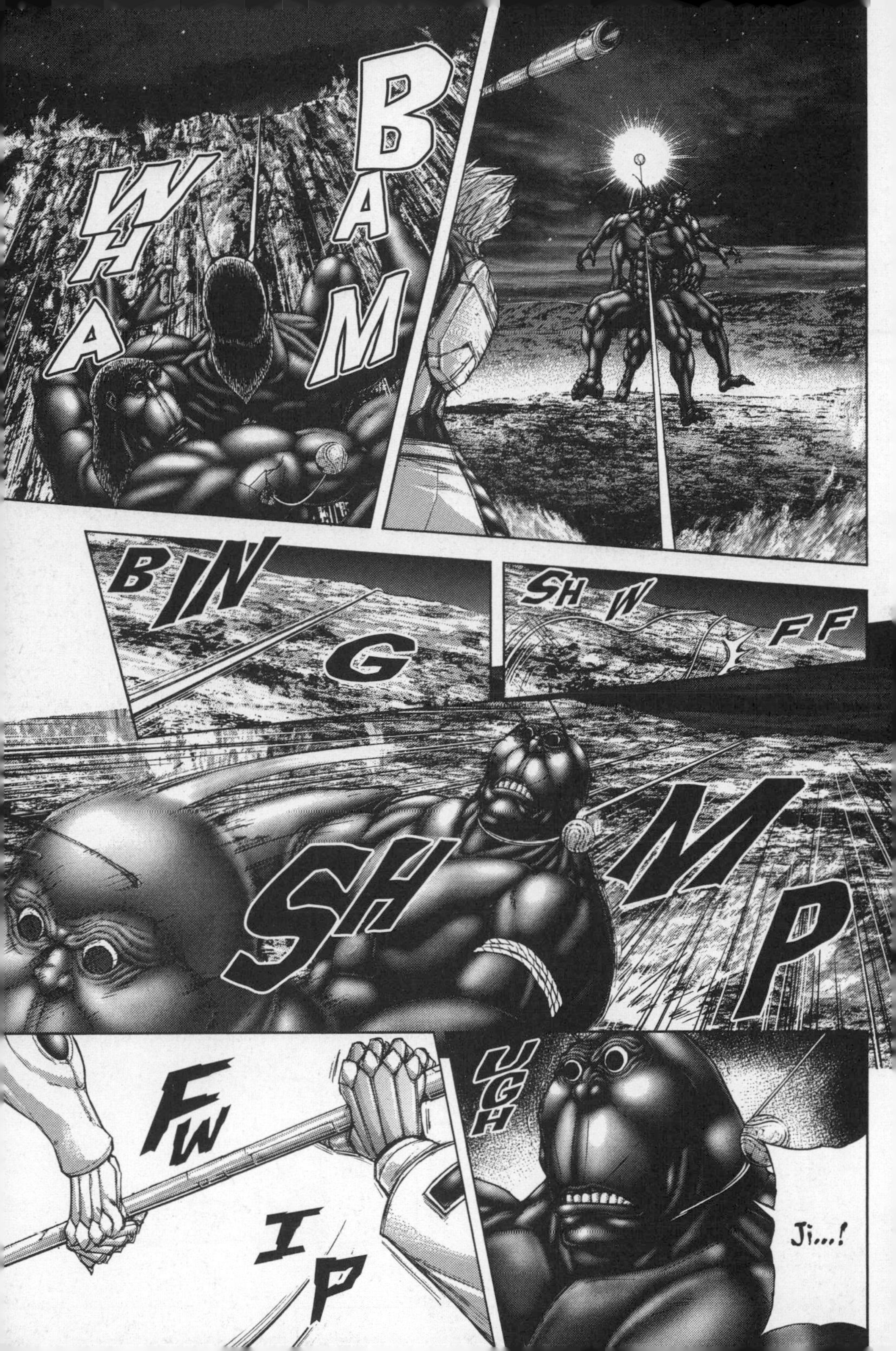
BAM
WHA
SHWFF
BING
SHMP
UGH
Ji...!
FWIP

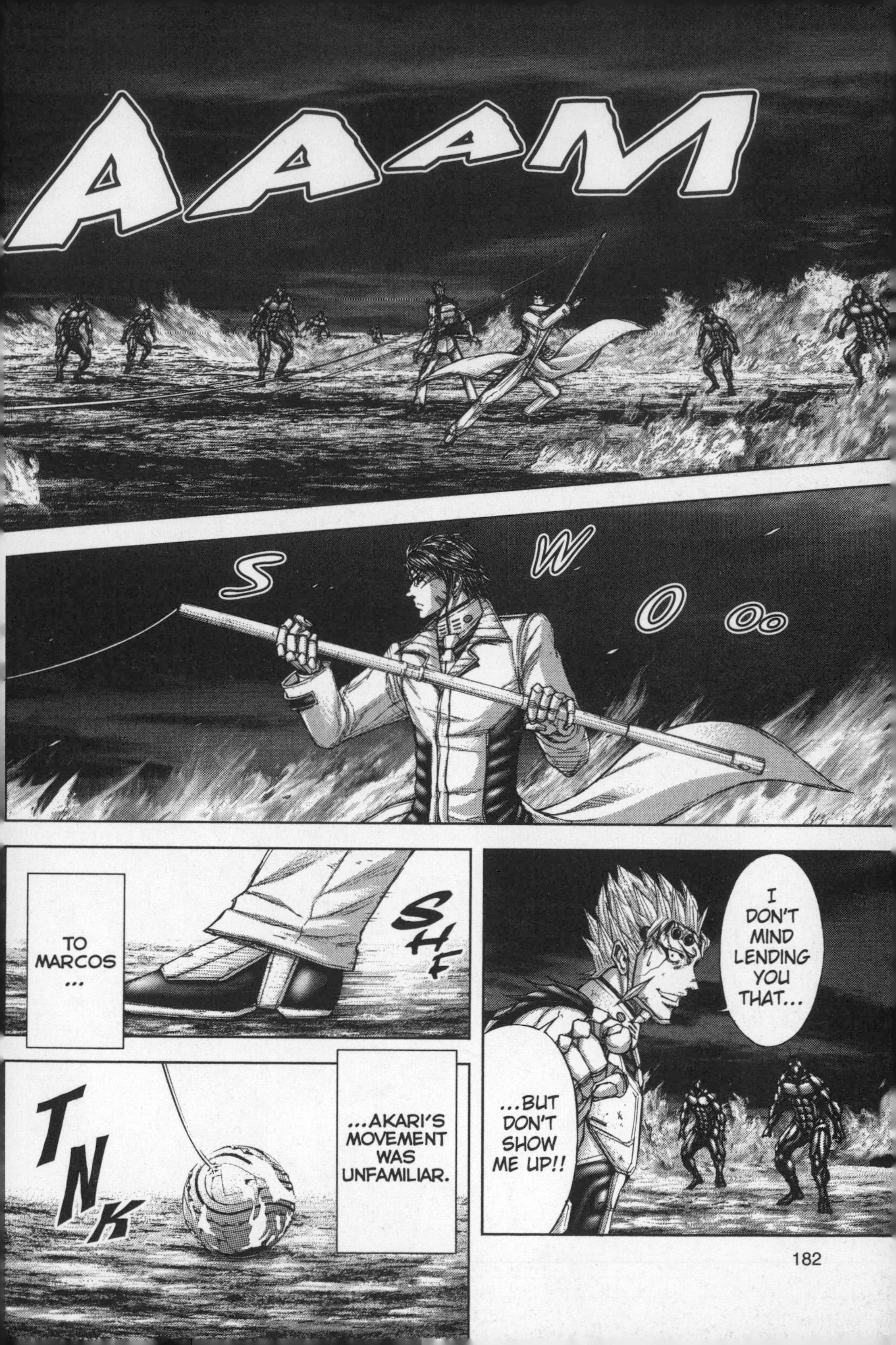
AAAM
SWOOO
I DON'T MIND LENDING YOU THAT...
...BUT DON'T SHOW ME UP!!
TO MARCOS...
SHF
...AKARI'S MOVEMENT WAS UNFAMILIAR.
TNK

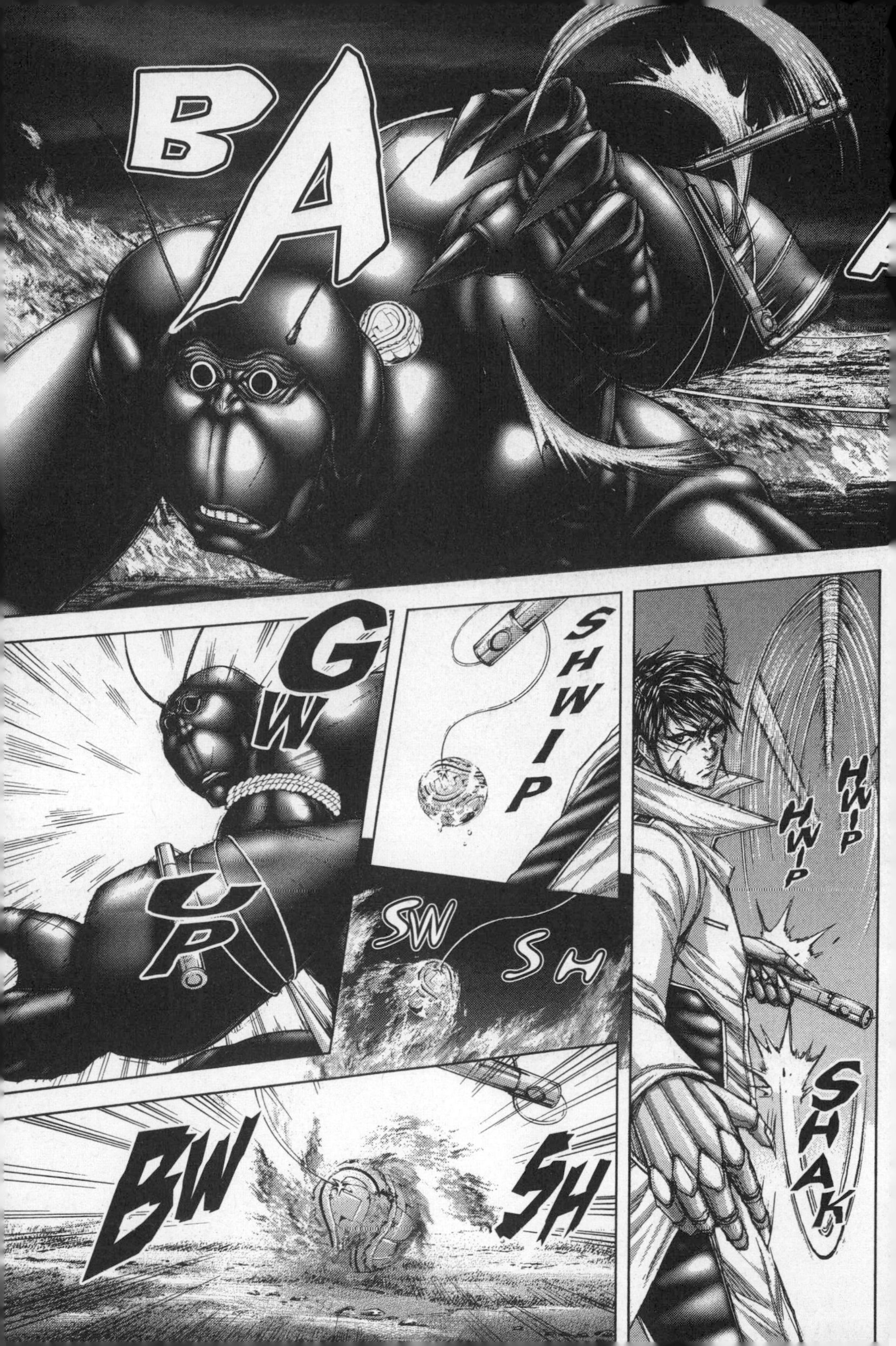
BA
HWIP
HWIP
SHAK
SHWIP
GWUP
SW SH
BW SH

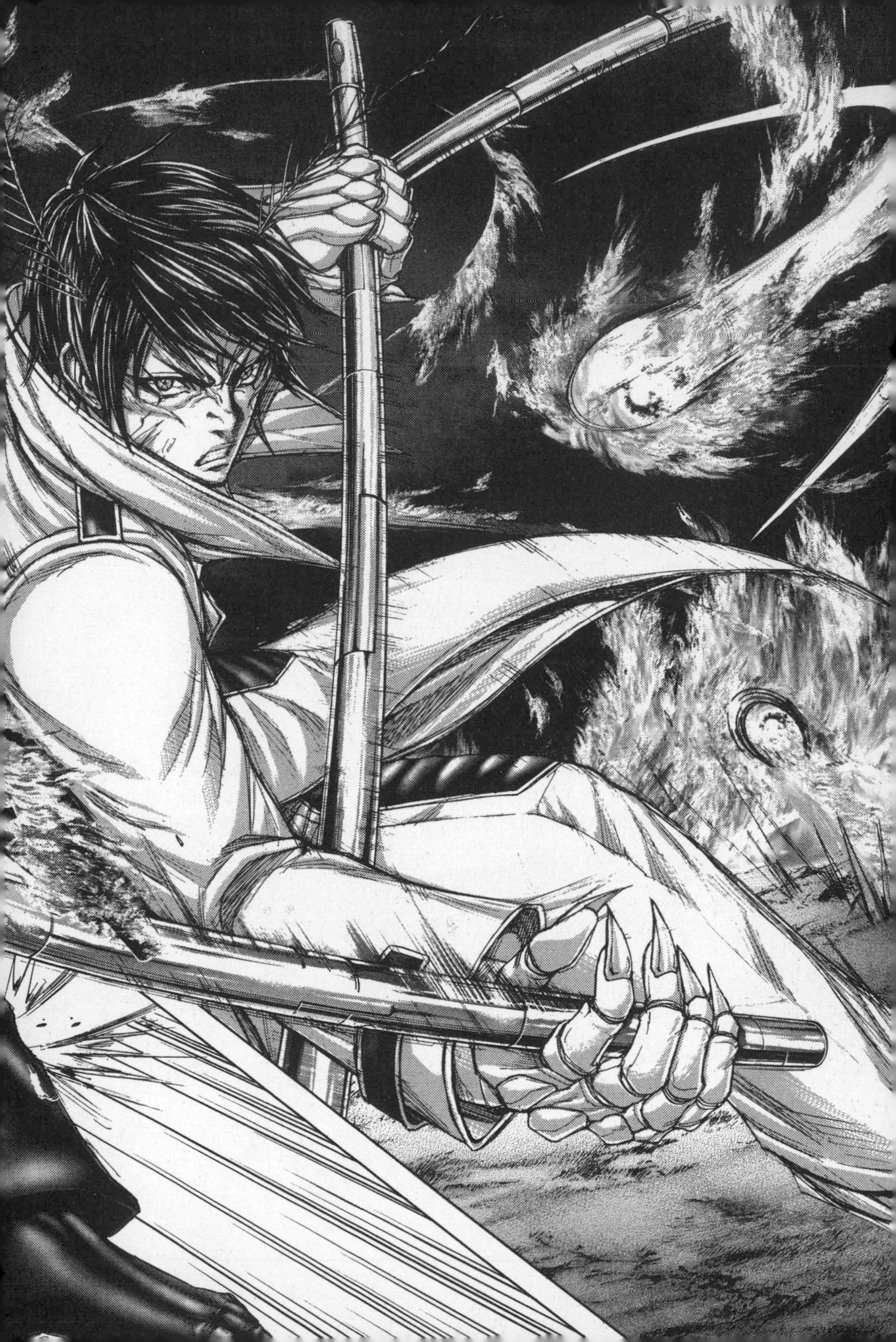

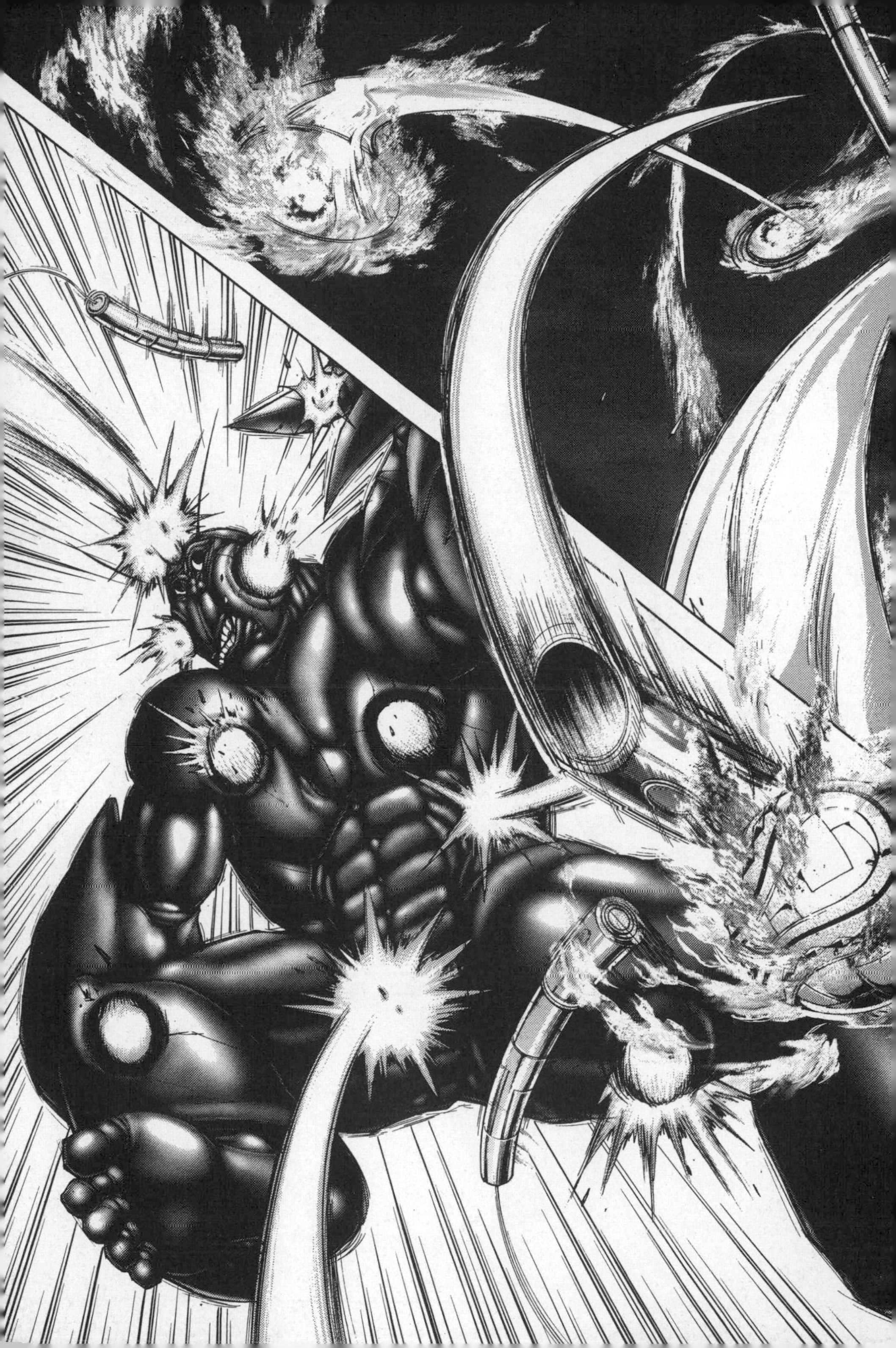

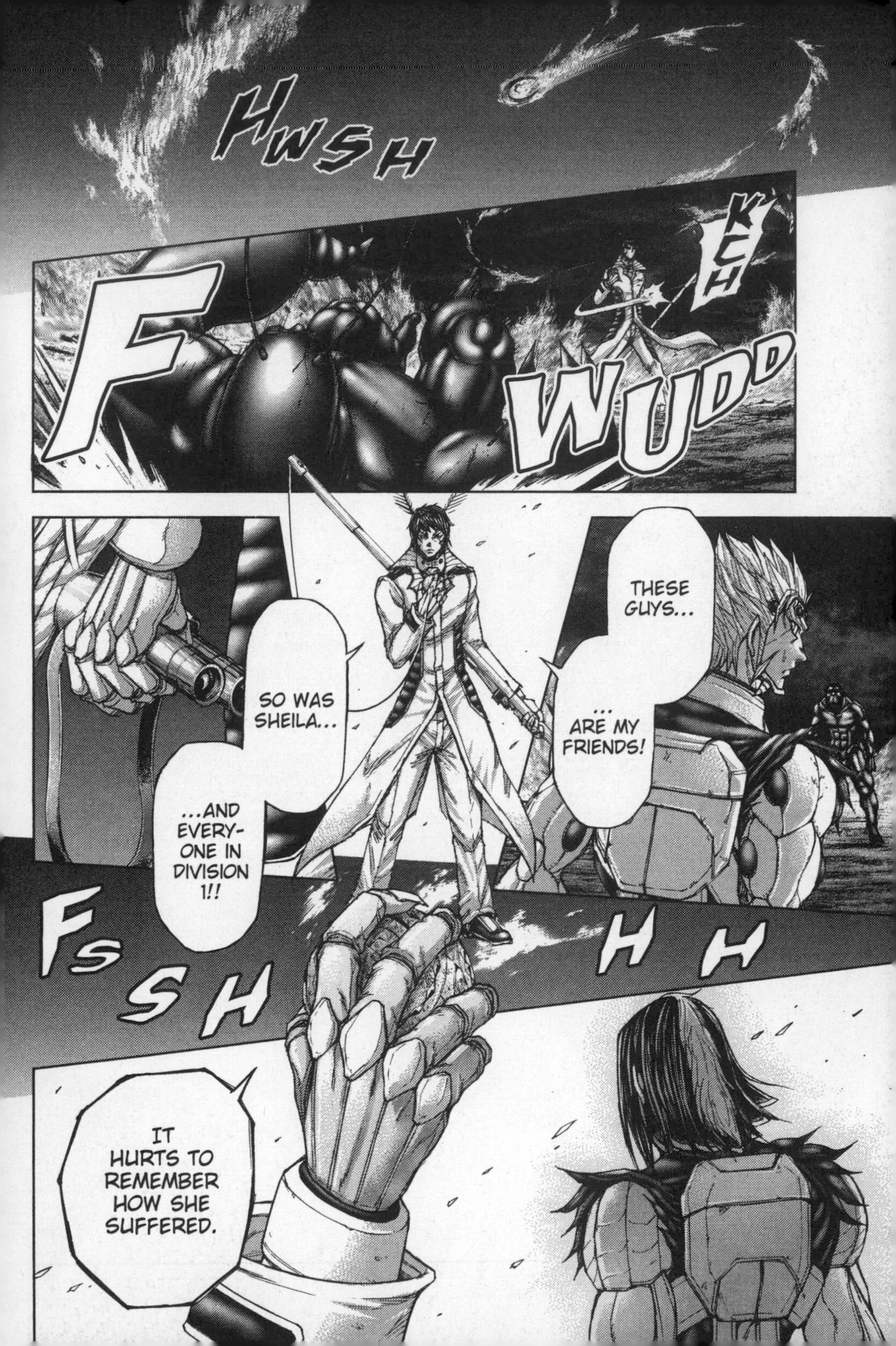
HWSH
KCH
FWUDD
THESE GUYS...
...ARE MY FRIENDS!
SO WAS SHEILA...
...AND EVERYONE IN DIVISION 1!!
FSSHHH
IT HURTS TO REMEMBER HOW SHE SUFFERED.

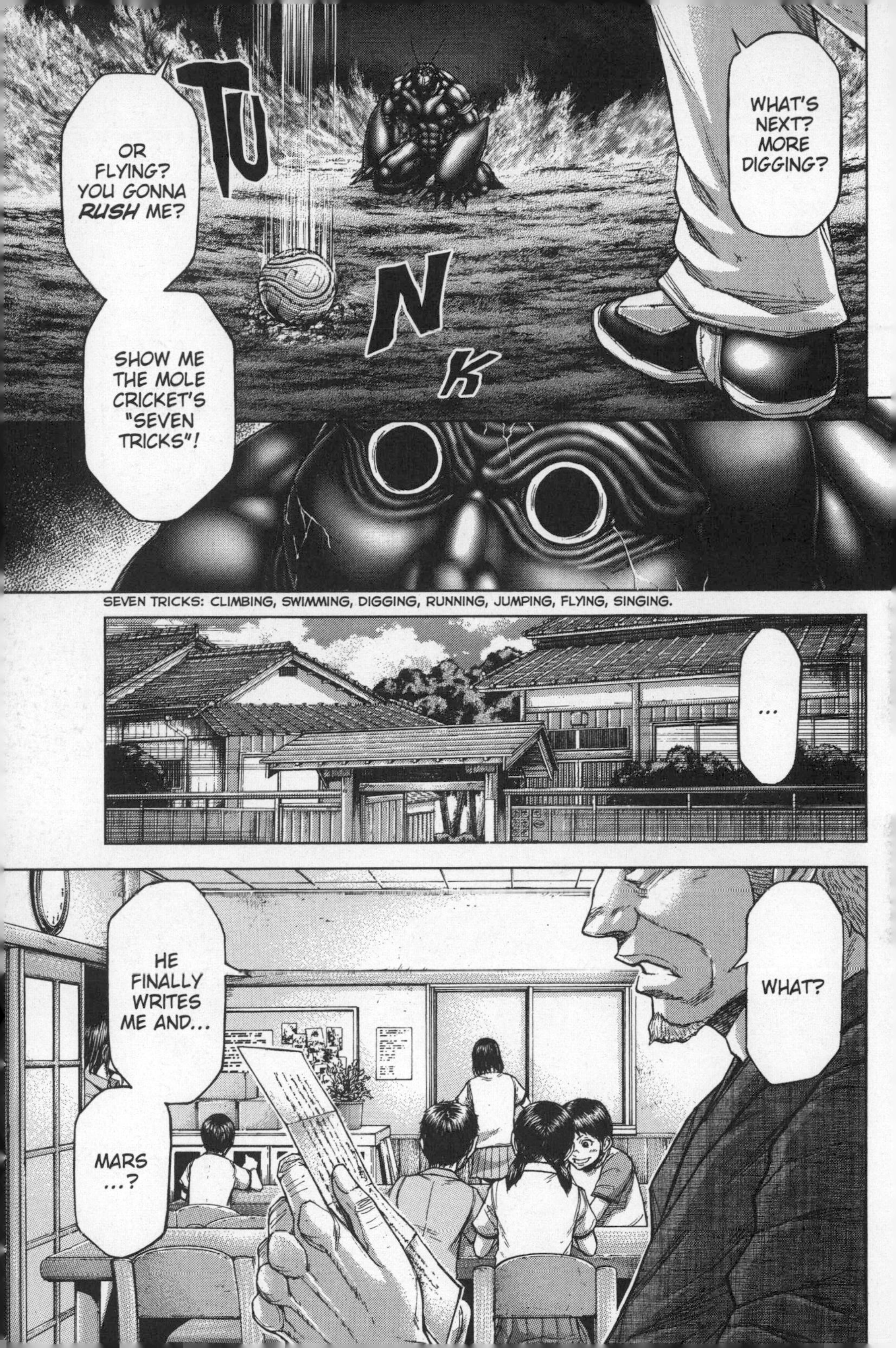
WHAT'S NEXT? MORE DIGGING?
OR FLYING? YOU GONNA RUSH ME?
TUNK
SHOW ME THE MOLE CRICKET'S "SEVEN TRICKS"!
SEVEN TRICKS: CLIMBING, SWIMMING, DIGGING, RUNNING, JUMPING, FLYING, SINGING.
...
WHAT?
HE FINALLY WRITES ME AND...
MARS ...?

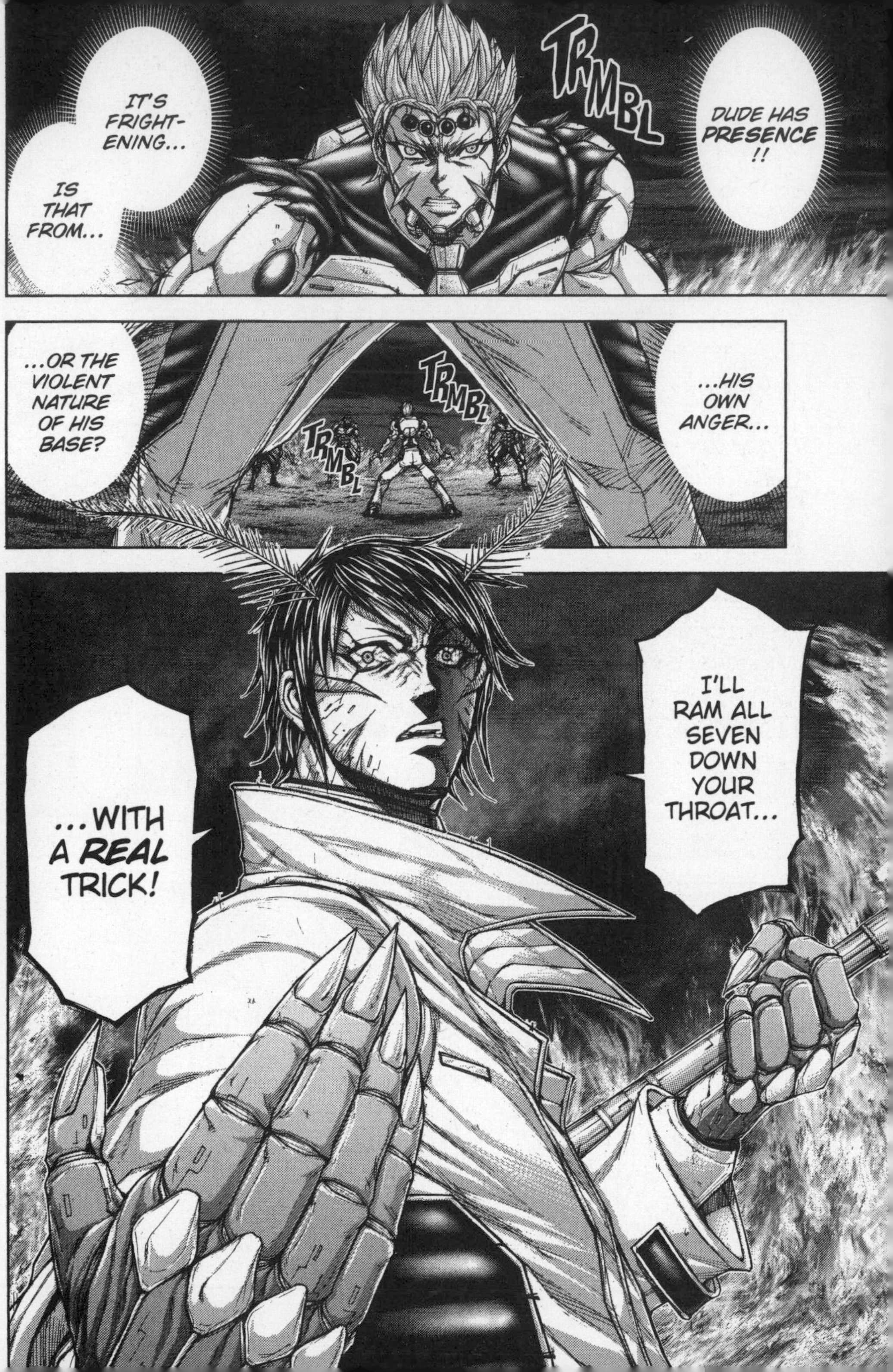
DUDE HAS PRESENCE !!
TRMBL
IT'S FRIGHT-ENING...
IS THAT FROM...
...HIS OWN ANGER...
TRMBL
TRMBL
...OR THE VIOLENT NATURE OF HIS BASE?
I'LL RAM ALL SEVEN DOWN YOUR THROAT...
...WITH A REAL TRICK!

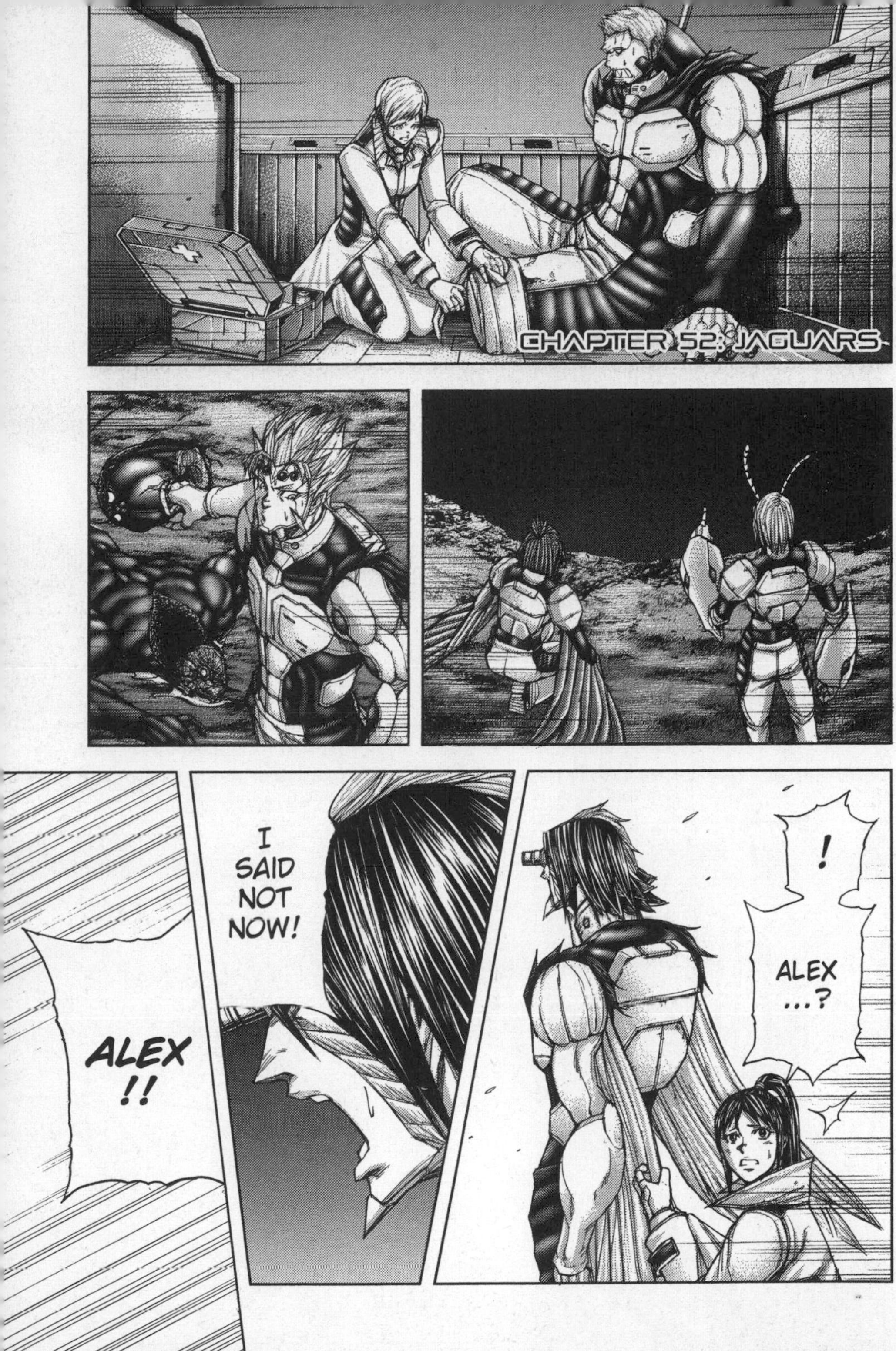
CHAPTER 52: JAGUARS
!
ALEX ...?
I SAID NOT NOW!
ALEX !!

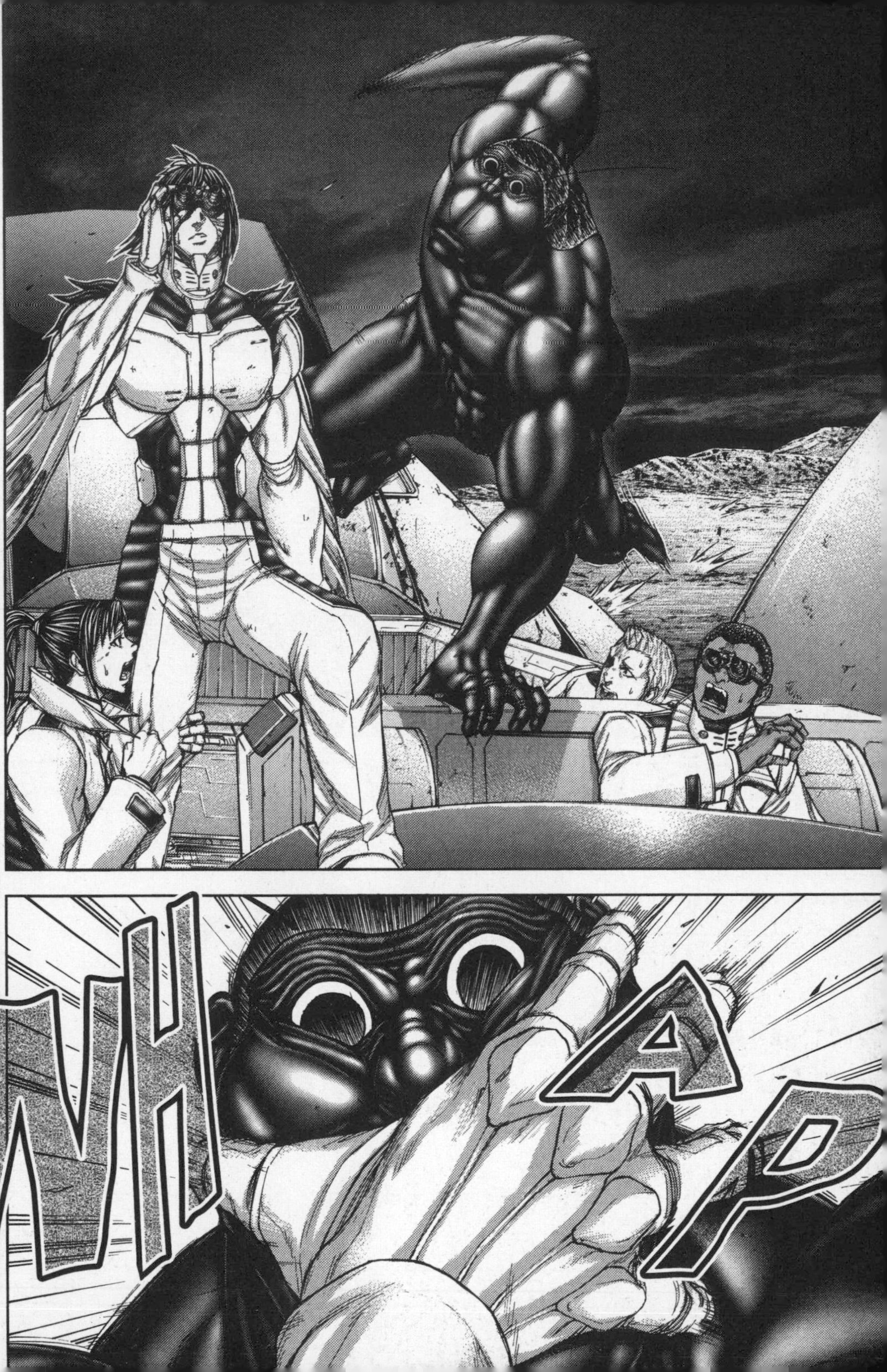
WHAP

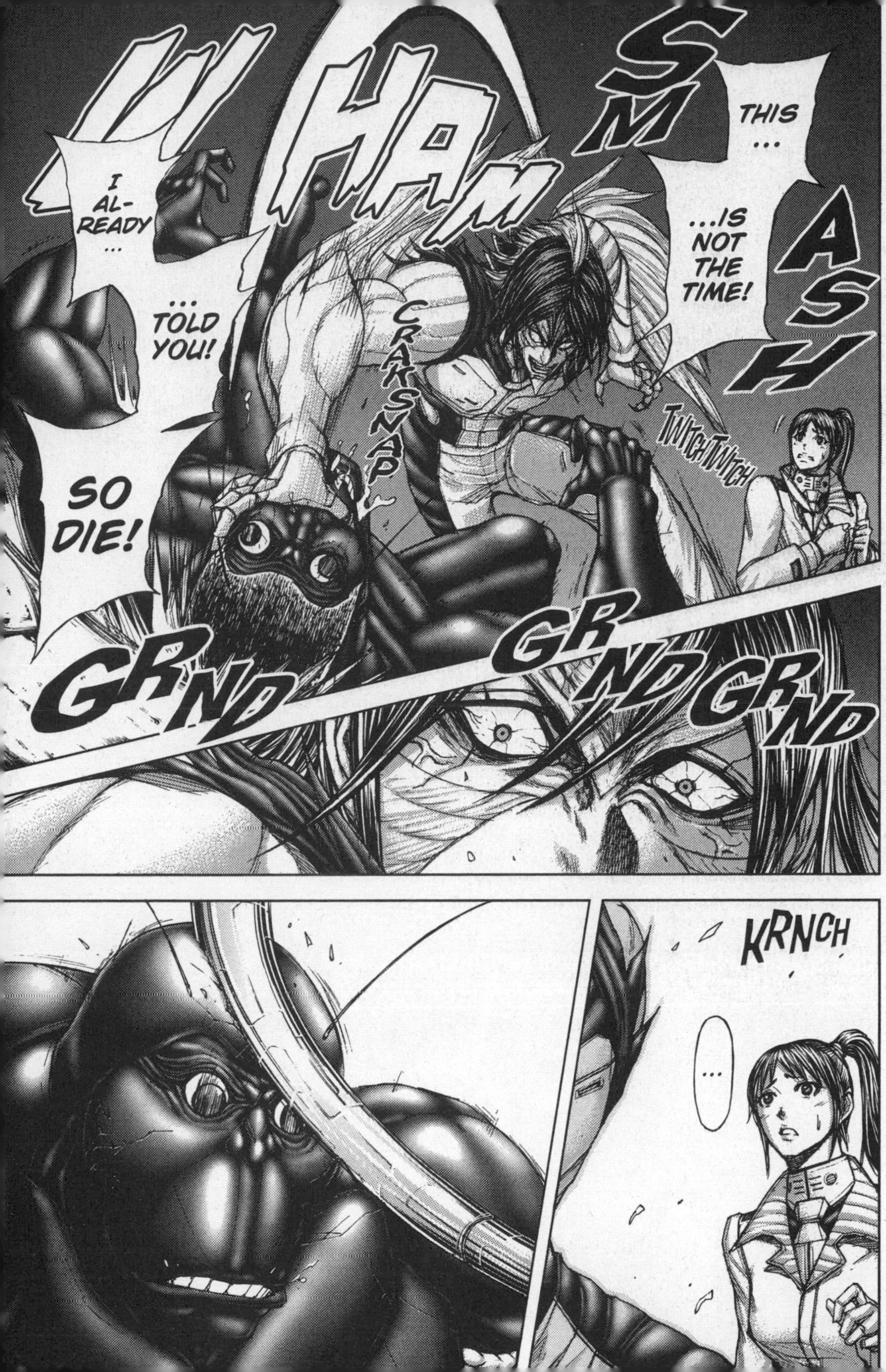
THIS...
...IS NOT THE TIME!
SMASH
WHAM
I ALREADY...
...TOLD YOU!
SO DIE!
CRAKSNAP!
TWITCH TWITCH
GRND GRND
GRND
KRNCH
...

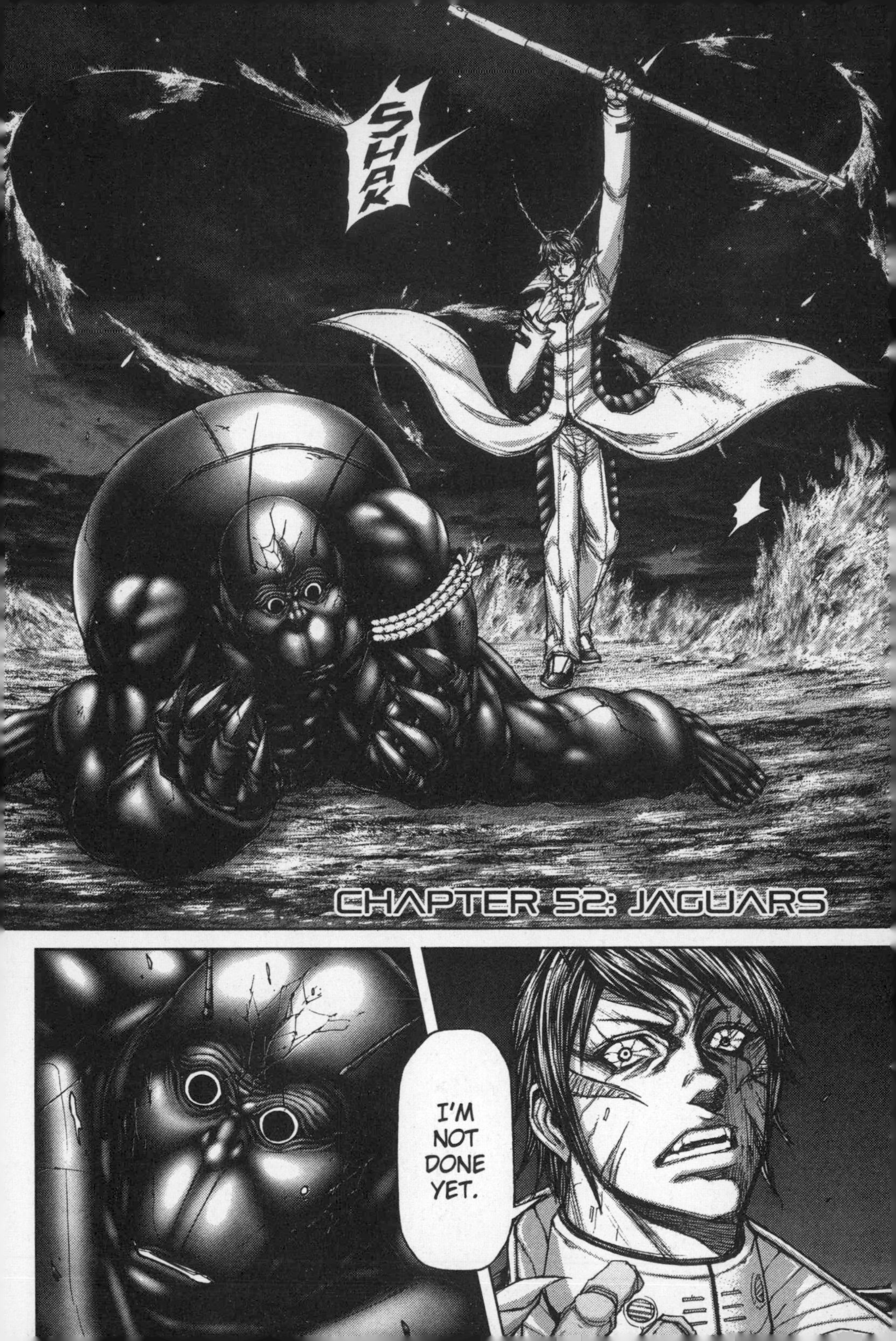
SHAK
CHAPTER 52: JAGUARS
I'M NOT DONE YET.

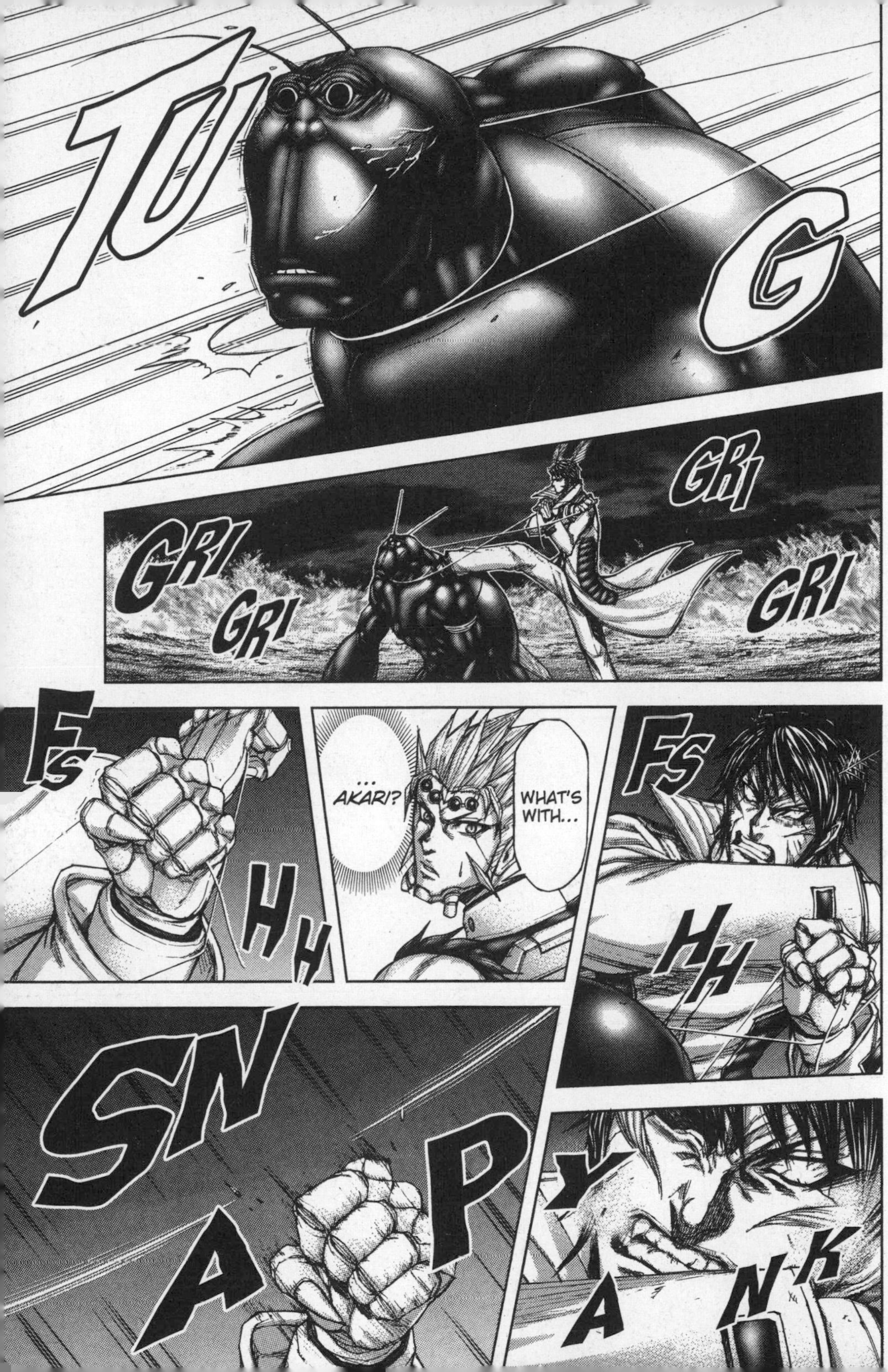

TUG
GRI
GRI
GRI
GRI
FSHH
WHAT'S WITH...
...AKARI?
FSHH
YANK
SNAP

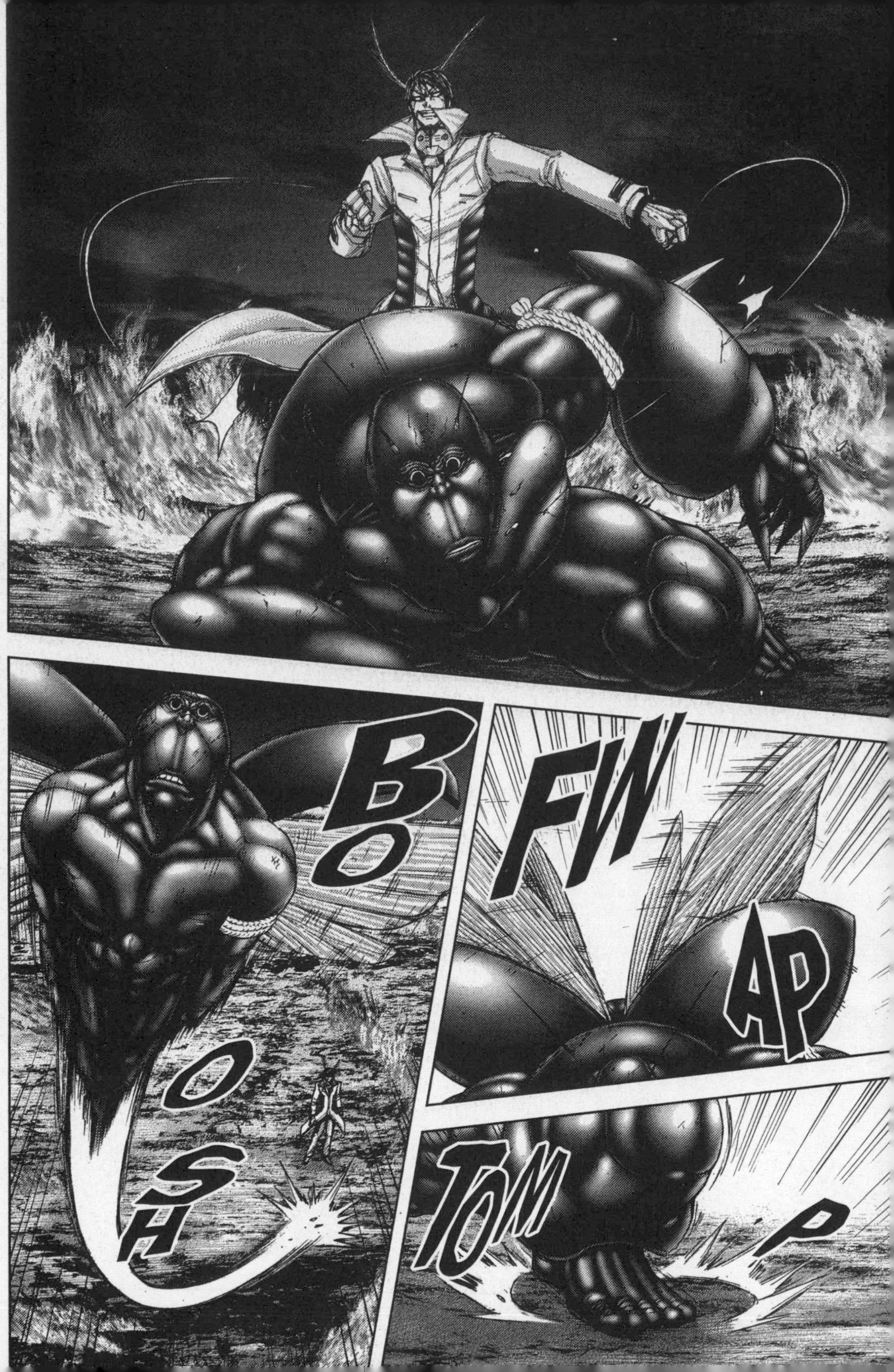
FWAP
TOMP
BOOSH

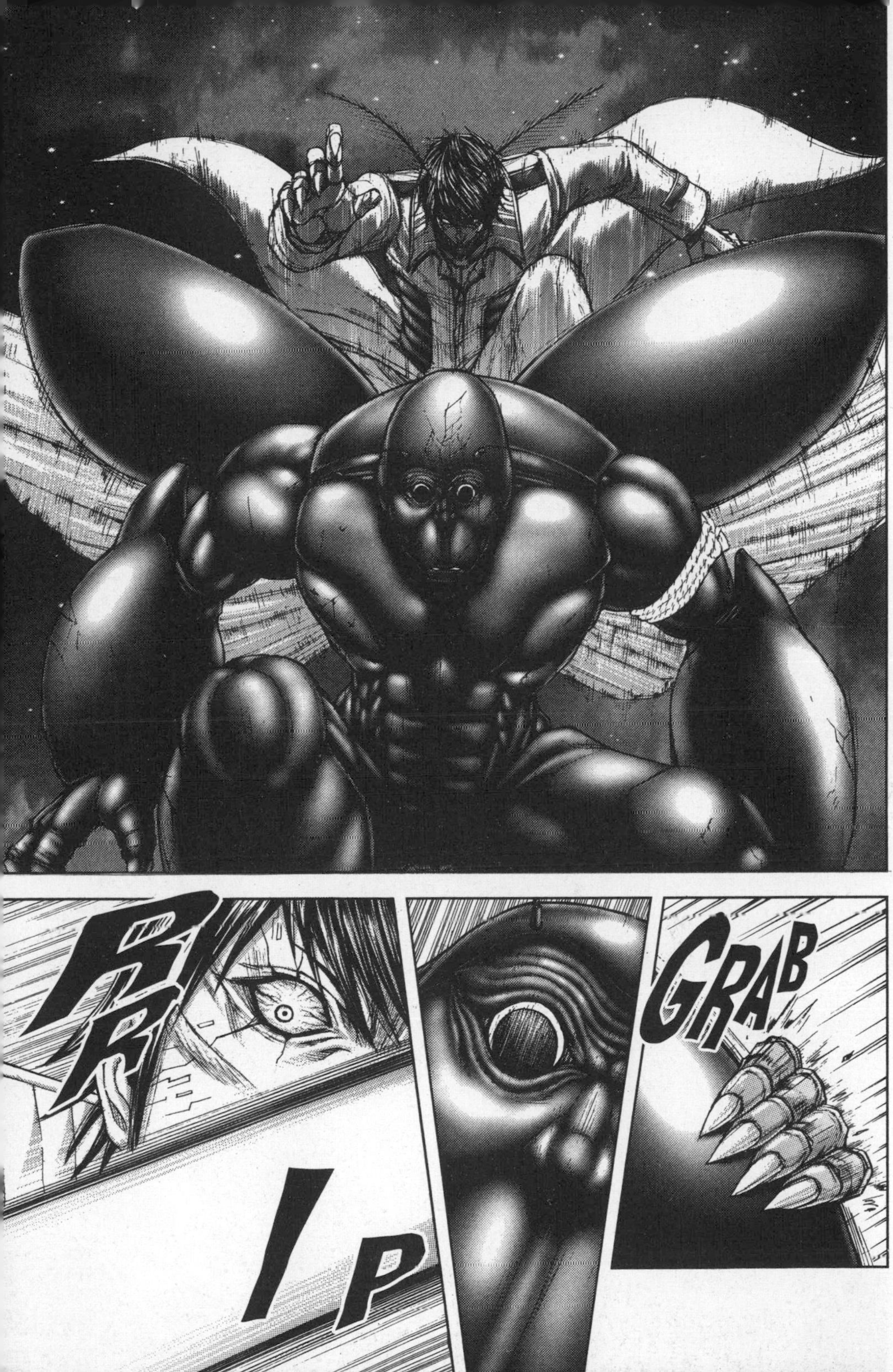
GRAB
RRIP

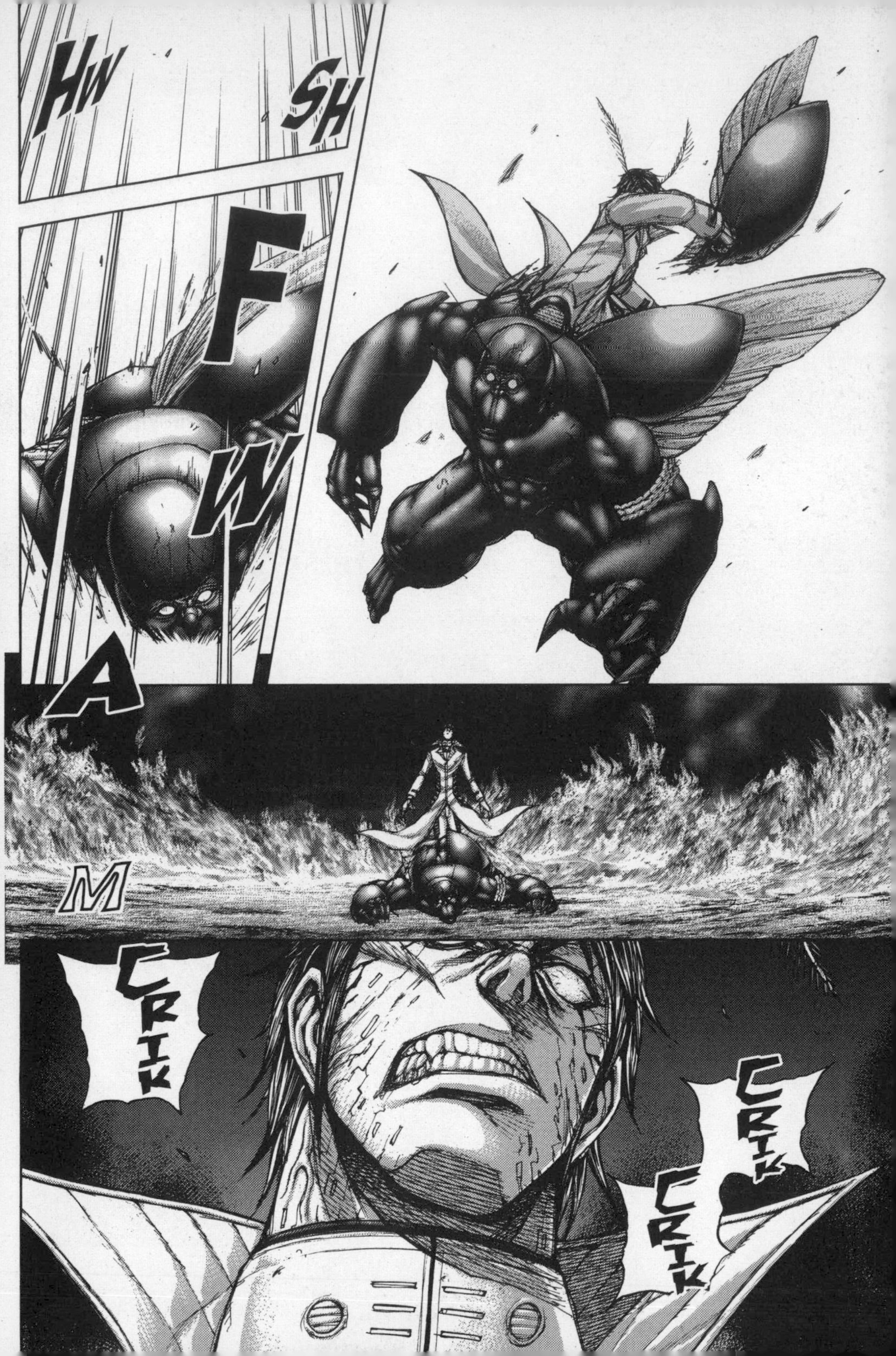
HWSH
FWAM
CRIK CRIK
CRIK

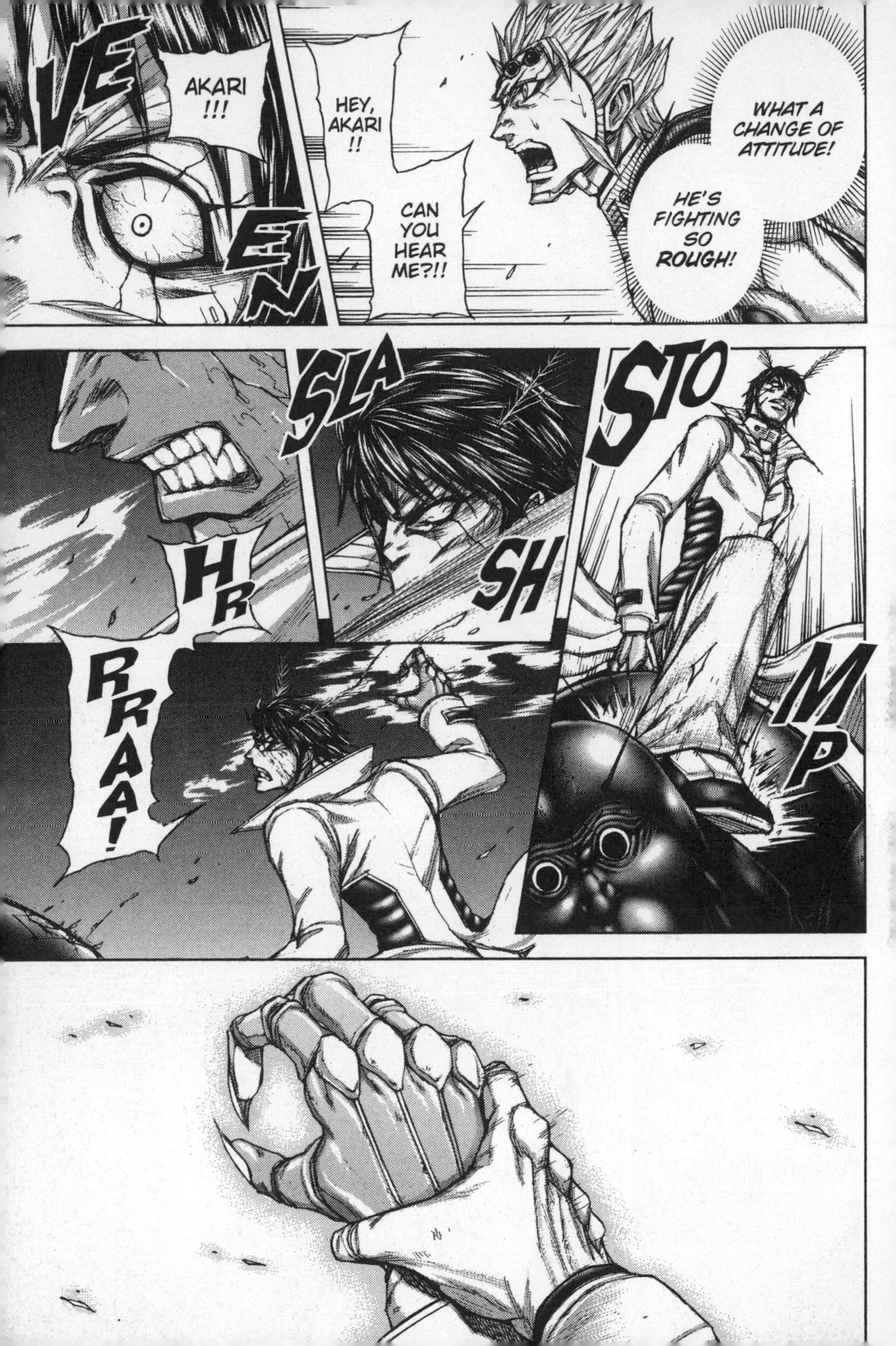
WHAT A CHANGE OF ATTITUDE!
HE'S FIGHTING SO ROUGH!
HEY, AKARI!!
CAN YOU HEAR ME?!!
AKARI!!!
VEEN
STOMP
SLASH
HRRRAA!

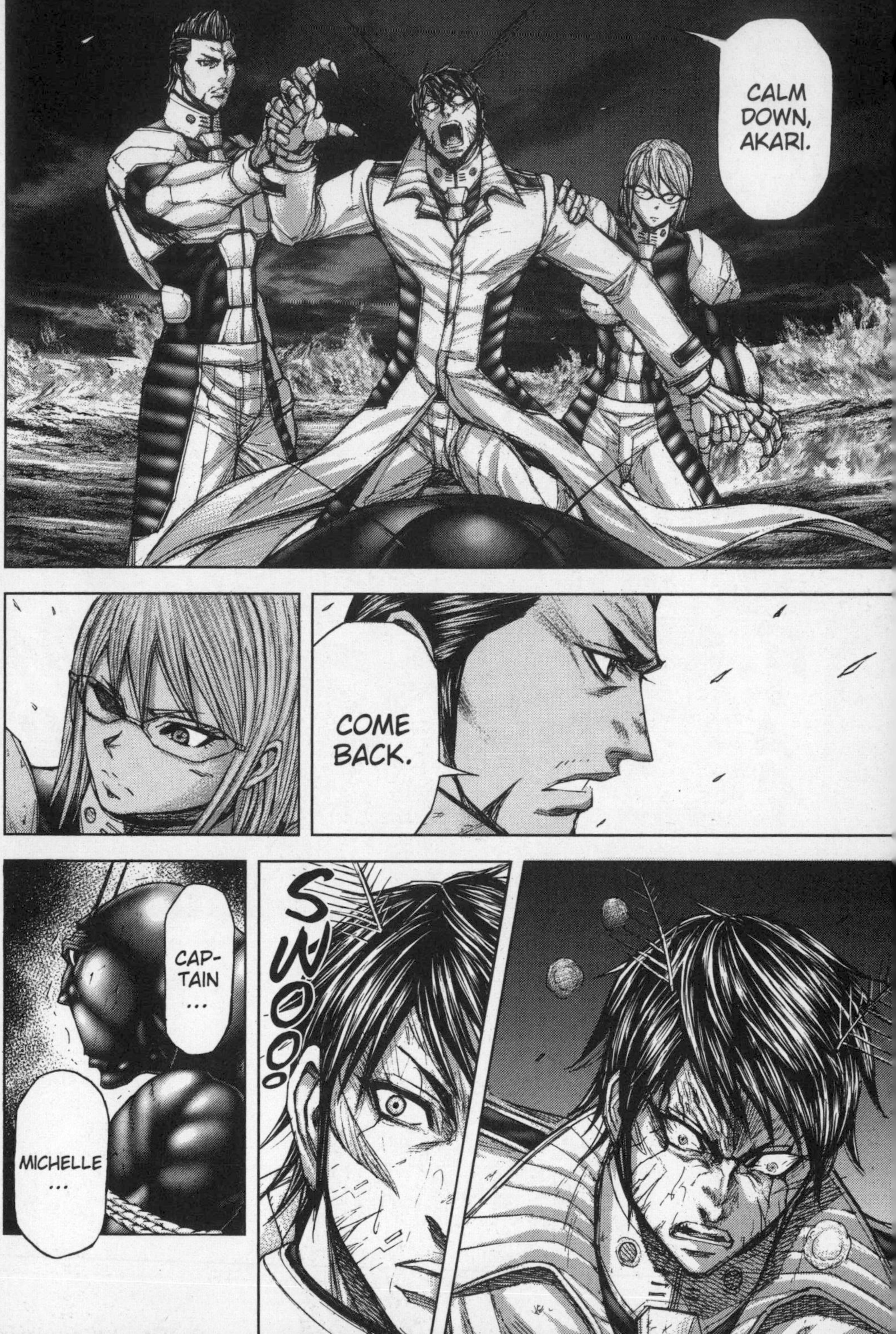
CALM DOWN, AKARI.
COME BACK.
SWOOO
CAP-TAIN ...
MICHELLE ...

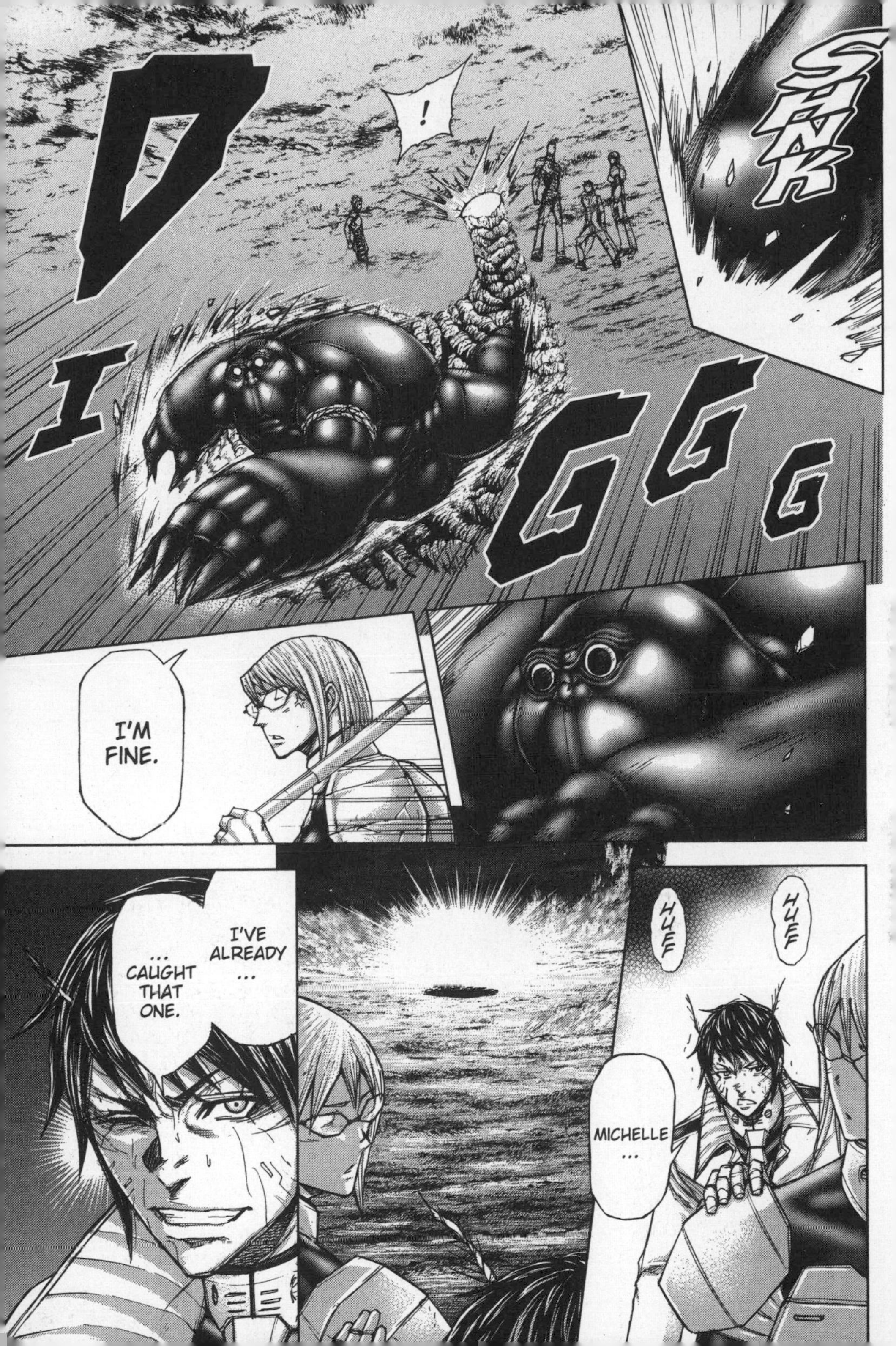
SHNK
!
DIGGG
I'M FINE.
HUFF
HUFF
MICHELLE ...
I'VE ALREADY ...
... CAUGHT THAT ONE.

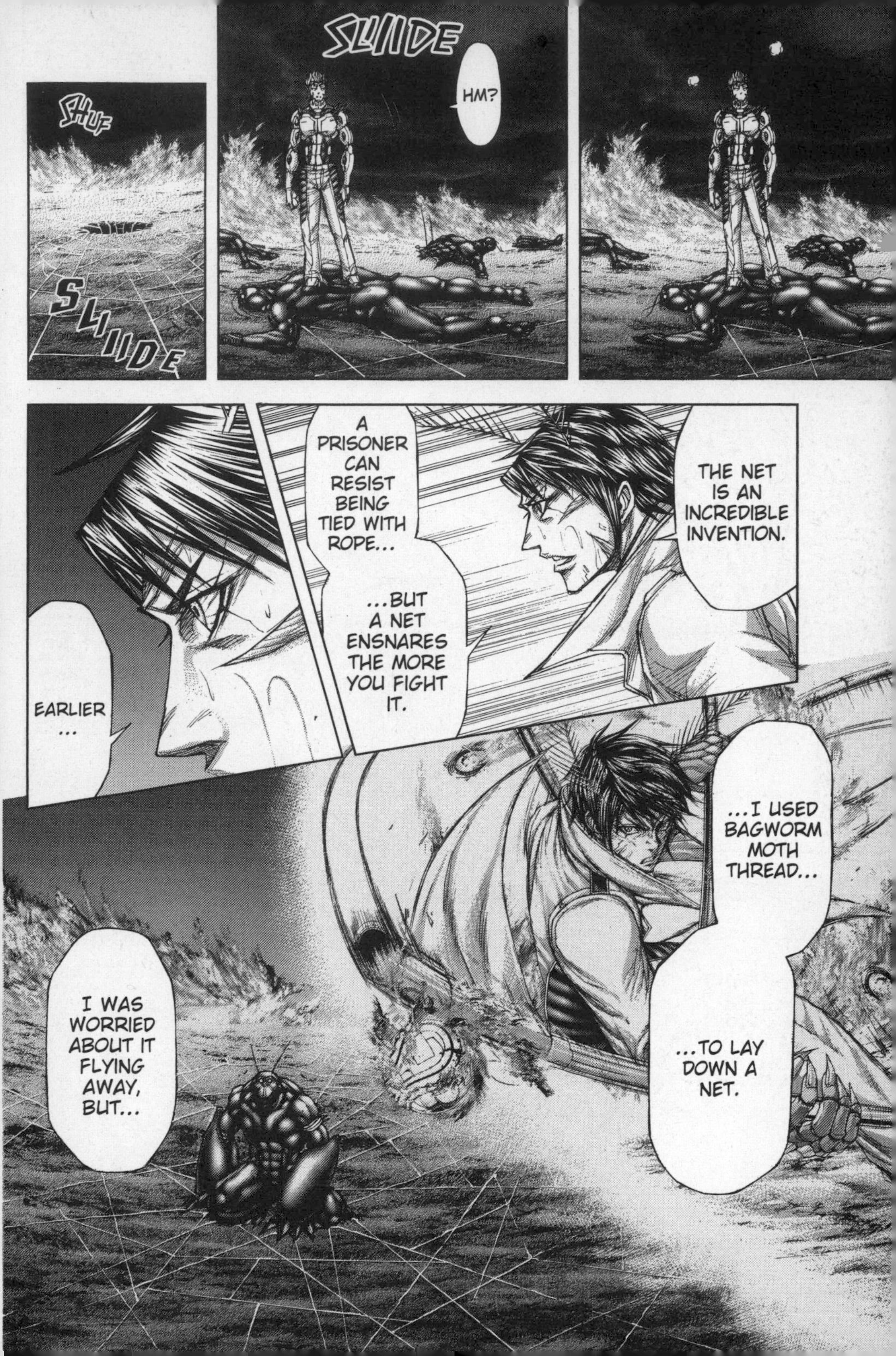
SLIIDE
HM?
SHUF
SLIIDE
THE NET IS AN INCREDIBLE INVENTION.
A PRISONER CAN RESIST BEING TIED WITH ROPE...
...BUT A NET ENSNARES THE MORE YOU FIGHT IT.
EARLIER ...
...I USED BAGWORM MOTH THREAD...
...TO LAY DOWN A NET.
I WAS WORRIED ABOUT IT FLYING AWAY, BUT...

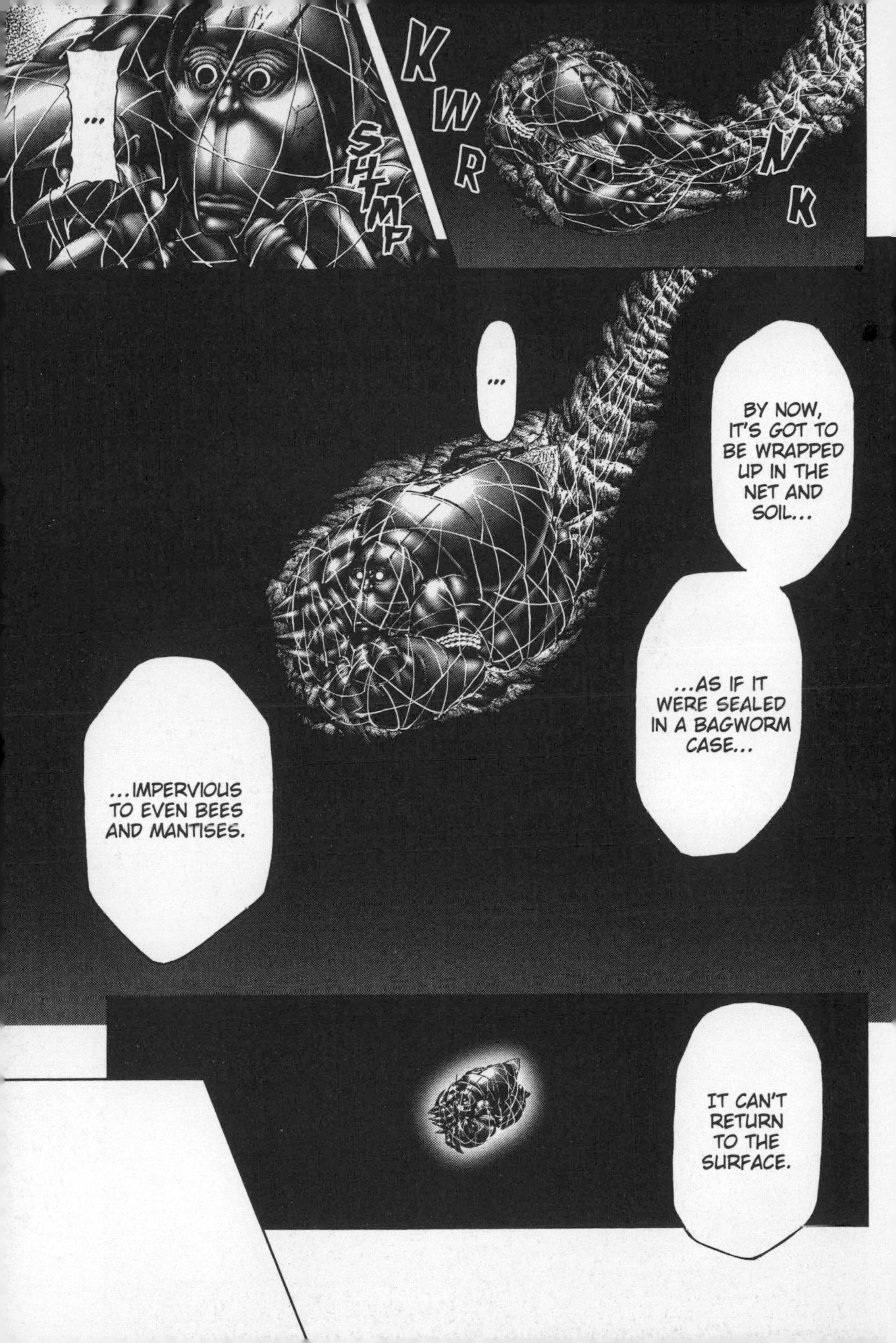
KWRNK
SHTMP
...
...
BY NOW, IT'S GOT TO BE WRAPPED UP IN THE NET AND SOIL...
...AS IF IT WERE SEALED IN A BAGWORM CASE...
...IMPERVIOUS TO EVEN BEES AND MANTISES.
IT CAN'T RETURN TO THE SURFACE.

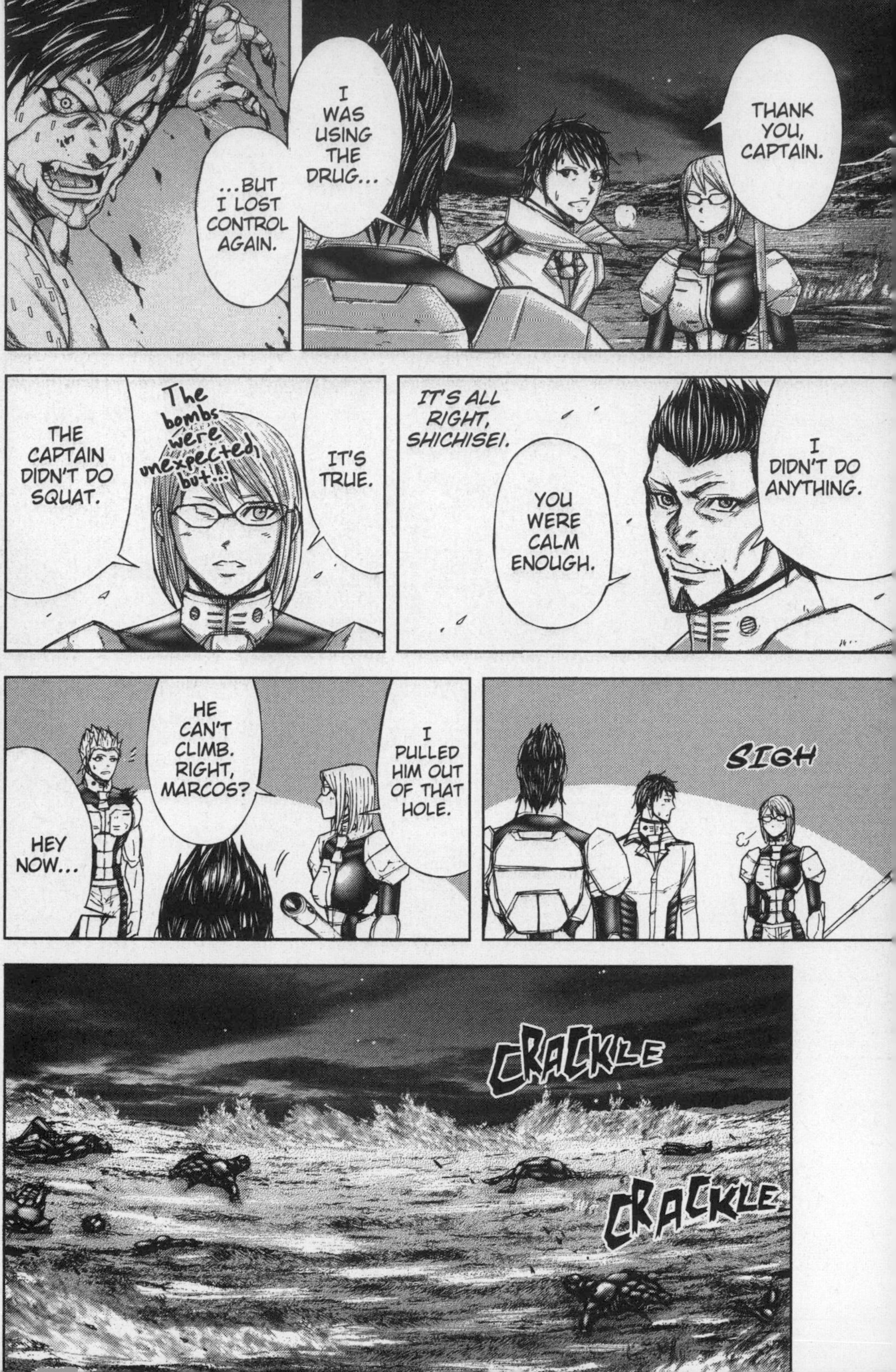
THANK YOU, CAPTAIN.
I WAS USING THE DRUG...
...BUT I LOST CONTROL AGAIN.
I DIDN'T DO ANYTHING.
IT'S ALL RIGHT, SHICHISEI.
YOU WERE CALM ENOUGH.
IT'S TRUE.
The bombs were unexpected, but...
THE CAPTAIN DIDN'T DO SQUAT.
SIGH
I PULLED HIM OUT OF THAT HOLE.
HE CAN'T CLIMB. RIGHT, MARCOS?
HEY NOW...
CRACKLE
CRACKLE

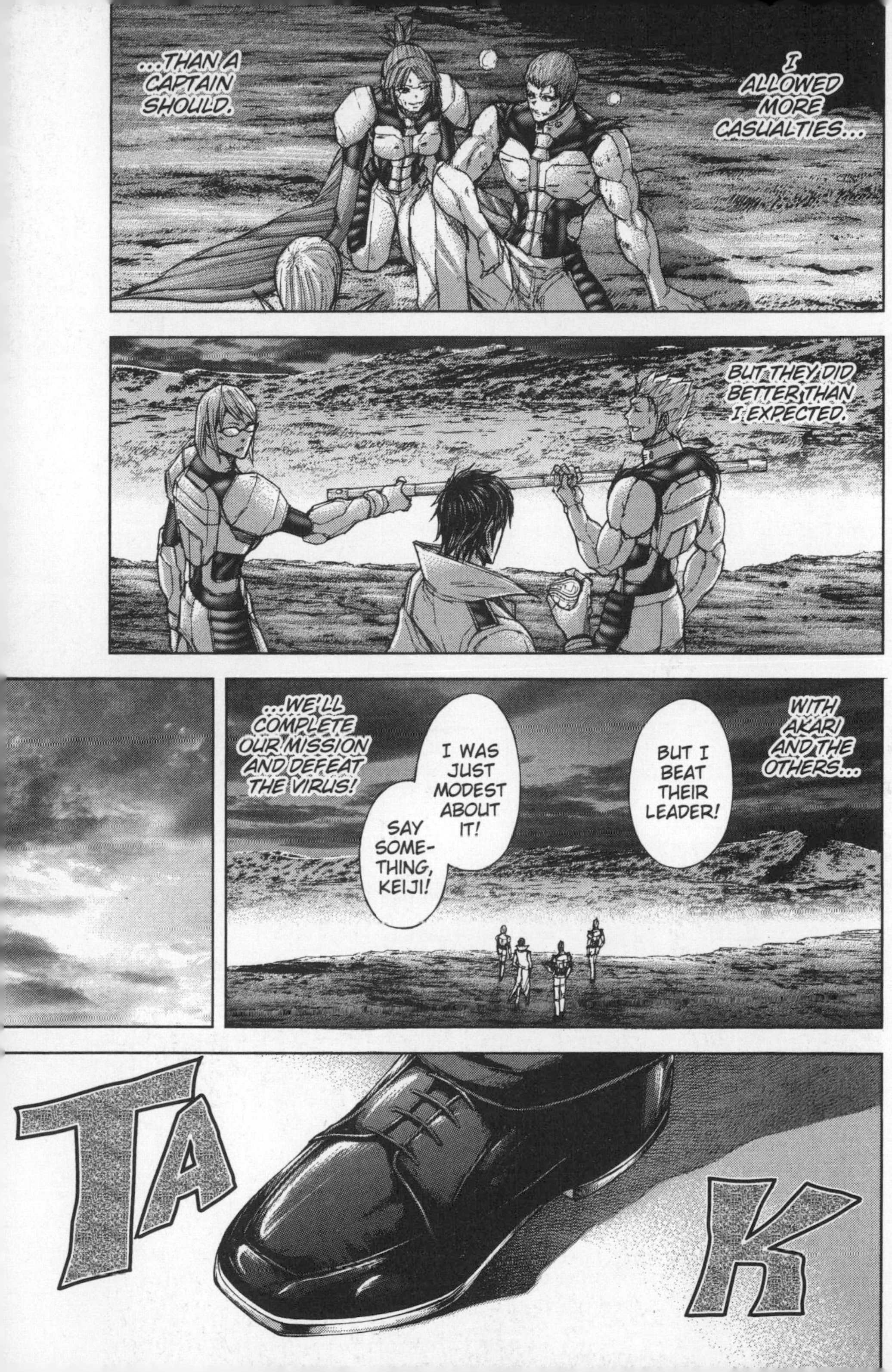
I ALLOWED MORE CASUALTIES...
...THAN A CAPTAIN SHOULD.
BUT THEY DID BETTER THAN I EXPECTED.
WITH AKARI AND THE OTHERS...
BUT I BEAT THEIR LEADER!
I WAS JUST MODEST ABOUT IT!
SAY SOME-THING, KEIJI!
...WE'LL COMPLETE OUR MISSION AND DEFEAT THE VIRUS!
TAK

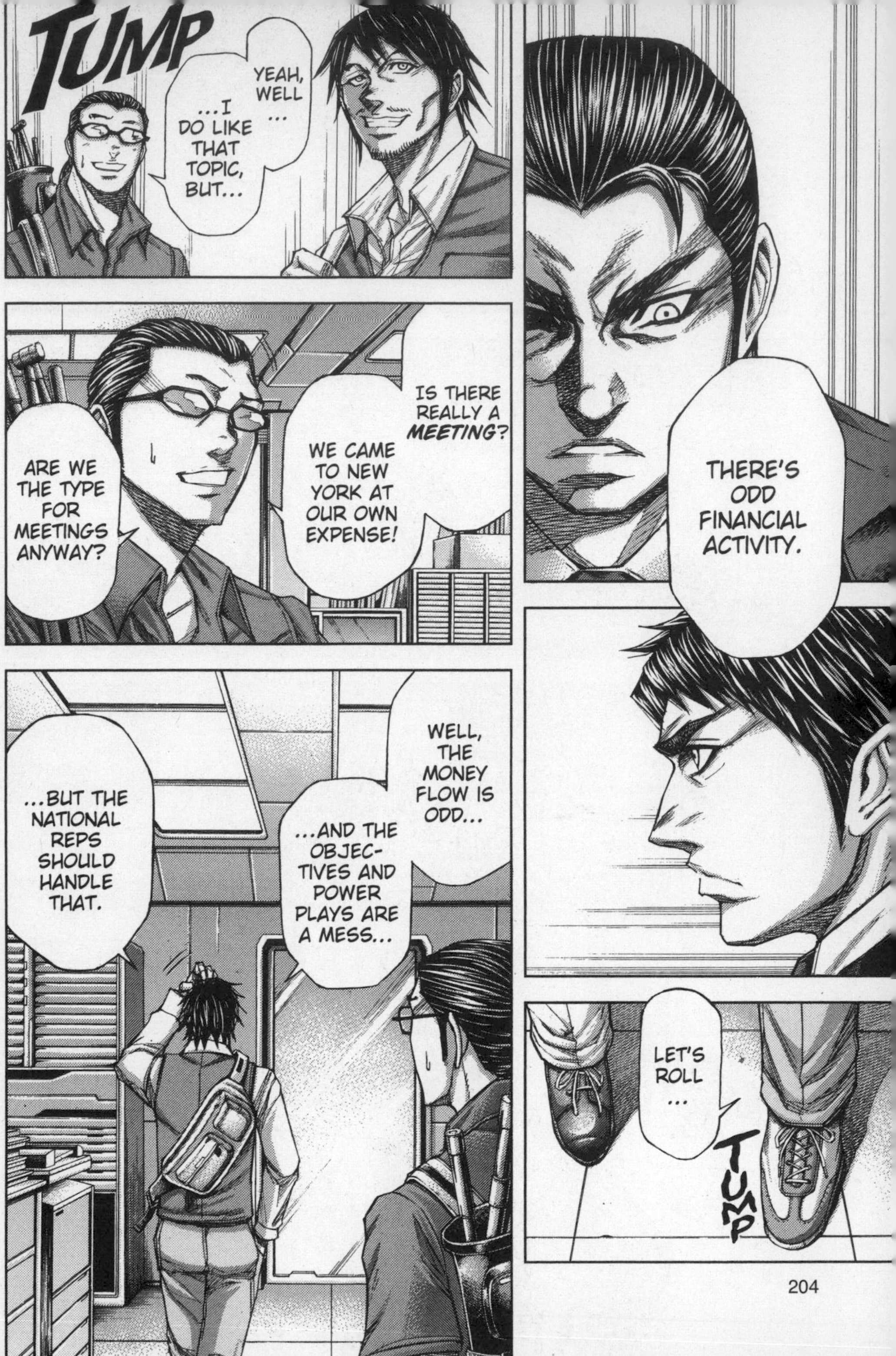
THERE'S ODD FINANCIAL ACTIVITY.
LET'S ROLL ...
TUMP
YEAH, WELL ...
...I DO LIKE THAT TOPIC, BUT...
TUMP
IS THERE REALLY A *MEETING*?
WE CAME TO NEW YORK AT OUR OWN EXPENSE!
ARE WE THE TYPE FOR MEETINGS ANYWAY?
WELL, THE MONEY FLOW IS ODD...
...AND THE OBJECTIVES AND POWER PLAYS ARE A MESS...
...BUT THE NATIONAL REPS SHOULD HANDLE THAT.

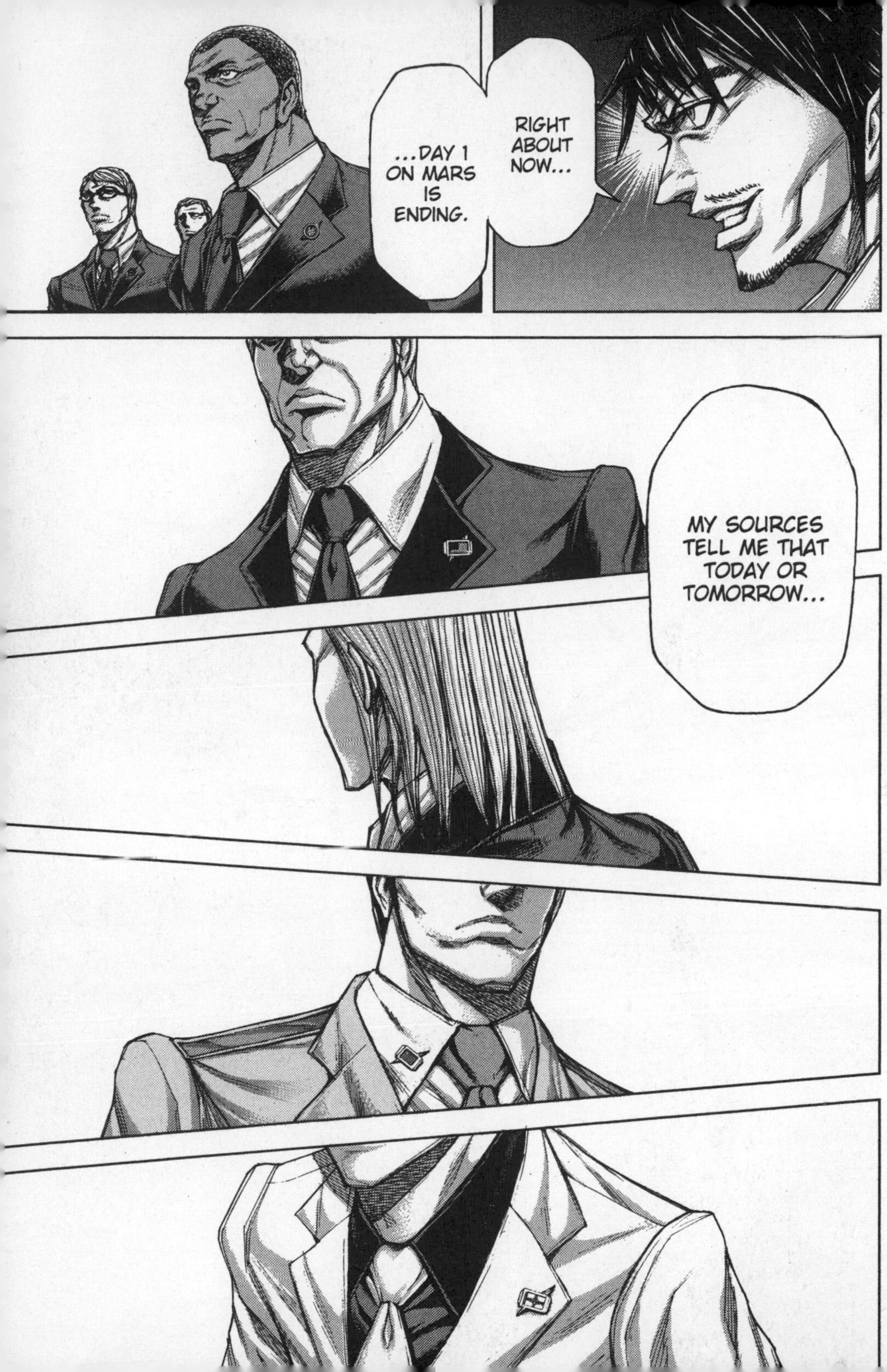
RIGHT ABOUT NOW...
...DAY 1 ON MARS IS ENDING.
MY SOURCES TELL ME THAT TODAY OR TOMORROW...

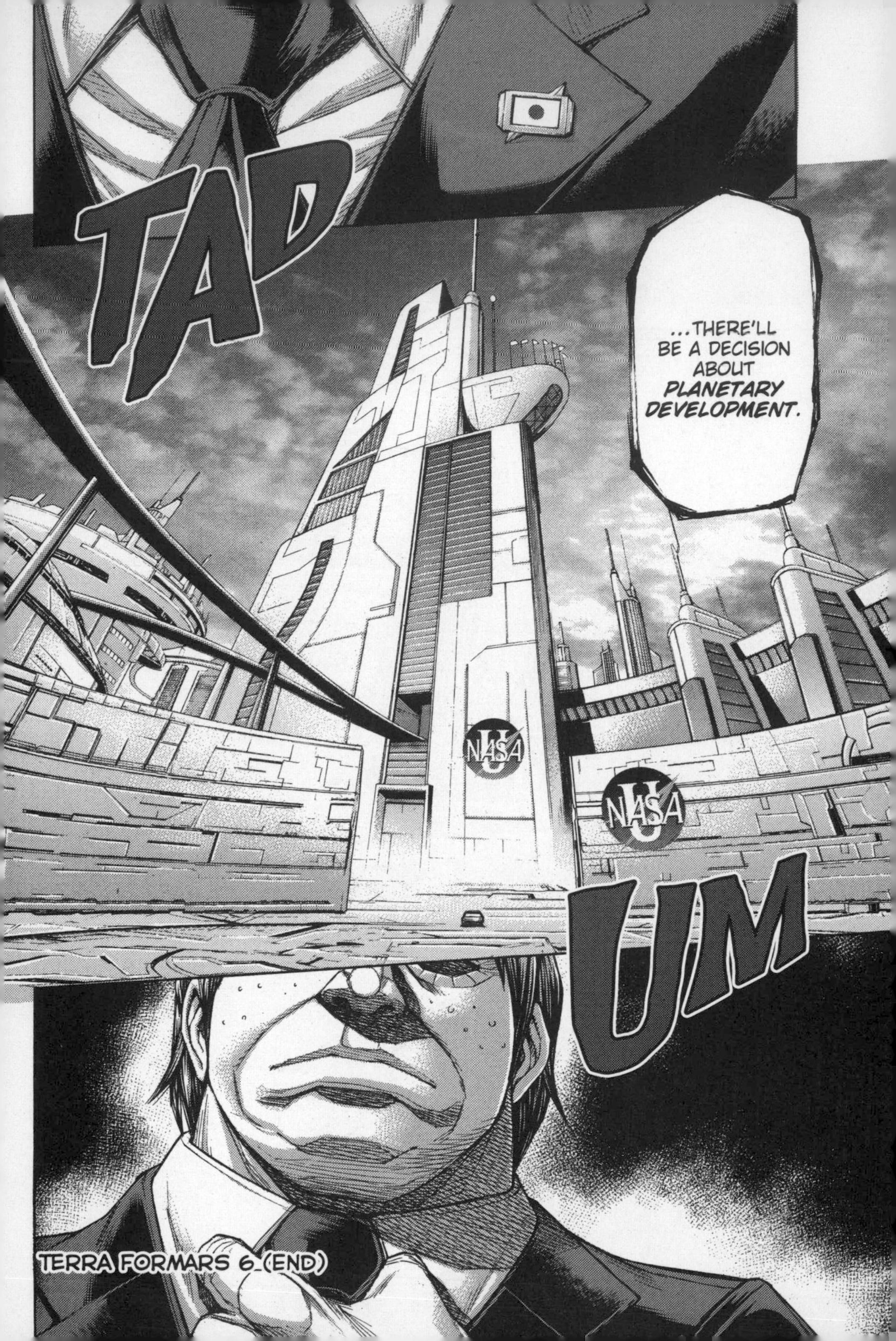
TAD
...THERE'LL BE A DECISION ABOUT PLANETARY DEVELOPMENT.
NASA
U-NASA
UM
TERRA FORMARS 6_(END)

TERRA FORMARS

Volume 6
VIZ Signature Edition

Story by YU SASUGA
Art by KEN-ICHI TACHIBANA

First published in Japan in 2011 by SHUEISHA Inc., Tokyo.
English translation rights arranged by SHUEISHA Inc.

Translation & English Adaptation/John Werry
Touch-up Art & Lettering/Annaliese Christman
Design/Izumi Evers
Editor/Mike Montesa

Printed in the U.S.A.

Published by VIZ Media, LLC
P.O. Box 77010
San Francisco, CA 94107

10 9 8 7 6 5 4 3 2 1
First printing, May 2015

www.viz.com

VIZ SIGNATURE

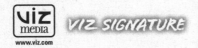

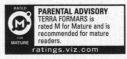

Hey! You're Reading in the Wrong Direction!

This is the *end* of this graphic novel!

To properly enjoy this VIZ graphic novel, please turn it around and begin reading from *right to left.* Unlike English, Japanese is read right to left, so Japanese comics are read in reverse order from the way English comics are typically read.

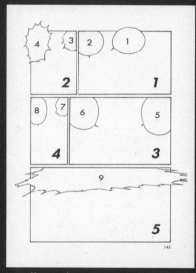

Follow the action this way

This book has been printed in the original Japanese format in order to preserve the orientation of the original artwork. Have fun with it!